On Behalf of Children

On Behalf of Children

A History of Judicial Activism in the Dade County Juvenile Court

Seymour Gelber

Copyright © 2007 by Seymour Gelber.

Library of Congress Control Number: 2007901339
ISBN: Hardcover 978-1-4257-5760-1
Softcover 978-1-4257-5756-4

All rights reserved. No part of this book may be reproduced or transmitted in any form or by any means, electronic or mechanical, including photocopying, recording, or by any information storage and retrieval system, without permission in writing from the copyright owner.

This book was printed in the United States of America.

This book is a publication of the

11th Judicial Circuit
Historical Society

And

To order additional copies of this book, contact:
Xlibris Corporation
1-888-795-4274
www.Xlibris.com
Orders@Xlibris.com
37435

Previous books by the Author

Hard-Core Delinquents—The Miami Experiment	University of Alabama Press	1988
Mom and Pop Elect a Mayor	Self-published	1994
The Gelber Family Memoirs	Self-published	2002
The 1972 Presidential Nominating Conventions in Miami Beach	Self-published	2004
Terrorism in Miami—The 1964 Shoemaker Bombing	Self-published	2005

DEDICATION

I dedicate this book to William E. Gladstone—judge and friend. As a tireless advocate for children, our entire community can look to him with pride and inspiration.

His voice has risen above all others—cajoling, shouting, and demanding that the powers that be open their hearts, minds and their purses to the cause. He is an individual with an inquiring mind who speaks out forcefully and with candor. Always on course, he never deviates from his responsibilities as a public servant.

He has been my good friend and colleague for many years, and has always been a strong support for me personally and to all the others who have had the privilege to serve with him.

Contents

Acknowledgments 11

Foreword 13

Introduction 19

Edith Atkinson 35

Walter H. Beckham 63

Dr. Ben Sheppard 113

William E. Gladstone 160

Seymour Gelber 238

Tom Petersen 281

Cindy Lederman 307

Activists Are Many Among Us 361

    Ellen Sue Venzer 363

    Jeri Beth Cohen 367

    William Johnson 370

    Steve Leifman 373

    Bonnie Rippingille 376

    Charles Edelstein 379

    Norman Gerstein 383

    Sandy Karlan 387

Afterthoughts 393

Index 397

Acknowledgments

Many hands participated in the creation of this book and many more brought it to fruition.

Edith Schwitzman Gelber, my late wife, served as my editor, a task she ably performed on my previous books. Edith, a foreign language teacher by profession and a strict grammarian, suffered through my ineptitude with the simplest of sentence structures. She frequently counseled me on the proper use of commas.

With caring and careful oversight, Edith had edited a large part of the first draft of this book before her unfortunate sudden illness and death. As with my other books, it was our intention to self-publish *On Behalf of Children*.

Her illness delayed the progress of this book for several months. Then Scott Silverman entered into the picture. Virtually, single handedly, he kept *On Behalf of Children* on a path to publication. As the Official Historian for the 11th Judicial Circuit, Judge Silverman enlisted the Historical Museum of Southern Florida and his own 11th Judicial Circuit Historical Society to sponsor the book.

Together, the Historical Museum of Southern Florida, the 11th Judicial Circuit Historical Society, and Xlibris nurtured and prodded *On Behalf of Children* through the various editing and publication stages. Throughout the process, Robert McCammon, President of the Historical Museum of Southern Florida, and the museum's staff contributed greatly to the finished project.

I also want to recognize the professional and helpful staff who work in the *Miami Herald's* archives department. They provided me with considerable assistance during my seemingly endless hours of research. I freely used *Herald* newspaper articles throughout this book as a major source of information about earlier eras.

Lastly, I would be remiss if I did not mention my son, Dan Gelber. During these troubled and difficult times for our family, Dan was a constant source of encouragement to me.

Foreword

The juvenile justice system, designed by social workers over a century ago, has been a fascinating experiment. Focusing on the best interest of the child, it has moved in gasps and spurts. Community idealists and juvenile court practitioners have struggled to keep the dream alive.

For eighty-five years Dade County juvenile judges have grappled not only with the plight of children but with the governing sources that control and fund the process. These include the county and state legislatures, the governor, and as well other private and public bodies whose philosophies often vary from the original concept of the juvenile court.

Mostly the burden to speak out in behalf of children has fallen to the judges. The very nature of the job calls for such performance, a responsibility they gladly have assumed. Whereas in earlier years the effort was more identified with reforming delinquent, crime-prone teenagers, it has moved in later years to greater focus on the needs of our younger deprived and dependent children.

The juvenile court is "special" in that, unlike the rigid criminal court justice system, it has a primary function to rehabilitate. Attempting to blend the two systems has been akin to placing round pins into square holes. A tough task. Has the juvenile court system been up to it?

This, over a hundred-year American mission to create a safer environment for children in trouble, has never quite made it. Even in those communities where the concept was born—New York City, Chicago, Denver—the goal has faltered. Similar to the United Nations' effort to establish a mechanism for world peace, too many jagged edges exist that have blocked this dream from realization.

Struggling against great odds, the idealists, the planners, and the implementers of this grand idea need to be noted in a historical context. Of the many who carried the torch for justice for children, and there are many, juvenile court judges have played a major role as standard-bearers.

Using the courts as a means to make distressed children whole again, is a magnificent concept that epitomized the democratic ideals of this blossoming nation. This concept rose during the mid-nineteenth century alongside the freedom efforts for blacks held in slavery and women suffragettes seeking equality. Whether a traditional court system, with the rigidity required to ensure fairness for all, could encompass this new totally humanitarian approach has always been open to question.

This book singles out seven Dade County Juvenile Court judges who from the inception of the Dade County Juvenile Court in 1921 have portrayed a special affinity for the betterment of children by speaking out strongly in their behalf.

With full due process for juveniles required by the 1967 U.S. Supreme Court *Gault* decision, and the rise of violent juvenile crime in that era, the role of the juvenile court was modified extensively from its early beginning in Florida. Through all of this, the "activist" judge has played a major part.

In some quarters, the term "activist judge" has become a pejorative description. Mostly this occurs in the conflict over the appointment of federal judges. There, the issue of strict construction, the "original intent" of the Constitution, as opposed to a broader, more elastic approach, often becomes a point of serious contention. This then surfaces as a heavy political matter with Republicans and Democrats—conservatives and liberals—marching to the barricades.

For the purposes herein, activist judges are defined as those who seek to improve the condition of children in distress by personal involvement beyond the regular call of duty on the bench. This includes championing private sector programs, urging enactment of positive legislation, offering critical analysis of rehab programs, and other forms of public commentary. In essence, these judges are forceful proponents for change.

This clarifying definition will not preclude critics from occasionally suggesting that this judicial activism, nonetheless, still strays too far from the traditional role of jurists. At times, it is charged by some that this activism may even impede the proper functioning of state agencies authorized by law to care for children.

The genesis of our activist judges takes many shapes. At the beginning, back in the 1920s and 30s, Dade County Juvenile Court Judges Edith Atkinson and Walter Beckham were pioneers in a totally new judicial concept. They needed to create a compass to fix the direction for this new court experiment. Both judges, with no preconceived visions as child savers and with different approaches, laid the groundwork for the future.

Some decades later, William Gladstone campaigned for elective office with a full-blown family court program aimed at resolving all the problems involving children in one family in one court. Gladstone also sought to replace the practice of "storaging" delinquents with active programs featuring rehabilitation. He also was a strong supporter for nonadversarial solutions. Gladstone was a true believer.

Still later, entering this twenty-first century, Cindy Lederman quietly set about addressing the plight of dependent children, long a neglected area of grave concern. She recognized that a direct correlation existed between violent delinquent behavior and children earlier declared dependent. Dependency cases, long the orphan child in the courtroom, found a home in the new Court Dependency Unit she created.

Some of the judges featured here came aboard with a sterling record of activism for children. Tom Petersen, perhaps the best example, before becoming a judge had already created self-help programs aimed at aiding children and adults in run-down black neighborhood housing projects. Even before him, Dr. Ben Sheppard, arriving on the bench, had established a community-wide reputation as a pediatrician serving poor children.

The juvenile court bench has always been a disparate group. Some have been conservatives of the "spare the rod, spoil the child" bias; others, liberal do-gooders always ready to give youthful wrongdoers another chance. In this mix, activist judges have thrived—all bound by the same common goal. Tempering any extreme approach was the one common thread: all had to satisfy the mainstream electorate.

The evolution of the court in Dade County has been one mostly of imperceptible change. A lot of it has to do with the circumstances of each particular era and as well the personality of those leading the way. Significant changes, however, did occur in a short span with the 1967 U.S. Supreme Court *Gault* decision and the 1972 revision of Article V of the Florida Constitution.

Before that, in the decades prior to World War II, it had been a struggle for recognition. Advocates for children, mostly women's groups, made a firm effort, but no fiery cause had emerged here as in the more liberal communities up North. Judge Edith Atkinson, the second juvenile court judge taking office in 1923, was the first of the flag bearers. Post-WWII, the impressive credentials of Judge Walter Beckham gave identity to the purpose of the court, but it was still a hard struggle to achieve a coherent image of the juvenile court. Too many obstacles existed for the institution to carry out its full purpose.

With the court going through a forced rebirth in the mid 1970s came William Gladstone as the vehicle for change. Could this one-man foray bring on a new and radical transformation? Hardly, but the time was ripe for a new focus. The mission now required more clarity. William Gladstone would set the tone for the leadership during the remainder of the century.

Change had been gradually moving into the system in both the areas of dependency and delinquency. At the onset, the concept of early intervention for the very youngest began to gain many adherents. Then, the value of early childhood development training in our schools made great strides beginning with Judge Edith Atkinson and continuing to Judges Tom Petersen and Cindy Lederman more than a half century later. The line of progress, in these and other areas, though perhaps indistinct, never faltered.

Always there were roadblocks. In response to a public outcry that juvenile judges were "soft" on hard-core youth, new legislation in Florida allowed hard-core delinquent youth to be tried directly in the adult court, via the state attorney's prosecuting arm, bypassing the juvenile court judge. The resultant data on children prosecuted in adult court never did show the expected tougher sentencing, or a decline in violent crime by sixteen- seventeen-year-olds. Nonetheless, it diminished the stature of the juvenile court.

The Dade County Juvenile Court, though surviving many life changes in its growth, has never quite reached its full promise. Nonetheless, this court with its strong rehabilitation purpose and the ability to attract change is still the most viable vehicle to influence children. However, absent activist judges, the goal to better the condition of troubled children often withers away. The absolute need for strong independent leadership willing to step outside the established line to initiate change is an essential element.

The inherent authority of the bench, along with the high respect the office of judge holds, strongly suggest that for this mission the judge is the logical leader. His and Her Honor's forceful voice, able to be heard above the din, can overcome the bureaucratic instinct to maintain the status quo.

This treatise, while designed to highlight judicial activism, is not intended to be a comprehensive history of the juvenile justice system in Dade County or to minimize the role of other components. The certainty and stability of the court system is provided, of necessity, by others quietly serving on a day-to-day, case-by-case basis. Activist judges, leading the charge, obtain much media attention, almost of a celebrity nature. A whole host of social service adjuncts to the court operation are, however, equally essential contributors to the efforts for children. Judges of the juvenile court are totally dependent on the performance of the several service units comprising the Court system.

Speaking out for children may have a universal appeal, but hardly is limited to juvenile court judges. Communities abound with public and private groups and individuals spreading the message. Perhaps, here more than in any other court system venue, the need to have citizen volunteers as monitors of both the child's progress and judicial performance is paramount.

Judicial advocates in each division of the court generally are the administrative judges (chosen by the chief judge of the circuit), who assume the role as spokesperson, innovator, or critic. Other judges, by virtue of circumstances of the moment, have also been drawn into the struggle. By their very involvement each has brought an added lift to a movement always requiring change. Judges have the power, prestige, and responsibility to do more. It comes with some peril from critics. Too often the undertaking is unnoticed, but few efforts are more worthy.

The author has selected those judges who regarded their most important function to be missionaries of a sort, speaking out forcefully at every available forum, including their own bench, to improve conditions for disadvantaged children.

The purpose here is not to describe the "good" juvenile court judges, or for that matter the "bad" ones. For example, some fine jurists like Mario Goodrich, later to serve on the Third District Court of Appeal, and Wilkie Ferguson, who was appointed to both the state appeals court and the federal bench, were also, earlier in their careers, excellent juvenile court judges (for too short a time). They, and others of high quality, are not noted in this presentation.

Although circuit court judges have a rotation system transferring them to a new division every three years, William Gladstone and I were exempt from this rule. Apparently the volatility of our division needed some stability and continuity. This policy has continued on in subsequent years.

The juvenile court judges featured herein as activist leaders have proven their worth. For the process and the progress to continue in the years ahead, many more will need to follow their pathway.

Introduction

Cook County, Illinois, has been the site identified as the first home for the newly arrived juvenile court in this country. The year was 1899, the final year of a century leading to dramatic changes ahead for children. It was the beginning of a dream come to life for idealists who had envisioned a new appreciation for children.

In the earlier years of the nineteenth century, the response to errant children had been harsh treatment. It had been lockups like the New York City Houses of Refuge, training schools, and other holding facilities, or nothing at all. Virtually all the approaches were found seriously wanting. For centuries children throughout the world had been abused, maltreated, and ignored with never a second thought from governing institutions, let alone the general populace.

Some few social advocates had favored separating delinquent children from adult criminals in the belief that children had less developed moral and cognitive capacities, therefore deserving special consideration and protection. This was a theory universally rejected in those days and not with total acceptance today. Even at the end of the nineteenth century when Illinois and Colorado were able to establish their new forward-thinking initiatives, progress was painfully slow.

The 1899 Illinois landmark juvenile court was a long time coming, but the grand visions of the early planners never did fully come to fruition. Dreams rarely come to life fully blown. The fresh look, however, enabled children in this country to attain a new standing that would point the way for viewing the troubled child in more compassionate terms.

Raising the child to full status as a human being may have arisen from the more democratic ideals taking hold as our country matured. Perhaps the Industrial

Revolution forcing children into onerous employment in factories pushed the button. Maybe the existing standard to punish erring children as adults violated the collective conscience of our people. Conceivably all of the above and other reasons brought the juvenile court into being. No matter what or why, it was one of the finest concepts ever conceived as part of our national being. A matter of pride for all Americans.

Now, a little more than a century later, the question often posed, has it worked, often draws a less-than-comforting answer: sure, in a fashion. Not at all like Jane Addams and those other inspired social workers at Chicago's Hull House had planned, when they envisioned this Child Saver project. By dint of the tireless efforts of these idealists the Illinois legislature in 1899 was persuaded to do the right thing. It was a beginning.

Not how Judge Richard Tuthill, a seventeen-year pioneer of the Chicago Circuit Court, or Judge Ben Lindsey, whose Denver, Colorado court followed the Chicago court into being, would have hoped or predicted. Judges Tuthill and Lindsey were the first two juvenile court judges to lead the way for judicial activism. They were like Johnny Appleseed, spreading the word, a new mantra implanting their concepts and vision wherever they went. Judge Tuthill was succeeded shortly thereafter in Chicago by newcomer Julian Mack, who continued to carry on the mission.

The resolute experiments in Chicago and Denver emboldened many groups in other states to push forward. Just as Chicago had been motivated by women's groups, the impetus to change the treatment of children in trouble came mostly through female persuasion. Judges Tuthill, Mack, and Lindsey, in large demand nationally, carried the crusade with great energy.

An example is cited from the efforts of the Des Moines, Iowa chapter of the National Congress of Mothers to invite the new national leaders to address the Iowa state legislature on the subject.

In response to an invitation from Cora Hills, state regent for Iowa, Judge Tuthill in his three-page letter dated December 1, 1903, expounded on the need for a juvenile court noting, "The State stands 'in loco parentis' to all children, and where a child for any reason has become delinquent for the want of proper parental care, the state should give the child such care."

He accepted the invitation writing, "As requested, I will come to Des Moines under your auspices and address the members of the Legislature as desired, for Fifty Dollars, paying my own expenses." And so he did.

Miss Cora Hillis, no wilting Iowa cornflower, continued her pursuit of national social reformers by following up with an invitation to Denver, Colorado's judge Ben Lindsey. The judge's January 11, 1904 response: "I think it very important to get a union meeting of the churches, as we found such meetings here did as much as any one thing to arouse public sentiment for our new laws. It would also be well to get the presence of the Governor and the Legislative Committee having charge of the bill."

Before even completing the speaking engagement for Ms. Hill's Congress of Mothers, Judge Lindsey wrote a letter to Iowa governor Albert Cummins dated February 3, 1904, beseeching him to look favorably upon the proposed legislation.

It was no easy task for these judges nor for their successors in the century that followed. Reaching the full potential of the juvenile court may be an unreachable point, but from the beginning there has been no shortage of advocates, particularly among the judiciary.

The early juvenile courts fostered by idealists and radical thinkers took the high ground, seeking a true emancipation for delinquent and dependent children. Theirs was the humanitarian approach. Public support, however, while sympathetic to maltreated children, was more practical, focusing mainly on simply keeping streets free of poor and vagrant children. These two differing approaches would continue to slow the efforts of the activists.

The large influx of millions of immigrants from Europe at the turn of the twentieth century gave large population centers like New York and Chicago a new ethnic flavor. Most arrivals, oppressed or impoverished, brought vast numbers of children in need: homeless, lacking parental control with little in the way of recreation or adult guidance available. Children of all ages roamed the streets; crime, both petty and serious, was their occupation and avocation.

This intolerable situation called for action. A Children's Aid Society report of that mid-nineteenth century era concluded, "For over half a century the street child has been an inescapable fixture of the nineteenth century. These street rats and gutter snipes gnawed away at the foundations of society undisturbed."

This strong language, by a social work agency no less, suggests the anger against the street children prevalent in those days. Language, it should be pointed out, not too dissimilar to that offered over a century later in the 1970s when the rise of violent youth crime frightened citizens walking the streets, resulting in an outcry for strong punitive action.

The focus of early court systems was to "save" the potentially criminal children from the fate obviously in store for them. "Saving" them consisted of harsh jail sentences meted out to serious juvenile offenders; others shipped to reform schools to be warehoused until release with no hope in store for them. Dependent children were recognized but not addressed for specific needs. Protection for these abused and neglected children was on the back burner. Way back.

New York City, as the entrance port for these mostly European refugees, bore the brunt of the children dilemma. The movement to separate children from adults actually began in the early 1800s, but then it meant only separate housing and did not distinguish between delinquency and dependency. New York City's House of Refuge, a separate juvenile facility, was built to house the more serious young offenders.

In 1874, in New York, the case of ten-year-old Mary Ellen attracted attention to dependent children. The child was removed from her home due to the cruelty of her custodial parents. Chained to a bedpost, beaten, underfed, and abandoned, she was so malnourished that, though twice the age, she had grown only to the size of a five-year-old.

With no laws on the books to protect such children as Mary Ellen, and no civic organizations to carry the flag, child advocates beseeched the Society for Prevention of Cruelty to Animals to intervene, since Mary Ellen was of the animal kingdom. A receptive New York court system provided her protection. In this city, where the problem was most pressing, the *Mary Ellen* case became the turning point in favor of children.

The *Mary Ellen* case resulted in the founding of the New York Society for the Prevention of Cruelty to Children. Other cities followed, and by 1900 there existed 161 such societies in the United States. At last, children were to be viewed as a separate species of the animal kingdom.

In 1893 Lillian Wald, a nurse activist of the Jane Addams genre, opened the Henry Street Settlement in New York's Lower East Side to provide a variety of medical and social services for poor immigrants newly arrived in the country. She eased the hard life among those she treated, organizing neighborhood grocery stores, holding integrated training classes on health subjects, and other forms of social interaction. Far ahead of her time, like Jane Addams, she also was a radical pacifist.

In 1902 New York would join the new juvenile movement, establishing a children's court. The *Mary Ellen* case and the work of Lillian Wald and other volunteer citizens were the impetus for the movement toward the creation of a juvenile court in that city.

Though other cities, like New York, were also moving in that direction, the full ray of light had already burst forward in 1899 with the first establishment nationwide of a juvenile court in Chicago, Cook County, Illinois. Led by radical social thinker Jane Addams, her Child Savers helped create the new law that would infuse the juvenile court system for the next century. Her Hull House, a sanctuary for abused women and children, was the central point for advocacy.

Perhaps Ms. Addams best described the plight of dependent children with this comment: "Poor mothers who had to work, would tie their children to a table leg, and go off to work." Hull House provided a basic safe environment for children—kindergarten plus a meal. Not a lot, but a good start. So much more had to be done.

Introduction

Slowly the movement developed. Jane Addams, the indefatigable social worker, and her mostly women colleagues earned distinction as the driving force for the creation of the model Chicago Juvenile Court. This court, the first in the nation, was built across the street from the Hull House as testament to its forebears. The creation of the Chicago court was just the beginning. Messengers were needed to send the word out to the world.

Judge Julian Mack of Chicago and Judge Ben Lindsey of Denver, identified by historians as early judicial advocates, had their work cut out. Both championed the bold idea for the court to serve, where necessary, as a substitute parent and as well to improve the lot of the child through counseling and education. This required total separation from the adult criminal court and a new mind-set toward the rehabilitation of the child.

Whereas, historically, the adult criminal court had styled charging documents "the State versus John Doe," the new juvenile court used the more compassionate salutation "In the interest of John Doe." The two phrases identified the world of difference between the two approaches. Juvenile courts in the modern concept grew quickly. By 1915, forty-six states had adopted versions of the Illinois and Colorado juvenile court system.

It was a job only beginning. Richard Tuthill, an activist at Hull House, became the first Chicago Juvenile Court judge, hearing the first case on July 3, 1899. The job of organizing the court fell to Judge Tuthill. Restructuring the style and nomenclature of this new court was the immediate task. Obtaining and training an able staff was also a need to be addressed. This was to set the standards for the monumental changes this new court would offer.

Judge Tuthill's effort to establish a workable process for administering the new court did not earn him the recognition later afforded Judge Julian Mack, his successor in Chicago. Judge Mack took on the more public task of reaching out to other states as the promoter of the new cause for the betterment of children in trouble.

Both these judges filled equally essential roles, but administrators usually work long hours unseen and unrecognized. The man with greater public visibility usually attracts the eye of the media. Chicago's Judge Mack was shortly joined by Judge Ben Lindsey of Denver, Colorado's court to carry the banner nationwide. Each with his own distinctive style.

Julian Mack, a Harvard Law School graduate, editor of the *Harvard Law Review*, later an appeals court judge, traveled the country bringing the message of the new juvenile court potential. A serious student of the law, an outstanding member of the Bar, a courtly man, he was the ideal messenger to sincerely portray the values of this new court.

Judge Mack, perhaps best described the new concept in words commonly used this day, but back then a rarity: "What must be determined by the juvenile court is not whether this boy or girl committed a specific wrong, but what had best be done in his or her interest and the interest of the State to save him from a downward career." A prophetic statement.

He saw the new juvenile court as a vast improvement over the past injustices foisted upon children, but his goals were not as far-reaching as those sought by Judge Ben Lindsey. From the first moment in 1902 when the Denver Juvenile Court was established, Ben Lindsey saw this as an opportunity to change the entire approach to juveniles. He, like Judge Mack, also traveled the chicken-and-peas circuit, addressing conferences and seminars throughout the country, extolling the virtues of this new kind of court for children. His action plan, however, differed dramatically.

According to an article authored by Ted Rubin, "Juvenile Justice Update" (February 1999), Ben Lindsey was the visionary pioneer who foretold the potential of a movement that could and should change the entire world for children.

Ted Rubin, a much later successor on the Denver Juvenile Court bench (1965-71), and currently a leading consultant and author in the juvenile justice field, credits Lindsey as having had the greatest impact on juvenile court development. Judges Julian Mack and his predecessor in Chicago, Richard Tuthill, are right up there in their concern for children, but Lindsey preached from a far different, more expansive mount.

Chicago, the pioneer city, through their advocate Judge Julian Mack, worked at modifying the criminal law to fit the needs of children in a special court devoted to them alone. Denver, through Judge Lindsey's assertive style, was "establishing an informal approach unencumbered by tradition or precedent." Lindsey and Mack preached the same message but Judge Lindsey's style was far removed from the staid, conservative approach expected of a judge bound by the letter of the law.

Judge Lindsey was an iconoclast, an irreverent, totally independent jurist whose mission to further the juvenile court saw no boundaries. He was a hell-raiser, constantly in conflict, always ready for a fight. And there were many for him. He disregarded statutes; formal adjudication was of minimal importance—rehab was everything. He called the adult criminal justice system a "medieval torture chamber." Judge Lindsey was more a friendly social worker treating children before him as "my boys."

According to author Ted Rubin, Judge Lindsey featured walk-in sessions, with boys and girls coming in on their own accord. Here, "Denver's young people could come to talk about matters, particularly sexual concerns, which they were unable to discuss with their parents or teachers." Lindsey believed lawyers and legal procedures obstructed the court's rehabilitative mission. He eschewed all the traditional court trappings, eliminating the wearing of a judicial robe and declining to sit above his audience on a thronelike podium.

Further, the Denver court under Judge Lindsey institutionalized only 6 percent of court youth, while the Chicago court under Judge Mack institutionalized 44 percent. These were two pioneer courts going in the same direction with the same purpose but with differing styles: one incremental, the other rebellious. In the years ahead juvenile courts would address their community concerns for children both ways: most from the vantage point of the conservative Judge Julian Mack and a few with the more radical approach of Judge Ben Lindsey.

Unlike Judge Mack, Judge Lindsey literally sought controversy, sharply reacting to conservative religious leaders opposed to many of his views. He advocated both birth-control education in schools and legalized abortion. He went so far as to open his own clinic to provide contraceptives to students. After serving for several terms, he was finally defeated for reelection in 1927, and then disbarred by the Colorado Supreme Court for practicing law while on the bench.

Apparently, he had testified as a witness in an estate matter in Pennsylvania, receiving a fee. His defense, that it was not a fee but a contribution for a juvenile detention building in Denver, was not persuasive to the Colorado Supreme Court. Lindsey supporters, and there were many, insisted this was a conspiracy among archconservative Lindsey-haters, but that argument did not impress the supreme court.

His losing election had all the forces he had angered over the years lining up against him including the Ku Klux Klan, then a powerful political force in Colorado. Upon leaving office, Lindsey built a well-publicized bonfire, burning all the children's court records. He is credited with saying he feared the KKK would be invading their privacy by gaining access to the children's records.

As a footnote, Ted Rubin, the Lindsey biographer cited here, also became a Denver Juvenile Court judge thirty-eight years later in 1965. With a "liberal" reputation and an activist bent, Rubin also was swept out of office in 1971 for displeasing the more conservative elements in that community. Activism, while good for the soul, is not necessarily a strong vote-getter.

Judge Lindsey viewed the established bureaucracy as the enemy. The story is told how in sending delinquents to the state school, Judge Lindsey would give them tokens for the trolley system rather than permit the sheriff's office to transport them.

Lindsey had heard that the sheriff's office was detaining the children in their lockup for several days in order to gain the housing stipend provided by the State. Perhaps not a critical issue, but it showed the constant division between the judge and other law enforcement authorities. Lindsey battled every issue, small or large.

Was he paranoid? Perhaps, but when the entire world around you is attacking, it may be reality, not a delusion, that governs your response.

Former Juvenile Court Judge Ted Rubin, in a recent interview with this author, had this to say about Judge Lindsey:

> Ben Lindsey was the greatest salesman ever for the new juvenile court, traveling all over the world, testifying to its virtues and potential. He was way ahead of his time.
>
> Such national figures as President Theodore Roosevelt and the acclaimed socialist writer Upton Sinclair praised his efforts and viewed him as a friend.
>
> In 1909 he succeeded in persuading President Roosevelt to call a White House conference on orphaned and dependent children that led to creation of the Federal Children's Bureau, which began the movement to influence issues such as lowering infant mortality and establishing birth registration.
>
> Judge Lindsey was constantly under attack by groups such as the KKK and as well by ultraconservative forces railing against him on morality issues.
>
> Those of us in the field today think highly of Lindsey's strong activism. He set the table for all the progressive ideas to be attempted in the future, many of which have come to pass . . . and others yet in the making.

Judge Ben Lindsey, the rambunctious firebrand, may not be the perfect model for the Dade County Juvenile Court judges displayed in these pages, but the goals he sought and the perseverance he possessed as the tireless advocate for children are standards also maintained by those that followed. And some, like Judge Lindsey, have shown a willingness to buck the establishment, as he so often did.

Lindsey, known as the Kids' Judge, was a showman, an innovator and a fighter—worthy attributes in any public endeavor. In 1914 a national magazine poll named him one of the ten greatest Americans of that era, probably the *first* juvenile court judge to have a national identity. He did not go silently or unknown.

In 1929 Lindsey, not deterred by the disappointing disbarment action of the Colorado Supreme Court, moved to California. There in 1934, he won election to the superior court, was reelected in 1940. He died in 1943 at age seventy-three, still on the bench.

Were a pantheon of judges to be selected for a national honor roll applauding leadership in the creation and furtherance of the new-model juvenile court, in all likelihood Colorado's Judge Ben Lindsey's name would be among the top.

Miami, with its slow development, was not as blessed as more progressive cities such as Chicago, New York, and Denver. Our city's law enforcement did not take on a modern hue until many years later. Back in 1840, when activism in behalf of children was beginning to be recognized as a national concern in many of our major cities, Miami was still fighting and losing battles with the Seminole Indians. Our early settlers had displaced the Indians, who were successfully fighting back.

In an August 9, 1840 letter seeking help from the governor, Dade County's acting clerk of court W. C. Maloney pleaded, "The Seminoles have destroyed Dade County and there is no way to canvass the votes in the recent election. The only thing left from the Indian attack is the State Seal."

It took a decade to 1850 before the state legislature did alleviate the situation by consolidating wobbly Dade County into the more stable neighboring Monroe County. In time the Seminole Wars were resolved. The state seal was saved, and Dade County was restored to its former status.

The city of Miami, then and now our major city, was incorporated in the year 1896. A mere 319 voters favored the move that heralded the birth of Miami officially as a city. Twenty-three years later, in 1921, when the Florida state legislature empowered Dade County to create a juvenile court, we were still in swaddling clothes compared to cities of the North. The Seminole Wars, though now only a distant memory, were still remembered by many.

Organized law enforcement was a novelty in Miami at the turn of the century. When the citizenry voted to incorporate in 1898, they also had on the ballot an election for marshal. That was the title for the first policeman for this community of fifteen hundred citizens. A man named Young F. Gray, a dynamite expert for Miami developer Henry Flagler, won election to the post.

Young was the lone policeman, driving a goat-drawn wagon, collecting stray dogs and law breakers. The historical item from which this information was extracted made no mention of children, but the author takes the liberty of assuming stray children were also included.

A new wooden jail opened in December 1896 with the jail on the first floor and city hall upstairs. Mr. Young Gray, the city marshal, was also the jailer and as well building inspector, street superintendent, sanitary inspector, and tax collector.

Several other towns—notably Miami Beach and Coral Gables, both not yet chartered, and others—made up the remainder of Dade County. In a few decades the land boom would strike the Miami area, bringing a new height of prosperity to Miami life. The land value bust that shortly followed the boom brought back reality.

At the turn of the century, however, these outlying areas were mainly undeveloped, mostly uninhabited, with saloons, gambling and bawdy houses running freely as portrayed in one of those old Wild West movies.

In September 1907 the Miami City Charter was amended, abolishing the office of marshal and creating a bona fide police department. By 1916 the department numbered twenty, and the first policewoman, Mrs. Ida Fisher, was hired. Under pressure from the Woman's Club of Miami, the police department had hired Mrs. Fisher to assist delinquent girls. Her "beat" was patrolling parks, dance halls, and other places where girls might find trouble.

Working with the City's vice squad and the County's probation officer, she mounted Miami's first direct police effort against juvenile delinquency. Miami mayor William Smith described her at a city council meeting: "A woman who can come up to a girl in trouble and appeal to her better side." This philosophy fit right into the creed of the new juvenile court yet to come.

In 1921 when the Florida Legislature created our juvenile court, we were among the last three states to join in that national effort. We lacked the Jane Addams-Lillian Wald fiery change-the-world leadership. But then again, Addams and Wald did not have to contend with the fury of the dispossessed Seminole Indians and the growing pains of the birthing of a new community.

Eventually, this Eleventh Judicial Circuit would produce some of the most innovative and productive judges ever to serve in behalf of the best interest of the child. The several enumerated here have in their own fashion carried on the tradition established by Judges Mack and Lindsey, as well as the work of such early pioneers, mostly women volunteers.

The development of today's almost century-old juvenile court in Dade County came about more by evolution than revolution. True, it was the women of Dade County once more leading the way. Yet the passion of those extraordinary world changers—Jane Addams, Lillian Wald, and other women—fighting for a cause was not the driving force. Here, it was more a down-to-earth equitable division of labor.

Back in 1911, the Florida legislature had added juvenile cases to the county court judge's calendar, increasing his already established assignment of civil lawsuits. Already with a full caseload, County Court Judge W. F. Blanton additionally had his hands full as committing magistrate for criminal cases, ex officio coroner, probate judge and as well control of the marriage and hunting license bureaus. Seeking relief from his heavy caseload, he had for some time been requesting the legislature to establish a separate and independent juvenile court.

Rather than accede to Judge Blanton's request for a new court for children, the legislature instead magnanimously provided him a lone probation officer for a four-year term. The governor thereupon appointed Mr. J. J. Combs, but the salary was small and Mr. Combs stayed only thirteen months. Five of the first six probation officers either resigned or were removed from office.

Apparently, many of these political appointees received very small salaries leading them to seek payments from parents whose children had been apprehended for a violation of the law. This petty bribery rarely led to the arrest of the culprit or the official involved.

Introduction

Quietly, a resignation was accepted and on occasion a complaint to the governor led to a removal from office. Eventually, this brought a legislative change allowing the probation officer's appointment by the senior judge and serving at his will. Being directly responsible to the senior judge resulted in more circumspect behavior on the part of the probation officers.

During those early years, there were few Dade County resources in terms of proper facilities to house those children found delinquent, thus magnifying the problem. Compounding the problem even more, the probation officers lacked training for their duties with children. Viewing the job as political spoils, the probation officers were constantly skirting trouble. County Court Judge Blanton, vexed no end, was forced to continue handling juveniles in this haphazard manner until 1921.

Our women did then again came to the fore. The Woman's Club of Miami (their spelling) and other groups and individuals spoke out for this new juvenile court. In 1921 legislation was introduced before the state legislature to establish a separate and independent juvenile court, but passage was no easy going. Our own Dade County Commission sent a resolution to Tallahassee strongly opposing the bill.

Not caring less for children, nonetheless, they bemoaned the extra expense of creating a new court. Reasoning that since the county judge already had authority to hear these cases and a probation officer was available, therefore a special court for juveniles was not justified, expensewise.

The *Miami Herald* (10/16/21) pitched in with an editorial scolding the county commission for their penny-wise, pound-foolish opposition to the proposed new law:

> The law establishing the juvenile court was enacted at the urgent request of the leading women of this County who have long seen the necessity for such a court to care properly for such backward, wayward and delinquent children, of which Dade County has all too many, although it cannot be said that the County has a very large element of incorrigibles among its children.
>
> It is hardly up to the County Commissioners to either abolish the court or cut off the salary of the presiding officer.

Joining the voices against the backward position of the county commission was the Civitan Club, a group of men comprising many leading citizens. These included family names that would lead Dade County for decades ahead: T. N. Gautier, H. Dale Miller, D. E. Sheehan, George Stembler, Fred Snedigar, Arthur Yelvington, C. H. Crandon, and others.

Chairman of the group Harold Wilson, who had authored the proposed legislation, said, "Maintaining a separate Juvenile Court eventually would be repaid with the better control and management of the delinquent child problem in this County." Not exactly a ringing endorsement with an inspiring message, but it represented the best mood of the Miami establishment.

State Representative Ben Willard, sponsoring the bill in the legislature, brushed aside county commission objections. He opted instead for the voices of the Civitans and the Woman's Club passing into law a special bill creating an independent juvenile court. Governor Cary Hardee signed it on June 14, 1921. It is to be noted that Rep. Ben Willard later became judge of the Dade County Criminal Court of Record, serving with distinction for several decades.

The law, identified as Chapter 8663z (No. 268), provided for a judge, probation officer, and clerk of court. Appointment was by the governor, with the judge's salary set at $2,400. Appeals from this special court to be heard in the circuit court. The Dade County Commission shall provide a courtroom and pay the salaries with expenses of running the operation to come from the court fine and forfeiture fund.

That the juvenile court started off in disfavor with the county commission was a foreboding of future relationships with not only the County but also with the State. This conflict with the ruling government agencies controlling the purse strings would continue on and on. A "special" court aiming for rehabilitation rather than punishment was to most citizens a strange being. Educating the public as to the worthiness of such a court would be a long-term project.

Once established, the early operation of the juvenile court consisted mostly of a stern lecture from the judge, a local lockup, or sentence to the Marianna Industrial School for Boys located in Central Florida. Marianna, a long trek for parents to visit their children, was also viewed as perhaps a too-harsh imprisonment for incorrigible youth. For those children declared dependent, it was usually a volunteer citizen willing to take custody in their own home.

It would take many years for this new offspring of the judicial system to gain recognition in the community and full acceptance among legal practitioners. Not created as a result of some anguished cry for justice as in Chicago, Denver, and other cities, it was looked upon more as some relief for an overcrowded judicial calendar rather than an experiment in governance. It was decades before lawyers even instituted appeals on a regular basis. The juvenile court, absent any fanfare, had arrived in Dade County. Wonderful, but where was it going?

Filling the judicial seat drew no heavy interest in the general community, but among civic clubs it attracted some attention. Three candidates appeared, but no political favorite was apparent in the contest. This was to be decided by the Dade County Democratic Party Executive Committee. One candidate was Harold Wilson, chairman of the Civitan Club. The others were H. W. Penny, justice of the peace for the city of Miami district, and Walter Payne, a successful businessman. Penney won but hardly by acclamation. Twenty ballots were taken before the winner emerged.

Introduction

Penney, first name Harry, preferred to be called H. W. Having a new law degree and already schooled in politics, he prevailed over George Wilson, who had drafted the juvenile court legislation. Wilson, by his strong interest in the office more likely would have been the kind of advocate earlier found in Chicago and Denver. That would have to wait.

Although this was a hard-fought contest, the new judge, Penney, did not appear to be overqualified for the job. He had some political experience, was a newly minted lawyer, but little to suggest what one might hope for and expect from a juvenile court judge. Ordained as a Methodist minister in 1898, Penney served in the Spanish-American War in Cuba. Upon returning to Florida he was ordered to serve among the Cuban population in Tampa and Key West.

After several years there, he developed an interest in law and resigned from the ministry. Harry Penney was admitted to the Florida Bar in July 1921 at age fifty-one. Along the way he had opened a large wholesale grocery store in Miami and had also found time to serve as a justice of the peace in District 3 in Miami.

Governor Cary Hardee immediately approved the Democratic Party Executive Committee recommendation and sent the commission of office to the new and first Dade County Juvenile Court judge. Meanwhile, Judge Penney was on a two-week hunting trip with his two sons on the west coast of Florida and could not be reached. Mrs. Penney said she would notify him by correspondence but was uncertain the mail would reach him in a timely fashion. Apparently there was no great hurry in the Penny family for him to take office.

An examination of the date sequence recorded in the County archives suggests Penney, admitted to the Bar in the first week of July 1921, signed his first order as a juvenile court judge on July 7, a scant several days after his admission. Most likely, the governor, knowing little about the importance of a juvenile court, viewed the post as more honorary than for a real purpose. In any event, clearly while the juvenile court was now here, judicial advocacy was yet to arrive.

Upon the judge's return from his hunting trip, the *Miami Herald* ran a front page story featuring Judge Penny's philosophy for the new court he would head. Here are excerpts of his statement:

> I believe the strict performance of duty of the Judge and the Probation Officer will to a large extent eradicate the depredations of children in fruit groves, and in other petty thievery and will also restrain delinquent girls from roaming the streets at will and committing immoral practices.
>
> The idea of the court, so far as the boys and girls will permit it, is to exercise a parental care over delinquent children, inducing them in every way possible to become good citizens of both Dade County and the State of Florida.

> I will try to always point out the inevitable results of living a life of immorality and crime and will help the boys and girls in every manner possible for the betterment of their condition.

Judge Penney concluded his statement advising that, in essence, his hearings would be private, "barring the curious" so as to avoid embarrassment to the children before him.

All in all, Judge Penney's declaration was in keeping with the standards that would govern Dade County's juvenile court mission in the years ahead. He actually performed as well as one might have hoped, considering the circumstances of his appointment.

The 1921 law enacted by the state legislature granted the new judge all the authority previously afforded a judge in treatment of juveniles as defined in Chapter 62116 of the Acts of 1911.

Back in 1911, the legislature had given the presiding county judge jurisdiction over juveniles. Now, ten years later in 1921, that authority was quietly transferred to the juvenile court judge. No fanfare, no fireworks. Although the juvenile court would become a full-fledged part of the circuit court some half century later, it was now a special court, limited to children not yet seventeen years of age.

In addition, the new law made it abundantly clear that the juvenile court judge had complete control as to the welfare of any child taken from the custody of a parent or custodial agency. In later years the introduction of state and county welfare agencies diluted the absolute judicial control of a child's placement, both in delinquency and dependency cases. Back then, at the beginning, the decision of the judge was absolute.

The requirements for serving as a judge were somewhat less stringent than exists today. The appointee had to be a citizen of the United States and Florida for at least one year, and not be less than twenty-four years of age, with a salary of $2,400 annually. The governor would also appoint the probation officer at a salary of $1,600.

Judge Penney's first case, as recorded in the official clerk's record, was indeed July 7, 1921. The defendants, Laurie Johnson and Irvin Hall, two sixteen-year-olds, were arrested for stealing mangoes from Mr. Ozohu's trees in the South Dade area. The arrest was made by Probation Officer Estelle Harris, one of the volunteers who manned watch over fruit groves.

The children were tried, convicted, and sentenced on that same date. The chief of police had urged prosecution, advising Probation Officer Estelle Harris that "the father of Laurie is not sufficiently concerned as to the welfare of Laurie."

Acting on his pledge to show concern and compassion for youngsters in trouble, Judge Penney suspended sentence so long as they "get to work and report to me every Saturday."

Miami, by then an agricultural and fruit-growing community of about fifty-thousand people, had problems with children infiltrating the orange groves, and guards were posted along many of the larger groves. A witness had observed the two in the act. Throwing themselves on the mercy of the court, they pleaded guilty. No records are available to show their later progress.

In the early years this personal involvement approach was the hallmark of the juvenile court. Court sessions were informal and in the absence of community-based programs and social work agencies, it was up to the judge and the probation officer to personally attend to the treatment aspect. The judge would preach homilies from the bench and personally relate to the child as both a counselor and as a stern parent. With only the probation officer to assist, the judge, by virtue of his high office, interacted as best he could.

Several decades later, the U.S. Supreme Court's *Gault* decision required that juvenile defendants receive the same protective rights afforded adults in criminal court, appreciably altering the role of what had been a friendly mom-and-pop court to an adversarial forum.

Organizing his new court required much of Judge Penney's attention, completing his otherwise uneventful term in 1925. Six months before the end of his term he retired, returning to his old position as justice of the peace in the district of Miami.

His successor, Edith Atkinson, arrived in 1912, at the same time Miami and Dade County were losing that virginal look. Still a sleepy village, it would soon blossom into a boomtown. In a few years, the land speculators would be coming to town in droves, dressed in resplendent knickers, hawking options on street corners, and making millions overnight. Florida land would suddenly sell at premium prices, bringing hordes of investors, grifters, criminals, and families—all seeking a share of the golden eggs suddenly available.

With this new surge of prosperity there was little thought in the community of the impact of this new-fangled court specially created for children. It did, however, have full meaning to new Juvenile Court Judge Edith Atkinson. She, along with other units of law enforcement, would have their hands full dealing with a sharp rise in juvenile crime brought to Miami by the influx of families joining the get-rich-quick crowd.

This was but one of the many hurdles to be faced by juvenile court judges in the years ahead. Having had but limited time as a practicing lawyer, Judge Atkinson hardly seemed to be the experienced hand with the doughty spirit called for in this situation. Was she up to the task?

Edith Atkinson

In 1912, the city of Miami had the semblance of a frontier western cow town, and why any sensible citizen from a relatively civilized place like Portland, Maine, would decide to find a new life this far South was hard to understand.

Edith Meserve, a young woman of Portland, and two friends chose to make the trek. Her friends thought it a great adventure. With Edith it was different. She had some health problems, and her doctor suggested she relocate to a warmer climate. Only a temporary lark for her friends, but to Edith Meserve it was to be the beginning of a new and exciting life taking her to heights never contemplated.

No job, no relatives in town, no plan—she was like one of those early pioneers striking out for the 1848 gold mine rush in California. Her doctor had recommended a warmer clime, but Miami then, as now, was an absolute hot-house eight months of the year. Unfazed, Ms. Meserve, a twenty-one-year-old, with all the optimism of youth, found work as a secretary and a variety of other jobs and began her acclimation to the new life.

Even back in Portland, Edith had been a go-getter. Here, with full responsibility for her own well-being, she accepted the challenge. Being a secretary was fine, but somewhere along the way, while working for a lawyer, Edith's ambition turned to the legal profession. At that time there were relatively few female attorneys in the country, and few, if any, in Florida, let alone in backwoods Miami. Her dream was not likely to bear fruition, but that didn't hold her back.

Henry Atkinson, her boss, was considerably older, but somehow he was attracted to this vivacious young woman, and she to this serious, scholarly lawyer. There's no record of their courtship, but there is a court record in the State of New York attesting to their marriage on September 12, 1916. She was twenty-five years of age; he fifty-seven.

Hardly settled into their December-May marriage, Edith's thoughts returned to pursuing law as a profession and the wonderful prospect of practicing with her husband. Even before finding a law school to admit her, she already could visualize the new sign on their office door—Atkinson and Atkinson, Attorneys at Law.

For a woman to gain admittance to law school would be no easy task. And due to her health it had to be a Florida school. As luck would have it, a newspaper article describing the new Stetson Law School, located in central Florida, solved her problem. As a sign of progress, Stetson had proclaimed in a news release it was now admitting women. Wasting not a minute, Edith applied, was accepted, and her new life truly began.

Top student in her graduating class, she had earned A's in every course except one. She never tried to explain that B, and the law professor responsible has been equally silent on his obvious misjudgment. At last it would be the law firm of Atkinson and Atkinson. But it was not to be. The very same day she had gained her law degree, husband Henry was appointed to the Dade County Circuit Court.

She spent the next few months as his secretary, helping him organize his new judicial office. Once done, lawyer Edith Atkinson was off to open her own private practice. Within a year, beginning as a solo practitioner, she was selected to be secretary for the Dade County Bar Association. Careerwise, she was the first woman lawyer to win a jury trial in the State of Florida. It was only the beginning of both a spectacular rise in her profession but also the maturation of an uncertain young woman to a person of considerable consequence.

As the year 1925 approached, Judge H. W. Penney suddenly resigned his juvenile court judgeship, and on January 2, 1925, Governor Cary Hardee appointed Edith M. Atkinson his successor. Apparently, Judge Penney's old position as justice of the peace had become available, and he chose not to complete the final six months of his term due to expire on July 1, 1925.

How and why Edith Atkinson was chosen is open to conjecture. A June 1922 graduate of Stetson Law School, a relatively inexperienced lawyer, and one of the few women practicing law in the entire country, her quick ascension to the bench, two years out of law school, ordinarily would raise eyebrows. Besides, the city of Miami was not viewed as some liberal enclave in support of women in public office.

She was, however, number one in her graduating class and by now had established herself as a competent trial lawyer. Nonetheless, for a neophyte lawyer to start in so important a post, though not quite the same level her husband had only recently attained, is still an impressive leap.

Perhaps above all, being married to Henry Atkinson, recently named as the chief judge of the Dade Circuit Court, provided her the big push. He had long gained a fine reputation as a criminal court judge and as well had been highly esteemed as a lawyer, representing most of the early pioneers, including Julia Tuttle. In those days judges were allowed limited practices as private lawyers.

Her claim to fame over the appointment was not her relative youth, gender, or peerless academic record at Stetson Law School. Rather, she and spouse Henry were at that time the only married couple in the entire nation sitting as jurists, a fact noted in the press throughout Florida and beyond.

It is not unlikely that since Judge Penney had abruptly left that post for greener pastures as a justice of the peace, perhaps the juvenile court position may not have been so prized an appointment as first projected. And as with the earlier appointment of Judge Penney, Governor Hardee apparently was a firm believer that one can learn on the job. After all, how many kids can be saved from truancy and an errant life of foraging fruit groves?

There is no record of a recommendation by the Democratic Party Executive Committee as existed in Judge Penney's pursuit of the job. Nor were twenty ballots required as occurred when H. W. Penny won the nod. The greater likelihood had Governor Hardee calling on Dade's chief judge for advice on the appointment. Since her term of office was only for the six unexpired months of Penney's term, no serious whiff of political maneuvering was present, and no negative community reaction emerged.

During the next few months Judge Edith Atkinson held court in a room in an industrial school building around NE Second Avenue and Fifteenth Street (later known as the Lindsay-Hopkins Vocational School).

This was a temporary shelter awaiting the completion of the Flagler Street courthouse, where the juvenile court would find a place on the fifth floor, joining the entire galaxy of judicial divisions as well as the offices of the prosecuting attorneys.

Edith Atkinson had hardly warmed the seat of her new chair when she was before the county commission seeking help. Two weeks after her July 2, 1925, appointment, she was before the county commission with requests for immediate action. She had two main objectives: the completion of the Dade County Farm for Boys and the securing of adequate quarters for the juvenile court.

Dade County Sheriff Henry Chase had notified the judge that he had instructed his deputies to accept no more boys for imprisonment in the county jail. Instead, he suggested the boys be placed in the girl's home, an idea Judge Atkinson promptly rejected.

Apparently the problem at the boy's home was a lack of a lighting system. Atkinson pleaded for a temporary lighting system or the County renting a private home to temporarily house the delinquent boys. The commission took that under advisement.

As to the quarters, Judge Atkinson stated that the present site was totally unsuitable, lacked staff, and that the increased workload made it impossible to function. The county commission directed Commissioner Cecil Watson to look into possibly renting a storeroom as quarters for the court.

The county commission had not rushed to oblige Judge Penney when he had become the first judge a few years back, and wasn't about to bend too forward for his successor. It would be several years later, before a new county courthouse was built (1929), that real quarters would be available. When completed, this new courthouse, rising fifteen floors and built on the same site over the old county courthouse, was not only then the tallest building in Dade County, but considered at that time one of the finest architectural structures of that era.

Neither Judge Atkinson nor her successors were satisfied until a separate building for the juvenile court was constructed many years later. As to a site for holding delinquents awaiting trial, that would take even longer. The county commission was obviously in no rush to properly house the juvenile court or the children it served.

Beyond the problems with the county commission, making the adjustment to her new post was no easy task for Atkinson. She was a northerner, a relative newcomer to the South, suddenly enthroned in a position of authority over a new court enterprise in a community where cultural distinctions differed rather sharply from her Portland, Maine, upbringing.

Her acceptance in the community required her to trod carefully to gain the respect of fellow townspeople. In addition she had to quickly display strong leadership qualities to certify her fitness to hold office. Serving as a judge might be a lot more difficult than getting the appointment. She would need a wisdom beyond her years to overcome those hurdles.

She had, however, an excellent mentor in her husband. His background and standing in the community might well carry the day for her. His impressive and influential position, however, was also bound to place her in his shadow. A shadow hard to emerge from.

Henry Fulton Atkinson was a true southerner, born in Savannah, Georgia, in 1861. His father, a civil engineer, had served with the Confederate forces at an arsenal in Macon, Georgia, manufacturing weaponry for the Confederate soldiers. His mother had died thirteen months after his birth.

Henry practiced law in Titusville, Florida, before coming to Miami in 1897. He soon became the city attorney, drawing up the first incorporation papers and the city charter for the City of Miami.

His judicial career earned him the highest of marks. As a criminal court judge, he had been assigned the most difficult cases. That practice followed upon his promotion to the circuit court, where Judge Ad, as he was called by his admiring townsfolk, also tried the tough ones. Lacking a blind filing system in those days, the chief judge made the case assignments.

No one could have envisioned that little Edith Atkinson, née Meserve, could or would rise to the reputation she eventually attained. Although the position of juvenile judge had a high-sounding status, it was a new venture, totally untested. That Judge Penney gave up this judgeship to return to a role as justice of the peace, a position much lower in the judicial hierarchy, was a telling commentary.

Maybe it was propinquity—being in the right place at the right time. Or being the wife of a well-known and respected judge. But whatever the reason, the bottom line was that she had to make a positive impact on her own. And that she did.

Undoubtedly, upon becoming a juvenile court judge, she had concerns about upholding her husband's fine name that she now bore. Also required was recognition that the traditions of the South needed to be respected. Not inconsequential was her role as a woman in what had previously been a man's profession. Although totally aware of these concerns, Edith Atkinson was not fazed.

She was an independent, confident young woman wise enough to realize there was a special role she had to play. As judge, she would have to move softly on the southern tradition that encompassed her community and her husband. There was also a judicial face and a public one in being a judge, particularly with a husband and wife duo, both being in the same judicial arena.

Furthermore, there were relationships to wrestle with. He, not only as a male elder in the community with an unimpeachable reputation, was entitled to be the lead player. She, of course, many years his junior, any effort to rise above a secondary role might well have redounded against her, diminishing her acceptance in the community.

To her credit, she handled their respective places in the judicial firmament with skill. Judge Ad was the unchallenged mentor to her as he was to most lawyers in Miami as well as with his fellow colleagues on the bench. He seemed to have come to that standing almost by birth. Edith had one thing going for her that no other jurist in Florida could lay claim to: being a woman.

In growing cities, particularly in the South, it was the presence of social and fraternal organizations that maintained the spirit, if not the soul of the community. Men's groups, like the six men's civic clubs then in existence in Miami, were strong participants in the life of the community, but actually the ladies' groups far excelled in both number and activity.

Judge Edith Atkinson, seeking quick access to important civic groups, quickly associated with her club sisters. It was a move that would enhance her reputation and serve as a strong political asset. In the years ahead, all office seekers would attempt to engage their support, but for a woman in politics, heretofore solely a man's game, these established groups were manna from heaven.

In 1925 there were twenty-three clubs of the female persuasion in Dade County, with a total membership of about three thousand. These were not firebrand activists taking to the streets, like many of the early northern suffragettes. They organized around garden clubs and other social activities, but underneath they sought to improve conditions for children and the general well-being of all citizens.

Organized a decade earlier, one of the most prominent was the Married Ladies' Afternoon Club, later becoming the Miami Woman's Club. They were in the forefront, seeking improvement for the plight of children. The first library in Dade County was started in 1912 by the Miami Woman's Club on land donated by Miami pioneer Henry Flagler.

Yes, the male Miami Lions Club helped establish the Children's Home Society, but it was the Woman's Club volunteers who staffed it to find adoptive parents. Other Dade County cities also joined the Woman's Club movement. In Coral Gables they established the first kindergarten classes in their public schools.

Later, dental clinics for school children in Coral Gables were added by the Woman's Club. Familiar family names of early pioneers such as Mrs. Alexander Orr III and Mrs. M. Lewis Hall were in the forefront. During WWII, the Miami Beach Woman's Club gave up their now-historic building and property to the U.S. Armed Forces for training the military.

The Miami Junior League was also a strong ally of Judge Atkinson. Following the pattern of the more matronly elders of the Woman's Club, this group set-up as the "The Miami Organization of Junior League Girls." In 1927 it was chartered as the Miami Junior League. This was not a group of girls primping for their debutante ball. They sought action in behalf of their community, mostly for the benefit of children.

One would expect these Junior League girls to be more interested in being debutantes attending cotillions as expected of proper young ladies of that era. Instead, they followed a discipline that has long since identified the Junior League—improving the lot of deprived children. They were serious about their efforts to the point of extracting a fine of fifty cents for absences from meetings and twenty-five cents for tardiness of more than half an hour.

The devastating 1926 hurricane saw them swing into action. The Children's Home Society had suffered immeasurable damage and sought relief assistance from the Junior League. Under the leadership of league president Kay Pancoast, the League took temporary ownership of the Children's Home Society, caring for the children during that period until the home was returned ten years later to the Children's Society in 1936.

Letters congratulating the Miami Junior League for its effort in operating the Florida Children's Home after the destruction of the 1926 hurricane were printed in the *Miami Herald*. Duly noted was the role Judge Atkinson played in bringing the Junior League to the assistance of the Children's Home, a private institution.

Martha Lummus, then president of the Junior League, led the membership in choosing "the most needed project," the Dade County Children's Service Bureau, to assist the home in further foster placement for children. Together these women's groups, along with the still-influential male groups, continued their focus on children and actively persuaded government to respond.

It was a plus for Edith when in 1925 a woman was elected juvenile court judge in neighboring Key West. After all, Edith had set the way. Key West Juvenile Court Judge Helen Williams was invited to visit Judge Edith Atkinson to observe her court operation. The press dutifully noted her visit, adding to Judge Atkinson's stature in the community.

These were the kinds of groups that Judge Atkinson teamed up with during her term of office. They supported her efforts with the legislature and gave her a platform from which she could be heard. She, in turn, was able to alert and advise the community through those appearances.

One thing these groups had in common, for certain, was their support for Judge Edith Atkinson. They seemed to literally adore this bright, energetic woman lawyer, who continuously cajoled, pleaded, and sometimes was even critical of their efforts. As husband Henry Atkinson was the strong legal voice in the community, Edith became the conscience. The two were looked upon as a team.

The novelty of having husband and wife as judges piqued community and press attention for a while. Both Atkinsons enjoyed the special attention it brought, but they realized Edith would have to make her own way on her own merits. Her husband, asked by a reporter if she would use her maiden name rather than her married one, responded, "I think she has got used to the name Atkinson, and likes it."

When asked the same question, Edith responded, "I have no Michael Strange proclivities." Michael Strange, a highly popular author and poet of those days, hobnobbed with celebrities and made the press with regularity. In fact, Michael Strange was the pen name used by Ms. Blanche Oelricks. In those days some women engaged in activities usually occupied by men chose to hide their gender. Edith wisely stuck with her married name.

The women's groups, more particularly, were themselves strengthened and emboldened to have so strong a leader as Judge Edith. When she spoke out, one could feel a sense of pride among her women supporters. This, in turn, gave her another level of political prestige among her judicial colleagues and unquestionably with her husband.

With bad days ahead—destructive hurricanes, land boom burst, and the Wall Street crash of 1929—Edith Atkinson would need all her assets to stay the course for children. The worst was yet to come.

Shortly before entering her first political battle to hold her newly appointed seat, she and Henry had a joint *Miami News* interview on August 2, 1925. Today, no public relations counselor would advise husband and wife jurists to try that maneuver. Too much chance of a disagreement assuring a headline tomorrow, pointing out marital discord.

The subject of the interview: why the high rate of divorce in this country? Judge Henry kind of rambled on, placing the blame on a society continuously on the move, population shifts causing instability. He cited situations in Florida where one spouse coming here to avoid the cold Northern weather might have a mate viewing the hot summer here as intolerable, thereby declining to join, with a divorce ensuing.

Judge Edith echoed his views, "That's a fact," citing how she had been trying to induce her folks in new England to join her, but "they still believe Miami is the next place to Hades."

Notwithstanding Judge Edith's support of her husband's thin effort, she then went on to detail the program she intended to pursue for the juvenile court. She felt that making home life better for children would decrease marital discord and thereby lessen divorces. A much more sensitive response than her spouse's approach of blaming the weather for the high divorce rate.

She came up with other strong ideas in that interview. Her Visiting School Teacher Program offered school aides to provide a direct contact with the parent at home, thereby improving family life. Also, the establishment of a child guidance clinic to assess the child's progress and proper placement in school, and as well the child's health condition. Her emphasis on a stronger family life to diminish divorces struck a responsive chord.

These were positions she would put forth with regularity in the years ahead. Although her proposal featuring the visiting school teachers and a child guidance center was a huge step for a neophyte judge in that era and in that community, nonetheless some of her visions came to pass sooner than expected.

In that interview, though her statements were somewhat more to the point than her husband's, Judge Edith still managed to support her spouse and, at the same time, promote her cause for children. It was a role she would continue to play: deferential to her husband on the one hand, yet being a strong advocate for children on the other.

Barely with time to place her nameplate on her desk, she faced the 1925 election. Unlike gut-fighting political races of later decades, this one had two gentlemen and a lady contesting, each of the campaigners playing within proper bounds. Newspaper accounts described the race as "hotly" contested, though little appeared in the way of acrimony.

Some guarded references were made to her youth, inexperience, and gender, but Atkinson handed out palm cards that said, Elect a Woman for a Woman's Job, directly addressing the gender issue. This was a rather sassy statement challenging her two male opponents head-on. It foretold she would be no pushover on any issue.

By addressing that issue forcefully—a point obviously in the minds of voters—she turned it into a positive asset. Although not of the same activist cloth as the Jane Addams/Lillian Wald types, this little political handout suggested that living in a more liberal environment, she could well have been with them right up there at the barricades.

Edith Atkinson, not only a woman of broad vision, also was a minimalist, in that she kept a ledger of expenses and law fees about virtually every transaction involving her early years. Her ledger, safely entrusted to the Miami Historical Society, lists the minutiae that made up her early life. Keeping this kind of ledger apparently was not followed into her later years, suggesting she may have outgrown the need.

Ledger entries describing her first campaign are probably typical of Miami political campaigns of that era. Most of her expenses were for newspaper ads. As in every summertime, this was the broiling period for Miami, and door-to-door campaigning was not the mode. Debating before civic clubs was only beginning to catch on. Besides, this was a new position, and the duties therein were not too clear to the public, nor was there a feeling in the community that the post was a significant one.

Judge Edith, the title that stayed with her all her years, had little time to organize the new court. She had an election to win for the full four years of the term. Not exactly the hand-shaking, baby-kissing type, she needed to learn fast.

According to her ledger, her 1925 campaign expenses totaling $1,800, had newspaper ads as a key expense. Running countywide, she managed to include not only the *Miami Herald* and the *Miami News* but local papers in Miami Beach and Coral Gables. The total cost to the *Miami Herald* for all weekly ads run throughout the campaign was $430. For the *Miami News* it was $250. Her big cost was $250 for a filing fee to qualify for office.

No fee was listed for a public relations man to provide spin, but a Burt Reiley was shown for $200 for advertising, and he may well have been her PR man. She also paid dues that year to a variety of organizations: Women Lawyers, League of Women Voters, Pan Hellenic Club, and a few others that certainly improved her election chances. She won the election handily.

The ledger did not reflect their living abode, but old reports point to them living at one time in a quiet neighborhood on Twelfth Street. They seemed to move every couple of years. One report had them living on a five-acre estate on the Miami River. Another had them staying at a Dallas Park apartment in Miami.

Entries in the ledger also provided other insights into her lifestyle. She and Henry didn't speculate in the land boom, but they did invest in land purchases. They purchased a lot on Hibiscus Island in 1924 for $5,400. No resale price is shown, but it probably produced a nice profit. Other lots were also purchased.

Later there was a dispute with the federal government over a property they owned in North Key Largo. Apparently the Fish and Game Department had a crocodile natural refuge adjoining this property, and the government sought to take the private land for environmental purposes.

A protracted court struggle for several years ensued with the entire neighborhood of property owners aligned against the government. When the federal budget allocation for the lawsuit ran out, the government finally agreed to a settlement with the landowners.

Her own law career as an independent lawyer, prior to going on the bench, showed her with an active practice. From the ledger entries, some of her clients appeared to be well fixed, but the ledger showed no fee over $150. Apparently her husband's prominence as chief circuit court judge had promoted no rush of law business.

Since her time in private practice was limited, and the ledger may not reflect the full extent of her practice, we can assume, based on her ability, that had she not gone to the bench, her talent would have placed her among the top flight of the Dade County Bar.

Involved in many youth projects and with so many civic groups, she became an activist in issues beyond children. The Miami Woman's Club sponsored a bill requiring all employees to be fingerprinted. The purpose clearly enunciated in the preamble was to protect citizens against tourists and undesirables who might tend to commit criminal offenses. She signed the petition but was not a spokesperson in behalf of the bill.

Perhaps the proposed legislation had a worthy motive, but were there other implications? In all likelihood, it probably had a racial purpose similar to that of the Miami Beach ordinance then in force requiring all employees to carry identification cards. This was enforced after 8:00 p.m. in the evening and was construed by many as an effort to keep Negroes off the Miami Beach streets after nightfall.

In those days Negroes were tightly segregated in Miami with actual lines virtually demarcating proper zones for each of the races. The Miami Woman's Club, as well as other civic groups, though seeking to improve conditions for all children regardless of race, nonetheless maintained a strict color line.

Commenting in tears, on the civil rights movement, Enid Pinkney, a student at Miami's Booker T. Washington High School, described an experience in the late 1940s. Asked by her teacher to attend a meeting at the exclusive whites-only Miami Woman's Club, she was welcomed but told she could not eat lunch with the members.

Student Enid Pinkney walked back to her high school, had her meal, and returned to the club, saying resignedly, "I was more interested in listening to the missionaries (at the Woman's Club) and getting a strong education."

Rather than struggle for the cause, student Enid had wisely concluded that, for the moment, her education was more important than her personal emotions. Her experience was a continuation of the custom twenty years earlier during Judge Edith's time. This was the racial separation that had become an integral part of America's fabric, particularly in the South.

In the 1920s and '30s, the civil rights movement had not yet become the heated issue it would assume a few decades later. The Woman's Club, longtime leaders for improving conditions for youngsters, was then and has always been a likely place to find assistance for children's programs involving all races. But the traditions of the South were still carefully maintained.

South Florida was not then a stronghold of the lingering emotions of the cause of the Confederacy. Nonetheless, the common street attitudes of Georgia and Alabama still prevailed. There's no history to show Judge Atkinson joining in southern race customs, but she likely acceded to the prevailing Miami view, certainly one her husband supported.

Back in the courtroom, things were changing considerably from Judge Penny's day some few years earlier. From the four hundred juveniles appearing before Judge Penney in 1922, mostly for vandalism and other acts of mischief, her calendar rose tenfold to over four thousand cases in 1926. Civilization had truly arrived.

Probably one of the strongest advocates for the advancement of women in Florida, she wrote papers and made speeches pursuing that cause. Her strong treatise on giving women the right to serve as jurors drew attention in legal circles. The debate that followed was somewhat inane, objectors claiming that providing separate bathrooms for ladies, along with overnight sleeping facilities for a sequestered jury, created problems for the sexes. Eventually those concerns were worked out.

Judge Atkinson wasted no time in taking full command. Judge Penney's term had ended Miami's period of quiescence. The real estate boom and a devastating hurricane had totally changed the face of Miami and the surrounding towns and cities newly incorporated. The boom would eventually explode, and the distress caused by the hurricane would wane. However, the impact generated by these events considerably changed the entire lifestyle of the community.

The land boom that began in the early twenties reached its peak in 1926. A city now with a two hundred thousand population, four times the growth in a four-year span, had been moving upward at an accelerated pace. In his five-year report to the City on July 1, 1926, Miami City manager Frank Wharton optimistically described the future. "No municipality has been confronted with situations as we have—unprecedented growth of city—not only population—but a stupendous building program and numerous large developments, necessitate the rapid expansion of the City."

Wharton chose not to describe the underlying cause of the prosperity—the land boom investments that had captured the attention of speculators from all of America, who had flocked to Miami for the kill.

Manager Wharton continued his report, outlining the needs of the community in terms of projects to be undertaken. These included harbor development, increasing fresh water conduits, proper sewage disposal, and also the establishment of traffic controls. Problems, it should be noted, that to this day still test the City of Miami.

This was a growing, thriving city on the move, and Manager Wharton was preparing it for the prosperity surely around the corner. For a frontier city, it had moved upward in fine fashion.

One hundred ten acres had been set aside for thirty-six parks to benefit the 22,000 children population with a $30,000 budget for program activities. Not a bad beginning for a city government that today takes pride in their parks system.

The numbers in the police department had risen from 56 in 1921 to 350 in 1926. Separate jail quarters for blacks and whites were provided; previously blacks had been housed in cagelike cells.

The first city commission elected under the charter consisted of five bankers. They ran at large as a group. The Bankers' Ticket, as they called themselves, won easily. With property sales as the major business practice, this appeared to be a wise choice. Hard to believe that in Miami today, five bankers would run as a team for election—and win.

Other factors, however, quickly entered the scene to disturb the rosy picture. Out-of-town land speculators, banks, and local property owners all ferociously joined the land rush. Land was a money pot, and greed the guide. One piece of land that had sold in 1914 for $1,500 went for a million and a half in 1926. Millionaires at the end of 1925 suddenly became poor by the time the hurricane struck.

A commentator of that time wryly noted, "Lots are bring sold by the gallon." Another noting the sparse amount of lodgings for out-of-town land speculators remarked, "Hotels are renting 'hot beds'—two to a bed, each on a twelve hour shift."

Then came the 1926 hurricane. Called the Big Blow (hurricanes were not yet designated by first names), it hit in September and devastated Miami and other areas up to Central Florida. It was a Category 4 hurricane labeled by the Weather Bureau as, "probably the most destructive hurricane ever to strike the United States." There was little the bankers' commission could do. Although they had performed credibly as city commissioners, this onslaught was beyond theirs or anyone else's ability.

The *New York Times* in a front-page story described Miami seeking to conscript twenty-five thousand laborers for repair duty. A flotilla of destroyers arrived from the Charleston Naval Base bringing typhoid serum. Storehouses, where liquor seized under the federal Prohibition laws was stored, were emptied to provide emergency medical use for doctors.

Both disasters, the natural one and the economic one, turned Miami upside down, increasing the work and responsibility of all law enforcement agencies, including the juvenile court.

It was a serious setback for Judge Atkinson's crusading efforts. The economic and physical damage had tragically disrupted families. She and the entire community of Miami joined in the salvage effort. Rooftops of homes battered by the hurricane suddenly sprouted spirited signs: "We are still here. Let's go!"

Judge Atkinson, taking heart from the spirit of her fellow citizens, accelerated her whirlwind activity. She appeared before every civic group, traveled the state seeking new legislation, did studies on crime and further identified herself as a moving force in behalf of children, locally and beyond Miami's borders.

Like Judge Ben Lindsey's style, her visions were far ahead of her time. Unlike Ben Lindsey and the other more radical activists of his era always pressing for a fight, she was comfortable with the local lifestyle, joining in with most of the conservative beliefs then prevalent. Thus, she avoided conflict with the establishment and made them more accepting of her new approaches to children.

Her early philosophy was more of a firmness approach than one of saving children from the evils of child labor that dominated thinking in the industrialized areas of New York and Chicago. This came from her own childhood where children were expected to work hard and obey both the civil law and the religious scriptures.

Her family, century-old pioneers in Portland, Maine, had a tradition of a strong family setting with children following the path of their elders. This, of course, coincided with the attitudes of her new Miami constituents. In an early speech she urged, "There's a growing need for old-fashioned parental control in America. Parents should assume their proper authority rather than pass the problems on to the public offices and the courts."

As she progressed, she realized that parents alone either could not or would not solve the problems of delinquent and troubled children. Almost all the programs she sought to institute were a serious departure from the existing structure. She encouraged parent involvement but began to recognize that government and particularly the courts would have to play a major role enforcing the programs and also assisting parents in their role.

Her campaign statewide for a constitutional amendment to establish a domestic relations court was in line with the new thinking. Why not a court that went directly into the home, providing efforts to save a family where possible, or to hold the pieces of a broken family together? It was a beautiful vision but a difficult task. When the going got tough, she always had Henry to call upon.

Unquestionably, husband Henry—Judge Ad—was a great asset to her career. Many years younger, she sought Henry's advice in all her ventures. For her project to have the legislature create a separate domestic relations court, she drafted all the big guns available, including her own esteemed Chief Circuit Court Judge Henry Atkinson.

Henry wrote a three-page scholarly paper, terming it only a "horseback opinion." His views coincided with the other heavy legal thinkers Edith had enlisted. Their conclusion: only a constitutional amendment could satisfy her intent.

Unanimously, all agreed with Henry that rather than a separate court, her domestic relations project be folded into the circuit court as a division, the same procedure as had originally brought the juvenile court into being. It wasn't until Judge Walter Beckham succeeded Atkinson that the domestic relations court was established, but the groundwork had been laid by Edith Atkinson.

Judge Atkinson also moved into an area that, at that time and for some time in the future, would receive only perfunctory attention. Beyond juveniles committing street crimes was the plight of children abandoned, neglected, and abused. Citizens preferred to focus on juveniles committing criminal acts who were a threat to the community. She created an awareness of dependent children—a class of children the juvenile courts would wrestle with forever.

Back then these children were deemed excess baggage in the community. The court's approach was to only storage them in homes or orphanages. In the last half of the nineteenth century, the pioneers of the child-saver movement in New York and Chicago first began to address this concern.

By the twentieth century, the concept of the "best interest of the child" became the philosophy of the new juvenile court. Parents would no longer have an absolute right to their child where abuse, neglect, and abandonment enter the picture. Under this new thinking, the court could and would terminate the rights of the parents. That was indeed radical thinking for a society that had viewed children, as property, under the complete domain of the owner or parent.

Judge Atkinson's advocacy moved slowly in that direction, setting the path for Dade County to begin to address it. Other states began years earlier in that direction, but Florida was moving up.

With or without husband Henry's help, she moved in all circles. She served as president of the national women's legal fraternity Phi Delta Delta at a time when women, not encouraged to practice law, were an absolute novelty in the legal profession. She also helped create the state Welfare Board and traveled the country advocating State aid to mothers via pensions.

Early on, in her determination to lower the crime rate among children, she once spoke in favor of sterilization of parents suffering from certain specified diseases. This, to prevent an increase of the socially unfit population. Back in those days, this concept was accepted in some scientific circles as well as among several law enforcement leaders. Fortunately, she quickly abandoned this concept because it seemed a frontal attack on the minority poor.

Following her predecessor's direction, Judge Atkinson was reluctant to send offenders to the State School for Boys at Marianna, Florida. Located in rustic Central Florida, the Marianna institution had inadequate facilities and a reputation for harsh treatment. This was a place for the incorrigibles. Many Florida cities, with virtually no local rehab programs, had no choice but to send their errant children to Marianna, where they often suffered inhumane treatment.

In order to create a presence in Dade County for delinquents not viewed as requiring lengthy incarceration, the Dade County government came into the picture by providing a residential boys home and a girls home on the outskirts of the county in then faraway Kendall. At the beginning, dependent children were also admitted.

With no neighborhoods in sight, this was a large tract of land, which then also housed the Old People's Home, the county hospital and a laundry and workshop. Also a chicken yard, later converted to a vocational area for residents of the boys and girls homes to learn animal husbandry for a possible future vocation.

To monitor the county's concerns the board of county commissioners created the Board of Visitors consisting of leading citizens to periodically visit these sites, reporting back to the county commission. This excellent approach involved leading community figures. It displayed a county commission, both caring and politically astute.

The early Board of Visitors also included important industrialists, winter residents in Dade County who sponsored programs for delinquents back home. The first board included James R. Mellon (of the Mellon family), president of an Allegheny, Pennsylvania, company, Industrial Farm, and George R. Hilton, president of Boys' Work, Inc. Mr. Hilton ran several children's programs located in cities on the eastern seaboard.

Locals on the board included the Junior League's Mrs. Joe H. Gill and Mrs. F. J. Ravlin, from two prominent longtime Dade County families. In addition to serving in an oversight capacity, the Board of Visitors raised money to augment the sparse funding provide by the Dade County Commission.

Judge Atkinson, a strong supporter of the Board of Visitors, made it a point to participate in all their activities. And why not? It was a perfect political vehicle in which to promote her concerns and surely brought credit to her as a strong advocate for children. Besides, the county commission had authorized the senior judge to make the Board of Visitors appointments. She would have complete control.

In later years that control would be a bone of contention between the senior judges and the county commission. Her successors in office also continued a strong affinity for the Board of Visitors. To their satisfaction, for the next forty years the Board of Visitors functioned as their gatekeeper to the county commission.

Near the end of the Judge Walter Beckham era (1933-1960), when criticism of the juvenile court became more pronounced, many county officials seeking to eliminate the board described the board as merely an appendage of the juvenile court judges.

Eventually, in 1963, during one of the many power struggles of that time between the judges and the county commissioners, the Board of Visitors was discarded by the County. By then the board had become an ancient relic with little power and no particular use to either the judges or the county commissioners.

True, the judges may have in some fashion used the vehicle of the Board of Visitors to highlight their own efforts. However, the Board of Visitors had been even more valuable to the county commission, who, since they had little taste for funding children's programs, would refer all requests to the Board of Visitors for screening.

Early on, lacking rehab programs, Miami used the court probation officer as the point person in terms of guidance for youth in trouble. A probation officer, having direct contact with the child and family was then the key operator in the court system. Further, the Marianna State School for Boys—a last, last resort for incarceration—offered no staffing for rehab purposes. Spotting these weakness in our system, Judge Atkinson took up the cudgels for additional probation officers.

First, she convinced the Florida legislature to replace volunteer probation officers with a paid professional staff. It was hiring one officer at a time, but before long there were three, including a woman. In essence, the probation officer was the social worker, the intake counselor, the court bailiff—the works. The beginning of a total court system was in process.

In order to provide programs, Judge Atkinson was instrumental in organizing the first City of Miami Recreation Department to create play areas and provide actual programs from what was barren land. She also was one of the original founders of the Miami Boys Club, an institution that to this day offers perhaps the best keep-them-off-the-streets recreational services for kids at loose ends.

This came about from a trip to New York visiting various settlement-house youth programs. There she ran into the head of the national Boys Club movement, a man named Atkinson (no relative). The Boys Club concept was then beginning to take hold throughout the country. Impressed with his program, she invited Mr. Atkinson to Miami at her own expense to spread the word among civic groups on organizing a boys club. As a result the SW Boys Club came into being. Today, several Boys Club branches exist here, and Judge Edith is still remembered there for her early efforts to bring the other Mr. Atkinson to town.

Bringing out-of-town advocates with fresh new ideas prompted her to invite other guest speakers from faraway cities to infuse Miami residents with new programs and concepts relating to child welfare.

One was Sophie Loeb, a wealthy socialite, head of the Child Welfare Committee of America. Ms. Loeb directed the Child Welfare Board of New York and was on a crusade to eliminate orphan asylums, proposing instead that public funds be provided for support in a home setting.

As the foremost promoter of welfare legislation in the country, Ms. Loeb came here to arrange a conference with Miami and Florida welfare workers to plan beneficial legislation for the relief of fatherless children in this state. She pointed out that forty-two states had endeavored to care for poor children directly in their homes whenever possible.

Providing relief for destitute parents eventually became part of federal programs during the President Franklin Roosevelt years. His social legislation for the poor became the key to overcome the economic depression then enveloping the country. Judge Atkinson did not publicly endorse Ms. Loeb's program, though part of it was similar to her own effort to offer pensions for destitute mothers.

In all likelihood, Ms. Loeb's plan to eliminate all orphan asylums may have been a bit too radical for conservative Miami back in 1927. Judge Atkinson did not hesitate, however, to welcome Loeb's presence with this progressive concept. It was a good learning experience for her club members to hear firsthand what those "damn Yankees" were doing about problems similar to their own.

It was a lot easier for well-educated wealthy women to adopt a "cause" and seek out followers among more receptive audiences in the more liberal communities of the North. Judge Edith had to be a lot more selective and bide her time to first educate her constituents and then to persuade them. No easy task.

She worked closely with a stalwart local women's group, the Junior League of Miami (JLM), which since its inception has been involved in children's issues. With her assistance the JLM began a child guidance clinic in 1926.

In the wake of the 1926 hurricane, followed by the Great Depression of 1931, the JLM came to the rescue of the Children's Home Society. Under severe economic constraints, the Children's Home Society turned to Judge Atkinson, who, along with JLM president, Kay Pancoast, worked out an arrangement for the JLM to take over responsibility for the home.

The Junior League ran the home from 1931 to 1936 when conditions permitted return to the Children's Home Society. Taking over the operation of an organization involved in so delicate a task as placing children for adoption was a difficult chore. Fortunately, Junior League members had been serving as volunteers and were also able to provide financial assistance to keep the home operational.

In 1929 Judge Atkinson also invited Mrs. Marjorie Bell, field secretary of the National Probation Association, to address the Kiwanis Club. At a luncheon meeting at Burdine's Department Store, Mrs. Bell described her recent effort in Tampa. There, her team of trained social workers had studied the manner in which court personnel handled the problems of underprivileged children and other methods used in juvenile court.

The team then presented the Tampa Juvenile Court with a set of proposals to improve their programs. This was no recruiting program to further a cause, but rather an effort to upgrade and professionalize existing programs. For the first time a professional expert had undertaken an evaluation of a Florida juvenile court.

Mrs. Bell talked about accrediting court probation officers as well acquiring college-degree social workers as court counselors. She pointed out clearly that all these changes were funneled through the courts for the judge's approval. "Slowly," Mrs. Bell pointed out, "the judges were acquiring official control of the total operation."

This was good news for Judge Atkinson. In her courtroom she had maintained control mostly by default. The question of, who's in charge? would not become an issue in Miami for another decade or so. Whether the court ran the show or county officials or state social agencies would become a major issue throughout the twentieth century and beyond.

Educating civic groups through outside national experts was the best way to not only bring a focus on modern approaches, but it emphasized the significant role juvenile court judges could play. In these efforts, Edith Atkinson was doing more than enhancing her own name and role. She was opening the way for juvenile judges of the future to step beyond the traditional adjudicatory role of only determining legal issues. Advocacy for children, on and off the bench, would find many judges following the path of Judge Edith Atkinson.

Edith Atkinson was into every new venture for children. Perhaps her greatest identification was with the Girl Scouts. An early leader in that movement, she has received international recognition for her service. Long after she had retired from the bench, she continued her association with the Girl Scouts. The newly sprung city of Miami, struggling from mangroves and alligators, woefully short in addressing the growth and development of their youth, had found a forceful leader in Edith Atkinson.

In the public schools, her Visiting Teachers idea to augment the regular teaching staff by providing aides to counsel troubled youth began to take hold. The Elks Club agreed to pay a thousand dollars for one visiting teacher, the Dade School Board picked up the tab for the other visiting teacher.

Judge Atkinson saw the visiting teacher as a combination classroom aide, someone to address specific problems for the child and also to involve parents. She went so far as to optimistically predict, "If this succeeds, it will do away with my job." One in every school was her goal. She persuaded the Kiwanis Club and others to also join in support of the effort.

By 1927, Judge Atkinson had fairly well framed her approach to the job. The advent of the motor vehicle had become a new factor. She wrote articles and conducted studies of automobile crime, predicting in one study that this new-fangled vehicle called an automobile is and will be responsible for many crimes caused by children.

Doing an analysis of ninety-six cases for the month of June, she found delinquent boys following a new path to grand larceny by stripping automobiles, something not faced a decade earlier with the horse and buggy. Not then a major concern, but she certainly had identified a problem that has bedeviled us for the past century.

Her research also came up with the surprising fact that dependency cases had risen to equal the delinquency caseload. The increase in dependency cases could have been attributed to the hard economic times prevalent; more likely the problem had been there but simply had gone unnoticed. In the past, delinquents causing damage in the community attracted more attention than dependent children in distress.

Only in recent times has the plight of abused and neglected children begun to receive the attention warranted. Innumerable studies now show that as many as 90 percent of delinquent children with five or more arrests have an early record of dependency. The link is unquestionable.

Judge Atkinson, back in 1927, was beginning to recognize more and more the true bane of children's criminal behavior, namely dependency. Not seriously addressed in Miami until the last decade of the twentieth century by Judge Cindy Lederman (see Lederman chapter), this recognition was a sign of great foresight so long ago from the bench.

Women's groups had been urging this direction early on, but a dichotomy had existed for a long time. In the early years the juvenile court was primarily viewed as an arm to fight crime. Juvenile delinquents were a menace on the streets. The connection between delinquency and dependency had been ignored. The affliction of dependency was a woman's thing, something that only do-gooder social workers addressed. Crime in the street delinquency was the male macho thing that aroused the community.

Although Judge William Gladstone (see Gladstone chapter) first recognized the failure of juvenile court judges to realize the relationship of dependency to delinquency, it may also have been the preponderance of male judges on the Dade County bench and the nationwide war on crime that slowed the full realization of the problem.

To be absolutely fair, it is more likely that the community's fear over violent juvenile delinquent behavior demanded that the courts first protect citizens before moving to alleviate the distress of dependent children.

Whatever the answer, it was Judge Atkinson way back then in 1927 who designed a program to address the total children problem—both for delinquents and dependents. She wanted an emphasis on addressing the dilemmas of youth at an early age and the resources to address them.

She sought greater public school training on home life, required courses in early grades that fit children for their eventual roles as parents and follow-up teaching in secondary courses on the care and training of children. Also, institutions to house dependent children and other kinds of recreational and curative resources. Hers was a worthy call, but at that stage only a call into the wind. The world wasn't quite ready.

Shortly thereafter, addressing the Association of Dade County Social Workers at the Hotel Granada in Coral Gables, she hit three main points: strengthening the child labor laws, the need for a state tubercular hospital, and creating a state welfare board. It is noticeable that almost all her movement at this point was in the direction of dependent children. This seemed to be the banner she was already beginning to wave.

Her new elective term was a continuation of the past. Speeches before groups, mostly activists for children, were numerous. Before the Kiwanis Club at the Columbus Hotel, introduced by her husband, she again gave a numerical report of her regular caseload study. This time dependent children exceeded delinquents, confirming her earlier study showing that dependents were present in greater number. Interestingly, in terms of race, there were twice as many white delinquents, and among the 170 dependent children for that three month period; only twenty were Negroes.

In all likelihood, the small number of dependent Negro children may have been due more to the unwillingness and fear of Negro parents to deal with the white establishment, or perhaps it was the lack of concern shown by white officials to address the problems of Negroes.

Judge Atkinson also noted the alarming large number of cases before her involving parents abusing their children. This, along with the sparse number of Negro dependent children, clearly showed the inadequacy in dependency care, a situation that would continue on for decades and decades.

The delinquency problem was not ignored. Chairing a meeting in her office at the Central School Building, Judge Atkinson called in every top government official to discuss ways to combat delinquency. More delinquency cases had been handled during the first nine months of 1928 than during the entire previous year.

Present at the meeting was the entire city and county power structure—city and county commissioners, police chiefs, prosecutors, chairman of the Board of Public Instruction, and the general manager of the Miami Chamber of Commerce, among other community leaders. Their presence made clear the importance of the juvenile court as well as her considerable rise in stature.

The major problem seemed to revolve around high school students frequenting nightclubs and men hanging around schools enticing young girls to take automobile rides. The police agreed to investigate nightclubs and provide better supervision. School nurses were to be employed to detect communicable diseases among school children.

Judge Atkinson closed the meeting with this strong admonition: "More drastic enforcement of the law and the prosecution of persons contributing to the delinquency of children in Miami is essential." There would be many more such meetings in the years ahead in the chambers of juvenile court judges. And many such admonitions. Some meetings effective, some for show, but all with the juvenile court judge in command.

Judge Atkinson had done well in building bridges to all the command posts in the community. It takes more than law enforcement to hold a community together. She had welded both government forces and the civic club circuit into responsible entities. Only time would tell how effectively, but it was a start.

These all-encompassing meetings with government officials were infrequent but important to keep lines of communication open. Recognizing that her real strength, both politically and as a judge, was dealing directly with citizens, Judge Atkinson continued to make the civic club circuit rounds her focus.

Back then, with government providing limited resources for communal activity, it was these local fraternal clubs that proved to be the center of the community. As an activist for children and as well a successful politician, Edith Atkinson was wise to play the club circuit. For her willingness to appear there and her candid assessment of the problems of children, she was a welcome sight.

Her public service ventures did not slow down the efforts to firm up the juvenile court process. Establishing the rules of court, she followed the standards set by the Children's Bureau in Washington, D.C., keeping in frequent contact with Washington officials to maintain her office as up-to-date as possible. In all of her endeavors, her underlying thrust remained Prevention, Not Detention.

Sometimes that was hard to follow, but she and most of her successors maintained that approach. These were the times for action, and she was the leader ready to accept change—rapid change. In her eight years on the bench, more had happened in terms of judicial activism than in any comparable period since. She had planted all the seeds.

Her reelection in 1928, for what would be her final term, passed with little incident. Now firmly established as a local, state, and national leader, she had but token opposition. Ignoring her campaign, she had spent a good part of the year lobbying legislators, never giving up on her pension bill for mothers, a form of which had passed in the U.S. House of Representatives and eventually came into law via the federal government.

The actual reelection campaign in 1928 was shortly coming up, and she found ample support among her followers and in the press. The *Dade County Times* in a half-page story on her qualifications said and accurately predicted,

"The success of Judge Edith Atkinson means, no doubt, she will be returned to office."

The *Miami Review* ran this support editorial on July 3, 1927:

> We made a little journey recently to visit Judge Edith Atkinson and learned something. Judge Edith runs a Court with a heart and soul big and tolerant enough to do the work.
>
> We do not believe any man will have the heart and courage to tackle the intricate problems presented. The work of her Court requires the intuition and wisdom that mothers of the ages have handed down to their daughters.

This editorial followed exactly the line that had propelled Atkinson to victory in 1924 when she first ran a campaign handing out palm cards to voters with the catchy line, Vote for a Woman for a Woman's Job.

This time she took out two-by-six inch political ads in the newspapers featuring her photo along with the copy "Mrs. Edith A Atkinson Who was first Elected in 1924 as JUDGE OF THE JUVENILE COURT Announces Her Candidacy for RE-Election to That Office."

Now, with these ads being fairly well recognized, along with her heightened appearances at local functions, she won easily against her two male opponents, gaining twice as many votes as both opponents combined. The 1928 election firmly established her total acceptance in the community and validated her political credentials.

The reelection campaign had hardly caused her to miss a beat in her activities. She obtained a concurrent resolution in the state legislature calling for a statewide survey of delinquent and dependent children as well as a study of the current juvenile court law. Her goal, a significant one, was to bring all state courts up to a high standard.

With juvenile courts then existing only a handful of years in Florida, and of low status among the legal profession, her effort to uplift the function and operation of juvenile courts was impressive. It would take many years before the changes she sought would even begin to gain a foothold. Not until the U.S. Supreme Court *Gault* decision in 1967 did Florida Bar committees and the Florida Supreme Court become actively involved in this pursuit.

The young woman from Portland, Maine, Edith Meserve, had risen in a decade from this uncertain young person to a leader in the children's movement in Florida. With a flood of firsts to her name, she would always be identified as the first leader for children in Florida.

Her final term on the bench in 1929 started positively, but the dark clouds had already spread an unwelcome message. The economic depression had worsened considerably. Tourism in Florida had disappeared; jobs had become scarce. Judge Atkinson labored as ever, but the economic bad times spread a pall over the community.

President Franklin D. Roosevelt (FDR) made a gallant effort to staunch the economic misfortune with a variety of alphabet agencies designed to address the social ills. These stopgap measures were helpful but not enough. The malaise, the feeling of hopelessness, was pervasive. No overnight cure in sight.

FDR, with his resounding cry "There is nothing to fear, but fear itself," fully captured the despair felt in every corner of the country. The 1929 Wall Street crash, which had stock brokers in New York jumping out of skyscraper windows, reverberated throughout Florida. The value of stocks dropped 40 percent immediately, and by the end of the year were down as much as 90 percent.

Lost among the national priorities was this new juvenile court effort, started some thirty years earlier to save the child and rehabilitate families. With unemployment and out-of-work breadwinners striking terror in families, there was not much room in that period for the voices of child savers. Finding food for the table was the dominant theme, not structuring stability in the court system.

What with a slow recovery from the mammoth 1926 hurricane and other calamities, Florida's tourist season and industries would take a tremendous hit for several years. Things got so bad that the Florida State Police stationed on the Georgia border only permitted people into Florida who could show a means of support. Ninety thousand families in Florida affected by the depression sought relief from the government in the form of federal aid to the needy.

In 1928 Judge Atkinson continued on with her court projects. While her zest was still there, her constituents had more basic needs beyond a court's ability to address. The collapse of the economy changed the face of the country, and at the same time changed the temper of the times.

Politically there was both uncertainty and indifference in Dade County in regard to local races. The contest between Herbert Hoover and Franklin D. Roosevelt for the presidency carried the full attention of voters. The malaise that had swept the country over the economic disaster included an attitude of apathy toward local races.

A disappearing farming economy, a slow recovery from the 1926 hurricane, and the land-boom disaster had added to the economic woes. Few would pause to care about the election of a judge or county commissioner.

FDR had become a beacon of hope for the suffering. The momentum appeared to be going his way. The *Miami Herald* of that day provided much newsprint of the progress of the national political campaign. FDR eventually swept the Republicans out of the White House in 1932 with promises to provide new measures to alleviate the ills that beset the majority of Americans. He is credited with having fulfilled those promises, but in truth, the man on the street had been so frightened at the meager prospects ahead that change in the national leadership was inevitable.

Locally it was somewhat different. Incumbents in office were not at risk. Or so it seemed. Few seats had ever been contested in the past, and good sense suggested that this election would be no different. Blame for the economic crisis was pointed toward Washington, D.C. Attention by the press to local campaigns was only slightly visible. In fact, the public attention to political races in Miami barely had a heartbeat.

Atkinson, by virtue of holding office, was able to obtain media attention more by her activity in office than by campaigning. A January 1931 *Miami Herald* story described the growth of her court, noting that five thousand more case were handled since 1935. The story described Kendall Hall caring for hundreds of delinquent and dependent children each year and concluded that Dade County can be proud of what it is doing for children.

That same month Judge Atkinson obtained a writ of habeas corpus releasing a thirteen-year-old Negro boy from jail. He had been sentenced in municipal court to four days in jail in connection with a police gambling raid. Atkinson had requested his transfer to juvenile court, where proper jurisdiction lay, but the municipal court judge had rejected her request. Atkinson prevailed on appeal.

Considering the race-relations standards of those days, that was a gutsy move on her part. Probably letting it slide and not creating a possible racial issue would have been more politically astute. The press noted her effort but gave the action no special attention. How it played during her election is hard to determine. With Negro voting of that day at an absolute minimum in the South, it surely gained her no votes.

She continued her extensive speaking engagements all over town to PTAs, the American Association of University Women, and other groups, mainly women. Attending a White House conference on children, she reported back to the Kiwanis Club.

In addition she was an invited out-of-town speaker addressing Loyola University in New Orleans, where she urged more playgrounds for children. While lobbying in Tallahassee, she was invited to address the general assembly of the Florida State College for Women (later to become Florida State University).

A careful review of the *Miami Herald* editions of the winter months in 1932 and spring 1933 found local political races virtually ignored. In the smallest print possible, requiring a magnifying glass to read the minute print, local candidates were at best listed. At least some were.

Among incumbent judges, only Dade County Court Judge W. F. Blanton was named. The county commissioners were listed as well as constables and justices of the peace. A lawyer named Walter Beckham had announced for Edith

Atkinson's post, but nary a line on that race appeared in the early going. Hardly a serious contest was the accepted view.

In later days, the *Herald*, still printing in type that reached below the lowest line on an optometrist's reading chart, reported that Buck Leatherman, a man destined to be elected Dade County clerk of court for a good part of the twentieth century, had no opposition. As well, all the justices of the peace were returned to office, and R. B. Chastain once more was constable in his district. Each of these men had long-standing support among their neighbors and had expected no opposition.

Edith Atkinson had been confident her past performance would hold her in good stead in her campaign for reelection. Always in her support, the civic clubs and her neighbors, would for sure be there for her. No likely candidates had announced early or was otherwise on the horizon. The newcomer Walter Beckham was a name barely known in her or her husband's circles. Hadn't she and her well-regarded spouse, the esteemed chief judge of the circuit court, been model citizens and respected office-holders?

One would expect under normal conditions her good efforts to be rewarded. But, normal conditions did not exist out there. These were troubled times, far more severe than ever before. Politics is an elusive strand of quicksilver. Today's favorite loses favor at the slightest quirk. One never knows how the ball will bounce.

Were one to measure the newspaper space afforded the juvenile court doings in those days, one could readily assume that the justices of the peace and constables ranked a lot higher in terms of the community regard. As a matter of fact, they did. Those offices had been held for decades by friendly fellows, always there to help keep the peace and be of service. As political appointees by the governor, they knew their place.

The juvenile court, then only a little more than a decade old, had been barely recognized as an important part of city life. Edith Atkinson had brought some attention to the office by virtue of being a female office holder and her affinity with women's groups, but it was still the constable and justice of the peace to whom citizens looked with their everyday problems.

Judge Atkinson had made the juvenile court something more than a place to adjudicate children. Separating it from the adult criminal court required more than a change of situs. By dint of her making the court a community effort, involving women's groups and advocating for more compassionate new approaches, she gave the juvenile court a special cachet. It was to be a style and quality that made children special. On or off the bench, she never stopped seeking the opportunity to serve children.

Apparently, those virtues, while perhaps appreciated, never fully registered with the voters. She lost the race to Walter Beckham. A shocking defeat, but she lost no stature. Retired, but still receiving the plaudits of organizations throughout the state, she sought new fields to conquer.

With new judge Walter Beckham, a man who would prove himself a tireless advocate in his own fashion, the work she had begun in Miami was in excellent hands. What next? She was hardly a wilting loser. Always optimistic and hopeful, she needed to address the challenges still out there.

Perhaps her failed reelection bid went beyond the dreariness of the bad times. It may have been that this community wasn't quite ready for these new approaches to children. Dreamed up by visionaries in northern cities, like Chicago and New York, Judge Atkinson, circumspect as she had been in her advocacy, may still have moved a bit too fast.

It might even have been her action in obtaining a writ of habeas corpus in behalf of that thirteen-year-old Negro child held in jail on a gambling charge. But that was only a matter of a dispute with the municipal court over who had the authority to hear the case. This had not been some stirring civil rights battle, of which there would be many in the South. But then again, after all, Miami was still a small conservative southern city, not ready for what some might have considered a radical racial move.

While the reason for her defeat may have been blurred, her activism in behalf of children did continue the path of the early advocates for bettering the life of children in need. Her approach was consistent with the early movers, though perhaps not as outspoken. Miami of that day, unlike New York and Chicago, was not exactly fertile ground for such powerful advocacy.

In a commencement address at Stetson University after her retirement, she focused on the need for more women to enter the practice of law. Wisely, as an advocate for women's causes, she chose not to enlist them in the many available causes of that day, civil rights then beginning to sweep the nation, or the dark clouds hovering over Europe pre-World War II.

Instead, her message for the new lawyers urged joining the law profession and then, by virtue of the status the law profession holds, find a niche where they could be in a stronger position to improve the quality of life. Her approach, gleaned from experience, was not to change the world with one burst of explosive energy, but to work hard, educate followers, and make incremental changes that in the end produce results. Good things take time aborning.

Today, women's groups in Florida credit her with being a strong pioneer leader in their behalf. She surely led the way for all juvenile court judges. Her careful approach, keeping one step ahead of her constituents yet avoiding controversy, staying educated as to the needs yet blending in with the community, all earned a job-well-done accolade for pointing the way for the long struggle ahead.

Edith Atkinson was hardly ready to fully retire. Both the state and the nation, still in the full throes of the Great Depression, continued to struggle to improve economic conditions. Edith, still full of the vitality and spirit that had carried her though the early days of her juvenile court tenure, and still relatively young, sought new frontiers. There were many.

Her aim, a worthy one, was to join the national effort to overcome the discontent that had enveloped the country. In 1932, newly elected president Franklin Roosevelt instituted a series of programs to counteract the bad economic times. The Civilian Conservation Corps (CCC) hired thousands of young men to build roads and new buildings. The Works Progress Administration (WPA) created other efforts in the arts and for children as a stimulus for the economy and to bolster the morale of citizens.

Aubrey Williams, administrator of the National Youth Administration, aiming to develop need programs for children, headed one of these many groups. Retired from the bench, Edith Atkinson sought this new avenue to support children, a never-ending pursuit for her. Thus began a campaign to be appointed Florida state administrator for the program headed nationally by Mr. Williams.

As a loyal Democrat and highly esteemed juvenile court judge for eight years, her choice was a strong likelihood. She and friends began a campaign to earn Atkinson the post. Past and present U.S. senators, governors, and politicians of every sort were on her mailing list. She enlisted them all in her pursuit of the appointment.

A local lawyer and friend, Mr. S. J. Barco, organized this 1935 effort in Edith's behalf. Letters and contacts were made with the entire Florida Congressional Delegation. These included Congressmen Mark Wilcox, Lex Green, Millard Caldwell, and W. J. Sears. Also, Senators Duncan Fletcher, Park Trammell, and others were solicited in her effort. All responded with fulsome praise for Judge Atkinson, but their efforts were to no avail.

Long-time colleagues of husband Henry Atkinson also pitched in, and local newspapers had friendly paragraphs about her goal. A likely and logical choice, it apparently was not in the cards. Certainly, it wasn't her lack of qualifications.

Politics is a strange animal. Not to derogate the person finally named—it wasn't Edith Atkinson. There's an old axiom in politics, "Once you get off the winner's merry-go-round carousel, it's hard to get back on."

Edith Atkinson was the true beginning of judicial activism in the Dade County Juvenile Court, and nothing or no one can ever take that title away from her. Her goals, many of which were not fully realized until later years, surely marked footprints for the future.

For the next half century, the standards for assessing delinquency and dependency would surely change. The national pulse, moving away from rehabilitation toward punishment, would make the road rocky for the child savers. But considering the negative posture of child saving in Florida and the South, Edith Atkinson had impressively opened the way in Miami.

Walter Beckham's defeat of Atkinson may have been an omen or only an obscure happening of that era. Whatever it meant politically or in terms of social progress, the process in Miami would go through many convulsions in the next half century. For certain the Atkinson era had been a beginning, a small one but highly meaningful.

Lacking the crusader approach at the onset and recognizing the need not to go too far too fast, she, nonetheless, earned her stripes as a true advocate. Had she arrived a half century later, she still would have been a true trailblazer.

In her later years she became the darling of the many women's movements, particularly in legal circles. When the push began to encourage women into becoming lawyers and seeking public office, Edith Atkinson was always the poster girl. Her name and image was portrayed as a model in most other efforts involving the quest for a more complete and equal role for women in both the private and public sector.

As late as 1979, she received major honors and accolades. That year the Girl Scouts of America honored her at a gala at Tropical Park on the fiftieth anniversary of her founding the Girl Scout Council in Miami. Six thousand people were in attendance. Not a bad turnout for a politician no longer in office.

She led a full life and a good one. Her job had not been easy. Starting virtually with a blank page, she managed to pick up on every concept developed by the early radical child savers, and translate those ideals into positions her more conservative southern constituents could find palatable. Her successors for the remainder of the twentieth century had many problems, but their task was somewhat eased by the temperate and wise manner in which she had introduced these progressive ideas.

Edith Meserve had come to Miami, Florida from Portland, Maine, in 1912 on the advice of her family physician cautioning her that for health reasons she relocate to a warmer clime. It should be noted that the Miami weather had really worked for her. Whatever her early ailments, she lived out all these many years here until her death at age ninety-two. She was a hardy soul in many ways.

Walter H. Beckham

If, by her approach, starting the court off on the right foot, Edith Atkinson gave the juvenile court a special cachet, Walter Beckham gave it a stature that earned the respect of the community. In every sense of the phrase, Walter Beckham was the juvenile court for the next twenty-seven years.

The almost three decades he served bridged Miami's history from the first old Ford wheezing along Flagler Street to the overcrowded modern metropolis we all enjoy. Though gathering some of the trappings of a modern-day operation, his court was then still of little note and of little influence over the conduct of delinquent and dependent children.

Judge Atkinson had done a fine job starting the process, but little was in place to further accomplish the purpose. Beckham, a strong, imposing leader, was exactly what the system needed at that time. This long stretch of time needed stability, not charisma. He was forceful, respected, and clear about what needed to be done. That he had attained national recognition among juvenile court judges was an added asset.

Although possessing a political background going back to his days in Georgia, Walter Beckham, in all his many years as a juvenile court judge, never indicated in any way that this was to be a stepping stone to higher political office. In those early years Miami and Dade County were two political entities constantly engaged in hot partisan struggles. A man of Beckham's background and temperament might well have succeeded to a higher-elected office. Fortunately, he chose to stay the course.

Walter Beckham came to Miami in 1925, at about the same time Edith Atkinson had earned her first election victory for a full term. Thirty-seven-year-old Beckham had served one term in the Georgia legislature but had no thought of resuming elected office on coming to Miami.

As an experienced lawyer, twelve years admitted to the Bar, a Harvard Law School graduate no less, his purpose in choosing Miami was purely business: the land boom speculation that was making millionaires overnight of investors. As many future Miamians would choose this city as a land of opportunity, so, back then, did lawyer Beckham.

It must be said that the Harvard accent never overcame the Georgia drawl. He liked having the credential of Harvard Law School, but it was Georgia and the South that stayed with him. Before law school he had been a high school principal, met and married school teacher Clara Marshall, and settled into the quiet life of a small-town lawyer in Albany, Georgia. It was not to be. Adventure beckoned farther South.

But, it was more than adventure that sent the young lawyer to Miami. He was kind of forced out of Albany. According to son Walter Jr., then fourteen years of age, there was trouble brewing between the local constabulary and his dad, a member of the Georgia legislature.

The city of Albany, Georgia, was a pleasant town, comfortable in every way for most citizens, except for one, namely Walter Beckham. An elected state legislator, Beckham, a man of conservative upbringing with two young boys to bring up, deplored the free-running red-light district on the edge of town. He had requested and implored the local sheriff to close down this den of iniquity, or at least make a reasonable effort at enforcement of the law.

In those days the local sheriff was a power unto himself. It was custom that in every southern town, the sheriff was the big man. Whether appointed or elected, his was a political job aimed at keeping order and protecting certain business interests. Law enforcement generally, and the sheriff specifically, tended to look away from law-breakers in the area of victimless crimes: gambling and houses of ill-repute, for certain.

Whether this particular sheriff resented the interference of this state legislator or objected to a possible loss of his own ill-begotten revenue, is not known. Son Walter Jr. says, "That Sheriff was spitting mad at my father and vowed to get him unless he laid off. Dad, however, would not back away and continued demanding the sheriff close down the red-light district."

With two unmovable forces, someone had to give. As it played out, the sheriff prevailed. He indeed was the powerful political force able to carry out his threat. As often happens in small-town politics (and large cities too), he found an opponent to face and unseat Walter Beckham in the next election. It was the last time in Beckham's life that evil would triumph over good.

Hurt by the loss but not defeated in spirit, Beckham began making inquiries about the land boom in Miami. Some of his friends had sent letters describing overnight riches attained by land transfers. Upon learning that Miami Beach Municipal Court Judge William Walsh was looking for a law partner, he immediately made contact.

A hurried train visit to Miami enabled him to firm up a partnership agreement with Judge Walsh and obtain a three-room flat for lodgings for his family. Beckham returned to Albany, satisfied his decision to move on was the right one.

Beckham Jr. described the trip to Miami,

> Before we knew it, the four of us were packed into Dad's old Essex auto and were on our way. The route from Albany to Miami didn't have the highways of today. It was mostly piney woods, obstructions all the way. Trying to locate gas stations and other necessaries, we felt like pioneers. If I remember correctly, we even had a few flat tires to fix late at night. That was about seventy years ago and I still recall that—rough trip.

Once arrived, Walter and Clara made a quick adjustment to the social and civic life of Miami. There's no record of the Beckhams and the Atkinsons having a social relationship, but in all likelihood Clara Beckham, with two boys of her own, closely followed Edith Atkinson's endeavors to improve the public schools. No doubt, with the small number constituting the legal fraternity in Miami, Henry Atkinson and Walter Beckham had, at the least, a passing acquaintance.

In behalf of one of their first clients, the new University of Miami, the firm of Walsh, Beckham & Ellis petitioned the circuit court for a university charter. It was formally granted by none other than circuit court judge Henry Atkinson.

The firm, occupying the seventh floor of the Olympia Building, came to the rescue of the University of Miami when their opening date, September 1926, was delayed for several months. Apparently the building the university planned to occupy had been severely damaged by the 1926 hurricane. The Beckham Law firm gave up half the floor they occupied so that the university could begin classes on time for the three hundred enrolled students.

Meanwhile the new law firm engaged in land purchases; the most impressive one was fifty acres near Titusville in what is now known as Cape Canaveral. They subdivided, built streets in 1925, and began to sell lots. Regrettably, the 1926 hurricane and the Great Depression that followed a few years later destroyed their potential value.

Had they been able to hold on for a few decades, all their dreams of wealth might have been reached. A modest estimate has that property worth at least twenty-five million dollars in today's market. Unfortunately, like most other investors buying options, the hurricane and the economic downfall combined to destroy both the value of the land and their investments. The firm of Walsh, Beckham & Ellis was forced to surrender their options.

Lawyers, like other professionals, were not doing too well in those hard times, and to augment his income, Beckham's partner, Judge Walsh, suggested he throw his hat into the ring for the office of juvenile court judge. Walter Beckham's background had included stints as a high school principal both before entering law school and then for a short spell prior to entering the practice of law full time. Nonetheless, he had not in his early endeavors made children a focus of his activities—certainly not in the idealistic fashion some of the early crusaders had envisioned.

Walter Beckham was more a goal-oriented pragmatist, singularly moving to be an able law practitioner and providing for his wife and family. His vision was centered, as with most lawyers, on being financially stable. The growing new Miami seemed to be an ideal place to attain that goal. As Walter Jr. stated, "The pay for a judge was only six hundred dollars, but we sure needed the money."

Nor had Beckham Sr. given thought to seeking a judgeship. He was still politically ambitious, but his experience losing his seat in the Georgia legislature only because he sought to eliminate a blight on the city still rankled him. Besides, the office of juvenile court judge, a new position, was also one of minimal status in the legal profession of that day. In addition, Edith Atkinson seemed firmly entrenched in the post, both politically and by her good service.

Nonetheless, the realities of the time continued to stare Walter Beckham in the face. Fortunately, his one session in the Georgia legislature had given him enough political smarts to organize a relevant campaign. His law partner, Judge William Walsh, also had experienced some political warfare in winning his seat in Miami Beach, and both understood that winning this election would be no walk in the park.

Judge Edith, unaware of what was brewing, went blithely along doing all the fine things that had brought her respect and acclaim. Along with her husband, the esteemed Judge Ad, as spousal support, she assumed all was well in her political world—a vision that has caused many a political ship to go asunder. Politics is too strange to assume anything.

Prior to announcing, Beckham paid a courtesy call on Judge Henry Atkinson, then senior circuit court judge. Atkinson, a political power in his own right and a judge before whom Beckham would continue to practice, was not one to ignore. Win or lose, he would continue to be an important part of Beckham's legal career. This was a courtesy not to overlook.

Candidate Beckham asked Judge Henry Atkinson directly, "Do you have any problems with my running against your wife?" A kind of ticklish situation for both, but Atkinson was cordial, telling Beckham, "No, this is a free election. No hard feelings." He made no effort to dissuade Beckham, nor any intimation that Beckham, win or lose, would be under any disadvantage appearing before him.

It was a very gentlemanly exchange, as one would expect from two upstanding members of the Bar. Although in more recent times, it is not unknown for sitting judges to have shown less restraint in enunciating their distaste face-to-face with potential opponents. Perhaps more so here where a spouse was involved.

Judge Atkinson, probably distressed at the sight and voice of an opponent for his wife, had no choice but to be courtly in his response. That was his nature, and that was then the style in political campaigns. Attacking an opponent was acceptable. However, unlike today's sometimes-virulent campaigns, even in judicial races, there was a self-imposed limit on excessive personal assaults on the character of an adversary.

Those were the standards of the time, at least in local races. In national races, the sky was the limit. Accusing a presidential candidate of fathering an illegitimate child was acceptable grist for the mill. This approach has always governed the conduct of national races in this country. Especially with the advent of TV, it has become an entertainment vehicle every four years for voters.

Henry Atkinson also realized that his wife had an unimpeachable record, her energy and devotion unquestioned. She had overcome her tender years—lack of legal experience and being of the wrong gender—by impressing townspeople she was the right person for the position. He could not conceive that this outlander could unseat her. Unfortunately, for him and for her, the public has a short memory for political officeholders.

The Beckham-Atkinson joust was really a strange one, at least in terms of the kinds of judicial campaigns that would follow in the decades ahead. For one, Atkinson's record was never at issue. The main point of contention seemed to be gender: was the male or the female better equipped to do the job? A secondary concern involved the impact of the poor economic times.

Beckham, assisted by Walsh, cooked up a campaign that at first blush seemed almost childish, but on reflection was truly smart. Edith Atkinson had been an excellent judge, and a frontal attack might antagonize the voters. After all, Walter Beckham was a virtually unknown office seeker trying to unseat a highly qualified incumbent. Although some political tacticians today in Washington are credited with remarkable skills, sometimes these shrewd operators tend to overplay their hand. Not so here. Theirs was a simple but clever approach.

Remember, in her first campaign her astute political move of handing out cards, Elect a Woman for a Woman's Job, had quickly eliminated the gender issue. Now, Beckham came out with a similarly clever platform: One Judge to a

Family. There's nothing more fickle in life than an electorate. On the one hand, ignoring records of accomplishment and even misdeeds, voters sometimes tend to be swayed by attractive catchphrases. Today we call these offerings sound bites.

This ploy attacked the very strength offered by Judges Henry and Edith Atkinson that together, they, the marital-duo judges, were a powerful and productive team. Instead, Walsh and Beckham turned the One-Judge-to-a-Family charge into a message that in these hard times with jobs in short supply, one breadwinner to each family was enough. Two government salaries for one family was an issue that could and did resonate with voters.

This attack brought the hard times citizens were now facing to the attention of the voter. The Atkinsons couldn't directly be blamed for that, but the very existence of an economic depression gave voters concern. Beckham didn't dwell on the two government salaries in one family issue; he merely wanted to raise the issue and give voters something to think about.

His real campaign was based on a series of questions he raised unrelated to her performance. Was a woman, who had no children of her own, best suited for the job? Did she have enough life experience dealing with errant boys to serve as a juvenile court judge? Wasn't a man with two young sons better equipped to handle rambunctious teenagers?

These issues were raised along with his theme: in bad economic times, why have two paychecks in one family? On their face, these issues were hardly enough to unseat Edith Atkinson, but slowly, quietly, they enabled Beckham to pick up steam.

Ordinarily, Beckham's approach might never have attracted much attention, except for the fact that Edith Atkinson herself had raised the sexist banner in her previously successful campaigns for the office—Elect a Woman for a Woman's Job. It had worked for her in earlier campaigns, but unfortunately for her she made the error of reviving it for Beckham's challenge in 1932. That theme, rather than her excellent record in office, became her standard for the campaign.

Beckham trod carefully. In this race, dealing with a well-liked, respected woman, the challenger needed to attack his opponent skillfully and with caution. He campaigned in traditional ways, mostly traveling the county in an old Buick that had replaced his rickety Essex auto. He made certain nothing untoward was said or done publicly, relying on his undercurrent themes.

On the top of his Buick he had affixed three triangular signs, three by six feet in size, each with a Vote for Beckham for Juvenile Court. It was an impressive advertisement touting his candidacy. When not driving around town, he parked the car in downtown Miami along the Second Street Bridge next to the old Hyatt Hotel, for all to see.

Although placards on moving vehicles became a fixture in political campaigns in later years, this was probably the first time any candidate had explored this technique, particularly aiming for the motor vehicle drivers crossing the bridge.

Sixty years later, running for mayor of Miami Beach, I used that tactic at the foot of the Julia Tuttle Causeway on Forty-first to attract Miami Beach motorists coming home from their day at work in the city of Miami. And to think I thought my little enterprise was an original and clever move.

Beckham didn't rely solely on his triangular signs. That was only for name identification. He attended rallies, spoke to friendly groups, focusing on the suggestion that his life experience and gender had better prepared him for the office. No way he could attack her record on the bench.

Atkinson, on the other hand, allowed his issue to make headway, focusing on her old theme that this was a job for woman. Had she instead directed her presentation to the fine record she had established and the new programs she had brought forth, little attention might have been shown to Beckham's platform.

Nothing of notice happened, at least outwardly, until about two weeks before the June 7 primary election when the voters began to show an interest in the campaign. The slowly developing response gave Beckham time to develop his stealth campaign. Apparently, the voters paid little attention, other than to become aware of his charges.

The modes of electioneering in Miami had already been firmly established. There were large debate-style gatherings in Miami's Bayfront Park with invited candidates, radio talks by the candidate or someone in their behalf, newspaper ads, and home coffees to "meet the candidate." Not quite the pressure of today's infighting, and no easy path for a challenger unless some special issues could be offered.

The kickoff in Bayfront Park on June 2 opened the final leg of the campaign. Several hundred were in attendance at this Democratic Party rally. The primary was then tantamount to election. Republicans were allowed on the ballot but never taken too seriously. It would be some time before states of the South offered a two-party struggle.

This particular rally was limited to local office seekers. The highest office at stake in this group was for election to the state legislature in Tallahassee. Other offices represented were county purchasing agent, school board member, clerk of the criminal court, and judge of the juvenile court.

The *Miami Herald* coverage of the event included statements by both Judge Edith Atkinson and challenger Walter Beckham. The *Herald* noted, "William Burwell, speaking for Judge Edith Atkinson, commended the efficiency of her work and explained that nature decrees that juveniles appeal to women instead of men for guidance. The greatest of welfare workers of the world are women."

The *Herald* reporter then went on to quote Walter Beckham who, unlike his opponent, spoke in his own behalf saying, "That office is a man's job since the majority of the cases are concerned with boys."

Walter Beckham, a man of few words, could have provided a stronger response, but felt that her spokesperson, by keeping the issue alive, had reinforced his charges. He also was probably helped by Mrs. Atkinson choosing not to speak in her own behalf.

Of course, Atkinson was playing right into Beckham's hand by insisting this was a woman's job. It had worked in her earlier campaigns, but now she had an excellent performance record to run on. Why enable her opponent to make his case for a man in the job? Bad strategy on her part? Probably.

The newspaper coverage, or lack of it, made campaigns for local offices most difficult. National and state elections were freely covered but for lesser offices only squibs appeared in the press. Courts, such as the juvenile court, rarely received any serious attention.

Those were difficult times, both economically and worldwide. The failed economy surely had a marked influence on the election, and the prelude to World War II would also herald a change in the lives of all. Times were bad. Other more important issues that affected their lives were now pressing the people, and would do more so in the coming years. Campaigns for local political office didn't impress the average citizen too much.

Raising campaign funds in those hard times was difficult, particularly for newcomers. About two weeks before election, newspaper ads began to surface, some for Atkinson, mostly for the office of Sheriff, none for Beckham. Judge Atkinson found it easier to raise money to afford the cost of ads; Beckham lacked the fund-raising contacts.

Alongside the political ads seeking votes was an ad best describing the pinched economic climate. The Bromley's Men's Wear at 28 West Flagler Street offered a sale reducing men's suits to $5.95 and $6.95, a price far below normal.

Despite the warning signs, Atkinson, still confident of victory, ran a campaign in absentia. Avoiding personal appearances, she had surrogates speak in her behalf and ran newspaper ads still touting her original position.

Beckham's approach was to have friends gather together a group at their homes to meet the candidate. There, he preached his theme, by now catching hold with audiences. He sent out press releases to the newspapers announcing these events: one in the *Miami Herald* was a six-liner announcing a meeting at the home of Mrs. A. H. Bartle, 1025 Castille Avenue, Coral Gables.

Endorsements and preferred slates were offered by groups. Labor's Citizenship Committee endorsed Franklin D. Roosevelt for president and a host of other local incumbents including Edith Atkinson. The Miami Beach Democratic Club had a full slate, but somehow the office of juvenile judge didn't make the cut. Nor was this juvenile court viewed important enough to be included in other slates. In the twelve years since creation in 1921, despite the efforts of Judge Edith, neither she nor the juvenile court had gained much traction in the public eye.

Beckham, meanwhile, continuing his slow move to the top, issued a press release to the *Miami Herald* that though only fifteen lines, had a sprightly heading: "Juvenile Court Race Now Lively Contest." The content would have warmed the heart of any public-relations whiz of today. Here's how it read: "From an unexpected contest the race for Juvenile Court Judge has developed into one of the liveliest subjects of discussion among voters. Walter Beckham has made a fast and peppy campaign making rapid contacts in all sections of the County."

The story went on to say that Beckham's campaign material distinguished him from his opponent by emphasizing his background as a family man and a parent with two boys of his own. Beckham's purpose obviously was to dramatize the traits that fully qualified him to preside over a court where most of the cases involved boys.

Coupled with the fact that his opponent and her husband held two judgeships in the same family, Beckham was able to highlight the hardships of the bad economic time then prevalent. The article concluded, "Beckham's campaign literature has been a familiar piece of literature at practically every political rally."

For windup speeches before the June 7 vote, three rallies were sponsored by the Democratic Party Executive Committee. The major races for governor and congress took place at Bayfront Park. The secondary level of candidates, including the juvenile court judges, met at Shenandoah Junior High. The third level, including school board and justice of the peace, held their session at Miami Beach Elementary School. The juvenile judge candidates were somehow spared the ignominy of being placed in the lowest category.

Judge Edith Atkinson, finally sensing her campaign was badly losing ground, accelerated her newspaper ad campaign. She ran a two column ad covering the length of the page and responding to all the charges and claims made by Beckham. It was a repeat of a radio address made in her behalf by a person she chose not to identify in the ad.

In great detail the ad pointed out women who had become leaders in the field: Jane Addams for one, and several other noted women jurists of the day. The ad even emphasized that being childless was no bar to serving as an effective judge. This in response to Beckham's claim that being father of two boys somehow made him more qualified for the job. Obviously, Atkinson was on the defensive.

The radio address may have been a great speech by this nameless person, but as a faceless political ad it was a zero. To make matters worse, the *Miami Herald* had omitted the line required by law, "paid political advertisement," and had to correct the error in the next day's newspaper to avoid Atkinson being accused of a campaign violation the day before voting took place.

Sensing she was in dire trouble, Atkinson had rushed off a telegram to a friend, U.S. Senator Hamilton Lewis, imploring a letter of endorsement. Senator

Lewis complied with a flowery letter extolling her ability. She quickly printed an ad with his endorsement, titling it "What the nation's most prominent Democrat (unsolicited) says."

Senator Lewis couldn't stem the tide. He hardly was the nation's "most prominent Democrat" (FDR might have disagreed), and certainly his letter had been solicited by her telegram. But in the heat of a campaign, all assertions are prone to error.

At this distance, almost eight decades later, it is difficult to judge tactics in a political campaign based on only a few sparse newspaper reports. Venturing an educated guess, one could say she probably should have campaigned more vigorously, certainly in person and avoided her emphasis on a woman for the job. Beckham's campaign had caught her off-stride. She never believed that his attacks would stick.

Beckham, an outsider and a long shot, ran a wily campaign, avoiding her outstanding performance on the bench, instead attacking her on her sex and lack of motherhood, as well as the economic factor of two judges in a family drawing two salaries.

Objective observers today would describe Beckham's tactics as smokescreens, and members of the Bar might be taken aback at the nonjudicial tenor of his campaign. But Beckham defenders today would point out that it was Atkinson who brought sexism into the campaign by introducing her campaign motif Vote for a Woman for a Woman's Job.

Walter Beckham, his political senses honed to both winning and losing election campaigns while running for the Georgia legislature, probably had stayed within the acceptable electioneering tactics of those days, but it was a close call. His was a smart, tough campaign. He had an innate ability to rise to every situation, as his future would bear out.

The final vote was a rout. It had him with almost a three-to-one margin. With seventy-one of the eighty-six precincts counted, Beckham scored 16,005 votes to Atkinson's 5,679 votes. The final vote tally was not reported in the press. This loss could not have been totally attributed to the poor campaign Atkinson ran.

Whatever she had done or failed to do, and whatever clever moves Beckham had made, none seemed consistent with the margin of victory. She had the long-held esteem of her fellow citizens; he was but a relative newcomer. It had to be a set of circumstances beyond the control of campaign tactics.

In all likelihood, the times were so difficult that voters were ready for a change. The harsh economic period, then prevalent, probably played a major part. Perhaps the progressive new idea of a woman in charge had lost its allure. As they say in politics, you need to be in the right place at the right time. Walter Beckham was at that spot.

That two of the most significant figures in the history of the Dade County Juvenile Court engaged in so puerile a campaign is noteworthy. Rarely is a leader of the quality of Judge Atkinson challenged, let alone defeated. Even more rare is the likelihood of a winner of such a race, becoming so important to the court in years ahead, as was Judge Walter Beckham.

On July 2, 1933, the *Miami Herald* announced Walter Beckham as officially installed as the juvenile court judge for Dade County. He had won the primary the year before and after the general election in November was formally named to the office by Governor Dave Schulz. It was a monumental day for him and for the juvenile court.

He had gained office at a time when people were apprehensive and fearful of the future. Times ahead were of a foreboding nature. Alongside that announcement of Beckham's installation ran a small paragraph in the newspaper with the heading: "Nazi Revolution in Germany Aimed at Communists." Datelined Berlin, June 22, 1933, it merely stated in a few lines, "One Nazi and two Storm Troopers were seriously wounded in a shooting early today. A Marxist who fired the shots was arrested."

This was all before Adolf Hitler was recognized by the world as a tyrant. How would WWII and all the other changes in America impact on the juvenile court during Judge Walter Beckham's long stay as head of the court? Would the suffering from the economic depression and the carnage resulting from WWII diminish the humanitarian approach fostered by child advocates of a few decades earlier?

Such heady questions were not under consideration for the new juvenile court judge. At that time the new judge, Beckham, had less worldly issues before him. His concern was now and today. A posture he would adopt all his days on the bench.

He announced he would remain a member of his law firm Walsh, Beckham & Ellis, and would devote a portion of his time to the court work. Under the law he was able to maintain his private practice while a judge. It all sounded like the judgeship would be a temporary diversion from his real career as a private practitioner. How little one can divine the future!

Queen Edith was gone! Long live the king! Walter Beckham had replaced an outstanding leader, mostly for a small salary to help him through the hard times of that era. No grand visions in mind. No plans to change the world for children. Then again, the young woman from Portland, Maine, had had no grand vision, not the slightest idea of what a positive impact her term of office would produce.

Now we had a relative newcomer in town taking over. He brought all the good virtues people of that day respected. A Southerner, born in Zebulon, Pike County, Georgia. A mature forty-two years of age and a Harvard Law School pedigree to boot. What more could any frontier town ask for?

His early training in government had come from his father, a Civil War veteran, who had served as clerk of court for Pike County, Georgia. Having a father who was a disciplinarian and a devout Christian made young Walter learn at an early stage many virtues. These included hard work, obedience, along with compassion. These would guide him the rest of his life.

As a boy he contributed to the family income by selling peanuts to passengers on trains stopping at Zebulon. Later, he attended Emory University, graduating at age nineteen, working his way through college selling peaches. In still later years, the Emory College tradition would continue through three centuries with four generations of Beckhams graduating Emory and more in the offing.

In the next three years he saved sufficient money from his teaching career—three years as principal at two rural high schools in Georgia—to enter Harvard Law School. His earlier training selling peanuts and peaches enabled him to gain a summer job with the Georgia Fruit Growers' Exchange representing them in New York, Philadelphia, and Chicago. The young rustic was seeing the bright lights of the big cities.

Walter Beckham assumed office July 2, 1933. At that time the court consisted of space on the fifth floor of the then new Flagler Street courthouse. As befitting the low rank of the court, his space was considerably smaller than that afforded the higher trial court judges. The job was part-time. It would take several more decades for the juvenile court to lose its "special" status and become a full-fledged member of the circuit court.

Judge Beckham had an immediate early success that imbued him with the possibilities for the future. One of the first tasks he assumed was to establish a better working relationship with the various police departments. Beckham instituted regular meetings with the several municipal police chiefs to create an appropriate understanding as to the proper treatment of juveniles.

By nature, Beckham was a law-and-order man, not inclined to coddle children, his own or delinquents appearing before him. Just as Judge Atkinson had made each child's case a roundtable discussion with all the parties engaged in how to help the child, so Judge Beckham chose to add the police in this kind of setting. A fine idea that fit into the advanced thinking of that day.

Several police departments had designated a member of the force as the juvenile police officer. Miami, the major Dade County city, created a formal Juvenile Aid Bureau staffed with trained officers and policewomen. This approach was a worthy accomplishment for that early era.

In a story recounting Judge Beckham's long service, *Miami Herald* staff writer Bert Collier described Judge Beckham's introduction to the juvenile court on his first day in office:

> Judge Beckham found his office filled with sad-faced mothers and pinched anemic children. This was the depth of the Depression. Parents

were pleading with the court to take the youngsters and feed and clothe them until a better day arrived.

There was no work, no food, and there were no facilities for hungry, dependent children either. There was little the new Judge could do.

It was a pathetic situation. He was a bit appalled on that first day to discover there was but one secretary for all the clerical work to be processed, and only three probation officers to handle the increasingly large number of juvenile probationers. Judge Beckham indeed had his work cut out for him for the next twenty-seven years.

His three small rooms on the fourth floor of the Flagler Street courthouse were always full: the judge's chambers, a closet-sized room for his secretary, and what might be viewed as a miniature courtroom. For his hearings he sat at a desk with the parties involved seated around the table. He wore no robe of office.

From the beginning he had determined that reading books was beneficial for youth, and shelves were built around the courtroom. He had solicited books from churches and schools for his charges to read. Really a splendid idea, but apparently never replicated.

In response to my question as to his father's courtroom philosophy, Beckham Jr. thought for as few moments, and then said,

> I suppose his philosophy about handling kids in court was the same as it was in how he treated his own kids. He was a strict, conservative man of the old school—a good Christian, following principles of the church. He was a Methodist, and as my mother, taught Sunday school for years.
>
> He made certain we followed the rules. On Sunday morning we read the comics and then off to church. Going to the movies was out. We were not allowed to indulge in vices at any time. Playing cards, gambling, or other vices were always forbidden.
>
> But as strict as he was, we always knew and felt that he loved each of us with all his heart.

Walter Jr. continued further as to how his father handled his court duties. After attending a few sessions watching cases in court, he asked his father why he had been so tough on a kid for stealing a car. The judge responded,

> When a young man comes before me who is stealing, I know in my heart he'll be back. Somehow whatever we do isn't enough. Usually I send them to our Kendall Boys Center, where maybe a stay there will

reeducate them, but I know in my heart, they will be back before me. I'm strict with them, but what else is there to do?

Interviewing Beckham Jr. over the phone, I empathized with the plight of his father back then. With no rehab resources available, it varied little from the situation that all his successor judges (Gladstone, Gelber, Petersen, Langer, et al.) faced working for delinquent boys. Despite all the new programs available, their results were too often not dissimilar to the situation and the concerns expressed those seventy-five years earlier.

However, Beckham, beginning his career as a juvenile court judge did not have time to bemoan the absence of clerical staff and probation officers. Often, youngsters arrested had to be placed in jail—the adult jail—until a hearing could be held before the juvenile court judge. He had to move fast to improve that situation.

Judge Beckham didn't realize it, but the three probation officers he had were there only because his predecessor, Judge Edith Atkinson, had over the years struggled with the Florida legislature to increase the number from one. At that time, gaining any additions to her staff was considered a victory. Beckham would promptly learn the difficult task ahead of squeezing funds from the county commission and the state legislature.

Quickly he became a strong activist with these legislative bodies to obtain new resources. Continuously and with determination he pushed for rehab programs, additional staffing, and other resources during his lengthy years of service. Many a child was aided through his good offices.

That the same problems remain can be expected. No court, juvenile or otherwise, can restructure the factors that make for delinquency. All that Beckham could do was to try to make things better, hope for the best, and be grateful for small successes. Beckham instinctively knew that seeking public credit for his small gains was the wrong route. He shied away from the press, fearing they were more foe than friend. This was a position universally accepted by most officeholders of that era, elected or appointed. Little has changed in that struggle.

Unlike Judge Atkinson, who came on at the beginning and was able to travel the state and country preaching the virtues of the new juvenile court, Judge Beckham, in his early years had neither the time nor the inclination to be an advance man selling the value of this new institution. Beckham was too busy doing the tasks necessary to further organize the court structure.

So many things had to be done. He needed to augment his staff of probation officers, establish rehab programs, find more space to house the court functions, and dream ahead of a courthouse solely for the juvenile court. It would take at least a decade before Judge Beckham could assume the full role of an activist judge, beyond the internal needs of the court.

Unforeseen to the new judge was the astounding fact that he would be reelected five times, actually serving office for one-third of the time since the court's beginning in 1921 to the date of this book's publication (2007).

Considering that he had sought the part-time office only to tide himself over the Great Depression era, this was a remarkable career turn. Stylewise, hearing cases early on involving delinquent children created no special problem for him. Their shortcomings would be addressed the same way his parents had treated him—with firmness and with affection and above all follow the Good Book.

Not being part of the children's crusade, Beckham had no preconceived altruistic plan to rescue children from the inequities of the criminal justice system. As a lawyer he would follow the statutes and administer justice as warranted.

In the beginning he was a tough taskmaster. Children breaking the law received no special consideration because of their age. The early tales of his firmness as a judge became part of the courthouse lore for years.

Pete Peterson, later a well-regarded City of Miami police sergeant, described his appearance before Judge Beckham,

> I was eleven years old and had stolen some things out of a store and was brought before Judge Beckham. We were all around a table. He was sitting in a large chair looking down at me. All he did was ask me, "Did you do it?"
>
> I nodded yes, and before I could explain what had happened, he reached over, turned me on my backside and whacked me with a big ol' strop. I was so scared I didn't even cry.
>
> "Now get out of here and don't ever come back" were his final words. That's when I decided to become a cop.

There aren't many other descriptions around of Walter Beckham's early style on the bench. The Internet did disclose a snippet from youngster Donald McCloskey growing up on Miami's NW Second Avenue where there were many mean streets.

Young McCloskey, later in life to become a name partner in the eminent Broward County law firm Ruden McCloskey, described sights of the 1930s Miami life, including "watching a Ku Klux Klan mob strap a Filipino man to a coconut palm tree and beat him near to death because he had married a white woman."

McCloskey came into contact with Judge Beckham arising from an incident where neighborhood toughs had accosted him in Lummus Park, roughed him up, and then threw his bicycle into the Miami River. As the victim, he was a witness in the juvenile court hearing. He described it, "Back then there was a juvenile court judge named Walter Beckham. The guys who beat me up went before him.

My eye was split. At the end the judge said to my mother, 'Well, boys will be boys.' I never forgot that. I did my own fighting from then on."

Some seventy years later, McCloskey bore no ill feelings toward Judge Beckham for what back then he may have considered a casual and indifferent ruling by the judge. McCloskey added this comment describing the aftermath: "Biding my time until I grew up in strength and stature, I went after my assailant and threw him in the Miami River."

While the McCloskey and Peterson cases are hardly illustrative of Judge Beckham's style or philosophical approach, it does suggest that he had no misgivings about corporal punishment. He also was a cool character, not inclined to go overboard on any issue.

As the years went by, he would recognize that children needed much more than coercion or the ability to survive on their own character and fortitude. As he and the system matured, he became more sympathetic to children in need and began to speak out in their behalf. The juvenile court spirit of compassion for children would come into play.

His service on the juvenile court bench encompassed the most significant era of the twentieth century. Starting with the Great Depression in the 1930s and FDR's introduction of dramatic social changes, Beckham's early terms saw the rise of Hitler in Europe, then World War II, and the United States' entry into the conflict and our eventual victory.

Then later, under the presidency of Ike Eisenhower, there came the rise of the USA to world-power status, followed by the cold war with Russia. And even more disturbing elements, the advent of McCarthyism in America, and the U.S. Supreme Court decision on *Brown v. Board of Education*.

The latter brought heavy, angry, violent racial strife to local communities, particularly in the South, some in Miami, resisting the now court-ordered integration of our public schools.

All of these events impinged in one fashion or another on local communities. The course of national events of this magnitude, occurring in the over a quarter century of Judge Walter Beckham's service, mostly obscured the noble national experiment to save children. The surge of other overpowering events also overshadowed the do-gooder approach sought by child advocates who had pioneered the movement.

His predecessor, Judge Edith Atkinson's fine beginning was fortuitous in that she started with virtually a blank page. She had created a skeletal Court structure; he had to add bone and sinew. The juvenile court in Miami still had many unanswered goals.

At the onset it had been one lone judge supported by civic groups, mostly women, who together would advocate for the betterment of children. Had it not been for the Miami Woman's Club and the Miami Junior League, along with a few male civic organizations offering support, Judge Atkinson's mission might have withered away.

Fortunately, amidst all the new concerns facing our nation, her successor was ready for the task. A lesser person might have accepted the dire economic conditions and other growth problems in local communities as signs to move slowly. Walter Beckham was determined to act boldly, but the times would not always oblige him.

Carefully he surveyed the situation, realizing that Judge Atkinson had made great strides in behalf of the welfare of children by working with women volunteers. It behooved him to follow her lead.

The *Miami Herald* in a social page note of January 1933, shortly after Beckham had assumed office, stated that he, in conjunction with the American Legion Auxiliary Women's Group, had provided clothing and other needs to one hundred underprivileged children.

In May 1934, still fresh from his election victory, he organized the Dade County Juvenile Council, installing Mrs. Dorothy Andrew as president. He, like Judge Atkinson, had recognized that citizen volunteers, particularly women, offered the best source of support, imagewise and at election time.

He continued working with the Miami Woman's Club and the Junior League and other civic groups in projects beyond the courtroom. This was a new court with a new concept that required extensive community involvement. The women of the community seemed more attuned to the needs of children. His political battle with Judge Atkinson had taught him that while this position as judge of the court did not necessarily belong to a woman, it surely would need the help of women to make it work.

His goal was to establish the juvenile court as an important entity ministering to children and to involve parents in the activity. To accomplish this, he first needed a proper physical setting from which to administer justice for children.

Problem was that their three small rooms in the 1928-built Flagler Street courthouse were rather cramped, and the circuit court judges, growing in numbers, needed courtrooms. Juvenile judges were still an anomaly—half-breed specialty judges, neither beast nor human. At least so it seemed at times to him.

Not until 1946 did Dade County voters authorize a $400,000 bond issue for building a court and detention center on a 245-acre tract at 800 NW Twenty-eighth Street. A two-story building, it provided a courtroom, offices for court attaches and lawyers. Included were facilities for doctors, a clinic, and recreation rooms.

Also, four dining rooms for white and Negro boys and girls served from two adjacent kitchens. All segregation rules were observed. Two detention wings were attached to the courtroom, and four fenced playgrounds completed the center.

Judge Beckham and Probation Officer Ira Hazlett served on the Juvenile Facilities Committee along with Chairman Mrs. Ellen Whiteside and other community leaders. County Commissioner Preston Bird, the designated head of health and welfare in the county, oversaw the project. On April 27, 1948 bids were opened and building contracts let by the county commission.

As generally occurs in public building construction, time estimates for completion were not met. Judge Beckham fumed, but the building contractors always had a ready reason for the delay. Three years later, in April 1951, the new Dade Juvenile Hall was dedicated, five years after the bond issue had been approved.

Judge Beckham had already moved out of the Flagler Street courthouse some six months earlier to make room for three newly appointed circuit court judges rising from the recent federal census. A fourth new circuit court judge was expected to replace a judge being severed from the Dade Circuit Court in order to join the neighboring Monroe County bench. Soon a total of ten circuit court judges would be there for Dade County.

Judge Beckham had hoped for a trackless change into his new quarters. However, due to the failure of equipment to arrive, installation problems, plus the delay caused by a hurricane, the formal court opening had to be delayed indefinitely. Although the building had been occupied for some time, the formal opening was delayed. He made do for emergency hearings at a makeshift courtroom.

Should anyone question where the bulk of the time in these previous five years had been spent by Judge Beckham, one need look no further than the creation of this building. He was neither the architect nor the construction manager, but this was his new baby, and like a good father he carried all the pangs of birthing.

Countless questions are raised at every new public building construction site. Sudden new changes are inevitable. Some are outdated by population changes before the building is completed. Often funds are diverted due to some emergency. Here, once the building had been finally completed in 1951 and the artisans had moved on, only Judge Walter Beckham, who headed the court, was on the premises available to respond to the faultfinders.

In any historical telling of the development of the juvenile court, Judge Beckham looms large, but in truth those early decades of his service were mostly holding the court in place and establishing the special status sought. Surely important purposes, but hardly memorable.

By virtue of the early nonadversarial trial approach, prior to the U.S. Supreme Court *Gault* decision requiring full due process for juveniles, little attention was afforded the activity of the court. Examining the microfiche of old newspapers in the public library, one could scan weeks of newspaper clips before finding any reference to the juvenile court. Along with the failure of county, state or federal governing bodies to provide funds pre-WWII, there was little Judge Beckham could do other than work at establishing some orderly system, and to create an image that would gain the respect of the community. This he did.

One of the legal problems vexing Judge Beckham from the very beginning of his term was the constitutionality of his office. Able lawyer that he was, he knew the question as to the special act creating the office would require his frequent presence in court defending his election to office. In several courtroom disputes, opponents had claimed that the legislature had erred in creating a special juvenile court only for Dade County.

The Constitution, they averred, requires that laws dealing with courts must be general and uniform, applicable to every county. Ours, a special act for Dade County, seemed to have been created only for our use. As indeed it had been so created for that purpose.

In 1953, a Florida Supreme Court majority, by a four-to-three vote, found that the law relating to the juvenile court did in fact relate statewide. It, they ruled, applied to all Florida counties since the less populated ones are capable of growing into the same bracket as Dade County. Some thought this a tortured opinion but the supreme court had spoken.

They had reasoned that problems in a large urban areas call for different treatment. Beckham breathed a sigh of relief over this close call. Though appreciative of the court's ruling, he told a friend he found the supreme court's legal reasoning questionable.

Carefully developing a program of his own, Walter Beckham was prepared to hew out a way to further his new responsibilities. But the course of events brought new problems. Seeking support programs for the children from the State and the County, he found these new government entities insisted on a role in the decision making.

There's an old political saying "Be careful what you ask for; your wish may be granted . . . to your later regret." Here, Judge Beckham, determined to be an activist judge to meet the needs of children in distress, suddenly found he had acquired partners seeking to limit his undertakings.

His efforts to further create state legislation to restructure the court had brought the state legislature as well as other state agencies into the picture. Beckham, by this time, was truly a skilled political practitioner. Judges were not then nor now permitted to endorse or engage in political campaigns. But this wise restriction did not prevent establishing good relationships with legislators, both county and state.

Beckham, already having served as a past president (1948, 1949) of the National Council of Juvenile Court Judges, knew his way around, teaming up with the powerful Dade County state senator George Holt. In those days, Dade County had but one state senator, and no local bill could be passed without his approval. Senator Holt had complete control over any Dade County local legislation sought.

The judge and the senator worked closely together to obtain passage of proposals sought by Judge Beckham. In later years the State granted home rule to Dade County, permitting Dade to bypass the State on local legislation. Back in those earlier days, however, it behooved local officeholders to have a friend in court like Senator George Holt, who later went on to become a long-serving judge of Dade County's circuit court.

Beckham's push for local aid for new detention facilities had also aroused the Dade County manager into action. The manager preferred limiting the juvenile court judge to the adjudication of cases, and his own County Welfare Department seeing to the well-being of both delinquent and dependent children.

To top it off, during Judge Beckham's tenure in office, one, then another juvenile court judge was added to the rostrum—well-needed additions to handle the growing court calendars. But new faces of power meant new ideas, not necessarily consistent with the views of each other. Struggles for sure among the leaders.

Also coming into the mix were civil liberty groups, along with our own Dade County Grand Jury now rising to question the "unbridled" power of juvenile court judges. Our Judge Walter Beckham rarely had moments during those twenty-seven years to suggest that this "part-time" job, a temporary stopgap in his career, would also include short peaceful interludes.

In his twentieth-year anniversary on the bench, the *Miami Herald* (July 1953) noted the longevity of his service with praise, citing the thousands of cases he had heard, never having one of his decisions appealed to a higher court. So impressive was this feat that *Ripley's Believe It or Not!* devoted half a page to Judge Beckham's singular success.

Discussing this admirable performance with his youngest son Robert Beckham, now a distinguished trial lawyer with Holland & Knight, he and I agreed that in those days there were very few appeals, if any, from juvenile court rulings. The reasons were obvious.

Lawyers finding their way to juvenile court were few and far between before the 1967 Supreme Court *In re Gault* decision. The few that appeared found appeals of little value, since by the time they were heard by a higher court, the child's sentence had been completed.

Further, the State provided no public defenders, although some few jurisdictions had a lawyer chosen by the court to assist in the proceedings. Some private lawyers, where the defendant could afford the cost, were also litigating concerns of their clients. On the whole, however, the juvenile court was not, for a long time, viewed as a chamber where adversaries truly litigated a case. The judge alone ruled supreme.

In *Kent v. United States*, 383 U.S. 541 (1966), those concerns that would strongly come to the fore in the years ahead were addressed. A legal commentator noted, "In theory, the juvenile court provided less due process, but a greater concern for the interests of the juvenile. This compensating benefit may not exist in reality, and the juveniles may receive the worst of both worlds."

When Walter Beckham took the reins in 1933, the parens patriae doctrine had been firmly established almost by default. The juvenile court would be a paternalistic forum providing solicitous care and rehabilitative treatment for children. There was community support for this effort. Not overwhelming but sufficient.

However, the full significance of this benevolent approach was appreciated only by its most avid supporters. In later years it became apparent to many that this court could not, absent strong criminal sanctions, be at the same time the compassionate surrogate parent, and still be the force to deter violent juvenile behavior.

In all the world's history the court and penal systems had always before offered nothing but harsh punishment for persons convicted of crimes against society, including children. In some instances the mere accusation was enough to inflict serious bodily harm on those charged.

In the nineteenth century, the novel idea that children might be treated differently had suddenly come upon a nation now becoming steeped in new democratic ideals. This would be a new pathway giving juvenile judges tremendous leeway. In those early periods, the juvenile court judges were the beginning and end of the courtroom drama. That era, prior to *In re Gault*, coincided with Judge Walter Beckham's early years on the bench.

All one needed to make the system perform as planned by the early visionaries was to have judges blessed with the ability to dispense wisdom, turn "bad kids" into upright citizens, and to provide juveniles with all the due-process rights demanded by civil libertarians. To many, these were unrealistic goals.

Going back to the days of Judges Penney and Atkinson and for much of Judge Beckham's lengthy term in office, juvenile court consisted of the judge listening to the child and his parents, if available, followed by a judicial ruling. Little or none at all of the adversarial hearings as carried out in adult court was present. The juvenile court judge would summarily rule, and at the same hearing determine the fate of the accused child.

Parents could be present, and except for the most egregious offenses, an informal approach with a benevolent result hopefully came forth. Many court hearings denied the presence of the public. Serious criminal charges might result in a residential placement; incorrigibles would earn a stay at the dreaded state school at Marianna.

As some few cases on appeal wended their way through the court system, and the rights of juvenile defendants became more of an issue, the courts began to become a bit more formal. But with children's offenses still relatively low in the order of high crimes, and courts with little in the way of rehabilitation programs, the juvenile court had not yet reached a significant position in the criminal justice system.

Perhaps the greatest influence on the courts following WWII was the sudden increase of violent behavior by juvenile gangs. The earlier movement to be more compassionate, had lost its panache. Juvenile court judges could no longer serve as the grandfatherly/grandmotherly benevolent caretaker "saving" all children in trouble. A frightened public would have none of that. The public cry was for punishment, with prevention placed in the backseat.

Judge Beckham's lengthy tour of duty took him through each of the changes that had altered the juvenile court system in those turbulent mid-twentieth-century decades. Remember, the juvenile court in Dade County was created, not for compassion over our children, but because of the overcrowded calendar of Judge W. F. Blanton of a few decades past. He had been the catch-all judge, hearing all criminal court cases as well as assuming a host of other judicial roles.

Creating a special part-time court to hear children's cases would only partially relieve Judge Blanton's caseload. Special compassion for the child was at best a secondary consideration. There also was no expectation this new court would sprout into one requiring resources far beyond the early imagination of the Dade County planners.

To cite but one example, in 1943, ten years after he had assumed office, Judge Beckham wrote to Preston Bird, then chairman of the Dade County Commission, seeking funds for additional staff, pointing out that his caseload might approach six thousand for the coming year. This request went unanswered as did others.

It was not until ten more years had passed that the state legislature in 1955 finally provided for a second judgeship. This, despite the burgeoning juvenile population in Dade County and the introduction of a new breed of violent juvenile delinquents. William R. Culbreath was appointed to the position of Dade County Juvenile Court judge by Governor Leroy Collins. Matching the number of judges to the rising numerical caseload also remained a problem for Beckham's successors. A report in 1986, forty-three years after Beckham's request to Commissioner Bird, with a now tripled community population, the juvenile court made do with but five judges on the bench.

Today, in the year 2007, there are eight juvenile court judges with a somewhat increased total caseload, but not too far off from the caseload of sixty years earlier when Judge Beckham had first sought additional staffing. The times, though, and the nature of the court are dramatically different.

The monumental due-process changes in the juvenile court set by U.S. Supreme Court rulings, and as well structural changes created by state legislation, have changed the picture completely. In addition, there are now multitudinous rehabilitative approaches offered by the juvenile court, particularly in dependency cases. All of these change factors, rather than the numerical caseload alone, are key factors in determining the need for additional judges.

It took those many years for the juvenile court to begin to impress upon the community the significant role this kind of court needed to play. No government planners at the local or state level had studied the future needs of this growing court, as to function, staffing or funding. Every incremental growth just grew, like Topsy, almost by accident. In later years government agencies would begin somewhat to address the needs, at least in a limited fashion. Citizen groups would also materialize to join the effort of aiding the orderly development of the juvenile court.

To Judge Beckham was left the sole role to marshal these forces to persuade the community of the need. A quiet, reserved man, lacking a dramatic flair, he may not have been the charismatic leader ordinarily arising in such situations. But this situation did not need charisma. It needed a sincere, honorable, tough person presenting the facts for the government leaders to see. That made him the right man for this assignment.

In the past, the state legislature had been sparse in their aid to Dade County. But Judge Beckham's ability to convince Dade County State Senator George Holt, and as well his successor in office, Senator William Gautier, to offer enacting legislation enabled the appointment of a badly needed second judge for the court.

That William R. Culbreath, a former Hialeah municipal judge, had also been legislative aide to Senator Gautier undoubtedly helped in his appointment. Well regarded in legal circles, Culbreath also had been an outstanding worker in youth activities at the Coral Gables Methodist Church. Judge Beckham was pleased to now have a colleague on the juvenile court bench.

The presence of an additional judge was helpful, but with the court's growing pains it needed a lot more to address all the problems ahead. What with the newspapers and the grand jury beginning to take critical looks at what had been a kind of private enclave, some dark clouds were on the horizon.

How did Walter F. Beckham, judge of the juvenile court, handle so difficult a situation? Beckham, not averse to slugging it out, had his share of pitched political battles. He lacked a political machine to clear the way, but what Walter Beckham had was a lot of patience. He was in for the long haul. Somehow he recognized this was to be a struggle that would not produce a resounding triumph with bugles in the background heralding victory.

This would be progress through incremental gains. He needed to move forward step-by-step, implementing each gain. Beckham made calculated moves. First, becoming a state and national leader, he thereby attained a reputation beyond local recognition. His achievements there were not only of benefit to himself, but also accruing to the stature of his local programs.

Moreover, he had to recognize that success depended mostly on his ability to portray himself as a reasonable man to whom the fate of our children could be entrusted. This was more important than displaying skills as a political leader. Above all, he had to, in some way, persuade the community that this court was "different" in the sense that it did a lot more than adjudicate the guilt or innocence of those appearing before him.

He also had to stay above the political skirmishes that subsequently marked the juvenile court in the immediate years after his departure. He chose instead to minimize these struggles rather than dramatize them, thus avoiding many glaring headlines that would accentuate the difficulties government was having in the efforts in behalf of children. He had his share of pitched battles but never sought them out.

It was an ever-changing scenario during the Walter Beckham years, requiring him to change with the times. For a man set in his ways this was difficult. His eldest son, Walter Beckham Jr., now an old lion of the Florida Bar, was succinct in describing his father: "He was very strict with us. Church on Sunday. Hard work. He taught us the right things. He loved to have young people around him." Adding the earlier quoted McCloskey and Beckham Jr. comments together, one arrives at a serious, old-fashioned, no-nonsense jurist, caring for children but demanding they assume responsibility for their actions.

His approach probably fit the times, at least for the Miami community. This city was hardly then ready for a Judge Ben Lindsey type. The child-saver style dominating the early formative years of the mission to improve the condition of children had taken hold mostly with social workers. In Beckham's day, judges, for the most part, had to focus on organizing their courts and obtaining more than the sparse resources offered. In later eras, the child-saver doctrine would reemerge from time to time, but for Judge Beckham it would be tough sledding to merely stay above ground.

Judge Beckham became a state, national, and international leader in the juvenile field. In 1935, Beckham had founded and was the first president of the State of Florida Probation and Parole Association. Consisting mostly of professionals in the probation and parole field, Judge Beckham's presence brought in several other Florida juvenile court judges, giving the organization more prestige.

In the 1940s during WWII, too old to serve in the armed forces, he threw himself into organizing the juvenile court system on a national basis. He had been one of the original founders of the National Council of Juvenile Court Judges (NCJCJ) back in 1937. Today the NCJCJ is one of the most powerful voices in behalf of children in the world. Then, they were but a handful seeking a forum to reach, to inform, and to lead juvenile court judges.

The NCJCJ had been making progress toward their goal when, in 1943, WWII forced an end to their annual meetings. A few, including Beckham, put together a news bulletin and articles to keep the members in touch during the war years.

Before the WWII hiatus, the NCJCJ had presented a multipoint program to a U.S. Senate committee urging the construction of adequate facilities for delinquent children, educational programs for policemen serving as juvenile officers, and as well federal responsibility for the return of runaways. The latter became Walter Beckham's major project.

Judge Beckham's efforts in this regard brought him much acclaim and honors. Perhaps he was best known within the profession for the establishment of the Interstate Compact for the Return of Runaway Children. Children on the loose was a national concern with Florida viewed as a haven for runaways. Cooperation between the states was then a long and difficult process, unlike today's routine exchange of letters between the authorities. This had been the first major effort by the NCJCJ to influence congressional action.

The proposal for federal funds to implement the Runaway proposal was enacted into law in 1949, a goal Beckham had advocated for passage since 1943. For six years he was the leader, instrumental in bringing about the enactment in Washington of a law providing funds for the states to develop the concept. It expired a decade later, but Beckham until his death continued his activity to create an interstate compact, binding each of the states and their agencies to do the job properly.

Beckham stayed with the project, volunteering to do the job to the finish. On the Wall of Honor in the Dade County Juvenile Court lobby, along with pictures and bios of Dade County Juvenile Court activists, is a framed copy of a letter dated August 12, 1956 signed by W. H. Beckham. It had been sent to each juvenile court judge in the nation, advising of the final additions needed for passage of the Interstate Compact for Runaway Children in their respective state legislatures.

These proposals had already been endorsed by the National Council of Juvenile Court Judges, as well as the Advisory Council of Judges, who had worked for years with Beckham on the project. It goes without further saying that this process was complex and involved undertaking that included conformity among the juvenile court judges of each state, their legislatures, and as well each of the social and welfare agencies dealing with runaway children.

Walter Beckham's tireless effort to create this compact to insure adequate cooperation among the states didn't come to final passage until several years after his death, but as long as he was alive he fostered the hope that brought it to reality. Starting this project in 1943, for seventeen years until his death he stayed with it. What a man!

Recognized for his activity with state and national organizations, he was elected NCJCJ president in 1948 and 1949. At the 1949 NCJCJ Convention in Miami, a few moments after Beckham had been reelected national president, Judge Walter Criswell, a Jacksonville judge who was present, recalled,

A few men were huddled around Judge Beckham in the hallway. I thought they were celebrating Walter's victory, but no, they were at work organizing the National Juvenile Court Foundation to print the *Journal* and serve as a standing committee to carry out the functions between meetings.

This was a follow-up on the newsletter and bulletins started back in 1943 during the war years. Walter drew up the Charter and made certain it would function properly.

In 1950, he was the NCJCJ's first official representative to attend the International Conference of Juvenile and Family Court Magistrates at Liege, Belgium. Later in 1958, toward the end of his service, he was once again honored, this time with the presidency of the International Association of Children's Court Judges.

This was mostly an honor awarded to judges throughout the world for being international leaders. It was a fitting tribute he could appreciate during his lifetime. When elected to this illustrious post, he wired a telegram to his family from Brussels, Belgium, where the meeting was convened: "The little tow-headed boy from Zebulon made it." No other Florida juvenile court judge, then or since, has earned either of these two honors, let alone both.

Beckham seemed to be active in every national event taking place. In 1949 Judge Beckham was on the planning committee for setting up the first White House Conference on Children and Youth, and in 1950 attended the conference as the NCJCJ's delegate. He was also active in promoting other important national legislation through the NCJCJ. Perhaps equally as important as the Runaway Compact was the Uniform Reciprocal Enforcement of Support Act.

This legislation, like the Child Runaway Act was crucial in aiding the welfare of children. It too is a compact among the states of the Union to enforce action against father's moving to another state to avoid paying child support. Today, fathers cannot hide in another jurisdiction to avoid paying child support. Virtually every county in the country participates in this program. The NCJCJ, with Beckham and other judges at the helm, were instrumental in its passage by Congress.

Interestingly, Judge Beckham received little local recognition in the press for his activism on the state and national level. The above information about those doings was gleaned not from Dade County newspapers but from "A Brief History of National Council of Juvenile Judges," by Judge Walter Whitlach, printed in 1987 in NCJCJ's journal.

He did not ignore local and state concerns, particularly in the area of probation. Following up the child's progress after a court hearing was perhaps the most significant role in the child's rehabilitation.

Obtaining resources for that purpose was a difficult task. Constantly he fought the never-ending funding battle with frugal county and state lawmakers, who by their cost-cutting limited juvenile court judges from sufficient control over delinquents in this crucial time of their lives after release from incarceration.

In 1951, the Florida legislature eliminated the need for creating juvenile court judges by special local option legislation. Henceforth it would be by regular statutory modes. With this enhanced stature, it was Judge Beckham again who led the juvenile court judges to form their own organization: the Florida Juvenile Court Judges Association. He also was named leader of this group.

Both the Probation and Parole Association, organized by Beckham back in 1935, and the statewide judges' group, his current project sixteen years later, continued to work together as lobbying groups for improved services and conditions in the field.

The Probation and Parole Association eventually became the Florida Council on Crime and Delinquency, an important organization for corrections officers and scholars in the field. The statewide Juvenile Court Judges Association is today an influential group advocating for children and staff resources.

The development of these organizations again drew no major headlines in the local press, but Judge Walter Beckham, playing a major role in their development, helped upgrade the stature of juvenile court judges. In the years ahead, these organizations would be powerful spokespeople for the cause of children. Other groups following their path had a model to follow. Advocacy comes in many faces, not always heralded or even noticed.

As an example of the growth pattern locally, whereas Judges Atkinson and Penney had struggled valiantly to increase probation officers from one to two and then three, during Judge Beckham's reign the number of probation officers rose to forty by the year 1960. The term "reign" is used advisedly, but competing for funds against other worthwhile needs required a powerful force. Beckham was that.

For his years of service, Walter Beckham's career was not all parades of roses. There was much of the gritty day-to-day conflicts he had to face: struggles for power, egos that had to be massaged, budget woes to be met, political elections to be won, and on and on—a never-ending battle.

Did Walter Beckham relish or dread the swordplay? Hard to tell. He left no record of his pleasures or displeasures. He was a man of little flourishes or fanfare, always "the little tow-headed boy from Zebulon." Always short on words, long on action. Whether selling peanuts to the passengers on a train passing through town, or dealing with the heads of state, it was more like he had a task to perform, and he did it.

Back to 1933 when he first assumed office, totally unaware of what was in store, the new judge faced a lot of uncertainty. Then, in the impressive new

Flagler Street courthouse, housing most of the entities of government, his court was afforded three crowded rooms on the fifth floor, with the children he served locked in the adult jail on the fifteenth floor. It would take twenty years more before the juvenile court operation was moved to a more spacious Youth Hall at 800 NW Twenty-eighth Street, devoted solely to the needs for children. Home at last.

During those twenty intervening years, Judge Beckham had become an activist in the true sense of the word, but the great and grave events of those decades slowed the progress of the court's development. The devastated economy flowing from the Great Depression years of the 1930s saw the disappearance of what little funding was available, and the events of WWII totally eclipsed concerns about child behavior.

In the 1950s, with a revived economy, the world and Florida returned to some degree of normalcy permitting ordinary concerns of citizens to come to the fore again. Judge Beckham, meanwhile, had not been idle. His activism at every level had earned him a national reputation. He would need all his credits to complete his mission.

Postwar Miami had undergone a dramatic change. The population had jumped in large numbers. WWII veterans were flocking to join the explosion of opportunity. The population was ever changing with new ethnic groups taking residency in Dade County. Tourism was now the number one industry, and better law enforcement had become a hot concern for this new medley of residents.

There had been a lot of marking time with barely noticeable progress. Judge Beckham was now ready to move on. The juvenile court had not been receiving much attention, but now the Dade County Grand Jury began to notice progress or lack of it in the treatment of children. For starters, the Dade County Grand Jury initiated regular visits to institutions that were housing wards of the court.

The fall term 1954 grand jury issued one of the first of many grand jury reports on juveniles. This one noted that the facilities of juvenile court and Youth Hall had been inspected. The conclusion: "The above facility contributes much in exceptional and worthwhile service to this community." The report noted an almost five hundred number increase in complaints investigated over the previous year. The new total was 7,649 complaints brought to the attention of the juvenile court.

That grand jury requested two additional probation officers to respond to the workload, as well as salary adjustments in order to retain qualified persons. This first of many post-WWII grand jury reports, devoting only thirteen lines to children, was somewhat informative but hardly provocative. Subsequent grand juries continued to regularly visit and appraise the juvenile court function, mostly in a critical fashion.

Not only was the grand jury now paying attention to the juvenile court, but both the *Miami Herald* and the *Miami News* were beginning to offer a full-court press of juvenile court doings. The days of a slumbering minor court were over.

Hard-core juvenile crime and hordes of runaway and abandoned children were becoming commonplace, and the general public was displeased with the rise of both. Who else to point to for blame other than the juvenile court where these concerns were supposed to be corrected?

Judge Beckham, still intent on creating a solid structure for his court, had never made grandiose claims as to his ability to prevent and correct the dire problems juveniles were creating or involved in. This was not a one-man or a one-court job. It would need a marshalling of many community assets and actors. He, a man with a national reputation in the field, was both the logical leader, and perhaps more importantly, an ideal target.

It started with a fifteen-year-old pregnant girl and her twenty-one-year-old boyfriend. The *Miami News* was distressed over reports that Judge Beckham had ordered them not to get married and forbade them to further see each other.

This story and others in the *Miami News* brought a swift denial from Judge Beckham, blasting the *Miami News* story as "unfair and prejudicial." The judge stated that his restrictions applied only to the period the young girl was in Youth Hall.

No sooner had the furor over the pregnant child abated, the *Miami Herald* came out with a critical series describing the shortcomings of the juvenile court. Beckham responded:

> Once the court is given added facilities and personnel to relieve our crowded quarters, many of our problems will be relieved. There has been no expansion of Youth Hall since it was opened in 1950. The rapid growth of our child population requires the Dade County Public School system to serve twice as many children as planned for.

With the strong interest shown by the *Herald* and the *News*, it was apparent that the juvenile court's long quiescent period had come to an end. All the honors Beckham had attained and the positive action taken over the years became things of the past. It was more like, what have you done for me lately? Public scrutiny of an intensive nature was in the offing.

It did not take too long. The spring-term 1957 grand jury report on the welfare of children was a complete reversal of earlier favorable reports. Encouraged by the newspaper series in both the *Herald* and the *News*, this grand jury was primed for action.

The jury concluded about the juvenile court: "Many phases of their operations were stagnant or had deteriorated to such an extent that immediate corrective measures are indicated."

The jury recommended support for creating a new Division of Child Welfare to be incorporated into Dade County's Department of Public Welfare. This new division would assume total control for placement of children in foster care, thereby eliminating the exclusive authority held by the court. This was a heavy challenge directed solely at Judge Beckham.

The seven-page grand jury section devoted to the juvenile court continued with other proposed changes, all of a drastic nature. Few areas were ignored. Their list included many grievances: harsh treatment of offenders, inadequate and antiquated filing and maintenance of case records, failure to provide receipts for confiscated property, inadequate number of office hours to hear citizen complaints, and other concerns, even pointing out the filthy condition of linen in the male section of the detention center.

The jury did not directly criticize Judge Beckham or newly appointed Judge Culbreath, but a declaration of war had been issued. The targets were obvious; it had been brewing for some time. The major recommendation of the jury relating to the operations of the Dade County Juvenile Court voiced opposition to the exclusive judicial jurisdiction. The jury, as they declared it, wanted "a more flexible control." The report concluded,

> It is recommended that immediate steps be taken at once to analyze existing laws and instigate necessary legislation to revise the statutes governing operations of this Court in order that over-all operations and procedures will be removed from the closed-door methods and policies which have existed for many years.

This was a killer report. The juvenile court had been criticized in the past, but never in such strong terms. The actual language though not couched in threatening terms, the intent was clear. On September 12, 1957, the grand jury then submitted a sealed report to Governor Leroy Collins recommending action on his part.

The press immediately joined the fray, endorsing the call for legislative action and demanding a new order. It was to be Dade County government in total control; the judges relieved of much of their power. The judges responded forcefully, but in fact the issues were real and perhaps some of the criticism warranted. But where lay the blame?

What a few decades earlier had been a fresh, newly minted juvenile court system with glorious visions now appeared to be deteriorating. It had survived the bad early years—the Great Depression and the aftereffects of WWII—but now was under an attack of a nature more serious than ever before. And to top it off, the man at whom it was directed was recognized as one of the juvenile court leaders in the country.

Was it neglect by the Florida legislature and local government? Was it the upsurge of violent juvenile crime? Public disinterest? The fault of the judges? Judge Walter Beckham was on the spot. A seasoned veteran, wise in the ways of the world, he realized that while a defense of the system was necessary, this was a battle not likely to be won.

A man acclaimed by his peers nationally, he was now denigrated at home. That adequate resources had never ever been afforded this new venture barely had been acknowledged. What had begun as a crusade to "save" the children now looked liked a losing effort to save the juvenile court as a bureaucratic institution.

Was Judge Walter Beckham able to marshal the forces to resist the tide about to overwhelm his court? He was in a tight situation. Responding to a negative grand jury report is difficult, almost impossible. The grand jury, a citizens' body designed to be totally independent of political influence, is in a sense the voice of the people. The grand jury is meant to be the ultimate tool of our checks and balances system. In the eyes of the public, a grand jury report is the final word on any issue. When the GJ speaks, all has been said.

This independent body of citizens, aided by the Dade State Attorney's legal advice and investigative staff, is an unfettered, free body. A circuit court judge receives and accepts their reports, and until released, all their efforts are secret. In addition to presenting indictments on capital offenses, the grand jury may issue public reports on current events of their own choosing.

In this situation, Governor Leroy Collins, at the request of the grand jury, had replaced Dade state attorney Richard Gerstein with Ted Duncan, state attorney for the Eighth Judicial Circuit. On occasion, when the grand jury or the state attorney sense a possible conflict, such a request to the governor will generally be complied with.

How responsible is a grand jury? Mostly on target, but the grand jury, like any other civil or criminal jury hearing a case, can also be in error or overstate a grievance. Emotions of the moment can overcome reality; the truth may get lost in the interchanges. Many things can go wrong.

In this case the grand jury appeared to be on the right track, but were some of their conclusions flawed? In their major recommendations they seemed to have missed some of the fine points of the juvenile court operation. By emphasizing many minor failings, it looked as if they might be reaching out to establish a full plate of wrongdoing.

Judge Walter Beckham and new associate Judge William Culbreath responded firmly as reported in the press of that day. Judge Beckham, disabled by a heart attack six weeks earlier and speaking from his sickbed, blamed the report on "misinformation and factual errors." He added a statement similar to his response the previous year when the press had attacked one of his earlier rulings. Again, he emphasized the failure of the State and the County to provide sufficient funding,

"For years I've been asking for many of the same things which the grand jury talks about. I've requested another judge and more probation officers to keep pace with our increasing population."

Judge Culbreath agreed. In addition, he outlined all the grand jury statements he deemed incorrect, refuting with specificity the individual charges. Culbreath's response, unlike the mere conclusions offered by the Jury, detailed a point-by-point reply, fully explaining the actual court process.

No matter Judge Beckham's plea for help and Judge Culbreath's defense of the court action, there was little response. A grand jury accusation, particularly when the conclusions reached are close to the mark, is hardly refutable. Despite the shortage of resources provided the court, the public expects maximum performance. Nothing less.

Courthouse rumors had the sealed grand jury letter to Governor Leroy Collins as requesting the removal of Chief Probation Officer Ira Hazlett. The grand jury report, made public, had condemned harsh treatment and corporal punishment of offenders and as well the presence of unqualified probation officers. This public report did not include any reference to Ira Hazlett by name, but the inferences were plain. He, the man in charge, would have to walk the plank. Or so it seemed.

The special trip to Tallahassee by Dade deputy clerk Richard Rice to personally deliver the sealed letter to the governor, with its secret contents, gave some credence to the rumors. Much to the surprise of the courthouse observers, it was learned that the governor no longer had that power to remove the probation officer. At the last session of the legislature, specific authority over the chief probation officer had been shifted to the chief judge of the juvenile court.

To the public's even greater surprise, Judge William Culbreath, then the legislative aide to State Senator William Gautier, had in that capacity proffered this change to the Dade County Legislative Delegation at the request of Judge Beckham. This change was in line with the authority of other chief juvenile court judges in Florida. To some it was clear proof of some kind of a political move by the judges to save Ira Hazlett's job.

No one connected with the Dade County Grand Jury would confirm or deny any recommendation as to Ira Hazlett in their sealed letter to the governor. Joe Grotegut, administrative assistant to the governor, only stated that the governor's staff was analyzing the contents of the "rather voluminous letter" sent by special messenger to the governor.

This was all a continuation of the political maneuvering concerning the status of Ira Hazlett. Several months earlier, Judge Beckham had sent a letter to Governor Collins informing him that an attempt would be made to have Hazlett removed from his position as chief probation officer. Beckham had then urged the governor not to fire Hazlett. Back in 1942, Judge Beckham had promoted

Hazlett to the chief probation officer slot. According to Beckham, Ira Hazlett had served long and well.

After fifteen years in office, Hazlett decided to save the parties involved any further embarrassment. He resigned as chief probation officer. Whether he was pushed, shoved, or worn down by this "Byzantine politics" chain of events is unknown, but obviously the major players were involved in some heavy gamesmanship.

While complaining about Hazlett's performance was the main focus of the grand jury, the report opened the way for a stronger, critical new assessment by future grand juries and the media. If nothing else, it showed the juvenile court no longer as the step-child of the court system. Mostly ignored in the past, now the juvenile court not only attracted attention to its virtuous goals, but as well to the glaring deficiencies. Out of the shade and into the sunshine, the juvenile court would forever after be a focus of attention.

Upon Hazlett's resignation, Judge Beckham promptly announced the appointment of James C. Smith as chief probation officer, saying he was the best qualified staff member for the job. Smith promised to continue past policies. Critics, disapproving of continuing "past policies," voiced opposition, and shortly thereafter Jack Blanton took the helm. New leadership at many levels was coming to the fore. More of Jack Blanton later.

Although the governor took no direct action on the grand jury report, changes began to occur. Judge Beckham, rather than contest the grand jury charges, moved to rectify. He knew that the time was ripe for change, and although he would not be the axis around which change would revolve, he could start the wheels moving.

On December 1, 1957, a joint announcement by Judges Beckham and Culbreath revealed a plan to place all court personnel under civil service. The Intake Department would be expanded, with better supervision of children in detention and probation provided. A bailiff would be available in each courtroom. Improved psychiatric services offered. An architect was named to draw plans for the expansion of the children's home. In addition, ground was to be broken for a new three-million-dollar boys' school at Okeechobee.

According to the judges, the present training school at Marianna was frequently overcrowded. Although not cited in the grand jury report, Marianna reputedly used extremely harsh "training" methods. Judge Beckham preferred a full more modern training program to better prepare these children for a full return to society.

These changes suggested a recognition on the part of Beckham that the old was out; a new beginning was on the table. He sensed that change was inevitable. A lesser man might have resisted progress. Here was Beckham, now ending a long illustrious career, accepting change, now traveling with a realistic new approach, consistent with the views of the grand jury.

But the major issue yet to be addressed—who's in charge?—was still to be faced. Will the judges continue absolute rule? What will the role of the County Welfare Department be? And where do the state agencies fit in?

This would be a continuing debate and struggle for the next half century. Judge Beckham played a role at the beginning of this epic battle. It would continue on and on with the State replacing the County as the main adversary to control by the judges.

In the midst of all of this, the sitting juvenile court judges had to find a way and means to further display their advocacy in behalf of children. Forced into action, Beckham and Culbreath began an immediate response aimed at implementing change. They would turn the grand jury criticism pointed at them to their favor.

Judge Culbreath appeared before the county commission requesting budget increases that would enable the hiring of five more probation officers and several more clerks for processing of cases. He cited the recent grand jury report as well as other studies showing increased caseloads and a staff numerically unable to handle the volume.

Judge Beckham, in concert with Jackson Memorial Hospital psychiatrists, worked out a plan for troubled youngsters in need of psychiatric care to receive outpatient treatment at JMH. This would be a major step in medical resources for the court. At that time, the court had a part-time, once-a-week visiting psychologist who did screening, but follow-up treatment was not readily available.

Under the new plan, outpatient facilities at JMH were to be expanded with eight to ten staff psychiatrists working part-time with juveniles referred by the court, a written follow-up report with recommendations to the court to follow. In the more serious cases, patients were hospitalized at JMH's Psychiatric Institute. In addition, should the mental health problems of the parents give rise to ills of the delinquent child, the institute would provide treatment as well for the parents.

This was a great comeback for Judge Beckham. The juvenile court was slowly coming out of its swaddling clothes. Having these top-flight mental health professionals available was a giant step forward in terms of maturity of the court program. This also was the forerunner of what would be the creation of the juvenile court's own on-site, properly staffed mental health clinic, only a decade away in the offing.

Did all the scorn tendered by the grand jury and the lashing by the press awaken Judges Beckham and Culbreath to the urgent needs of their constituents? Had they been asleep at the switch?

Not at all. The juvenile court judges from the onset, going back to Judges Penney and Atkinson, had implored those who held the purse strings to invest more in the well-being and welfare of delinquent and dependent children. In a sense, the sudden furor aimed at the juvenile court caused a backlash that warned the legislative and executive branches in control of the budgets that it was indeed time for them to act.

Was Judge Beckham, the venerated longtime senior judge now out of the woods with the many positive changes in store?

No way. The power struggle was only beginning. Judge Beckham's early plans to avoid the spotlight on his court was never about to happen. Wise and well-meaning as he saw the situation, the genie was now out of the bottle. The juvenile court would forever be a full-time player on the public scene, both reacting to the critics and offering new approaches to save the system. That's how it should be.

The attacks kept coming. This time it was a more powerful Dade County Commission attack from a new source. Metropolitan Home Rule, recently enacted by the state legislature, gave Dade County authority to govern itself independently of the state legislature. At that time, this was a major change in governance. Metro, as it was called, no longer needed State approval in local matters. Emboldened by this new power, Metro chose to show off its clout. What better target than the embattled juvenile court?

This was the year 1958, with twenty-five years of Walter Beckham's term in office already behind him, yet the few years ahead would see him in the midst of constant battle. Despite failing health, he held up well.

Promoting Jack Blanton to chief probation officer brought a helmsman sincerely liked by the youngsters he had worked with for ten years. Blanton also had earned the respect of police and social workers with whom he shared their job of dealing with recalcitrant youth. No longer would probation officers be part of the patronage system. Not with Jack Blanton in charge.

This was a fortuitous appointment by Judge Beckham. The probation officers of that day, numbering nineteen, carried the full court workload. They processed incoming cases, made home studies, presented cases in court, checked out the conduct of those on probation, and other security functions.

The probation officer was the jack-of-all-trades, the forerunner of our current counselor/social worker. Not until later were specialists assigned to many of their tasks. Five of the nineteen on Blanton's staff were women. Two members, Ike Withers and Hillis Holman, later rose to department heads in the County's child welfare system, and one Donald Stone eventually became a circuit court judge, sitting as chief juvenile court judge. Dewey Knight, one of the best probation officers, would also rise to be Dade County manager in the years ahead.

Jack Blanton's leadership was of immeasurable aid to Judge Beckham in the struggles they faced. Choosing to go under the Metro Civil Service, the probation staff had improved their job security, meaning they could not be removed without cause.

For the first time, a true professional, Jack Blanton, was their leader. Starting back in 1942, he now had sixteen years working with children and their families. He also had served as a court administrator who had exerted significant influence in the formation of juvenile court philosophy and direction.

In the twenty years ahead he would help develop the children's psychiatric clinic and in addition set up court operations and staff training programs. Prior to the Blanton days, many of the probation officers were deemed "controversial" for their lack of professionalism and lackadaisical performance. Under Blanton's control and direction, they were viewed as an efficient, high-quality group.

Conflict was brewing with metropolitan government. This began the slow chipping away of Judge Beckham's authority. It was the first of many forays by County and later state officials to take over. Beckham's effort to low-key the problems were no longer able to resolve the issues faced.

As Judge Beckham approached the end of his tenure, his health began to fail and one crisis after another with the County began to emerge. He still had the skills and experience to handle most, but the quantity and magnitude of the changes were so massive that neither Beckham nor his successors could slow the tide.

Judge Beckham had a singular vision for the juvenile court. He was a systems person, relying on what had been tried and true. He had had his share of judicial advocacy, but now the real struggle for survival was close at hand. The loyalty of his staff, men like Jack Blanton and Donald Stone, aided him considerably. They were fierce supporters and worked hard with soldierlike precision to maintain the stability he sought.

Beckham, in essence, was a General Douglas McArthur type, determined to keep the fort going. Deprived of adequate resources all the years of his office, and now the subject of attack from many sources, "General" Beckham had kept his soldiers focused on retaining what was left of the child-saver concept.

Operationally, Beckham sometimes showed little empathy with court counselors or even the children before him. Being rooted into the defense of the juvenile court system and with his own personal health problems, he needed all his energies for the struggles ahead.

He still wanted children to be treated fairly, but more importantly he chose to save the system. Jack Blanton was there at his side to support him, and a few years down the road, one of his later successors, Senior Judge Donald Stone, would in similar fashion struggle to stem the tide about to engulf the court.

For the next several years, the judiciary of the juvenile court would be under severe attack. Beckham held the fort and established a pattern of resistance that would enable followers to continue the struggle. Judicial activism now would include not only speaking out for a humanitarian, therapeutic approach and the development of programs thereof, but also a defense of the very existence of the juvenile court.

The attacks came in quick succession. First came a metro ordinance taking operation of the Kendall County Home for Children away from the juvenile court, placing it under the control of the County Welfare Department.

This action arose from a critical survey made by the Welfare Planning Council of Dade County chiding county officials for failing to provide an adequate program of welfare service for dependent children. "This," their study stated, "caused the juvenile court to assume responsibility for these children."

It added, in a manner equally critical of the court's control, "Most of the children there are planned for and supervised inadequately by unqualified personnel, and are being damaged in the process." The Welfare Planning survey was based in part on a study done a year earlier by the National Probation and Parole Association.

Both Judge Beckham and Jack Blanton had their work cut out. Growing in gasps and spurts as the court had moved in the past decades, absent not only adequate funding but virtually no external controls, had to mean a kind of mom-and-pop operation. Activism, spreading the message for children, needed a lot more than the spirit of the moment. Many more controls by the judges would need to come into play before the community fully accepted both the concept and the individuals administering the program.

Mr. O. W. Campbell was the manager of Dade County under the new Metro government. Metro permitted the Dade County Commission the independence to pass local laws in many areas without the need for approval by the state legislature.

Manager Campbell was more an efficiency expert and less a leader ready to fight political battles. He saw Metro as an experiment to provide greater flexibility for large metropolitan governments by freeing them on local matters from the yoke of State control. To him, an independent Metro was a great opportunity to develop Dade County to its full potential. Tangling with the juvenile court judges over obscure issues, however, was not in his vision or part of his agenda.

Campbell came to Dade County with a reputation as being a highly competent manager. The County plan to decimate the authority of the judges was hatched by his department heads as an effort to do a little empire-building of their own. They had been patiently waiting for the opportunity to go on the offensive.

Manager Campbell, hoping for compromise, stayed at arm's length in the debate that followed, while allowing his department heads to move forward in their demands. This issue was one of the first tests of the new authority of Metro. Campbell suggested that "both sides sit down and talk it out."

For the judges it was a kind of countdown. Having the County, the media and the grand jury aligned against them, and by now probably the public, made for heavy artillery to overcome. The debate was civil, but the undercurrents were fierce. County Welfare Director Robert Nicholson was the lead debater for the County, and he had all the department heads ready and raring to go.

The "talk it out" conference on June 26, 1958, started on the wrong foot when William Scoville, the county budget administrator, responded to Judge Beckham's reasonable complaint that the proposed new budget made no provision at all for more funding help and expanded facilities.

Mr. Scoville candidly admitted that the funding omission was really only a "tool" to gain concessions from the judges in the bargaining process—a kind of opening gambit in a chess game. For a pencil-pushing bureaucrat to admit that this was but a clever strategy move was totally inappropriate and somewhat foolish.

Judge Beckham, grasping the moment, icily responded with, "I'm very resentful of that statement." Beckham paused for a moment, then added, "I can't be threatened."

County Manager Campbell, a bit embarrassed, broke in with a peacekeeping effort, denying that the County was using the budget as a club against the judge. "There is no dispute over the need. I hope that through a joint effort of the Welfare Department and the judges, we can meet those needs." Score one for Beckham. He was against the wall, but still not giving an inch.

Budget Director Harry Toulmin said his recommendation for relieving the judges of their administrative duties was made on the basis of studies by independent welfare agencies. He added for emphasis, "There has been very little attempt made by the judges to upgrade the staff. And what has been done was made only after inquiries and studies made by these outside groups."

Beckham took that opening to lash out at both county and state officials for their repeated refusal to properly fund the juvenile court. It was a refrain regularly offered by the judges, but in the context of this meeting much more dramatic.

As the meeting broke up, new Judge W. R. Culbreath pleaded with the county officials, "Give us qualified and sufficient personnel, and let us have a whirl before you jerk the rug out." No one responded to Culbreath's plea.

After the meeting County Manager Campbell said he had not yet decided about recommending an increase in the juvenile court budget. By Campbell leaving that issue still on the table, it was plain the Judges had captured some of the momentum.

Beckham was patient. If his illness had slowed him up, it wasn't too apparent here. Outside his opening comment, he allowed Culbreath to do most of the speaking. Knowing these were only preliminary opening salvos, he was keeping his powder dry.

Two weeks later, Beckham let go with both barrels in a *Miami Herald* press statement, giving a point-by-point rebuttal. He started with the legal conclusion that the proposed Metro plan to strip juvenile court judges of much of their power "offers no improvement for child welfare" and additionally is "illegal."

Further he stated, "The cost of setting up separate Welfare Divisions to take over many Juvenile Court functions would be overwhelming. Besides," he pointed out, "the proposal simply gives carte blanche authority to the County, but says nothing about the requirements or limitations within which to operate." Finally, he noted in a parting shot, "Asking the court to delegate court services is in direct conflict with the State law."

Judge Beckham, a fine lawyer, had given the Dade County legal staff more than ample legal research to undertake. He closed his newspaper comment with this observation: "Metro authorities had drafted the plan without consulting the Juvenile Court Judges." His comments were mostly for County Manager Campbell's benefit, knowing Campbell was a man who strictly adhered to rules of process and the concept of team play.

It's not likely that the department heads were overcome by either Beckham's logic or his legal arguments. But Beckham's approach did reach the county manager. Offering a friendly move, County Manager Campbell called for a peace conference to take place on July 11.

Campbell, facing other pressures involving his job, preferred to remove this issue from the front burner. At the appointed date, the county manager wisely chose not to attend, leaving County Welfare Director Robert Nicholson as his spokesperson.

In an "all's good with the world" powwow, both sides announced a compromise. As one participant described it, "This will give a better break to kids who get into trouble." The judges will cooperate with and get assistance from the County Departments of Welfare and Personnel. This was far better than the proposal first offered by Welfare Director Harry Toulmin that he be named as an agent of the court to control the Probation and Detention departments. The ultimate effect of the compromise announced in a *Miami Herald* story had judges continuing to boss the entire juvenile delinquency program.

The concessions made by Judge Beckham did not seriously diminish his authority. He would still appoint probation officers but from a list supplied by the County Personnel Department. The detention centers, Youth Hall and Kendall, would be run by employees named by the county commission, and hiring and firing would be under civil service rules. Finally, the judges agreed to give consideration to future recommendations offered by Director Nicholson.

All in all, this was a clear-cut victory for Walter Beckham. He had played his cards like the wily old gent he was. This had been a power grab by the county department heads. Their plan focused only on the weaknesses of the court operation, but offered no substantial program to offset it other than a transfer of control to their departments. With County Manager Campbell enmeshed in other significant struggles, and not looking to open another battle front, powerful Judge Beckham prevailed. He had maintained the upper hand, at least for now.

Following up on this victory, Judge Beckham, through his new Chief Probation Officer Jack Blanton, announced the creation of the Probation Services

Division. This far-reaching new reorganization would limit their duties only to juveniles on probation. The officers in this new division would no longer carry the tasks of prehearing investigations and receiving reports from parents of juveniles on probation.

Previously, according to Blanton, these youngsters had received no follow-up supervision after release on probation. His new division would focus on providing follow-up supervision for children placed under probation by the court. A staff of three officers would be assigned this task with three more to be added. Blanton concluded with this statement:

> Overworked officers have been so busy booking youngsters they haven't had time to do much else. Casework has been lacking, offering only a lick and a promise. We've just had to let the kids ride along with a weekly check-in by phone.
>
> Now, these officers will be able to work much more closely with juveniles, parents, schools, churches and community centers than was possible in the past.

The *Miami Herald* story called it a "trailblazing" venture. Time would tell how effective it was, but the positive response to the announcement made it all worthwhile. Probation is an important court function, and Jack Blanton's program was a big step in the right direction.

Politically, the new deal was a great boon for Beckham. He had made a wise decision forgoing any announcement of his own on the creation of the new Probation Division. Too often ignored due to lack of personnel, following-up on repeat offenders is a significant goal for a juvenile's rehabilitation. Professionals in the field view this as the missing link in aftercare efforts.

Had Beckham, rather than Blanton, announced the change, it might have appeared as a defensive measure to cover up shortcomings alleged to him. Judge Beckham had attained both a national and international reputation, but there are always naysayers around seeking a change of faces in the political gallery of officeholders.

Serving for as many years as Beckham had recorded can develop a strong cadre of followers. Beckham, however, never capitalized on this in a political sense. By personality he was a reserved man, avoiding publicity, tending to his court business and his family. He won reelection easily in each race, rarely having an opponent. In those earlier years no one could find an issue to contest a race with him.

With Jack Blanton—a fresh, popular young figure—proclaiming perhaps the first new major approach of the juvenile court since inception, Beckham realized that this fresh approach could carry a lot more validity coming from a new generation man. As part of his earlier duties Blanton had run the Youth Hall

Detention Center as well as the new Kendall Residential Placement Institution, which earlier had enabled Judge Edith Atkinson to place delinquents in a local setting rather than in the adult-type Marianna institution.

This big step forward gave Jack Blanton the image of a man who can get the job done. Blanton's department also provided aftercare for delinquents released from the Marianna institution, where our most serious offenders were sent. In the past, delinquents released from Marianna had only to check in with local authorities.

Now, under Jack Blanton's energetic rule, his probation officers assisted and kept tabs on all youngsters released from incarceration; all omens pointed to better times ahead. That grand jury report and replacing Ira Hazlett had produced dividends.

Hazlett, as part of the past, had performed in a manner the community had accepted. Like all government functionaries of that era, he followed the status-quo approach of the senior judge. Beckham's was the way—the only way. Now, at the end of his career, Beckham was also falling in line.

Jack Blanton offered the beginning of a new approach, and Beckham appreciated his involvement, but the juvenile court was too far committed to the past for any serious change to occur from the inside. It would take a lot more action for the court to keep up with the times.

Before the year was out, trouble again loomed. The Dade County department heads, still smarting from Judge Beckham's "victory" of a scant six months ago, once more gathered their forces to gain control of the juvenile system.

In July, 1957, Beckham had weathered their challenge by declaring that Dade County had overstepped their legal authority in the effort to divest control from him. At that time the County backed away from Judge Beckham's strong opposition. Now, in a counter attack, the Metro budget director sought an opinion from Dade County Attorney Darrey Davis. Highly regarded in the legal community, Darrey Davis certainly carried much weight.

Budget Department head Toulmin again sought to strip control of the juvenile detention facilities from the hands of Judge Beckham by placing the facility under the County Welfare Department. In addition, he asked that the Board of Visitors, a citizen group appointed by Beckham, be abolished. Decades earlier in the 1920s and '30s, this group of well-meaning citizens had an important role at Kendall Youth Home. Now in the decade of the 50s it was only an anachronism—mostly window-dressing.

Dade County Attorney Davis issued an opinion saying it would likely take a charter amendment to accommodate Budget Director Toulmin's purpose to take control. Beckham quickly added, "This Court has a responsibility to work directly with Youth Hall, and the transfer of jurisdiction to the County would cause confusion and retard the efficiency of the Court."

In his response, Judge Beckham ignored the reference to the Board of Visitors since he saw no real value in their continuance and had planned to eliminate them in the near future. He further administered a coup de grace, charging that this latest effort to wrest control was a violation of an agreement entered into between the judge and the county manager to cooperate in every way possible.

Judge Beckham then offered a willingness for the County Welfare Department to take over the plight of dependent children, an area receiving little attention in juvenile court. Toulmin, as budget director, offered no response to either Beckham's criticism or his offer. The issue quietly receded. County Manager O. W. Campbell, never too enthused about this dispute, apparently was satisfied the issue was out of the way,

Interestingly, county officials were becoming more cooperative. They began to recognize that the strong judicial position in delinquency matters was directly tied to the operation of the court. They could, however, through the County Welfare Department, become a strong partner in developing a variety of programs relating to delinquency rehab, drug programs, and mental health treatment. In dependency matters, the County also began to work jointly with the court in many aspects, particularly in the mental health field. At least for the moment, the court's struggle with the County abated.

Judge Beckham realized that this was only one of those truces that periodically occur. The power struggles between the court and both the county and state child welfare agencies would, on various issues, continue ad infinitum. Judge Walter Beckham had the stature to fend off most of the attacks, but the years ahead would require some extra special, skilled maneuvering at the judicial end.

Both the county and state welfare bodies, as part of the executive branch of government, usually had the county manager and the governor on their side. These two political leaders had a lot more clout with their respective legislative bodies than the judges when it came time to enact legislation governing control over children. That is why having a big hitter like Walter Beckham in the batter's box helped immeasurably.

It took some time before the struggle between the court and the County diminished. Finally, it seemed to lessen considerably. Rising to the fore in an adversarial posture were new players: the governor and his state social agencies along with the Florida legislature. The legislature, as keeper of the checkbook, and the governor with his veto power, regularly played checkmate with the wishes of the juvenile court judges.

More so than in other court divisions, the senior judge (later to be titled the administrative judge) of the juvenile court must be an advocate able not only to develop new programs and initiatives, but also one ready to take on a whole host of adversaries out there, whether real or imagined.

Being a strong advocate to improve the plight of children gone astray requires not only the desire to do good, but as well a keen sense of political reality. Walter Beckham was one of these judges whose ability and experience qualified him to perform at every level. He defended the fort with skill, though never knowing for certain what form the conflict might take or which side the cavalry would come to rescue.

Judge Walter Beckham died October 24, 1960. At his funeral, his successor, Ben Sheppard, offered perhaps the most accurate estimate of the man's career. Sheppard, recently returned from the National Council of Juvenile Court Judges Convention, stated, "You had to attend a national gathering to appreciate the high and wide esteem in which this Dade jurist was held. He was a real pioneer." Indeed he was.

Although the juvenile court had not yet begun to draw the attention it warranted, Beckham's death was a significant event. Memorials attesting to his stature were posted among many organizations. The *Miami Herald* chronicled his passing with a lead story, characterizing him with a single word: "Fighter"—certainly one of the terms that described him appropriately.

In a tribute by Judge Criswell, a Jacksonville colleague, printed in the *Journal of the National Council of Juvenile Court Judges*, Criswell wrote,

> He never quit the fight. When stricken a few months ago his family and friends urged him to retire and take it easy, but he stubbornly chose to limp along and discharge his duty.
>
> In the hospital on the last day of his life, he arose early, shaved, had breakfast, dressed and walked down the corridors, giving a cheery greeting to those whom he knew, announcing, "Later in the day, I am going home."
>
> Those were prophetic words. What he meant was that he would be going back to his Coral Gables home to rest a few days before taking up his duties at the Court again. But the GREAT JUDGE had decreed otherwise.

In 1962 at a dedication ceremony changing the name of Youth Hall to Walter Beckham Youth Hall, Daniel Redfearn, a noted lawyer of that day and good friend of the judge, described Walter Beckham, the man,

> In private life Judge Beckham was a loyal, devoted husband; a gentle guiding father; a friend without guile; and a fair and bold antagonist.
>
> He was unfailing in his courtesy, and never overstepped the bounds of propriety or hit below the belt. His mind was keen, analytical, fertile and resourceful. He delved deeply for the truth, taking nothing for granted.

Judge Beckham, despite his monumental twenty-seven years of command, holding together the existing structure of the court, always had to prove himself. Rarely, if ever, did he fail in this task.

Activists come in different shapes and sizes. Some are applauded for the visionary humanitarian goals they espouse. Others, by their personal warmth, are able to establish one-on-one relationships with children that open new vistas and hope for otherwise disenfranchised youth. Some are systems designers.

Still others are powerful leaders. All their energies go into making the system work. Walter Beckham had some of the qualities in each of the above categories, but mostly his was the image of a man that created confidence in his ability to lead. No matter the crisis, he would find a way.

A kind of loner, Beckham avoided the media. Like many past and present elected officeholders, he was a bit wary of the press. His tenure in office never came close to the positive media attention received by others who followed him (Gladstone, Gelber, Petersen, Lederman) who struck a responsive chord with program efforts that heralded dramatic progress.

By nature a retiring, self-contained person, Walter Beckham neither sought media attention nor appreciated it. Often embroiled in conflict with county and state authorities, seeking out the scriveners to impress a point or to laud a new effort was not part of his arsenal.

His task was immense. He was the shepherd of a court in its infancy, with little if any support services available. The juvenile court was at the bottom of the priority list when it came to County and State funding. Gaining an adequate staff and space in which to operate this ever-enlarging enterprise was a huge task in itself. Getting all the disparate parts of the court system and the rehab programs to mesh so that the wheels ground properly was an immense challenge. Beckham's goal had one direct line—"make the juvenile court system work."

Organizing other judges into a state organization and then playing a major role in development of a national group were massive undertakings. These were groups that eventually played major roles in the acceptance and development of the inner workings of a proper juvenile court both statewide and nationally.

He laid the groundwork for his successors by building on a structure that gave the juvenile court the special identity it so urgently sought. Furthermore, he gave not an inch to those who sought to lessen the impact of the court as a healing device. He truly personified a staunch and lofty leadership.

In retrospect, looking back at his twenty-seven years of service on the bench, Walter Beckham was a unique personality. Not fiery or charismatic, he was the very essence of integrity. Those serving with him respected him for being a private person who did not pursue the importance of personal popularity. Beckham was a man who kept his own counsel; even his colleagues on the bench had difficulty engaging him in other than official business. Searching for press clips covering his years, his are few and far between. He fought his share of public battles but mostly in a gentlemanly fashion, in keeping with his own sense of fairness and character. No dramatic displays on his part. The positions he fostered, and the goals he sought were enough to carry him through each struggle.

It is unseemly for a judge to seek recognition for duty well done, but the juvenile court, unlike most others, often involves new programs requiring strong community backing. In a sense, selling such a new concept to community leaders often calls for persuasive support from the bench. Beckham declined to promote his programs, insisting that the positive results would speak for themselves. From the old school, restrained and dignified, he managed to quietly portray his Dade County court in the most positive manner on a local level and as well nationally and internationally.

A few appearing or serving in his court thought he was not the inspirational personality the court required, while some others viewed his work in keeping the court afloat as the major purpose of his administration. History has shown that the latter approach was exactly what the situation in that era required.

Looking back in perspective, one can not help but appreciate the fact that the firmness and resoluteness of Walter Beckham was precisely what the court then needed. If ever a Judge had the credentials to address those many years of the Court's growing pains, he was that person. This era was destined to belong to Walter Beckham.

With an ultrastrong hand he ruled every aspect of the court, maintaining its effectiveness, keeping all the participants on course. The fault lines that periodically emerged in the structure were setbacks that he took in stride, continuously moving forward to address them, and then move on.

At times those early dreams of the juvenile court seemed to disappear into smoke. Was the juvenile court in Dade County only a false apparition? Do away with the court? Not likely. Too many positive things had emerged. The dreamers were in abeyance, but they too would appear again.

That the juvenile court lacked recognition in those early years goes without saying. It took thirty-five years since inception in 1921 before a second juvenile court judgeship was established. The 1955 appointment of W. R. "Bill" Culbreath as a second juvenile court judge was a signal that things were about to change. Judge Beckham had already served for twenty-two years as the sole juvenile court judge. He had been "the man." Culbreath's addition didn't alter Beckham's control, but it presaged a major turnover in judges as well the transformation of the total juvenile court operation and function.

Five years after the newly appointed judge William Culbreath appeared on the scene, Judge Beckham died. Then began a splurge of new faces on the bench. It seemed strange, after all those years of sole Beckham rule, that the rostrum had a whole new set of black robes, vying with each other and offering new approaches.

But from all that new talent, it would be hard to find one of his successors who had his durability to perform in each of the eras of transitional changes that he had survived so well.

The addition of several new judges would ordinarily mean new opportunity and the certainty of change. However, those new faces on the bench in the midsixties made only a minor impact compared to the almost revolutionary changes brought on by the Florida Constitutional Revision of Article V relating to the judiciary, and even the more significant series of U.S. Supreme Court rulings starting with *Kent* and then the blockbuster *In re Gault*. The juvenile court would never be the same again. But more importantly, would it be better?

The rise in the number of judges did have its own impact internally. For a system so long under the wing of one judge as powerful as Beckham, the reverberations of change had to be meaningful. The benevolent dictatorship, in the era of King Beckham, had lasted for half the years of the total juvenile court existence in Dade County to that time. Change was inevitable.

Would it mean a protracted struggle for power among his successors? Possibly, but other court and legislative changes overshadowed any personal moves by the newcomers. Would the juvenile court fare better with a change at the top? Under ordinary circumstance, perhaps, but in addition to the legal changes imposed upon the court, the times were changing, and new faces would bring fresh new approaches.

Judge William Culbreath, the first new addition to the judiciary, to his credit, recognized the importance of Judge Beckham's stature and loyally supported his leadership. Judge Beckham had been there through almost three decades. His was the only name the public knew bearing that title.

Failing health had slowed Judge Beckham in his last years, and Culbreath attempted to fill the gap in terms of relationship with the Court staff and taking the lead when Beckham was under the weather. Long active with children's activities at his church and with a strong legislative background, Culbreath brought some new personality facets to the bench.

An outgoing, convivial fellow, highly personable, and even entertaining, Culbreath tried to be a friend to each child, an approach Beckham had avoided. Beckham loved children but personality-wise was not one for displaying affection publicly. On the bench he was the epitome of business. He expected caseworkers to do their duty, brooking few excuses. With lawyers he had been firm and direct.

Culbreath's warm approach to the kids was reciprocated. In him, they also saw a common bond as one who had suffered deprivation. Judge William Culbreath had only one leg but managed his life not only with skillful mobility, but with a cheerfulness that inspired others. He had acquired such dexterity at dancing that at social gatherings he performed to great applause. Many of the children and their parents appearing in his court were aware of his handicap, and along with his warm personality, he was viewed with great favor.

Beckham, accustomed to rule alone, did not encourage a close personal relationship with his new bench mate. Judge Culbreath deferred to his elder but chafed a bit in his secondary role. He had no choice. Beckham literally lacked the time to favor Culbreath had he sought to mentor him.

Upon Beckham's death, the governor appointed Dr. Ben Sheppard, a well-known pediatrician with a law degree, to fill the unexpired term. Dixie Chastain, who had been a staff attorney in juvenile court for nine years, announced her intention to contest Sheppard in the upcoming election. Suddenly, the leadership of the juvenile court, uncontested for twenty-seven years, was at issue, and likely to upset the equilibrium of the court.

After Beckham, for the next several years the turnover of judges was rapid. Judge Sheppard would defeat Dixie Chastain in her effort to unseat him. Six years later, when Judge Sheppard suddenly resigned from office, Sid Weaver was appointed by Governor Haydon Burns and won election for the full term. In that same year Dixie Chastain was appointed the third judge. Unfortunately, those were the years of dramatic change both of a state constitutional nature and Supreme Court edict. The juvenile court needed stability, not constant turnover.

It had become a game of musical chairs. A week after Beckham's, death Dr. Ben Sheppard was appointed his replacement with Judge William Culbreath becoming senior or, as the new title called for, administrative judge. Donald Stone, after defeating Judge Culbreath, was sworn in on January 5, 1965, Judge Ben Sheppard then becoming administrative judge.

Dixie Chastain appointed by Governor Haydon Burns in 1965, won election for a four-year term in November 1966. Sidney Weaver, the final new judge in that cluster, appointed upon Judge Sheppard's resignation, was then elected in November 1966.

In the half-dozen years after Beckham, new faces arrived and departed with rapidity. The public hardly knew who was on first. In the final move in that flurry, as a result of Judge Sheppard's resignation, Donald Stone took over as senior judge. Three judges were then on the bench, with a fourth to come soon.

Beckham's departure was the end of an era in more ways than one. His years preceded all the many changes determined by the U.S. Supreme Court and the state legislature. It's hard to tell how he would have reacted to *In re Gault*, although in all likelihood he, as did his successors, would have strongly rebelled at the U.S. Supreme Court's total revision of the juvenile court process. Add to that, the flurry of new judges joining the bench, and we have uncertainty entering the picture. Fortunately, the new judges had, for the most part, been schooled in the Beckham style and were able to carry on in his steady manner.

Walter Beckham's twenty-seven years may not have been filled with enduring change, although some of his turning-point accomplishments are of a landmark nature, but his was almost three decades of relative stability and of acceptance by the community. Not an activist judge in the sense of the early turn of the century pioneers who preached the gospel of the humanitarian approach, he was a man who faced the practical problems of creating a court structure that someday might fully accomplish that goal.

He was not a born leader who, by his own personality, could create ardent followers. His support came from the integrity and character he possessed. His probation officers, starting with Jack Blanton, pledged undying loyalty as though Beckham was an army officer leading a charge against an overwhelming force.

Donald Stone, having also served under Judge Beckham in his earlier days as a probation officer, said, "He was the greatest judge we ever had. He was a strict old-time southerner. He ran everything: the court, Kendall, Youth Hall. It all went through Judge Beckham. Everyone serving under him respected his leadership."

Stone, still somewhat in awe of Beckham, described an incident that had touched him, and that he now recalls:

> When Beckham died, I went to his office to retrieve his personal belongings. In one of the desk drawers I found a small safe with a warm inscription from William Jennings Bryan to him.
>
> Apparently, Beckham and Bryan had served together in their younger days in the Georgia legislature, and their friendship had continued on over the years.
>
> I realized then that Walter Beckham had been more than a local leader in Miami. He was a legend. His life experience had taken him far beyond what we knew.

Those first fifty years were indeed a trial and the strength of Walter Beckham had carried the court. Each of those judges, before and after Beckham, could point to judicial activism, at least to some degree. Some more than others. But judicial activism can thrive only in an environment of acceptance. More than the judges, the community must be accepting, and support from the media is significant.

Judge Beckham's style of unquestioned rule was due for a makeover. What it would be was hard to foretell. With new faces at the top, different voices surely would begin to be heard not only from the bench but as well from county and state agencies involved in child care. When vacuums occur, a power struggle usually ensues.

Judge Bill Culbreath, on becoming senior judge, hoped this was an opportunity to display his own brand of leadership. He had faithfully followed Beckham's path, and felt entitled to the leadership reins. Upon Beckham's death, Culbreath, at one of the memorials for his departed chief, had said, "It's more like losing an institution than a man." Now he wanted the opportunity to follow in that man's path.

Judge Ben Sheppard, already an established medical doctor and an individualist who had long attracted much community interest in several of his endeavors, was not one to sit quietly waiting his turn. Barely had Culbreath taken over the administrative judge role than the two were in constant disagreement, drawing unfavorable press comments. A WGBS radio editorial describing it as a "running feud" had this to say: "Differences between the two judges have been distressing and have damaged the image of this judicial branch in the eyes of the public."

It probably was inevitable that upon the departure of Judge Beckham, that his successors might differ strongly as to the course of the juvenile court. The Culbreath-Sheppard struggle lasted from the day in October 1960 when Sheppard succeeded Beckham, until May 1964 when Culbreath, defeated in his own bid for reelection, was replaced by Donald Stone. During the period in question, Culbreath was administrative judge, a fact that rubbed Sheppard the wrong way.

Although no outward manifestations of the low esteem he carried for Culbreath showed, it was apparent to courthouse observers that he viewed Culbreath as less than his equal. Culbreath, on the other hand, patiently waiting for Beckham's departure, looked forward to being the spokesperson for the court. He had, in essence, paid his dues.

Judge Sheppard did not in any way demean his colleague publicly. He merely moved into whatever issues of the moment arose, barely consulting with his younger but more senior associate. Their coolness, if not outright hostility, lasted until Judge Culbreath met defeat at the polls. Culbreath had tried hard to be a good judge and as administrative judge, a forceful spokesman for the juvenile court, but sometimes fate intervenes, playing harsh tricks. It wasn't, however, his differences with the popular Judge Sheppard that did him in. It was the Cuban Missile Crisis!

At about that time, American reconnaissance flights had discovered Russian missile sites located in Cuba, pointing toward Florida shores. The U.S. blockade of Cuban ports and interception of Russian ships heading toward Cuba had caused South Florida to be placed on a war alert. The possibility of a nuclear confrontation with Russia was frightening and, to some, imminent. To many Dade Countians, the proximity of Miami to Cuba posed a serious threat to their safety. This was no idle threat, being well within the range of the Cuban missiles.

My recollection is that most Dade County residents took the concern in stride, treating it as the usual parrying with Russia during the cold war. Almost like another hurricane threat approaching our coast. Others took it more seriously. As a young assistant state attorney, I recall our staff placed on an alert to be on call should circumstances warrant our services.

In our office, none of us felt a Cuban attack on Miami was imminent, fully aware that any such military action would bring a quick destructive response from the United States—a fact Fidel Castro was certainly aware of. In all likelihood, some few of our citizens, concerned about the welfare of their families, may have departed for safer inland sites. The newspapers did not report any wholesale exodus—only Judge Culbreath's flight was noted.

Judge Culbreath and his family left town for the safe haven of relatives in Mississippi or some other southern state. No one was certain where he had gone because he had offered no official notice to anyone about his departure. He and his family simply left town for parts unknown.

Somehow when the crisis was finally averted, and things returned to normalcy, the idea that some residents had left town in fear suddenly took on an ugly image. It was viewed as unpatriotic, some form of deserting fellow Americans. Particularly so with a public official performing a duty to stay and protect our children.

The Culbreaths returned, and all seemed to be forgotten, although some snide remarks still were tossed about the courthouse. Come election time, the radio talk shows picked up on Culbreath's sudden departure, and it became an issue. Donald Stone, the eventual victor, had not made it a part of his campaign, but the talk show hosts carried the day. Culbreath lost the election.

With both Beckham and Culbreath now gone, it was Judge Sheppard sitting alone in the catbird seat. He was to be the administrative judge and the official leader of the court. This was not a role for which Judge Sheppard needed any rehearsal. Long accustomed to being outspoken, the public attention was something for which he was totally equipped. In truth, amidst the turmoil, the public needed a personage with good credentials, fully accepted in the community and someone willing to take on all comers and all issues.

Sheppard at age forty-five was a seasoned veteran of public life. Question was, would this be only a pause in his wanderings, or would he settle in and rise to the tough tasks ahead? This was a golden opportunity for Sheppard, along with the hope that under his seasoned experience, the juvenile court could now settle down and begin to move in the direction that many of the planners had envisioned.

Dr. Ben Sheppard

Ben Sheppard's three predecessors heading the bench during the first fifty years of the court's existence for the most part had sat alone. For them, being the senior judge was a nice but still only a vacant title. Only one voice was there to speak for the court: theirs. As the court was drastically changed by both Supreme Court decree and state constitutional revision, additional judges were added, each becoming a voice alongside that of the senior judge.

In the new situation, the senior judge had the views of his colleagues to consider. Collegiality became a factor. Some differences came along with their arrival, but few serious problems. Mostly they worked together and tried to be supportive. Still, though their impact was not as strong as that of the administrative judge, they chose to be heard.

Ben Sheppard, unlike his predecessors, came to the bench as a star. He already was a prime activist in the community with a sterling reputation. Assuming a leadership role came easily to him.

Dr. Ben, as he was known to his patients, came here in 1947 from his private medical practice in New York, becoming director of Polio Treatment at Miami Variety Children's Hospital. Quickly he became known as the only doctor willing to go into the polio isolation ward to treat his patients.

Later he established several clinics: for unwed mothers, for alcoholics, and for drug addicts. Many of these projects were sponsored through the Catholic

Services Bureau, the organization that supported his efforts through the years. Through these activities, Ben Sheppard seemed to be involved in every community crisis involving the young.

His reputation as a pediatrician brought only praise throughout the community. Former Dade County mayor John B. Orr was heard once to whisper to a colleague in the midst of a heated political argument with Ben Sheppard, "How can I get mad at the guy? He came in the middle of the night to take care of one of my sick kids."

In similar vein, Robert Taro, then director of Kendall Youth Home, later head of the State of Florida Health and Rehabilitative Services (HRS) operation in the juvenile court, had this to say:

> Dr. Sheppard never slept more than three hours a night. He would call me anytime during the night to talk about medical problems the kids in Youth Hall had. I never complained about my loss of sleep. Anyone who cared that much could wake me whenever.
>
> Was Dr. Ben a good pediatrician? He brought up my four kids and in addition took care of my mother-in-law's shingles.
>
> As a private doctor he charged $5 to $10 for a visit. Once when I reminded him that he forgot to charge my daughter for a visit, he said, "Consider yourself lucky."

Ben Sheppard's appointment to the bench was widely praised. Not identified as a politician, he was viewed as a *people person*, a perfect fit for the position. He had handily defeated Mrs. Dixie Herlong Chastain for the seat. Dixie Chastain, with a long and well-regarded record in the juvenile court, started as a court investigation officer and then sat as a special master. She was admired for her conscientious efforts over the years and for her contribution to the court development.

Chastain, later to earn a seat on the juvenile court bench, however, lacked the charisma of this man whose name alone brought heaps of praise. Her excellent record of service and the strong political ties of her husband, who had served for many years as a constable, were not enough to sway the voters against this hugely popular pediatrician. She went down to a clear-cut defeat.

Ben Sheppard, with about 65 percent of the vote, won easily. It was if some divine source had decreed that it was time to rise for a leader who could truly bring the message and inspire allegiance to the cause. Doctor Ben's arrival was timely, to say the least.

The *Miami Herald* story by staff writer Lawrence Thompson announcing Sheppard's wide-margin victory over Chastain was replete with many accolades. "A man of many accomplishments . . . Dr. Sheppard has so many talents and activities that it is hard to classify him ... He probably knows more about the treatment of polio than any man in the South." Reporter Thompson garnished his article with many other choice phrases of approval.

Dixie Chastain probably deserved the office, but fate and politics don't always provide the proper due that people may have earned. Interestingly, the issue of Sheppard's lack of legal experience never entered the campaign. Night-schooling it, a 1952 U of Miami Law School graduate, he had handled a few cases in juvenile court. In a magazine article, writer Arthur Henley recalled a court-appointed juvenile court case that Dr. Sheppard handled, involving a sixteen-year-old girl charged with auto theft.

Dr. Sheppard, then and when he later sat on the bench, always first sought to determine possible medical problems of accused children. In this case he determined, "She had too much insulin in her blood" and convinced the judge that probation and proper medical treatment would best serve her rather than "sending her away to straighten her out" as the prosecutor had suggested.

Unquestionably, Sheppard's medical defense was warranted, but he, as well as other juvenile court judges, would learn from experience that a medical deficiency is but one of many characteristics that make up the cause for an offender's misbehavior. But bringing his medical expertise into the picture made other judges more aware of the complexities involved in analyzing human behavior. Most likely, Sheppard upgraded the consciousness of his fellow judges to the need for more forensic approaches in understanding the total picture.

That the juvenile court may have finally arrived was evident when he came on the scene as Judge Beckham's successor. It was 1960, and the times were changing. Prior to Dr. Sheppard's arrival, each of the preceding juvenile court judges had been chosen or elected by political chance. None had arrived with the brand "children advocate" clearly visible. Although the spirit of the court had eventually moved each to at least some level of activism, waving the flag or leading the charge for the cause of children was not on their immediate agenda.

Ben Sheppard, a practicing pediatrician and a community leader, always looking for new challenges, was for Dade County a new breed seeking public office. Practicing as a doctor for twenty-five years, his practice alone marked him as a man for children. He also had branched into many areas of medicine along with extensive involvement in other community projects. Despite an overflowing medical schedule, he had found time to attend the University of Miami Law School at night, earning admittance to the Florida Bar.

Becoming a lawyer was not one of those sudden "climb another mountain choices." In his earlier years in New York, already a physician, he had registered twice to enter Brooklyn College Law School, but his medical demands prevented attendance. Instead he took correspondence courses in law, finally satisfied with a diploma (night school) at the University of Miami Law School.

This dogged determination was evident in everything he undertook. Sheppard, like many of us, had harbored many dreams during his lifetime, but unlike most of us, he had never given up on any of them.

In Dade County, he became well known and admired throughout the community for his work in several areas. In 1952-1956 he had been Dade County medical examiner as well as medicolegal consultant for the state attorney and the sheriff's department. Besides taking court-appointed cases in the juvenile court, he became an instructor at the University of Miami in legal medicine. Each of these assignments was virtually a full-time effort, but somehow he managed to carry them all in his portfolio. This was a man of action.

Judge Sheppard was a startling change, adding a new dimension to the office of judge. In the beginning, back in 1921, Judge Penney, a respected public official, had taken office quietly, allowing the public to see the juvenile court merely as an ordinary, nonradical appendage to the existing court system. Following him, Judge Atkinson became an activist but within the bounds of the community standards of that day. She made few waves as she strove to introduce new concepts into the community.

For the six terms of Judge Beckham's tenure, he was the captain of the ship, keeping the tiller straight and guiding the court though the perilous times of the Great Depression, World War II, and the shifting debate as to the true purpose of a juvenile court. He effectively maintained the status quo while earning a reputation as a national leader, which inured to the benefit of the court on which he served.

Mostly by choice or circumstance, none of the judges immediately preceding Judge Sheppard had captured the imagination of the populace as had Judge Sheppard. In truth, it was time for someone like Ben Sheppard to come into the picture.

Ben Sheppard, by dint of his own personality and ability to bring important issues to the attention of the community, was exactly the kind of leader needed. Somewhat like the outspoken Judge Ben Lindsey of Colorado had been in the infancy of that court, but our Ben was a lot shrewder in the political sense.

For one, our Ben continued his community contacts as before. He maintained his pediatric office for families he had served. His reputation continued as the family doctor, always on call, no matter the time or place. This was an image that kept him in good stead with his constituents. He also continued to teach at the U of M Law School and serve as chair of the Florida Bar Medical-Legal Committee. These activities enhanced his image more than any popular decision he might make as a judge.

Denver's Judge Lindsey had sought conflict for the sake of conflict, always ready to go the barricades against the enemy, real or imagined. Miami's Judge Sheppard, equally combative, picked his spots and attacked when appropriate, made his point, then stepped backward to fight another day. Sheppard, in his new role as a judge, was determined to act as the conscience of the community rather than function as the community scold.

Viewing himself in this new office as the essence of the juvenile court, Ben Sheppard found strong community support, but hardly unanimous. Several of his bench colleagues were not absolutely enamored of him, and both the County and the State were in the process of strongly contesting the court's authority. In addition, new voices were beginning to recognize and adopt the position of child savers so important a half century earlier when the children's movement first began.

Lawsuits challenging the courts, heretofore barely a part of the process, were coming to the fore. Sheppard, not one to step back from a battle, pitched in with all his might in defense of the court operation. But it was not to be an easy fight, nor necessarily a successful one for him.

Becoming a part of the juvenile court system, Sheppard did not require a welcoming party. He served only six years on the bench but packed in a lifetime of action. He was already there as a volunteer physician for the Dade Detention Center since the budget for the detention center only called for a nurse and a part-time visiting doctor. A physician of Sheppard's caliber was essential although, upon his assuming the bench, some later criticized Sheppard's dual role.

Sitting as both a juvenile court judge and performing as the detention center medical doctor made it virtually impossible for any internal monitoring to oversee and appraise his service. Were the delinquents held in Youth Hall receiving adequate medical attention? Were proper medical records kept? What program existed to curtail suicide attempts in lockup? Nobody around would dare question the medical credentials of a sitting judge?

Barely into office, Sheppard and County Manager Irving McNayr began a struggle that would continue as long as both remained in office. There was no shortage of issues. Two strong-willed men, neither one accustomed to backing down. The first of many jurisdictional issues loomed ahead. These issues were contentious. The fight for power was nothing new. The opening face-off was a kind of preliminary bout.

Back in 1957, Metro government had assumed jurisdiction over juvenile traffic offenders, placing them in Metro court. Sheppard, adamantly demanded traffic offenses be returned to juvenile court. Perhaps not too significant an issue, but it was a turf battle that the participants chose not to avoid. Sheppard lost that one, but it was a warm-up for the really big struggles ahead.

These came quickly. Dade County welfare officials had never ceased to demand that dependent children—those neglected, abused, or abandoned—be placed under County control. The nub of the problem had judges demanding continuing control over both the adjudication of dependent children and their placement. A recurring issue with many nuances, never clearly defined by either side or by an appeals court. Prior disagreement had been avoided by temporary compromises but never fully settled.

The County also opposed programs, favored by judges, that institutionalized foster care children. Instead, they preferred programs that keep the children at home, providing aid to the parents, thus keeping the family intact. The County had maintained a watchful distance from the juvenile court in the past, but as the court sought a greater allocation of funds, the County had no choice but to become an active player.

The latest grand jury report also joined the contest, criticizing the lack of progress made for dependent children by both the court and the County. The report bemoaned the fact that the County approach to rehabilitate the family by case workers visiting the home, rather than removing the distressed child from the home was a dream never fulfilled. As well, the grand jury regretted that the court philosophy for an expanded residential foster care program had, over the years, also failed to be the full answer.

Although the differences between the court and the County seemed to be of a philosophical nature, it really was all about adequate funding. Both sides wanted the best for children but there never seemed to be money available to carry out the promise. That problem persists to this very day.

Hovering over all these issues was the proposal to finally rid the county of the now useless Visitors' Board, a relic of the past. Politically, in the early days, the Visitors' Board had had been a perfect buffer, a vehicle to avoid conflict. By now, it had become only a symbol around which a power struggle ensued as to the future of the juvenile court. Also, the Visitors' Board, appointed by the senior judge, was viewed as being under the court's influence, making the board less effective as a monitoring group.

In the beginning, the county provided only a small amount of taxpayers' money for the court. Now the demands were increasing at a fast pace. The struggles with the County continued for years, and no matter the resolution of the moment, always in the long run the same issues would resurface. Had County Manager McNayr displayed a more conciliatory approach, much of the judges-versus-County struggle likely could have been avoided or at least deferred.

Many concerns were beginning to be voiced publicly as to the rising juvenile crime rate and the ability of the juvenile court to stem the tide. The *Reader's Digest* had published an article about a judge in Montana whose get-tough policy included releasing the names of delinquents charged with a crime to the newspaper as a deterrent. Miami radio station WGBS, intent on bringing inadequacies of the court to public attention, brought the matter to Judge Sheppard seeking his views.

Sheppard, strongly opposed to publicizing the names of children who have been charged with a crime, contended that the subculture of delinquent youth want attention, and this would play into their hands. This was the first of many charges accusing the juvenile court system of being overprotective and soft on juvenile offenders. It was no easy task for Sheppard and those who followed to defend a system totally dedicated to "the best interest of the child."

Responding to radio station WGBS, Sheppard stated in a strong fashion, "The only time a name should be published is when the offense is sufficiently dangerous to society that society needs protection by awareness." That issue faded away, but it was the beginning of what would be a concerted effort to chip away at the special protection afforded children.

The whole juvenile court concept pointed to treating children differently than adults. Now, a rising public demanded that we curtail children, not provide them more freedom. This effort focused on no longer allowing juvenile court judges to determine the fate of serious juvenile crime offenders. Place these culprits in adult court to impose appropriate penalties was the cry.

The rise in violent juvenile crime nationally was beginning to bring a sharper look at the role of the juvenile court. The radio station WGBS campaign and other local media reflected a national concern over rising juvenile crime rates that questioned the effectiveness of a soft, humane approach for delinquent children. A get-tough attitude was quickly moving over the nation.

Releasing names of delinquents and lessening other protections afforded children in juvenile court were gaining heavy support among the citizenry. In Florida, the proposal to bypass the role of the juvenile court judge with direct filings by the prosecutor brought heated discussion and debate. The old-fashion way of meting out punishment was moving back in style.

Though defending the philosophy of the juvenile court, Sheppard, wise in the ways of public imagery, would not allow himself to be tagged with a Let 'Em Go Ben title. By nature, his soft side as a caring pediatrician was offset by the sometimes brusque, impatient, often a not-too-gentle man in debate. And one who rarely tolerated fools.

He was ready for the rough and tumble of his office. At the onset, upon assuming office, his announced policy to "get tough on the toughs" was warmly received by his constituents. Philosophically, Sheppard fit into the mold of the early child savers, but his own life experience, growing up in the hard streets of New York City and treating hard-core drug addicts as patients, gave him a sense of reality about the difficulties in fighting crime.

As to the general populace, hard to tell which of the two concerns—the lack of treatment for dependent children or the menace of the assaultive delinquent—gained greater public attention. Undoubtedly, the latter group provided the greater menace. Nonetheless, this time, it was County Manager Irving McNayr brandishing the dependency banner.

McNayr, one of those tough tall bureaucrats looking to make a name for himself, was ready to respond at the slightest moment of his displeasure. He passed up no opportunity to engage in battle. Unlike County Manager O. W. Campbell, his predecessor of a decade earlier, McNayr, rather than his department heads, personally took on the attack mode. Again, the county manager had a grand jury report to back up the charges.

This grand jury, supporting the county position, urged separation of the dependent and the delinquent children and removing all dependent children from the Kendall cottages. The County's solution to eliminate foster homes by rehabilitating the children at home, instead of placing them for eventual adoption, meant cutting out any role for the State of Florida or the juvenile court judges. It would be carried out entirely by the outreach workers from the Dade County welfare departments.

Sensing that the far-reaching, idealistic County proposal offered by the Welfare Department for dependent children was unrealistic and doomed to failure, Sheppard readily agreed on a compromise. So long as the court retained jurisdiction over the actual trial process, he would not object to the county effort. Placing the children for adoption would remain unresolved for the time.

This same struggle with the County had played out during Judge Beckham's years, and he had successfully repulsed the takeover effort. Absent State funding and other resources, there was little likelihood that the County could or would attempt to totally replace the judicial focus on adoption.

McNayr, more than a neophyte politician in his own right, was playing his cards with skill. Recognizing that each of the grand jury reports resonated with the rising public demand for action, he latched on to their findings. With each of his broadsides against the judges, he gained more media support.

Looking back at it, his goal more likely was to shake up the judges rather than to seriously diminish their roles. McNayr, unhappy with the performance of the juvenile court, sought change, and he wanted to be the one to bring them about. It was unlikely, however, for the Dade County welfare departments to alone assume these difficult responsibilities.

McNayr expected, and properly so, that the state legislature, with not only a vested interest in the welfare of children but also a duty, was not likely to relinquish this responsibility solely to a single county seeking it. Nor, absent State funding support, did the County want to take over this burden for dependent children. It was indeed a clouded issue.

The three-pronged contest among the judges, the County, and the State for control over these court programs would continue on and on with the grand jury in the middle, prompting the activity. Every report would sound the call for action, but absent adequate funding only slow movement, very slow, could result.

The County Homes for Boys and Girls in Kendall, located on Dade County-owned land, was the focus of this McNayr-Sheppard dispute. This was large acreage considerably distant from the juvenile court building in midtown

Miami, consisting of cottages that housed children sent there by the court. Rehab programs in place were rudimentary, with the result they were mostly used as holding facilities.

Some of the more serious dependency cases were sent to private treatment programs in the community. Since the main thrust of the court program for dependents was eventual adoption, this County Homes placement for children was viewed as "temporary." Unfortunately, adoptions were few and far between, and that temporary stay took on a much longer life.

These interagency squabbles infected the contesting parties with emotions rising high, but with nothing of consequence happening. Absent, however, sufficient funding, little likelihood existed for resolution. Eventually state government would become the major player, but in this period there was little movement.

This was really the early beginning of the change-over years for dependent children. The issues were mostly details of operation, such as which agency would be in control and what philosophy to adopt. These were important to the players—the courts, the County, and the State—but had little resonance with the public or the media.

The grand jury, meanwhile, had placed Kendall and Youth Hall on their "make a visit" for each of their sessions. Every six months the grand jury members would board a bus, visit the installations, hear the woes directly from the children, and write a report expounding on the lack of services provided children in Dade County. It was always the same story: lack of funds.

These enervating struggles over an issue that seemed to not have a ready answer, may have sapped some of Sheppard's desire to stay longer on the job. Squabbling with McNayr over control of dependent children was not to his liking. He preferred to be a lead actor in large events with notable results.

Had he stayed on he might have participated with relish in the struggles arising from the explosive changes soon to be coming from *Gault* and the new provisions in the state constitution as well as the expanded role of the State. Ben Sheppard was the kind of man who preferred being the catalyst of change rather than being lost in an endless struggle.

The mere fact, however, that the juvenile court was on the table, under constant fire, could rightly be construed as a sign of progress. The regular, critical grand jury reports alerted the press and the public to the shortcomings. Virtually ignored before, at least now the juvenile judges were getting attention, perhaps not laudatory but in the midst of the action. Considering that historically children were among the last of the deprived groups to receive proper attention, the progress was probably right on schedule.

There were some positive signs about. Housing conditions at Kendall and at Youth Hall were improving. A new juvenile courthouse was constructed with more probation officers available. Even an additional judge was added, with another one in the offing. Growing pains were gnawing at the system. All part of the natural growth of a movement, slow as it was.

Judicial advocacy was limited to defending the control of the court process. Citizen advocacy had not yet matured as either a support for the system or as a critic of the failings. Soon the State would begin to assume more budgetary responsibility, and the County role diminished. Not enough to avoid conflict with the judges, but sufficient to keep the pot at high boiling temperature. Changes, major changes, were in the offing. Our judges would soon be wishing for a return to the good old days when the juvenile court was an unknown quantity.

How Judge Ben Sheppard really felt about all this uncertainty is hard to determine. Ordinarily, a man of his stature and ability, with even the minimal community and government support, would be forging ahead. Certainly, he, among any of the past leaders, was capable of capturing community support, introducing programs and offering visions to guide the way. But virtually alone, with no visible support, only critics, he was forced to the barricades constantly defending the very existence of the juvenile court philosophy.

Meanwhile, several other cases brought criticism to the juvenile court and further distress to Judge Sheppard. One involved a juvenile held in detention for several months without a hearing, and the second, a court ruling tossing out a confession to a murder made by a juvenile before he was transferred to adult court.

Both these matters were newsworthy, attracting public attention and causing consternation in the community and a considerable amount of distress to the sitting judges. There had been difficult times in the past, but never involving negative public reaction in this way. Nonetheless, the good doctor/judge pressed onward addressing major concerns.

Judge Ben Sheppard, in the midst of these moves, attempted to maintain an activist role. No matter what massive change was in the offing, he moved steadily along on his own agenda to improve the operation of the court. His first big move was to put the finishing touches on a psychiatric clinic. This had been on the front burner for years, going back to Judge Beckham's days when the goal was to install the clinic in the then new juvenile court building. Promises had been made in the past by the county to fund this important project, but whether it was the continuous wrangling between the county managers and the judges, or funding shortfalls, it found only delay after delay.

Perhaps Sheppard's stature as physician now serving as volunteer in Youth Hall, was able to make him more persuasive. His description of the situation to the county commission, as reported in the *Miami Herald* on July 3, 1963, certainly impressed his listeners as to the need for assistance.

> Every working court day of the year there are one or two children that need mental evaluations. In many cases long-term treatment. The need for this Clinic beggars description. In the past we've either had to wait our turn at the JMH Child Guidance clinic, or find a private psychiatrist to volunteer.
>
> Our Clinic will be the first in a Juvenile Court in the South. With our own Staff we will be able to get things done.

Hearing this from the doctor handling these kids in court made a positive impact on the county commissioners. Dr. Sheppard also seemed to be developing a better relationship with County Manager McNayr, and that may have also been a factor in winning over commission support. This would be the first major change in providing mental health care since the early 1920s when juvenile court children had been sent to the county hospital for examination.

Sheppard then set about to recruit a psychiatrist willing to accept the meager salary offered to head the clinic. No one doubted his ability to complete the mission. This was a big score for Sheppard and the court.

The Dade County Commission also responded to a 1963 editorial (WGBS Radio Station): "For too long there have been recurring reports of overcrowding, of homeless children jammed in with emotionally disturbed, and lack of adequate personnel." The editorial had also urged that Youth Hall facilities be turned over to County Manager Irving McNayr and sought the end of the Board of Visitors.

The county commission acted by abolishing the Board of Visitors, which had been nonfunctional and had outlived its usefulness. Whereas the Visitors in 1921 had then served a useful purpose, in the ensuing forty years this vestige of the past had at best served only as a passive response to the needs for children. The dynamic, gung-ho approach sought by the child savers of yore was absent, if it had ever existed in Dade County. The Board of Visitors, as the name implies, were in truth, only *visitors*, not advocates.

The struggle with McNayr's top staffers continued unabated. This time, in 1963, County Welfare Director Robert Nicholson fired the first shot: "Although the court has for years accepted the responsibility for dependents, it is not by rights a court function." He proposed jurisdiction of dependent children be taken away from the court.

Several years earlier, the same request had been made by Welfare Director Nicholson, using virtually the same words. Then, Senior Judge Walter Beckham had successfully warded off the takeover effort. Beckham had wisely perceived that the county department heads, not County Manager O. W. Campbell, were leading the charge. At that time, Campbell was immersed in other County problems and chose not to engage. Beckham had then deftly worked out a compromise.

Tempests continued on between the Dade County officials and Judge Sheppard. At one point in 1965, Welfare Director Ray Goode, later to be one of Dade County's most able county managers, found himself in a hassle with Sheppard by refusing to accept two delinquent youth sent by Sheppard to Kendall Children's Home.

Ray Goode, as county welfare director, felt it was his decision, not Judge Sheppard's, as to who would be admitted to Kendall. An angry Judge Ben Sheppard ordered a contempt of court hearing, and only the friendly intervention of County Attorney Darrey Davis persuaded Judge Sheppard to withdraw the order. The volleys were coming from all sides.

When Manager McNayr offered to lay down his cutlass, at least for the moment, and peace appeared, new adversaries emerged. This time a running feud between Judges Sheppard and Culbreath over control of the Visitors' Board had rendered the board immobile. Judge Culbreath had become senior judge upon Beckham's departure, but Sheppard was not one to stand back to the proprieties of office. Not a flaming battle that attracted serious public attention, but surely annoying to Culbreath.

Where were the citizen groups to mediate these differences? Nowhere to be seen or heard. Not for decades ahead would private sector voices truly emerge to play a major role. There were lone voices and small groups speaking out, but their influence was negligible. Not until the twenty-first century arrived with the Children's Trust, a group headed by David Lawrence, did a strong citizen's constituency emerge. They organized a campaign and passed a self-tax on property, the proceeds to fund children's programs. This group would become a major player in Dade County in the children's movement. But no such body existed in Sheppard's time

Most of the misdeeds of the past in juvenile court were relatively minor, considered indiscretions. Now a closer look at court activity found serious concerns. Other than the grand jury drop-in visits, no serious professional assessment of the court had ever been made.

The other shoe was about to drop, pushing aside the local quarrels. The long-anticipated new directives from the U.S. Supreme Court and the state legislature aimed at the juvenile court in a sense began the process for looking more closely at the court operation. The fractious struggle with McNayr, aggravated further by these soon-to-be directives from the Supreme Court and the state legislature, probably cut short Sheppard's tenure as a juvenile court judge.

Sheppard was willing to be a true soldier, staying the course, but these events had locked him into a position that made his role untenable. He was a man who wanted to see results immediately, if not sooner. In the turmoil of the 1960s this wasn't possible.

County Manager Irving McNayr continued his onslaught, going once more on a rampage (*Miami Herald*, March 31, 1964), this time including the State as a target,

> County Manager Irving McNayr blistered Juvenile Court and State welfare officials today in a pull-no-punches report on Dade's child welfare problems.
>
> McNayr charged the Juvenile Court Judges with violating the rules of detention in sending youngsters to Youth Hall and alleged the Court's judicial practices are so inconsistent that many agencies no longer refer cases to the Court.

This was a withering attack. The story went on to quote Judge Ben Sheppard's response: "The Court has a good image, I defy him to name one agency that will not refer cases." Sheppard's probably correct about the role of Judges, but the manager was probably right on point in his criticism of the State's role. The State of Florida had been a kind of absentee landlord, rarely jumping in with assistance in the way of funding or other resources.

The county manager's sharp comments were aimed mostly at the state's failure to provide funds for operation of Youth Hall and the juvenile court. He accused the State of ducking its responsibilities to handle delinquent and dependent children and treating Dade County unfairly. McNayr offered a long list of State failures not only for funding but also for providing services to Dade County children in need of services from the court system.

Although the interchanges between the judges and the county manager were old hat, this was the first direct attack on the State by the highest Dade County official. McNayr, operating out of frustration, perhaps realized that there was little the juvenile court judge could do, absent funds to do the job. He may have changed targets, but whatever respite Judge Sheppard may have gained from McNayr's attack on the State, it was lost in the next crisis.

Judge Sheppard was hoping for a quiet period. Not to be. New criticism of the court had been offered by the Congress for Racial Equality (CORE) for assigning caseworkers on a racial basis. CORE coordinator Dr. John Brown had complained, "Negro caseworkers handle only Negro cases, and White caseworkers handle only White cases."

This was the era when *Brown v. Board of Education* would bring racial violence to a peak in the South. Bombings of Negro residences in Miami's Carver Village, a section of Liberty City, had brought race relations to a low for the county. Prointegration supporters were threatened by the Ku Klux Klan and other violent racist groups.

The home of the editor of the *Miami Herald* had been bombed for his prointegration position by a violent cell with KKK connections. Many other community leaders were on the list as targets. In these tenuous times, the last thing the juvenile court needed was racial disorder, or even the charge of racial bias.

Judge Ben Sheppard and Chief Probation Officer Jack Blanton were candid in their responses, denying discrimination and explaining the need for segregating the system. Judge Sheppard said, "It is done for a substantial reason. They (Black Probation Officers) understand the background. They know the neighborhood. It has always worked to the best advantage of the child."

Jack Blanton added to Sheppard's words, "There is no use beating around the bush about it. Negro caseworkers do casework on Negro families. To do the work they have to know the culture. In addition it would be difficult to send a White officer into some areas of Dade County at night." He further noted, "I see integration of the caseload in Juvenile Court in the future, but not at this time."

Unquestionably weak responses in today's racial discussions, but back then they struck a responsive chord. CORE's leader, Dr. John Brown, recognizing the realities of the situation, accepted the explanations. He stated, "CORE is satisfied with progress toward integration of Youth Hall and also at Kendall Children's Home. Youth Hall is already desegregated and progress is being made at Kendall."

In those perilous race-relation days of the 1960s this was indeed an important point to have reached. Judge Sheppard and Chief Probation Officer Blanton had handled it well. And their word was kept. Within a decade, the juvenile court became totally integrated at every level.

Sheppard's major problem fighting with the County over control kept him active. Judge Walter Beckham had in the past warred with County Manager McNayr and his staff, always coming to some compromise that only provided a hiatus in the struggle. Once again, McNayr and his subordinates were on the offensive.

The Sheppard-McNayr battle continued on, with high and low explosions on the part of both. Eventually, after McNayr left the county manager post, these difficulties were resolved with an amicable division of authority. The judges retained total control of the adjudication and disposition process, and Dade County staffed, funded, and controlled a variety of rehab programs.

Not until the State of Florida entered the picture with a willingness to fund these programs did the county fully recede into the background with a lesser though still-important role. Judge Sheppard handled these negotiations with skill, perhaps the first sign of forward movement in a long time.

With all these dramatic power shifts, it was obvious that we were at another turning point. The needs were apparent. The system needed an overhaul to be able to keep up with growing demands. This one called for the creation of a full-service agency, designed to address the problems of delinquent and dependent children in Florida in a comprehensive, holistic manner.

Adequate funding and resource services able to blend the court and the rehab agencies into a seamless operation would be required. Perhaps the dreams of Chicago social worker Jane Addams and Denver's juvenile court judge Ben Lindsey could come to pass in Miami and all of Florida. Nothing of past experience suggested that possibility. It would require some miraculous overhaul. A bolt of lightning, perhaps.

Lightning finally did strike in 1967, compliments of *In re Gault*, 387 U.S. 1. *Gault* hit Dade County like one of those stealth bombers the Pentagon always brags about today. It landed on an unsuspecting court with full force, almost flattening the system.

There had been a series of local warnings to the court of imminent danger ahead. However, it was hard to foresee that what had gone quietly along with only minor tremors for almost half a century would suddenly erupt like the atom bomb over Hiroshima.

Gault, in essence, changed the whole scenario for delinquents in juvenile court. Most particularly, it handcuffed the court in the adjudication process by providing all due-process rights to children that adults possessed, plus many structural changes in the system. New problems quickly arose: Would *Gault* now make the juvenile court a pale image of the adult criminal court? Could the present juvenile court judges handle so drastic an adjustment? Would judicial activism be shackled? Maybe yes, maybe no. For sure, things would be a lot different.

It had all started many months earlier when a new frightening apparition appeared on the scene—anything to make Ben Sheppard's life a bit harder. The Florida chapter of the American Civil Liberties Union (ACLU) filed suit over the disposition of indigent juveniles. Several test cases were in the offing, and a full-frontal assault was ahead.

Noted Miami civil liberties lawyer Tobias Simon, leading the ACLU charge, contended that Judge Ben Sheppard had deprived children of their constitutional rights: to a full hearing, to be provided bond, to choose an attorney, and to have a speedy trial. Lawyer Simon had been successful in gaining such rights in the U.S. Supreme Court for indigent adults in the *Gideon* case and now sought to do likewise for juveniles.

Never before had the Dade Juvenile Court been faced with so direct an attack by so strong a legal opponent. In fact, the court had never before attracted legal opposition as to its existence and purpose in any manner. For the almost half a century of the juvenile court operation, members of the Bar had viewed this court as some abstract institution whose real value to the community had yet to be determined.

Juvenile George Dennis was one of the ACLU respondents. When Tobias Simon appeared in court with his demands, our judges took his words in stride, feeling confident our state appeals courts would uphold their rulings in favor of the status quo. They were correct up to a point, but the handwriting was on the wall, plain to see.

The *Dennis* case would wend its way through the courts beyond Ben Sheppard's stay in office. It began back in 1964, and Simon's appeal to the circuit court surprisingly found Circuit Court Judge Henry Balaban ruling for Simon's client. Had it fallen before another circuit court judge, a different ruling likely would have emerged.

Judge Henry Balaban was not a wishy-washy kind of judge. Totally independent, he had won office on a platform that featured the overriding of stare decisis. As a candidate for the office, Balaban had declared, if elected, he would no longer follow established precedent in the law. No matter how appeals courts had ruled in the past, every case before him would begin fresh as a new born child.

This was, of course, an election campaign approach that bordered on judicial heresy. Balaban had run for elective office before in the city of Miami and knew that campaign rhetoric was not binding once elected.

Sure enough, when finally defeating his opponent, Judge Balaban went back to following the law as it has been designed since the days of the Magna Carta. In his ruling favoring the ACLU, Judge Balaban proceeded to spell out the constitutional rights to be provided the child. He ordered confrontation of the complainant, cross-examination of witnesses, and a court-appointed lawyer, if indigent, among other rights already afforded adults. On a rehearing in 1965, Judge Balaban again ruled in Simon's favor, thus extending the U.S. Supreme Court's *Gideon* decision to include juveniles.

Judge Sheppard continued to defend the juvenile court arguing, "Are we going to use an adversary (adult) proceeding, or are we going to be allowed to deal with the best interest of the child?" He added, "My feeling on these kids may be Neanderthal, but I feel there has been too much confusion between rights and liberties, as compared to rights and license."

Sheppard sought allies, asking the Dade County Bar Association to intervene in behalf of the juvenile court. Peter Nimkoff, chair of the Bar's Committee on Children, declined saying, "We feel the constitutional rights of the child would be better protected if they were established as a matter of right." The Dade Bar Association had helped the court in the past, but not this time.

Judge Sheppard kept insisting, "I don't see how you can claim the judge is denying the rights of a child when the judge is trying to rehabilitate him, when all our work is being done in his best interest." Meanwhile, the ACLU continued to file cases in the juvenile court.

Our juvenile court judges promptly dismissed each of these ACLU petitions. But it was to no avail. On appeal to the circuit court, Judge Balaban would find for the ACLU. Next stop, the Florida Third District Court of Appeal, sure to overrule Balaban. All through 1966, this was the dance, as if choreographed by some unseen hand.

As the *Dennis* case and others moved their way through the state appeals courts, the direction was becoming apparent. Florida's appeals court would support the past, but once in the federal courts, things would be different.

And that's how it played. In April 1966, the Florida Third District Court of Appeal upheld Judge Donald Stone's ruling that the *Gideon* case only applied to adults and did not apply to minors in terms of a juvenile's constitutional right to be provided a lawyer or be told of his rights. Nonetheless, the ACLU's Tobias Simon continued filing suits, fully expectant that based on the *Gideon* case he would eventually prevail before the U.S. Supreme Court.

In 1967, one day after the arrival of the final U.S. Supreme Court decision in *Gault*, the picture changed completely. Tobias Simon went before Dade Circuit Judge Ray Nathan seeking the release of a juvenile committed by Juvenile Judge Dixie Chastain and sent to the Kendall Children's Home. Judge Nathan released the youngster, but lawyers representing Chastain asked for more time to prepare for the ultimate question: was the U.S. Supreme Court ruling retroactive?

This was a significant decision since hundreds, if not thousands of cases could be affected. The juvenile court standard-bearers would fight to the bitter end. Should Judge Nathan rule the Supreme Court decision retroactive, chaos was likely to ensue. Finally in June 1967, Judge Nathan ruled the Supreme Court decision retroactive.

Judge Donald Stone stated for a *Miami Herald* press headline, "The Retroactive Rule on Juveniles Won't Bind Court." No question as to the accuracy of Stone's statement, since Nathan's ruling was limited, but the writing was clearly on the wall. The *Gault* decision was about to change the lifestyle of the juvenile court.

Of interest, particularly to lawyers, these same issues litigated before the U.S. Supreme Court in *Gideon* (1966), involving an indigent adult, had also been heard in lower court cases involving children, but no broad ruling had yet been issued.

The Supreme Court had ruled as late as 1966, in *Kent v. United States*, 383 U.S. 541 (1966), a case involving a juvenile, that the child may receive less due process if a "compensating benefit" came with the lesser protection. Referring to the evidence, the court ruled, however, that this compensating benefit may not exist in reality. *Kent* foretold the likely direction of the Supreme Court.

Eventually, the 1967 Supreme Court *Gault* ruling historically changed the face of the juvenile court. Apparently the Bar, other than the ACLU lawyers, had been asleep for a long time or the juvenile court was viewed as a quasi-court of no real consequence. With *Gault* the gates were opened. A juvenile court trial would no longer be a casual gathering of interested public officials trying to discern what to do about "the best interest of the child."

In re Gault, 387 U.S. 1 (1967), tied up the package in 1967, putting the finishing touches on the old system. The case itself was kind of simple. Gerald Gault, a fifteen-year-old Arizona youngster, made a crank telephone call to an adult neighbor. His sexual innuendos—"Are your cherries ripe today?" and "Do you have big bombers?"—caused his arrest and detention.

At the adjudicatory hearing, the victim did not appear, and the court, without resolving the issue of whether he had made the obscene call, committed him to a training school until he would turn eighteen. The maximum sentence for an adult would have been a fifty-dollar fine or two months in jail.

The Supreme Court ruled that juveniles had a right to notice and counsel, to question witnesses, and to be protected against self-incrimination, The opinion stated, "Juvenile Court history has again demonstrated that unbridled discretion, however benevolently motivated, is frequently a poor substitute for principle and procedure."

The reaction among our judges had been quick and precise: horror and despair. The immediate problem was the large number of cases that might be involved in Judge Nathan's ruling, making *Gault* retroactive. Judge Dixie Chastain had one of her old cases before Judge Nathan on the retroactive issue, and she was concerned.

Florida assistant attorney general Arden Seigendorf, defending the judges against the ACLU onslaught, said at that time, "Making it retroactive could seriously disrupts the administration of justice." Tobias Simon merely pointed out that in *Gideon*, the Supreme Court had made it retroactive, and the likelihood for the same determination here was apparent.

Judge Nathan had addressed this issue directly in his ruling by quoting the language in *Gideon*: "The present posture of the law is that when fairness of the trial, the very integrity of the fact-finding processes are under attack, retroactiveness will be recognized."

As it turned out, ACLU lawyer Tobias Simon was right, and Juvenile Court Judge Donald Stone was wrong. Once in federal court, the retroactive status of the Supreme Court ruling was upheld. Our judges were satisfied that doing the right thing for children was more important than providing all the advantages of due process. They recognized that with the limited resources available, the child would suffer rather than benefit.

The issues were coming hot and heavy for the juvenile court judges. From their point of view, none of it was good news. In the midst of the turmoil, Judge Ben Sheppard resigned. Here was the one stable figure, a man of distinction, a voice to be listened to, and he was gone. Why would this man, an indomitable warrior, leave in the midst of this struggle?

While on a trip to Birmingham, Sheppard had phoned Judge Dixie Chastain, telling her he had sent a letter of resignation to Governor Haydon Burns and asking her to notify the county commission of his resignation. In his announcement to the press, he said he had accepted a university teaching post: "I have two offers and I am making that decision within a few days. After six years on the bench I have had enough of the fight." Was there more to his departure? Further inquiry needed to be made on that question.

Were the changes of so overwhelming a nature? A layman might assume that the implementation of the U.S. Supreme Court decision was but an administrative reconfiguration; a closer look would prove otherwise.

Each of the Supreme Court's new directions encompassed major changes in the court operation. All the new legal requirements meant large numbers of additional clerical and professional staff as well as a technical updating to devise means in which to collect data, enabling the system to run properly.

Additional numbers of clerical staff, hiring and training a batch of state attorney prosecutors and public defenders required immediate attention. More court hearings also meant additional judges and their staffs. How about space to house them and the additional courtrooms in an area already cramped for size. And on and on and on. And who would organize the total effort? Who had those skills?

Had Ben Sheppard stayed on, he might have been the best one to handle it. With his numerous community contacts and with all the chits owed him, he could have brought in a team of volunteer auditors, efficiency experts, and legal scholars to perhaps line up the process in a week or two.

Don Stone, the new senior judge, a bright young practitioner with experience in the court going back many years to his days as a probation officer, had an overwhelming task ahead. He had the ability to handle it, but actually running the Court system and handling his own Calendar would leave little time for this significant undertaking. Placing the restructuring burden on his shoulders alone would have been a Herculean assignment, and an unfair one. Planning and implementing required a skilled hand, someone part of the system, but yet in need of many other outside skills to blend the effort together.

In the midst of all these momentous happenings, the Florida Legislature had been quietly working on revamping the state constitution. Every ten years a commission is appointed to consider changes offered by the legislature and individual citizens. In 1968 and later in 1972, a major revision of Article V (Judiciary Section), offered by the state legislature, was approved by the voters. In essence, it changed a fragmented system of judicial feudal fiefdoms and created an orderly two-tier system: independent specialized courts and municipal courts would become part of the state's circuit court or county court.

Heretofore specialized courts, like the special juvenile court and the probate court, now became divisions of the circuit court. Municipal judges and justices of the peace and constables were eliminated, and their duties assigned to the county court, where misdemeanors and lesser civil liability cases were determined.

The Florida Supreme Court would play a major role in the manner of selection and maintaining office, and a Judicial Qualifications Commission would monitor and take action against improper behavior of judges. No longer would part-time judges serve; salaries would be paid by the State of Florida. Some exceptions to these rules were made for the smallest counties to provide for their different circumstances.

This was a major overhauling of the judicial system, making it a unified operation. Separate entities, such as the juvenile court, had been independent, but it also meant there had been no central structure governing the court system. In essence, each of the separate units had competed with the others for funds and recognition.

The circuit court, our highest trial court, was first in prestige and political clout. The special juvenile court was as far down as a court could be. Would this rise in class be an important step upward for the juvenile court?

In the 1970 reorganization effort, the Florida state legislature also created the Department of Health and Rehabilitative Services (HRS) and several other state authorities that together would control all functions outside the actual trials in juvenile court. The HRS Division of Youth Services would provide post-trial services, although the judges would insist on a major role in determining program assignments for children appearing before them.

The old days, when the juvenile court meandered along providing minimal services while struggling with the county over control, were gone. With the State of Florida now in the picture and exercising both controls and providing funding, the earlier squabbling with Dade County began to appear inconsequential.

Despite the struggles that would ensue with HRS, in the long run it was a colossal do-over. These changes would totally alter the complexion of the juvenile court forever. For the moment, however, the top crisis for the juvenile court was the *Gault* decision and the havoc it could possibly wreak.

New Senior Judge Donald Stone and the latest addition to the bench, Dixie Chastain, were both old hands in the juvenile court. Each had held positions as probation officers and hearing officers and knew the drill. But neither they nor anyone else associated with the court had ever dealt with the demands of *Gault* or the revision of the state constitution's Article V, the Judiciary Section.

How the juvenile court got Janet Reno for the job as advisor for these major changeovers is an interesting tale. Reno, later to be Dade County state attorney and subsequently to head our U.S. Justice Department in Washington, D.C., had recently returned from a tour as staff director for the Florida House of Representatives Judiciary Committee.

Her job in Tallahassee entailed revising the Florida court system by an overhaul of Article V of the state constitution. In that effort she was fully aware of the implications of the *Gault* decision. Upon completing her job with the state legislature, Reno had returned to Miami and campaigned for and lost a seat in the state legislature. With her talent she had no problem landing a job with a top Miami law firm.

Therein lies the story. State Attorney Richard E. Gerstein had for years been dissatisfied with the cases transferred from juvenile court to his office for prosecution as an adult in criminal court. Those cases heard by a juvenile court judge for a probable—cause hearing usually arrived at the office of the state attorney deficient in many ways for successful prosecution.

Prior to *Gault*, no assistant state attorney was present full time in juvenile court, and the files sent up were often lacking proper form. In addition, the Dade County Grand Jury, for whom Gerstein served as legal advisor, was consistently critical of the inadequate manner in which trials were held in those courts.

In the past Gerstein had suffered these problems quietly to avoid conflict with the juvenile court judges. Besides, he had no authority to change the system. Also, this was an independent court that neither sought a regularly assigned prosecutor, nor was there a quantity of work requiring the assignment of one.

Gerstein, not the type to suffer quietly, suffered quietly. What could be done to speed up changes in the juvenile court process to both implement *Gault* and at the same time lessen Gerstein's problems? For some time he and I had been discussing these myriad concerns. (I was his administrative assistant at that time.)

Never one without problems, Gerstein was at this time in one of his many flaps with the *Miami Herald*. As part of my job, I was the deflector of criticism aimed at him. We were both into some deep thinking as to how to overcome the bad press the *Herald* occasionally directed toward him. No wrongdoing on his part, and really no animus on the part of the *Miami Herald*.

It was more a cultural divide. The *Herald* bigwigs, mostly staid community—minded conservative midwesterners, were not accustomed to dealing with a derring-do WWII vet who, thanks to a wartime triage by his hospital doctors, had barely escaped with his life as an Air Force navigator flying bombing missions over Germany.

On his return from combat, Gerstein had vowed that, as a battered and almost not quite whole veteran, he would never again bow to the ordinary rituals required for success. He would always be his own man, deferring only to his own conscience, enjoying life as he saw fit. This was a tough standard for a politician, but Dick Gerstein was part of the John Kennedy WWII new breed veteran.

The *Herald* brass respected Gerstein's legal ability and his resolve, but they expected—nay demanded—that in his own personal life he follow the proper standards of how a prosecutor behaves.

On weekends Gerstein loved to go to the race track to bet on the ponies, and his taste for jazz music often found him at some nightclub enjoying a topflight musician. The occasional snide *Herald* editorial remark was not to Richard's liking. He wasn't about to convert to what to him appeared to be the dictates of stuffed shirts, sticking to his more open way of thinking. But then again, although the *Herald* tried, they couldn't beat him in an election.

In some convoluted manner, Gerstein had surmised that by hiring Janet Reno, the daughter of the highly respected family of Reno newspaper people, his image at the *Herald* might be uplifted. Her father, Henry Reno, had a long career with the *Miami News* as a courthouse reporter; her mother, Jane Wood, was also a reporter; and her aunt Doris Reno was the last word on music and art in the *Herald*.

Janet Reno, the prodigal child, working to create a new Article V for the revamping of the state constitution, had earned high grades in the legal community. Hiring her would be a plum catch for Gerstein. Whether this hiring would upgrade Gerstein with the *Miami Herald* higher-ups was questionable.

When Gerstein sprung his plan on me to offer Janet a job as an assistant state attorney, I was less than overwhelmed—considerably less. It was my job to make recommendations to Dick for new assistants. Usually I would interview the applicants, and then present those I favored to the state attorney for hiring. On a few occasions he would bypass me and hire a political favorite or a friend's recommendation. This was one of them.

Janet hardly made my list. No experience in trial court, and in my view one of those uppity lawyers who felt Harvard was the least qualification one should have for any position of significance. Never having earned an undergraduate degree myself made me a bit sensitive about class.

Finally I blurted out to my boss, "What do you plan to do with her?" Disdainfully he responded, "That's your job." And that's how Janet Reno got the assignment to redo the juvenile court to conform with the *Gault* Supreme Court ruling. Turned out to be a brilliant idea, even though accidental. We not only would improve Gerstein's status with the *Herald*, but we also would hasten bringing the juvenile court up-to-date.

Calling Janet Reno into my office her first day at work, and barely concealing a small smirk, I told her the assignment. Janet didn't blink, gasp, or utter a word. She said, "Thank you," and walked out, asking not one question. I figured this to be at least a three to four month job.

Pulling together all those discordant groups, who now needed to work in unison, along with satisfying the three judges who now made up the juvenile court bench had to be an effort that would keep her busy for some time. Some scant thirty days later, she walked in, dropped a report on my desk, still not asking a question.

Reno had designed an excellent organization chart and provided a specific plan for each unit so that they could perform their duties, have the ability to interchange, and meet all the requirements of the U.S. Supreme Court. How she charmed the juvenile court judges to cooperate had to have been a highly skilled performance.

Representing State Attorney Richard Gerstein, the top prosecutor in Dade County as well as its most powerful political figure, Reno could have tossed her weight around, but tactfully she played it cool. Senior Judge Donald Stone, himself a former assistant to Dick Gerstein, did not have a full recollection of her role but in a recent interview remarked thusly:

> We needed all the help we could get. I don't remember what she did exactly, but she was absolutely fair with everybody. I believe she worked mostly lining up an assistant state attorney to appear as a prosecutor. She also pitched in with all our problems. Never had a moment of grief with her.

Wisely, at that time, neither Gerstein nor I had discussed her role with the judges. From our view the judges were in no position to complain about a skilled, forceful volunteer aiding them. Particularly since she understood the criminal justice system and was providing gratis some expertise sorely needed. Reno would go on to aid the judges develop a workable system.

Janet, with her work in the state legislature revamping the role of judges in the new Article V of the state constitution, became the expert on the scene. The new provision in the constitution had also provided for the State taking over the functions of the probation officers and the staffing of the court clerk's office and other units heretofore the burden of Dade County government. Her knowledge, along with her innate administrative abilities, later to be fully revealed in the high offices she would hold, stood her in good stead for this assignment.

When many years later I finally asked Janet Reno what she had done, she responded modestly, "All I did was make certain that all those rights children were entitled to became part of the law." The same question posed to Marlyn Smith, then an HRS supervisor, later to head the HRS operation in juvenile court, drew this response:

> Janet put the whole thing together. Before her arrival, Court sessions were kind of haphazard. She set up a process assuring that all the witnesses participated in the trial. Police officers were required to testify and offer their written reports to the defense.
>
> It took on the appearance of a real trial. They were now presenting evidence in a court of law. Before Janet, it was mostly the probation

officers as the only witnesses. She was the one instrumental in revamping the whole trial system.

The final word on Reno's role in the makeover of the new post-*Gault* juvenile court came from Tom Connors, the first assistant state attorney to serve there back in 1973. Connors did a short stint in that capacity, going on to this date to become a defense lawyer in juvenile court. According to Connors,

> There were four newly appointed assistants, one for each of the four judges (Stone, Chastain, Weaver, Gladstone). Janet was in charge. None of us had much of an idea what was going on. Our big goal was not to mess up and anger our boss, Dick Gerstein.
>
> We had overlooked the new speedy-trial rule in a case against the son of TV Seven newscaster Wayne Farris, and Judge Gladstone was about to dismiss the case for lack of prosecution.
>
> Reno was in a frenzy. The state attorney's office would catch hell, and Gerstein would surely hold her responsible. Reno appeared before Judge Gladstone and practically begged for an extension. Gladstone was kind enough to oblige. We were all saved.

Tom Connors concluded that Reno had been the glue that kept the whole process together until all the kinks had been worked out. Connors memory coincided with mine. Janet Reno, indeed, had shaped up the new juvenile court so that it resembled the kind of operation the U.S. Supreme Court had envisioned.

For years, after Janet Reno became the attorney general of the United States, reporters would quiz me on how she accepted and performed her first assignment as an assistant state attorney. That's the story.

A year later, resigning to accept the position as director of the Criminal Justice Program at the University of Miami, I recommended her as my successor. I pride myself on knowing a good thing.

Senior Judge Donald Stone was helped considerably by Janet Reno's assistance. Her obvious skills as an administrator and knowledge of the law were a boon to the judges. Here, as a resource to the senior judge, she was able to structure the new juvenile court concept and bring in all the players at some even keel.

Gault had been the ultimate blow. Included, of course, was the revision of Article V and the emergence of the state HRS as the powerful service agency for the rehabilitation of children. Together these three-pronged movements forever altered the juvenile court system. What had been, in the past, a special, informal approach to children by avoiding traditional court practices, was now reverting to the old courtroom ways. The philosophy of the juvenile court was intact, but would its philosophy be impeded by the new strictures and control?

That these reforms all struck at the same time may have been a blessing or a disaster. For a while it seemed like the latter. Now, Judges would need to readdress their roles and attitudes, still maintaining the goal of making the child whole again. No easy task.

Gault was the key, along with reordering the judge's place via Article V of the Constitution. These were mandates with no choice but to follow. Not so with the State of Florida establishing a statewide decentralizing program for HRS so that each local district had independent control. This later addition meant an entire new life and struggles with the HRS agency to determine the relative authority of the judges and the state HRS similar to those in the past with Dade County officials.

Technically, when the juvenile court had started in Florida, the senior judge had been complete master. Slowly, Dade County government began to contest and lessen that judicial authority. Now with Article V, the role of the Dade County Commission would be of yet smaller consequence, only a minor player. On the horizon was HRS, ready to become perhaps the largest state welfare agency, about to divest the judges of even more authority. Or at least make the effort.

These state constitution changes, along with *Gault*, made for an impossible task for the sitting judges. For the three sitting judges, with larger caseloads plus full-blown trials where virtually none had existed before, there seemed no relief in sight. Along with undermanned staffs and lack of resources, Senior Judge Donald Stone faced a daunting challenge.

These changes provided added stature to the court, making it an office to which many lawyers would now aspire. Under the new court rules, the circuit court now included a juvenile court division. No longer a special court of lower rank, the status of the judges and the court itself now ranked as equal with other divisions.

The Florida Supreme Court would exercise control of the state courts with a Judicial Qualifications Commission to oversee judicial conduct. Judges were to sit in a division no longer than three years, before being rotated to another division, thus providing a cadre of judges with expertise in all aspects of the law. It was big-time now.

Strange indeed. Where the juvenile court had been a kind of stepchild of the judicial system, it now had gained stature, not for the important services provided the families of the community, but as a result of administrative and technical changes within the bureaucracy.

The emergence of the State of Florida Health and Rehabilitative Services (HRS), scheduled to be fully operational in 1971, was a formidable addition in the new children's structure. Dealing with Dade County officials had been difficult enough, but now with HRS, a new powerful agency likely to have the support of the state legislature and surely the governor, things might get more difficult than ever envisioned.

Before, no more than a concept in the sky, HRS would soon be an enormous giant perhaps swallowing all in its way—including what had been the absolute authority of the judge. The intensity of this struggle would dwarf the spitting contests of past years between County Manager McNayr and Judges Beckham and Sheppard.

In essence, where once the senior judge had total control of all the court staff and Dade County provided funding, now authority and funding would shift to the State of Florida. The court staff, hired by the senior judge in the past, would now be under a new line of authority. Query: would their conduct and allegiance now shift away from the judges?

Marlyn Smith had joined HRS as a court counselor in 1959 at the tail end of Judge Beckham's stay on the bench. She continued on all the way to Judge Tom Petersen's term as a judge in the 1990s. By the time she retired in 1992, she had reached second in command under Bob Taro, running the day-to-day operations of the Juvenile Division of HRS. In our continuing dialogue until her untimely death in January 2006, she gave me her version of both the pre- and post-*Gault* days:

> Before *Gault*, it had been the usual bureaucratic power struggle. First, at the beginning, there was an adversarial relationship between the juvenile court judges and the Dade County government. Then the judges fought the HRS leadership.
>
> Even before *Gault* we never approved total control by the judges. Just as the struggle between the judges and the County had gone on for years, so it continued with the HRS.
>
> The Judges wanted total command. It really was all about money. Had the funding for programs been there, the struggle would not have been necessary.

Smith was no fan of the judges to which I could personally attest. Now fifty-some years later, she still had that sharp tinge in her voice talking about our judges:

> Judges insisted that they had the inherent power to make the major decisions, while the social work and rehab staffs wanted to limit judges to control only court hearings.
>
> We worked with the children and knew their problems. The judges only knew the law. And sometimes not even that.
>
> After *Gault* it was our time. We thought we were in charge. We wanted social work agencies to determine the treatment for children. But it was the same old story. The judges still kept pushing us around.

Marlyn Smith, a skilled counselor and later an excellent administrator, fought hard over the years for her point of view, always looking somewhat askance at the performance of judges. In my own dealings with her, we were often at odds. As an administrator for HRS, she stood up firmly against the judges, although powerwise she usually came out second best.

A strong supporter of the *Gault* decision, Mrs. Smith saw the Supreme Court ruling as finally leveling the tide against the powerful judiciary. In her view, prior to *Gault*, the judges, as a whole, never really addressed the problems of the children.

> There were no rules to follow. The judge, the parents, and the child had a roundtable discussion. I, as the probation officer (later called a counselor), told the judge what I knew of the case. The judge then ruled.
>
> Most of the time I felt like a spectator, not a participant. It was all so cut and dried. More like a private conference at which outsiders could never be heard. I had the feeling of an interloper.
>
> The judges seemed to be only going through the motions. Nothing else.

I asked Mrs. Smith for her evaluation of the judges of those past eras. Still feisty, now in the year 2005, she had few good grades to dispense:

> I arrived when Judge Beckham was old and ailing. He was absent a lot and often seemed detached. People were afraid of him.
>
> I thought Judge Culbreath tried to give some meaning to the cases so the child and parent would want to join in the discussion.
>
> Judge Stone seemed overwhelmed by all the changes. As the senior judge, it all fell upon him. He had a very big load to carry.
>
> Judge Sheppard, with his experience as a medical doctor, could have been an excellent judge, but to me his mind always seemed to be somewhere else.
>
> Overall, the judges seemed confused and uncomfortable on how to handle the *Gault* decision. Not until Gladstone and you came on the bench in the 1970s did the court really settle down.

My final question to her concerned the manner in which the HRS court staff had performed after *Gault*. She responded, "We made a lot of mistakes, but we gave a damn about what was happening. We cared for the kids, and had Jack Blanton, our chief probation officer, to carry us through."

Former top administrator, now retired, Marlyn Smith still bore the scars of those earlier years. She had been there in that transition period at the end of Judge Beckham's reign all the way to the 1990s. Her estimate of those days was still skewed in defense of her field workers and court counselors who, in her mind, had suffered the failings of an underfunded system and a community that really didn't care.

The theme she enunciated then and now focused on her plaint that most of the failures of the juvenile court were unfairly attributed to her colleagues. The judges, she felt, were part of the problem, but they rarely, if ever, came to the defense of those mostly anonymous workers in the field.

In retrospect, Mrs. Smith's assessment had some merit. But this was no college football team where an "all-for-one-one-for-all" spirit prevailed. Too much was at stake, the judge's responsibility too great. The court, always in a state of urgency, didn't have time to provide comfort for those in the pits. Each of the units of the court machine, including the judges, had to produce immediate results. There was little time for reflection or sympathetic understanding of co-workers.

The period surrounding *Gault* was indeed tough days for all. Back then, as they prepared to conform to the many new conditions, the juvenile court judges collectively were aghast at the implications of the *Gault* decision. Senior Judge Donald Stone, normally a low-key team player, first tried to calm the community with his appraisal.

In the *Miami Herald*, July 1967, he assured the public of his support for the *Gault* ruling, stating, "I am keeping my fingers crossed that the new restrictions on the Court won't backfire on the progress the Court has made." These preliminary remarks were to assure the public that the changes would be followed, and while burdensome, would be carried out. A kind of whistling-in-the-dark assessment.

Stone recognized his responsibility as senior judge required a cautionary approach, but his follow-up clearly expressed his true concerns. *Gault* would, in fact, change the face of the juvenile court forever, and Stone felt it his duty to spell out the realities.

Quoting him further in the same July 1967 *Miami Herald* article, he added these comments:

> The *Gault* case could lead to an increased delinquency in Dade County. With attorneys now pleading and trying juvenile cases in court, trials will be much longer. I predict the number of lawyers will increase by 300 percent. In turn it will also take much longer to get cases to court.
>
> A backlog is bound to develop. Each of our three Judges now handle about 2700 cases a year. That number will leap as juveniles, knowing free lawyers are available, will prefer a trial to settlement of the case.

> Youngsters awaiting trial for months without having a Court intercession are likely to commit more crimes. The Court will need a lot more staff—probation officers, prosecutors, clerks, and bailiffs.
>
> Unless provided more funds, juveniles awaiting a trial, now taking from two to six weeks, the time will surely double unless we receive additional staff.

The latter part of Judge Donald Stone's response reflected his true feelings. Avoiding any high-flying rhetoric about "the best interest of the child," he offered a reasoned appraisal of the impact *Gault* might have on the operation of his court.

Some forty years later in 2005, Judge Stone gave some added insights as to his earlier reaction to *Gault*:

> My problem then wasn't about the *Gault* decision. I knew it had to come eventually. But the Supreme Court decision hit us like a round of buckshot. With our small staff and no money to do a thing, there was no way to implement it.
>
> I debated ACLU attorney Tobias Simon on the Larry King radio show and said I was going before the county commission and beg for funds. We needed lawyers, and I was telephoning all over the country to recruit them.
>
> That's how we got Tom Petersen to come back. He had a job in New York City, and I phoned him telling how urgently we needed him. He came down on the next plane.
>
> We were really in bad shape. None of the judges had bailiffs. We weren't anywhere near ready to comply with *Gault*. As a joke, I even asked Toby Simon, the ACLU lawyer if, rather than continue to sue us, he would come to work for the court.
>
> We were in a desperate situation.

Judge Stone was really up against the wall. He had worked hard to rise to his present position. *Gault* and the other changes were the last thing he had expected. A local product, forty-five years of age upon assuming the bench, he had early on chosen to be a U.S. Navy airplane pilot. Passing flight training, he was ready to join during the Korean War.

Meeting a young woman, later to be his wife, followed by a summer job in the law library of the Industrial Claims Commission changed things for him. He had developed a liking for law and asked advice from his future father-in-law, a successful lawyer. He was told, "You'll never know until you try it." Off to law school.

Asked today, if he had any regrets, he replied, "Going through the trying times and struggles with *Gault*, if I had my druthers, I think I'd have chosen being a pilot." Stone had then settled for joining the Navy Air Reserve.

As if in counterpoint to the early child savers and the plaints of the ACLU, Judge Stone had brandished a new phrase in 1967. Responding to the ACLU call to Protect the Rights of Children, Judge Stone touted the call to Protect People's Rights. It was a phrase that could resonate with voters for years to come in many a political campaign, directing the court to punish rather than rehab children violating the law.

Meanwhile, amidst all the furor over *Gault*, there was more than a passing interest in the sudden resignation of the esteemed judge Ben Sheppard. I too had not forgotten my quest to determine the reason for his departure.

I asked Stone for his candid assessment as to Sheppard's departure, expecting "inside" revelations. Stone responded, "Ben Sheppard was the most unforgettable man I ever knew. He always had a yearning to move ahead. He feared no problem and never ducked one."

I followed with a question as to the differences Sheppard had with Culbreath as a possible reason for his leaving. One observer of those court days, still around, had viewed Sheppard as somewhat temperamental, causing internal problems among the judges. The observer had suggested that Sheppard and Culbreath didn't quite hit the same keys.

Stone didn't recall any conflict between the two. He viewed Sheppard, his predecessor as senior judge, highly, "Ben Sheppard never had a cross word for anyone. Couldn't say no when asked to help someone."

My own views as to Sheppard's exit revolved around his battles with County Manager Irving McNayr and the county Welfare Department heads over control of the court. Those struggles surely had impacted upon him. The constant rattle fire of the ACLU lawyers, claiming children were being deprived of their rights, added to his woes. And the seemingly never-ending flow of grand jury investigations did not lighten his load. Later he told a reporter, "I resigned in 1966 when they told me I had to treat children as criminal adults. I couldn't accept the shift in philosophy by the Supreme Court."

Known as an ornery infighter, "quitter" wasn't part of Ben Sheppard's makeup. He actually enjoyed a battle, never avoiding a confrontation. He added in still another press statement,

> One of my dreams is to have a family court where parents and children could come to have their problems dealt with by professional people who earnestly wanted to help them. I'd like to be remembered as a guy who tried to help adolescents and their parents to deal with all their problems in a meaningful way.

Interestingly, Judge Edith Atkinson before him, and Judge Bill Gladstone after him, had also voiced that dream of a unified court to handle all the problems of family in one court before one judge. Both Judges Cindy Lederman and Sandy Karlan would bring it into reality by the end of the century.

Sheppard's final words to the public, said with earnestness seeping through his words, was as good a self-description as one could find for him:

> I'm a man who needs time. There is not enough time in the day for me to do all the things I want to do. That's what I really want. I have not bought a suit in five years. I haven't had the time.
>
> I forget to get haircuts. There aren't enough hours in the day for me. I only need five hours of sleep, and I wish I could get by on less.

Dr. Sheppard never did accept any of the teaching posts offered him. Instead he went to the Menninger Clinic to study psychiatry for six months. Did he come back to Miami fully refreshed from his sabbatical to resume his medical practice in pediatrics?

Yes, he always was a pediatrician serving his patients, of whom there were many in Dade County. He also took on a position as executive director of the Catholic Welfare Bureau, with the Archdiocese of Miami. This was but a temporary stopover.

Almost as an afterthought, he then announced for the Dade County School Board. Interestingly, the *Miami Herald* declined to endorse him, but Sheppard won easily. Although viewed as past his prime by the *Herald*, he served until his death in 1980 at age seventy-seven.

While on the school board, he became associate director of the Catholic Service Bureau, overseeing such substance abuse programs as Genesis, Miami Bridge, Overtown Recreation Center, Bethesda Manor, and St. Luke's Center.

For five of those years on the school board he was chosen by fellow school board members to be chairman of the board. Did the cantankerous Sheppard cause disquieting ripples on the school board? Not at all. The school board, like the juvenile court, always had its share of swordplay, and Ben was still agile enough to hold his own. Compared to the juvenile court, however, the school board was a rest haven.

But he was still the old Ben Sheppard in terms of his community activity. For one, he continued his activity as a volunteer medical doctor at Youth Hall. On the school board he instituted the Pride Program, a nationally recognized counselor-in-the-classroom program aimed at counteracting delinquency. His concern for problems arising from unwed mothers made him the leader in the development of sex education classes.

The never ending problem of drugs plaguing the community led him to organize the first methadone maintenance clinic for heroin addicts. He pioneered the unrestrained distribution of methadone to heroin users; an approach that had the drug enforcement community in an uproar. At the beginning, weaning users off heroin with methadone, viewed as a less addictive drug by Dr. Sheppard, was rejected by veteran police officers. Today, it has become an accepted form of therapy for heroin users.

In later years until his death, he and Bill Haast, director of the Miami Serpentarium, experimented with snake venom as an antidote for multiple sclerosis, cancer, and other incurable diseases. People flocked to their snake venom clinic from all over the world and attested to its effectiveness.

After Sheppard's death, the *Associated Press* ran an account of their relationship written by newsman Tom Wells. In it Bill Haast describes the involvement of Dr. Ben Sheppard:

> In the late 1970s a Miami physician named Ben Sheppard suffered rheumatoid arthritis. Sheppard took PROven. This was the medication produced by Bill Haast. The doctor, pleased with the result, began injecting patients who had a variety of diseases. Sheppard's clinic became famous. It was featured on the CBS-TV show *60 Minutes.*
>
> Eventually, Sheppard was treating six or seven thousand MS patients. People came from all over the United States and from other countries. The drug really helped them, but the Food and Drug Administration (FDA) was upset because Sheppard had not done clinical studies first. The FDA then shut down the clinic and banned the drug for not having been properly tested or licensed.
>
> The Multiple Sclerosis Society still gets so many inquiries about the Drug PROven that it felt compelled to publish a story on the drug last year.

The Associated Press article further notes the drug has been suggested as a treatment for arthritis, lupus, herpes, muscular dystrophy, Parkinson's disease, and sclerosis. Time will tell whether Haast and Sheppard were prophetic in their belief that the snake venom can be beneficial to mankind.

Why Sheppard, a highly ethical pediatrician, did not seek clinical testing to satisfy the FDA is unknown. Probably because of his constant battle with time. He always claimed he needed more time to accomplish all the deeds he sought to perform.

It should be pointed out, according to the Multiple Sclerosis Society, that while PROven has been banned in the United States by the FDA, a similar mixture known as Horvi MS9 is sold legally in drugstores in Germany.

So this is our activist Ben Sheppard. Growing up with Italian-Jewish parents on the Lower East Side of Manhattan, he lived with his family on Henry Street deep in New York City's downtown ghetto. He was a kind of bookworm, a nerdy kid, not quite fitting into the neighborhood street gangs of that era.

His father, a poor housepainter, headed a family always trying to make ends meet. Ben, sickly with rheumatic fever and arthritis, ailments that stayed with him the rest of his life, put himself through college and medical school by selling his blood to blood banks and waiting on tables.

He wanted first to be a writer, but his father, after reading a few of his stories, told Ben he was to be a doctor. And that was that. According to Sheppard, "My father wasn't very permissive with me as a child. He was a very firm person. He had never heard of Dr. Spock. When he wanted my opinion, he would tell me what it should be."

The choice of profession may have been mandated by father, but the medical inspiration likely came from mother. "My mother was the neighborhood nurse," he said. "She made folk medicine using garlic, honey, and herbs. She believed anything could be cured with garlic and honey. I carried garlic around my neck all winter."

Ben Sheppard was a dynamo with all the potential for a great leader. In fact, he was a great leader. Devoted, he had chosen Catholicism as his religion. Perhaps a bit eccentric, surely different, he was stubborn always following his own instincts. Born to lead, and lead he did.

Could he—and should he—have stayed the course with the juvenile court through the morass enclosing it? Of course, he should have. But if he had, he wouldn't have been Ben Sheppard. This was a man who forever needed new challenges for sustenance. In his vision he always saw himself answering an SOS with a life preserver. He wanted to help people—now.

To turn the juvenile court around in his tumultuous era required activists with a never-ending patience plus the will to compromise. Neither virtue was exactly Sheppard's long suit. He also saw no outpouring from the community in support of his "in the best interest of the child" philosophy. Perhaps had he found another Ben Sheppard type with him on the bench, he might have been inclined to stay the test. But with his individualistic approach, how long would their union have lasted?

To learn more about what made Ben Sheppard tick, I turned to Ed Swan, whose children he had treated and had been his law partner of fifteen years. Swan, an assistant state attorney with me some fifty years ago, had, upon going into private practice, a long successful career as a trial-lawyer practitioner.

Like most everyone else ever to come in contact with Sheppard, he described him as a caring man whom the world adored. Swan confirmed all the wonderful things I had heard. As his law partner for fifteen years until Sheppard's death, a new side of Sheppard emerged:

> He was an excellent lawyer. Very thorough. We'd go over every case as if he was diagnosing a medical ailment. He loved being a lawyer, insistent on knowing every facet of the case.
>
> He did a lot of medical malpractice cases as a consultant with some of the biggest trial firms in Miami, like Blackwell, Walker & Gray, also Sam Powers, and others.

Swan, like countless others, first met Sheppard as his pediatrician. "What did the good doctor do that so endeared him to the parents of the children he treated?" I asked.

> Unquestionably, he was a great doctor. But importantly, he showed how caring he was. If you weren't in his office, he was on the phone or in your house tending to your child. He was always available.
>
> He'd have breakfast every morning at Allen's Drug Store, where Red and Bird roads meet. Usually, he sat in a booth or at the counter. With all the people who showed up, it was like a medical clinic.
>
> Variety Children's Hospital was nearby, and from the drug store he'd go over to the hospital to make his rounds. He raised a ton of money for the hospital. He, much like Dave Walters later, was a big, big fundraiser for the hospital.

After learning that Ed Swan ran Sheppard's campaigns for public office, I asked what kind of politician had Sheppard been. Swan laughed in response.

> He was a laid-back, lousy politician. I tried telling him to pay attention to the big money givers. He insisted on stopping to talk to people on the way. Everyone seemed to know him and flocked around him like he was a movie star. He never really campaigned, but he always won easily.

I told Swan I had concluded that Sheppard resigned as judge due to frustration over the *Gault* decision. Several of Sheppard's friends agreed with me that he couldn't accept the change of philosophy—treating children as adult criminals. Those wars with County Manager Irving McNayr didn't help either.

"How had Sheppard talked about his reason for leaving office?" I asked Ed Swan. He responded,

Funny, he had never mentioned it. I think he quit on a sudden impulse. It wasn't that he disliked McNayr so much, which he did, but that McNayr stymied him with the budget, denying him funds to properly staff Youth Hall.

He was the doctor there and wanted to make things better for the kids. McNayr knew that and did it out of spite.

I had known Irving McNayr fairly well and found him tough to take in our dealings, but I didn't know him as a mean-spirited fellow. Then again, in the heat of battle, tough guys go for the most vulnerable spot. McNayr knew Sheppard's strong feelings about Youth Hall. Maybe Sheppard was right about McNayr.

Looking at all the mountains Sheppard had to climb in the juvenile court, I found it hard to envision the kind of success a man with his qualities expected. There seemed no end to wrestling with Manager McNayr and jousting with the ever-threatening ACLU. The final blow, the dreadful (at least to him) *Gault* decision, was more than he was prepared to accept.

So, if not Sheppard with all his virtues, what kind of a judicial activist could lead the way after *Gault*? Well, for one thing it had to be a long-term commitment. Secondly, his successor had to expect progress to be incremental. There's no way for a brilliant social planner to come in with a dream and then engineer a system that has more turns than a DNA genome. Too many spare parts to blend together. Too long a history of disappointment.

Judges of the juvenile court do not usually declare themselves activists. The task is thrust upon them, and they can assume as much of the burden as they choose. Some will ignore that higher calling and do commendable jobs simply handling their calendars. Some few will rise above. Both groups recognize the immensity of the challenge. Some few will accept the challenge.

There probably are no set of traits that assure an activist will go the full route. Like everything else, life sets the tasks; circumstances usually determine the outcome. Judicial activists who further a cause like Denver's Ben Lindsey may be heroic figures who give themselves up for the cause, or dramatic personalities like Miami's Ben Sheppard who need a stage with strong light beams to perform feats of magic.

Or they may be judges like some who stay the course, give it their all day to day, and in the end, having fought the good fight, are not concerned how success is measured, nor even being identified as such. We'll wait and see who among Ben Sheppard's successors grasps the mantle and goes for it all.

This was but a way-stop for Ben Sheppard, one among his many benchmarks. He did more than his share. Unlike others sitting on the court, his life story is exalted more by the variety of projects he attempted than by a career highlighted by a stay as a jurist. For one, in later years he would be deified for his work with drug addicts. A *Miami Herald* story (Jan. 31, 1971), not too long after he resigned from the bench, described him best: "Patron Saint of Junkies: Man Who Can't Say No."

Fifteen years later, six years after his death, *Herald* columnist Charles Whited memorialized Sheppard in a column (March 12, 1986) discussing the drug epidemic of that day. Whited wrote about a postcard Ed Tutty had sent to Sheppard's widow Thelma, writing, "He still lives with us, in us, through us." Ed Tutty was then the director of the Dade Juvenile Court Mental Health Clinic, a post he held for over twenty years. Tutty added, "Doc's work helped us galvanize the rising drug menace even before we knew how bad it really was."

Donald Stone, his successor, probably of all our juvenile court judges, lived through more sudden changes than anyone before him and probably any of his successors. All the transformations hit with such suddenness that the impact of each had hardly been recognized before another suddenly came along. To his credit, Stone weathered them all, with the system having enough flexibility to survive and go forward.

Tom Petersen, later a juvenile court judge (see Petersen chapter) fresh out of Columbia Law School in 1966, was an early observer of that turbulent transition period n the juvenile court's history.

Rather than accept an offer from one of those stodgy Wall Street firms, young Tom, an idealist, chose to become a VISTA member. Training in Oregon to work with Hispanic migrants in California, instead he found himself shipped to Miami where he was assigned to the Public Defender's Office. In 1966 Petersen became the first VISTA member to work in the Dade Juvenile Court. Shortly thereafter, Petersen passed the Florida Bar and in 1967 became the first full-fledged assistant public defender in the juvenile court. He described the years immediately before the *Gault* decision:

> It was a homey affair. No state prosecutor or public defender. No courtrooms either. Hearings were held in chambers. The idea was to have all the parties sit around a table discussing ways to help the child. Didn't even have a bailiff. You just sat around and talked it out.
>
> There was a court attorney, appointed by the senior judge to provide legal assistance. No assistant state attorney to represent the State. Nor a public defender. On some rare occasions a private lawyer appeared for a defendant who could afford one. Not many of those. A probation officer appointed by the judge was present.
>
> Testimony was rarely transcribed. Only when a private lawyer was present was a court reporter used. And that wasn't too often. Usually no trial occurred.
>
> The probation officer investigating the case would advise the court of his findings, and the judge would then rule.

> It was all an intimate, private discussion taking place in the judge's chambers. That's what the juvenile court was supposed to be when instituted back in 1898, and it hadn't changed much in Miami when I got there in 1965.

Tom Petersen found his initiation into the court as the first public defender in 1967 a rather unsettling event. The court probation officers viewed him with suspicion.

> Marlyn Smith looked at me as if I was an alien from another planet. She and the other probation officers thought I was there to get the kids off on some technicality. Here, they had prepared a case for the judge, and now this interloper was about to gum up the works.
>
> The judges weren't too keen on me either. They worried lest I introduce court reporters to the scene. They knew having a court reporter on the scene meant appeals. The last thing judges wanted was an appeal of their rulings.
>
> Not only was I the first public defender to appear in juvenile court, I was the first lawyer to appear there who wasn't appointed by the senior judge. It took me awhile to become a member of the club.

Petersen resigned as a public defender, went off to New York for a short stay, and returned at the behest of Judge Stone, as the juvenile court lawyer. This position placed him now on Judge Stone's staff. In essence he was the prosecutor to present the state's evidence at trials in both delinquency and dependency cases.

Hired by the senior judge, he found these pretrial conferences created some conflict-of-interest issues, but *Gault* was still months away, and the issue never arose. Petersen did have some misgivings about his role. Prior to *Gault*, everything happened through the judge. Everyone else involved in the process was a functionary of the judge.

He explained it thusly,

> Back then it was the judge being paternalistic, protecting the child against the cruel world. So long as the court tried to help the child, it didn't make much difference the route taken.
>
> I acted as the prosecutor, but going over all the evidence with the judge (my boss) beforehand, prior to trial, was not viewed as improper. We all knew the judge would do the right thing.

Tom Petersen was correct about that. No question that both the judge and the prosecutor would surely do the right thing no matter their employment relationship. Courtroom life, however, was changing dramatically in the seventy years since Jane Addams had fired up the world to care for children.

Did *Gault* now mean the end of the imperial judgeship? Was the juvenile court now better designed to address all the problems brought on by violent youth crime? Are those friendly chats with the benevolent judge a thing of the past.? Where does punishment enter the picture? How about prevention and rehabilitation programs?

When asked about the quality of punishment meted out pre-*Gault*, Petersen mulled it over for a few moments before responding,

> We really didn't have much in the way of rehab programs. It was still the probation officer kind of looking out for the kid. Or he'd be sent to the Kendall Home in Dade County. If he was real bad, it meant the state school in Marianna, a place for the real bad ones.
>
> By the time I arrived they had already built a state school at Okeechobee for the southern half of Florida. The school at Marianna was there for the delinquents from north Florida.
>
> Although the law called for it, our kids were rarely bound over to adult court. Our judges preferred resolving the cases here rather than transfer to adult court.

There had been a rash of complaints around that time about racially segregating the delinquents held in Youth Hall and about some excessive punishment of children. After a quick investigation, nothing came out of it. I asked Petersen to recall those events as best he could remember some thirty-five years later.

> We had some high quality black probation officers in those days, but their caseloads were limited to black children. Dewey Knight, later county manager, and Israel Milton, who later joined Knight as a top county administrator, were two of the best probation officers.
>
> Nonetheless, being black held them back. It took some years later before the color line in juvenile court was finally broken down.

Petersen found the attitude on the part of the probation officers, both black and white, not too harsh toward their charges. Segregation as part of the community standards was enforced, but racism was not practiced.

He emphasized that Chief Probation Officer Jack Blanton would not tolerate any unfair treatment of blacks. Everyone looked up to Jack Blanton. He was a man of character and honesty, traits with which the judges sought to be identified. From Senior Judge Donald Stone, who had his first job as a probation officer years before under Jack Blanton, all the officers of the court had only the highest regard for Blanton.

There were unwritten rules in Youth Hall; good behavior by an inmate meant a prized status as an assistant to a probation officer. On occasion, exemplary conduct permitted the inmate an outside visit to a movie or party, accompanied, of course, by a probation officer. These occasions were officially unauthorized, but excellent for inmate morale.

Summing it up, Petersen declared,

> It was more redneck than racist. The whole operation was run rather loosely. Judge Stone had a tough job keeping things together. He was fair and even-handed, but too many things were happening in the two years I was there for one person to handle it all.
>
> Besides, all the judges weren't always on the same page. The most popular judge was Dixie Chastain. She was a woman of the old South. A real lady. The most sympathetic and most lenient. No pretense about her. She didn't wear a robe. Only tried to help kids.

A concept as powerful as the child-saver movement required dramatic change. However, none of these changes in Florida were bottomed by the altruism of a demanding public hoping to keep the dream alive, nor were the judges of the juvenile court coming to the fore seeking these changes. These were all legal pronouncements by the highest court actually limiting judges, and the action by the Florida legislature, now establishing the process and structure for the future.

Interviewing Judge Donald Stone, asking about his activism, Stone responded, "Didn't have much time for that. Too busy trying to stay afloat." Long retired from the bench, Stone did recall some areas of his extracurricular activity.

On the heels of the Supreme Court edict, Miami, as well as many other urban areas, was feeling the impact of violent juvenile crime. The juvenile court with its professed purpose of rehabilitation, was bearing the brunt of community outrage.

In response to the problem, Judge Donald Stone issued an edict—"a major policy order"—aimed at curtailing juvenile "hoodlums." He directed police departments to take into custody for fingerprinting and photographs juveniles in possession of a gun or suspects in any other crime of violence. His colleagues, Judge Dixie Chastain and Judge Weaver, concurred in Stone's action.

At the next legislative session, Miami's state senator Robert Shevin announced his intentions to enact legislation supporting Stone's position. The existing law then only permitted juveniles charged with a capital offense to be fingerprinted and tried as an adult. Eventually, all these would become the law of Florida, but

Shevin's legislative effort, along with Stone's order was the opening salvo in an effort to bring hard justice to hoodlum delinquents.

The Get Tough on Juveniles became the key slogan among public officials and candidates for elective office in the decades that followed. The soft, humanitarian approach that had introduced the juvenile court concept in the early twentieth century was beginning to fade.

Judge Stone's other foray into judicial activism was a personal thing. Brought up with a religious background and the father of four children, Stone was unhappy with common-law marriages derived from the old English law, originally designed to prevent fathers from avoiding responsibility as parents.

Stone believed strongly in the sanctity of marriage as the cement that binds families together. He began a one-man crusade drawing up the legislation, buttonholing state legislators, urging the change in the law. He neither sought church support nor media attention. This was a personal morality issue with him. Although he was never credited with the passage of his proposal, it did become law. Common-law marriage was taken off the books.

Judge Stone may or may not acquire the title "judicial activist." I did not inquire as to his wishes in that regard. But in his nine years on the juvenile court bench he had made a strong contribution to the furtherance of the juvenile court in the most hectic period of the court's existence.

Dixie Chastain had joined the bench in 1965, appointed by Governor Haydon Burns. She had lost to Ben Sheppard in the race to succeed the departed Walter Beckham. In a support letter to Governor Burns, Judge Ben Sheppard had this to say about the woman he had defeated: "She should have won our election. She is the greatest thing that has ever happened to the Juvenile Court. She has depth and warmth for children that can't be beat."

This was more than political talk by a gracious winner. In her own quiet way, Dixie Chastain had already amassed a reputation as a loving and caring individual. Never raising her voice, she was the maternalistic mother superior tending to her flock. The juvenile court had been her home and her life.

In her younger days, she had been the court reporter who transcribed the testimony of Giuseppe Zangara in the attempted assassination of Franklin Roosevelt in 1933 in Miami. Chicago mayor Anton Cermak, riding with the president, was shot and died from the bullet wound. From court reporter, she became the first woman graduate of the University of Miami Law School, graduating magna cum laude in 1930.

Shortly thereafter she became investigating attorney in charge of the Domestic Relations Division. This was the unit handling dependent children and nonsupport cases. Judge Beckham had also appointed her as a referee to hear these dependency cases. For nine years she also sat as a juvenile court hearing officer handling overflow cases for the now-burgeoning court calendars.

Interestingly, Judge Beckham had been one of her law-school professors. Finally, with the Governor Burns appointment, she was vested with the robes to sit as a full-fledged judge of the juvenile court. Chastain really had paid her dues. Recently, she recalled for me with fondness the early days of the court.

> In those days it was all informal and friendly. The judge, the child, and the parents discussed the problem and then did something about it. Legal requirements were observed, but not emphasized.
>
> There were a lot of changes going on around the courthouse and a lot of differences among some of the judges. I stayed out of controversy. My job, as I saw it, was to take care of the kids. And that's what I did. That's all I did.

Not quite. She did a lot more. With all the turmoil created by Supreme Court decisions, constitutional changes in Article V, and the turnover among juvenile court judges, she had a full platter in her role as senior judge. Dixie had no plans to introduce new, visionary approaches. She was tied to the past, and her efforts were to build on all the good things she had accomplished in her many years on the job.

An old-fashioned mother of three, all the virtues she had instilled in her children were those she sought for the delinquent and dependent children coming before her. In all her years of service to children she remained constant with one theme: "Children are the mirror of the community. As long as there is any weakness about the morality or ethics of adult life, it will continue to show up in our children."

Many changes would take place over the years in the juvenile court: by higher court decree, legislative change, and by new approaches designed by judicial advocates. Dixie Chastain, however, stayed faithful to the practices her family and her church had ingrained in her. She always had an innate feeling about the ultimate goodness of people. As a judge she followed the law but guided herself by her family and church upbringing.

She treated each case with a delicacy not usually found in the court system. These were her children, and she would cajole the youngsters, plead with their parents, seek whatever court assistance was available. No one left Dixie Chastain's courtroom without feeling better than when they entered.

She sought few innovative new approaches, while never critical of programs purporting to have an answer to the problems. She stuck to the sermon her minister may have used that Sunday. Dixie had a kind of Sunday-school spirit about her approach that made all who appeared in her courtroom, children and adults alike, respect her sincerity. Everyone knew she was making an all-out effort.

She began her service on the bench at the tail end of her career when it was time to think of retirement. After Judge Donald Stone, seeking newer challenges, had been rotated to another division, Chastain became senior judge. It wasn't a role she had coveted. Dixie was more into changing the life of a single child for the better than having authority over a total court system.

Chastain probably realized that the juvenile court would no longer be an informal gathering place where all the parties could discuss family problems with a benevolent judge, hopefully to find a solution. The new directives called for the establishment of formula-type systems that ignored the personal touch. Most of all, the U.S. Supreme Court *Gault* decision, forcing the juvenile court into the image of the adult criminal court, ran against the traditions she had come to live by.

For several years, like a good soldier, she stayed the course, supporting Judge Sheppard and Judge Stone in their struggles to manage all the changes forced upon them. It wasn't that she opposed children in her court having all the due process to which they were entitled. Dixie measured all the changes against her standard of providing for "the best interest of the child." Judge Chastain had never given up on that concept.

Her last major project was the building of a new juvenile court at 3300 NW Twenty-seventh Avenue. Now the senior judge, she rose to the task, although not trained or experienced in this construction enterprise. Dixie had long been ready to retire, but this new structure was a symbol she wanted her imprint on.

This was to be a complex that would house not only the judges and their courtrooms but as well the prosecutors, public defenders, and the offices and staff of the Division of Youth Services of the State Health and Rehabilitative Department, identified as HRS. Also Youth Hall, the medical clinic and court intake. It was the whole works. Every agency involved in the process would be housed together.

With the State and the County sharing the cost, as senior judge it was her job to oversee putting this all together. Progress was slow. The county had already demolished the old Aviation Building sitting on the site. Unfortunately, moneywise they also were close to a million dollars short for the cost of construction estimated at close to six million dollars. The State had offered three million with the federal government remaining mum about a contribution.

No sooner had construction begun, then the federal government opted out of contributing. With a considerable shortfall ahead, alterations to cut the cost down were in the offing. Dixie, moving between her temporary courtroom and the construction site, wearing a hard hat as overseer of the construction, took well to the job. At least as well as could be hoped for. She badly wanted this modern new building for the children of Dade County.

Although ready to retire, she was determined to stick it out until completion. When the first shovel was lifted, Dixie Chastain was there for the groundbreaking, sporting her hard hat and full of smiles. The juvenile court judges now numbered four.

The first floor would house all the ancillary services and the HRS staff. In the outer areas would be Youth Detention Hall and other service departments. On dedication day she was there officially to open the doors. It took another year to add on the second floor to house the chambers and courtrooms for the judges.

There never was any question as to the naming of the second floor. It is called the Dixie Herlong Chastain Building. With completion at hand, Dixie asked to be relieved of her role as administrative judge (the new title), the post going to Bill Gladstone. She stayed on as a judge until 1979, having served for fourteen years until retiring. Dixie was not a judicial advocate in the sense this book portrays. She was just everyone's grandmother who wanted only the best for all the Lord's children. And she left a strong long-remembered mark in that capacity.

Judicial advocates are dynamic people, with fire in their system, but there's a lot of room for loving, caring surrogates who only want to do good in the only way they know. That's Dixie Chastain. In all likelihood, it is judges like Dixie whom the children going through the court will likely remember and treasure most. What really bothered Judge Chastain most about the *Gault* decision was Circuit Court Judge Nathan declaring that the Supreme Court ruling was retroactive. This involved a case of a fifteen-year-old she had sent to Kendall Youth Hall for six months due to repeated truancy.

No notice provided parents and failure to advise the child of his rights were the basis for Judge Nathan's ruling That hers would be the first case resulting directly from *Gault* really rankled her. For a judge who had so effectively nurtured the children before her, understandably, this was hard to take.

Judges Ben Sheppard, Don Stone, and Dixie Chastain had all been the senior judges in those few years of 1967 to 1973 when *Gault*, Article V of the new state constitution, and the creation of HRS, all converged like bolts from the sky joining forces to totally restructure the juvenile court system.

The latter group—HRS—was the culmination of a slow easing into the juvenile court process by the State. Starting as observers, both the legislature and the governor, let alone the state bureaucrats involved in children affairs, were hard-pressed to keep a hands-off policy. The cities and counties had been in no way equipped to bear the cost for children services, but whenever something went really bad, the State heads always drew the criticism and were asked to bear the costs.

Getting the State into the act—paying for a large part of the rising costs—was an important step forward. HRS was the vehicle and the State Legislature the driver. It had been a slow process but inevitable. Since the State was bearing much of the costs and getting the blame for local failures, centralizing these resources to run out of Tallahassee was a logical course. That the state HRS also offered to decentralize, by having local districts carry out the mission, made sense.

In 1969 the fledgling state Division of Youth Services, then not much more than a title, became part of the large state Department of Health and Rehabilitative Services. The duties, to begin with, were to develop a system of intake and probation services, and monitor these services.

It was a short hop in 1973 for them to take over responsibility for full operation of the eighteen existing detention centers statewide. The next jump was obvious: reorganize the system by setting up administrators in eleven geographic districts to operate within an integrated statewide system with Tallahassee as the nerve center for all services to children.

The State wisely retained all staff workers assigned to what was the former County dependency and delinquency cases and assumed their salaries. Since their health insurance and retirement benefits were superior to the County, there was strong local support in the work force for this takeover.

Not so with the judges. The old-time Beckham-style power was now going out the window. Judicial authority was shrinking by the minute. Bad enough sparring with county managers, followed by the Article V revision and the *Gault* decision, now even a bigger ogre was not only on the horizon—it was here.

The Florida Legislature still in the hands of a Democratic majority, with a Democratic governor, were determined to decentralize all social services giving local communities fuller control. The Dade County delegation, consisting of liberals like Senator Jack Gordon and House member Elaine Gordon, had passed legislation completely reorganizing the existing system of providing aid to those in need, including children, so that control shifted toward local communities rather than be determined in Tallahassee.

Appointed as HRS District XI (Dade County) administrator in 1975, Max Rothman had his work cut out. Under his command was the local Department of Health and Rehabilitative Services (HRS), which included the Division of Youth Services. The latter agency covered services for the juvenile court. A lawyer by profession, social worker by choice, Rothman was former legal director of South Florida Rural Services. HRS was responsible for virtually all the welfare and social services provided by he State. A large responsibility indeed.

One of Director Rothman's main goals was to create an interaction among his several departments that would enable clients, particularly children, to more readily obtain services with another provider agency without going through tons of red tape. For example, a child with special and perhaps costly surgical or rehabilitation needs could be directed to the appropriate agencies without requiring the child to apply for admission to each.

This HRS reorganization was so complex with an overabundance of moving parts that it could never quite function as planned. Too many of our grand schemes litter the roadways because the eyes of visionaries are much greater than the body politic can absorb.

The legislature and governor, well meaning as they were, never provided the funding to support so massive a turnaround as was contemplated. According to local HRS Director Rothman,

> The reality faced in construction never quite caught up with the blueprint envisioned by the planners. It took almost five years to restructure the agencies so that they could gear up to do the things that had to be done.
>
> Then we had disasters like the Mariel Boatlift from Cuba where over a hundred thousand refugees suddenly hit our shores. HRS had to transfer staff people to respond to that influx.
>
> We also had riots in Liberty City and stark budget cuts from the President Reagan administration that further diminished our staff and programs to help those in need, particularly children.
>
> We were spread so thin responding to crisis on a daily basis that I rarely had time to react to the judges complaining about the overcrowded Youth Hall Detention Center.

Rothman's vivid description as to how bad things were about thirty-five years ago gave me thought that perhaps my criticism of him and HRS might then have been a bit too strong. But then again it was their job to produce, no matter what.

The entrance of the state HRS in the picture was almost a replay of the original 1899 movement to create a juvenile court in Chicago. Idealism easily brimmed over the top, but implementation was a task that needed more than good wishes.

For the next several decades it would be the juvenile court judges struggling with the State of Florida (HRS). In prior years it had been the Dade County managers and commissioners who had faced off with the judges. Ahead was a new set of judges ready to take on the HRS state bureaucracy.

Interviewing Max Rothman, now head of a well-respected gerontology research and teaching program at Florida International University, I lamented the constant warfare that had ensued, as he did, during his stay until 1983. The judges repeatedly lambasted the department for their failure to provide adequate services for the children, and they in turn resented the judges interfering with their decision making. It was a repeat of the wars with the Dade County managers, but this time it was mostly with lower-level field workers that the judges could more easily push around. Max Rothman's view: "The constant demands of the judges, notwithstanding our lack of resources, dejected and demoralized our staff people in the field. We would have appreciated a more sympathetic judiciary."

My attitude toward Max Rothman became perhaps more understanding than it had been several decades ago when we were jousting . . . but the content remained the same. My response to him, bringing our differences up-to-date, was the same I had delivered way back then: "Our job, as judges, was to mobilize the thin resources available. The fact that your troops were in short supply, and they were part of a bureaucracy you inherited, was of no consequence to us. Like soldiers in battle, they and you were expected to perform."

Max and I, as two old war veterans, adversaries recounting tales of battle, let it go at that. In the intervening years, he and I had joined together in the cause of the elderly and rarely discussed our controversial days of the long ago.

Walter Beckham, Ben Sheppard, and the judges of their era had had their fill of conflict with other arms of government. Unlike other divisions of the judicial system, where the courts are an integral part of the establishment, deferred to and looked upon with esteem, the juvenile court judges always are in need of establishing their bona fides. Always some crisis arises with children that requires judges to repeatedly defend theirs and the system's worth.

Ben Sheppard was important for the period between Walter Beckham and Bill Gladstone. This was the time when a virtually new and strange structure had been imposed upon the court. A man of Sheppard's stature was essential. In the turmoil and disarray of these massive upheavals, he, by his lofty reputation and identity as a man of accomplishment, was a symbol that gave the community a sense of security about the future of the juvenile court. So long as Dr. Ben was thereabouts, people felt things were all right. His presence as a strong voice also enabled and encouraged his fellow judges surrounding him to feel more assured facing the new challenges.

Despite his larger-than-life stature in the community, Ben was a humble guy. Besieged with awards, his thoughts always went back to those days growing up on Henry Street amid all those pushcarts and immigrants escaping the poverty of Europe. It was hard to be anything but grateful for successes he had attained. When asked once in his later years how he wanted to be remembered, he summed it all up with dignity saying, "At times I felt like Don Quixote, but then I am one of those people who wound up tilting and jousting with windmills. I think I'd like to be remembered simply as a guy who tried to help people."

This very stressful transition period, and the turmoil in the court that followed, full of disruption and dispute, required steady leadership. Aided by the impressive work of Judge Donald Stone and the support of Judge Dixie Chastain as well as Chief Probation Officer Jack Blanton, our Judge Ben Sheppard was able to carry himself and the court through this difficult life change.

In addition, the voices of Judges William Culbreath and Sidney Weaver also played a role, as well as the cooperation of HRS leaders Max Rothman, Bob Taro, and Marlyn Smith. Facing all these challenges was not a solo effort. Nor did the players necessarily all perform as a team. Jointly and separately they managed it through.

The major change had come, not from activist juvenile court judges, but from powerful outside sources recognizing that the newest entry in the judicial firmament needed emergency repair. The juvenile court systems throughout the nation hadn't met the expectations of their pioneers. What had been visions of a new day in the lives of children had not yet materialized.

Scoring the progress of the Dade County Juvenile Court, one could say that the court had experienced many changes, some consistent with the early visions of the past, others deviating somewhat to satisfy the needs of an evolving society. On the whole—still a long way to go.

Would community expectations for the next half century be more modest? Would a new breed of judges appear more attuned to the times, make positive changes, and begin a new trend? Would the state HRS be more amenable to working together with the judges than had the Dade County officials? Only time would tell.

William E. Gladstone

No matter how one measures it, unquestionably *In re Gault* killed the juvenile court, at least the court we had come to know in Dade County. The first fifty years saw the child-saver philosophy fade away not only here but even in places like Chicago and Denver where, at the turn of the century, the concept was birthed. Programs bottomed wholly on idealism may leave a lasting memory, but thoughts of a perfect model generally fail to survive the hard facts of life. We all have learned that in order to survive, there needs to be a flexibility to meet changing conditions.

Judicial activism needed a revival in Dade County. Who would rise to meet the challenge and lead the way in the image of the old child savers? Hard to predict who among the judges gracing the juvenile court bench for the next fifty years would turn out to be the fiery crusader leading the march for children. Not likely the choice to be William Gladstone.

A staid member of the Bar for fifteen years, handling civil trials and real estate, and a graduate of proper prestigious schools—Mercersburg Academy, Washington and Lee University, and, of course, the Ivy League Yale University Law School—Gladstone was well on the route to a spot as an esteemed member of the downtown legal establishment. He was a cinch to provide a career, most likely to enshrine him in Martindale-Hubbell. Maybe in the cards someday, a later appointment on the federal appeals court bench.

But the juvenile court? The lowest status court among lawyers; the burial grounds for any lawyer with higher political aspirations. And then again, how qualified and prepared was Bill Gladstone for that quagmire at this stage of his career?

Gladstone had rarely practiced in the juvenile court, the post he now sought. His connection came from working on children's problems as a member of committees of the Dade County and Florida Bar associations, plus activity with the Dade County Mental Health Association. His juvenile court credentials for election as a juvenile court judge were far from reaching the long personal involvement of his two main opponents for that office.

How then do we account for this leap from a career as a proper Miami barrister to election and service as community flame thrower? There's no accounting in life for how the ball bounces. Bill Gladstone had a purpose, a dream, and a plan. He knew what his mission was to be. And he followed it.

Despite the close relationship we had over the years as colleagues on the bench, I never had inquired as to his election victory or what had impelled him to seek the office. We both had arrived at our goals; different routes taken, and the individual paths didn't seem important. Now, more than thirty years later, as a historian of sorts, I was questioning him as to his early aspirations.

SEYMOUR: You were a successful lawyer, with a good future ahead, never remotely touching active politics. What made you run?

WILLIAM: At that time, working on family committees of both the Dade County and the Florida State Bar on matrimonial matters, I was inspired with the new concept of a family court. Studying it made me believe it could solve intrafamilial problems in one court before one judge.

This was an idea making headway in several other States in the country. I envisioned a replica in Florida and Dade County. The basic underlying approach was to move away from the old adversary system that had encumbered all the trials of the legal profession.

To me it was an obsession. I just felt that one court could include all the problems of the family in a nonadversarial setting. Everything about the child—delinquency, dependency, divorce, custody—in one court before one judge. A true healing process featuring mediation and agreement with very few court trials.

SEYMOUR: With no political experience, and little financial support, what made you think you could unseat an incumbent?

WILLIAM: Nothing personal against Juvenile Judge John Ferguson, but even after *Gault* the court seemed to be standing still. To tell the truth, the prospect of installing a family court so obsessed me. I knew I had to be elected to do it.

I realized that is what I wanted for my career. I never looked back. This was going to be my life.

SEYMOUR: What ever happened to this vision?

WILLIAM: Chief Circuit Court Judge Ed Cowart set up a family court assigning six judges to hear not only the matrimonial aspects of a case but also to work together with juvenile court judges on other related issues in their courts.

SEYMOUR: How did it work out?

WILLIAM: It was a disaster. The assigned judges rebelled, wanting out. The high-priced lawyers handling the big-money matrimonial cases did a lot of judge shopping on custody matters, filing many separate petitions before different juvenile court judges.

In less than a year, the project collapsed. The new judges disliked coming to the juvenile court complex, located far away from the Flagler Street courthouse where all the important action took place.

More than that, the resources and staffing for this complex undertaking were totally lacking. After a year, the experiment was over.

SEYMOUR: Is there a family court today?

WILLIAM: We now have an excellent family court structure. Many judges now seek to sit in that division. Judges Cindy Lederman and Lester Langer have been structuring it so that the appropriate juvenile court cases are sent to the family court.

SEYMOUR: Are you satisfied with the current structure of family court?

WILLIAM: It's fine, but it's still not what I want. The family court should be totally without court trials. Florida Supreme Court Chief Justice Barbara Pariente and our own Dade County Chief Judge Joseph Farina are each working on plans to provide adequate support and staffing to make it work.

Gladstone's idealistic approach for the family court way back then had many doubters among the judges. To this day, three decades later, many questions still remain (see chapter "Activists Are Many Among Us": Sandy Karlan). When Gladstone concluded with, "The Dade County Family Court turned out a lot different than I had envisioned," I sensed he still might, somewhere along the way, be lending an oar to make the family court more to his liking.

Unlike a lot of visionaries, Bill Gladstone doesn't give up on his dreams easily. Don't count on him sitting by idly if the moment stirs him. However, should Gladstone and his successors in this cause rise, they have a bit to go. But then again his won-and-lost record on his other dream programs is rather impressive.

Gladstone's political baptism, running for elective office, was an adventure. In a moment of candor, he commented, "Had I been politically astute and really understood the political process, I'm not sure I would have undertaken it." Then a moment later, as if withdrawing that statement, he said, "I'm sure I would have run anyway."

Along with his vision of a family court, Gladstone had a broad circle of friends to draw upon for an election campaign along with his own spirit. Somehow he attracted people to his cause. His view of the benefits of the family court may have been contagious, but I suspect it was Bill Gladstone, the person, more than his ideal that drew people to him.

Nonetheless, he had to overcome the burdens every candidate faces, namely, persuading the mostly indifferent voter that Gladstone was their man. The traditional requirements for political campaigning were not his strong points. The first task assigned by his campaign advisor was to contact a list of neighborhood political leaders located in different sections of town.

In Miami Beach he met with Revy Balkin, a popular political figure who supposedly had access to the elderly Jewish vote in South Beach. She liked Bill, introducing him to the neighborhood leaders, mostly octogenarians, whose command of English was slight. For some unknown reason they were unimpressed with our usually impressive Bill.

Gladstone, a bit nonplussed at his rejection, inquired of Revy as to his failure to impress. He was told, "They can't vote for you. They don't believe you are Jewish because you have a Southern accent."

Then sent to another part of town, he was told to meet with this union official involved with the trucking industry. The man had had a bad press recently over some union misdeeds, and Gladstone wisely passed that opportunity by. Gladstone, a man who genuinely likes to talk to people, found himself uncomfortable at these one-on-one power-broker meetings.

In his election campaign handout, he offered a seven-inch throw-away sheet, folded in half, boldly stating his theme—Dedicated to a Family Court. On the inside flap under that heading was his philosophy:

> The family in trouble produces the child in trouble. We can now have one Court dedicated to the preservation of the family. We need a Court to promote healthy, inter-personal relationships of the family members. These include the sensitive resolution of family problems by reason, understanding, self-examination and mutual respect.
>
> The courts need no longer be an emotional background where the children too often are both the weapons and the victims.

A fine philosophical piece indeed but not exactly the handout to attract people in the street to your cause. Bill Gladstone truly was a novice in politics. He had never run for public office, disliked politicians, particularly the self-aggrandizing, often-corrupt ones. A highly ethical lawyer himself, his standards were high above those that even the best of our elected officials practiced.

He did, however, know and admire a few progressive Dade County legislators who satisfied his standards. Those included state House members Sandy D'Alemberte and Marshall Harris, State Senator Ken Myers, as well as State Senator Bob Graham (an occasional Gladstone tennis partner). These friends, highly regarded in government circles, were moving upward.

D'Alemberte would rise to president of the American Bar Association, as well as dean of the Florida State University Law School, and eventually president of FSU. Harris, viewed by many as the most able member of the House, was later an unsuccessful candidate for lieutenant governor. Bob Graham, then considered a likely candidate for governor, won that office and went on to become a Florida U.S. senator.

From these wise politicos and others, Gladstone received advice. Gladstone also had a host of friends in the South Dade area, mostly medical doctors and college professors. Dr. Ron Shellow, a close friend and highly regarded psychiatrist practicing in the juvenile court, also gave Bill some insights as to the court operation.

As a neophyte candidate, this was to be for him an adventure to remember. He chose a sitting judge, John Ferguson, as his target. In the evolving game of musical chairs of recent years in juvenile court, John Ferguson had defeated John Bilikes, a recent Governor Haydon Burns appointment to the juvenile court. Gladstone had no animus toward Ferguson in selecting the seat he sought.

Until his election, John Ferguson had been a hardworking, diligent assistant in State Attorney Richard Gerstein's office. In his two years on the bench, his record showed no scars, and the press had never found occasion to make light of his work. As a colleague of mine, working together in the state attorney's office, I found him worthy of my support for election to this post.

At that time, working in Dick Gerstein's campaign for reelection, I ran into Bill Gladstone in the parking lot of one of those giant Food Fair stores that then covered Dade County. Along with about twenty other Gerstein staffers, I was buttonholing voters with handouts for Gerstein while Gladstone sat alone at a bridge table in a shaded corner with his own campaign literature. Occasionally, he would offer one of his Gladstone cards to a passerby and even try to engage the recipient in conversation.

Never having formally met him, I had nonetheless known of his candidacy since we both had friends in common, mostly of the liberal persuasion. I introduced myself, whereupon he began to tell me of his desire to remake the juvenile court, the actual words of the conversation I do not recall.

Conversing with him at his Food Fair table, I found his words of little interest, recognizing his naiveté in politics, knowing he could never unseat an incumbent with only a dream and that little bridge table. I bid him well and moved on approaching potential Gerstein voters.

Gerstein won in a landslide. Not Gladstone. His was a tough battle to the very last minute. I think he won because he willed it so. He was so determined to prevail that his small band of followers beat the bushes in his behalf so that he had to win.

In those years, I too had thought of one day becoming a juvenile court judge but felt it was a long way ahead careerwise. A year later I was appointed to the circuit court, assigned to juvenile, and found myself sitting on the bench alongside him. So much for my astute political foresight.

His opening campaign announcement in the *Miami Herald* on March 18, 1972, drew two small paragraphs stating he was a partner in the law firm, August, Nimkoff & Gladstone, and had served as chairman of the Juvenile and Domestic Relations Committee of both the Dade County Bar Association and the Florida Bar. Not exactly a pronouncement that would induce fear in the heart of an opponent.

Not until September 23, six months later, did the Ferguson-Gladstone race make it in print in the *Herald*. It was now a three-man race with James Kyne, who had been chief juvenile court attorney for seven years, joining the roster of candidates. The addition of Kyne made it more difficult for Gladstone since both his opponents were considerably more experienced than he in the actual operation of the court.

Ferguson, a lawyer for thirty-four years, had run unsuccessfully for the state legislature in 1947 and 1949, and then had served for nine years as an assistant state attorney. He was running on his unblemished record as a newly elected (in 1968) juvenile court judge.

Gladstone drew an extra line in that small news article for being the only candidate awarded a Dade Bar Association stipend by agreeing to follow a Bar reform rule on campaign ethics. He also had raised $22,800 compared to Ferguson's $7,579. Half of Gladstone's funding was a contribution he had made from his own limited savings.

On Behalf of Children

On October 1, the day after the primary election, the *Herald* reported that Ferguson led Gladstone by 1,643 and a runoff would ensue. Jimmy Kyne was far behind. The next day the *Herald* printed a retraction saying that while Ferguson was ahead in the early count, at the end of the day Gladstone was the front-runner.

The following Tuesday in the runoff, Gladstone forged ahead amassing 49,146 votes to Ferguson's lesser number of 45,233. The *Herald* reporter had characterized the race as noncontroversial. And that was that. No personal issues ever emerged.

Gladstone's strong support for the concept of a family court was very meaningful to him. He still maintains to this day that issue won over the voters. Longtime political observers viewed it more likely the deciding factor had been his dogged campaign.

This race was a lot like the one where Walter Beckham came out of nowhere to unseat Edith Atkinson back in 1928. Here, decades later, the juvenile court still hadn't emerged from its lesser standing to one of importance. Like Beckham, who in his long service on the bench had moved the court up several notches, would this newcomer have a similar impact?

Judging his campaign by any of today's political standards, Gladstone's effort was hardly one to produce a winner, let alone defeat an incumbent. More so since no serious fireworks between the two had emerged. Voters enjoy an underdog who stirs the water a bit. Most aspiring politicians organize a campaign, not only with funding but with some experienced hands around who can actually plan it as a military campaign.

It may have been that voters actually recognized the value of his family-court plan that won for him. Or perhaps the voters admired this plucky young man for his support of a new approach. Whether or not they truly understood the impact of such a family court is questionable. Even the *Miami Herald*, which in later years would literally adore Gladstone, chose not to make an endorsement in this campaign.

My own political assessment: I never could fathom how Bill did it. I'd like to believe his unquestioned belief in a family court did it. More likely it was other factors. I think the voters were impressed with his sincerity. He oozes it. Not too often does a candidate appear whom the voters can truly trust. Spend five minutes with Bill Gladstone, and you know whatever he's for is probably good for everyone.

Then again, maybe the almost-religious belief and faith he had that the family court was the only salvation may have spilled over on the voters and converted them. If nothing else, the campaign showed Gladstone's character and his conviction. He wasn't a man to be treated lightly.

Would newly elected Bill Gladstone be the standard bearer to lead the way? Surely, he arrived to the court brimming with idealism, but could he blend that burning fire with the realities and roadblocks in his way?

His predecessors—Beckham, Sheppard, Stone and others, even way back to Atkinson—each had ideas that would both markedly separate the juvenile court, yet give it equal status among the various court divisions. Each in their own way had contributed not only to keep the ship afloat, but to further the idea that children were deserving of special treatment. But in fact, this ship hadn't really gained much steam until Bill Gladstone came along and took the wheel.

It was a challenge he accepted with relish. But could one's passion alone enable a successful struggle through the morass of this massive, confused bureaucracy? Was Gladstone the kind of man equipped to carry out this mission? Could anyone?

His early years might give some hints. His fondest recollections of those days revolve around growing up in Birmingham, Alabama. His family, in the mercantile business, was fairly large, and he recalls with relish growing up Jewish in a southern city. He was enthralled with his grandmother Anna speaking Yiddish with a southern accent and often regaled me with his version of her delivery.

Bill Gladstone enjoys telling tales of growing up in the South among his large extended Jewish family. The South was a strange place for all the Gladstone folk. His father, Irving, and mother, Essie, moved from New York City to Birmingham where Bill was born. His great grandparents, only one generation removed from immigrants escaping Europe, had somehow found their way from New York to Blockton, Alabama, deep in the Deep South.

Longtime Dade Circuit Court Judge Sam Silver was a cousin, and always I was amused listening to them relive their childhood adventures growing up in Birmingham. Somehow in their conversations, both reverted to their southern accent acquired in Birmingham, but long gone as a result of associating with their many northern friends in Miami.

Another cousin was Mel Allen, the famed baseball radio announcer known to all baseball fans as the Voice of the Yankees. Also with a southern twang. It's fine to have gone to school with famous Yale graduates as did young Bill Gladstone, but Mel Allen was a huge name for kids who followed the New York Yankees, I among them.

The Gladstone family—wife, Marilynn and children, Calvin, Lee, and Adam—are a well-knit group. Marilynn, an activist in her own right, has been a leader in the women's rights field and in many diverse activities since her youth. In high school she was a national champion drum majorette and, if asked nicely, will tell about twirling those fire batons at famed Ebbetts Field, home of the Brooklyn Dodgers baseball team of another generation.

Marilynn has an impressive list of accomplishments in her own right. She's the founder of the Women's Fund in Dade County, raising a quarter of a million dollars at their annual luncheon of a thousand women, proceeds going to worthy causes. She was the first executive director of the Donor's Forum, a national group advising private corporations on appropriate gift-giving to the community.

She has traveled to Bangladesh to learn about microlending by which banks loan small amounts of money to very poor people. It is a revolutionary banking concept used in third-world countries. Mrs. Gladstone later helped introduce that concept in this country in places like Appalachia and even in Dade County after Hurricane Andrew. Planned Parenthood is another one of the organizations in which she extends herself as a board member.

For her own fun, at an age in which she should have known better, Marilynn participated in an outward bound physical test program fording rivers in the Florida Keys. For quiet hobbies, she is a past president of the South Florida Calligraphy Guild. Hard to tell which of the two, Marilynn or Bill, is the inspiration for the other. Being a community activist has certainly become a family trait.

Fresh out of law school, Bill Gladstone came to Miami in 1955 to begin the practice of law. Marilynn arrived here in 1958; her first job was teaching in an elementary school. For fifteen years Bill and his law partners handled real estate closings, marital disputes, and other business matters. Gladstone was a successful young lawyer, well on the way to a career entitling him to the usual rewards of such enterprise: the good life and large home mortgages. Some inner compulsion literally forced him to give up this almost-assured future for the uncertainties of political office.

Activists in the juvenile field in the 1970s generally were more likely to be mainly ACLU types demanding we provide due process, and on the other side, hard-liners aiming for tough new laws to rein in juvenile street violence; both approaches responded to the paramount issues of the time. Gladstone did not specifically fit the mold of either group, but was comfortable with both.

A point of pride with him were his classmates at Yale, a veritable who's who of luminaries in the legal field for decades to come. Yet the one man whom he most often talked about was the Reverend Pat Robertson, who attended Washington and Lee two years before Gladstone and later was his classmate at Yale Law School.

He remembers Robertson as a rather quiet person, not identified with the strong conservative views that later would define him—certainly not some of Robertson's more shocking recent utterances, such as a statement suggesting the United States assassinate the Castro-leaning president of Venezuela.

Was the time ripe for a Bill Gladstone to arrive on the scene? Yes, it was. The turmoil arising from *Gault* and the other current major court changes had brought the juvenile court into a major transition mode. Was it now ready for leaps and bounds? Was Bill Gladstone the heroic figure coming to the rescue? You can bet on it!

Could he succeed? Well, just as the knights of the round table had several impossible tasks ahead, so young Lochinvar here, with a swagger and a spirit, might move to the challenge. Not waiting a reasonable time for acclimation, he started on the run, never slowing down in the several decades ahead.

Today, Gladstone's early dream has arrived. There is a family court division. In his capacity as administrative judge of the juvenile court, Gladstone supported the creation of this division. Not yet precisely the one Gladstone had envisioned in his campaign for office, but one that has attempted to further many of the principles on which he campaigned.

The day he took office he became a man in motion, hurrying from one project to another. His black robe flying behind him became the Gladstone signature as he sped from chambers to courtroom to meeting room—to meet the next challenge. Sitting on the bench did not restrict his constant activity. Listening intently to the testimony offered before him, he simultaneously used the battery of telephones on his desk, imploring or demanding of governors and other such high officials for the assistance needed for one of the children in his court.

I recall once walking into his courtroom when he had just finished a telephone conversation. Describing the call, he had a grin of satisfaction on his face.

> The U.S. secretary of defense is a decent man. I had this navy recruiting officer in my court trying to help one of my delinquents enlist. I directed my secretary to call the secretary of the navy in Washington, D.C.
>
> It was four o'clock in the afternoon and no one had answered the phone at the Navy Department. Then asked my secretary to call Casper Weinberger, who heads the U.S. Department of Defense. An admiral answered, identifying himself as the legal advisor to Secretary Weinberger.
>
> Told him my problem. Ten minutes later he called back saying that Secretary Weinberger would take care of the problem, and that in the future the Navy Department would be more prompt answering my phone calls.

Incredulously, mouth agape, I inquired of my colleague, "You called the highest ranking person in the U.S. Defense Department—a cabinet member—as well as the secretary of the navy about a kid's case in your court?" I followed with a bit of sarcasm, "Why not start with someone a bit higher in the chain of authority?"

Without breaking stride, still with a big smile on his face, he responded, "You'd be amazed at how much influence a judge can have dealing with the military bureaucracy. I always call for the highest rank available. Even if the top man isn't there, I never fail to get action on my request."

This little incident told me a lot about Gladstone's modus operandi. He moves forward, no matter what. I also learned something of importance: always take your problem to the top man for results.

Comparing this eager new judge I first got to know in 1974 when I took office, to the man before me today, decades later, I could see the evolution. Perhaps I was best situated to assess how he had lived up to his expectations. Few of us are able to objectively judge our own progress. He, least of all, would lay any excessive claim of success at his own feet. At times he even downplayed his part, but in his heart I know he has always been proud of his effort.

It wasn't that Gladstone had recognized all the many shortcomings of the court, and that the promise of the child savers of decades ago had been unrealized. In a historical sense, he may not even have been fully aware of the efforts of social worker Jane Addams in Chicago or Judge Ben Lindsey in Denver. He did not view himself as the savior of the institution. He knew things were bad for children, and that cause was enough motivation.

He had but one immediate goal in mind to address the problem: follow through on the Florida Bar committee's recommendations to institute a new family court. In his gut he knew that was the thing to do for the betterment of children. What better guide does one need than one's own instinct for good?

Early on, Gladstone recognized that the situation was indeed complex. A lot had to be done. A major failing of the juvenile court, he discovered, was the lack of contact with the school system. The Dade County School Board was like a foreign entity, speaking a different language with no effort by either side to create a common approach. Under federal privacy laws, school records were inviolate.

Schools functioned as if a student in trouble coming before the juvenile court was no longer a concern of theirs. Since these were usually the problem kids in school, it was a kind of good riddance to troublemakers. Rarely, if ever, did a school principal or school official contact the juvenile court to learn the fate of a student in trouble with the police.

This lack of communication was almost a tradition, not a problem to be resolved quickly by some judicial fiat. Instead, Gladstone moved slowly, initiating weekly meetings with Superintendent of Schools Leonard Britton to discuss the lack of communication.

Slowly, but surely, a relationship developed. School records began to be available without the need for the subpoena process. Lists of arrestees were made available to schools. Problems of children under court jurisdiction became the concern of many school principals. It took some years before the solution to the problem was fully formalized (described later in this chapter).

Hard to believe that the bureaucracy of two agencies devoted to the same purpose could be so distant and divided. This togetherness concept finally evolved, but it took some doing on both sides.

All the judges worked together with the school leadership to make it happen but, absent those early weekly discussions between Judge Gladstone and Superintendent Leonard Britton, the court today might still be viewing the school system as it was then: an isolated entity, almost in an adversarial mode, unwilling to join in the effort to aid the child in trouble. Those beginning conversations, unnoticed by others, began the movement toward an understanding between two of the most significant public programs concerned with the welfare or children.

Bill Gladstone is a modest person, though often he assumes the role of absolute right and virtue. He chooses the latter role because of his strong convictions as to his efforts to create a better life for children. Describing himself as "obsessed" with the value of a family court says a lot about him. The dictionary definition describes "obsessed" as an overriding passion, a fascination, even a fixation—words that aptly describe his strong determination in all his years on the bench.

But his modesty overrides his ego. That is based on his own recognition that creating change, though acclaimed for the moment, is at best temporary. Honored for his efforts frequently, he is not a man to take bows. He is well aware that in the area of child welfare, today's panacea can easily become tomorrow's debacle.

Gladstone joined the debate on formation of the new family court, fostered by Dade County Chief Circuit Court Judge Gerald Wetherington and as well by the family committees of the Florida Bar. This was no simple task; the struggle would continue for years. Gladstone remembers it well.

But the immediacy of the problems awaiting Gladstone were more telling. In his first several years in office, the new courthouse was completed, although the second floor housing the judges' chambers and courtrooms needed to be added. In the meantime, Judge Donald Stone rotated to the Civil Division, with Judge Dixie Chastain taking over as senior judge. Waiting until 1978 for the completion of the first two floors of the building, Judge Chastain then gave up her construction hard hat and stepped down as senior judge of the juvenile court.

The new senior judge was William E. Gladstone. A quick rise, but this transformation period of the last decade had been so abrupt that Gladstone's sudden ascendancy went unnoticed. Also unnoticed during all the turmoil was Judge Stone's replacement in 1974 to the juvenile court, newly minted to the circuit court, former Assistant State Attorney Seymour Gelber.

Reconstituting the juvenile court through the vast due process changes required in the courtroom by the *Gault* decision, plus the revamping of Article V of Florida's constitution, and also the new State role in the courtroom via the State Health and Rehabilitative Services (HRS), certainly upgraded and set new standards. This also meant a new potential that hopefully could create a fully functioning and better court.

Much had changed in the structure of the court since these changes began, but still vestiges of the past had slowed progress. Newly arrived senior judge

Gladstone fully accepted these changes, but where was the wherewithal to accomplish these goals? The rehab resources, the inadequate staffing, the dreadful Youth Hall Detention Center, and the new medical and psychiatric centers were all wanting.

Funding from the State of Florida was no improvement over the meager contribution by the Dade County Commission in the past. Staff morale was at a low. No way that a one-man crusade could change this world. A lot had to be done. Gladstone was more than willing to give it a try.

In the midst of these vast concerns, each a monumental one, there still stood the final construction on the second floor, housing the courtrooms and judges' chambers. It was at a standstill—a difference between the County and the State as to who foots the bill. All very complicated.

Dade County provided the land, the State paid for construction, then the County turned over the title to the new building to the State. All well and good, but the high overruns and construction delays left no money to complete the second floor court section. Only a shell was visible, but walkways and other necessaries to accommodate courtrooms hadn't yet left the drawing board.

Judge Gladstone quickly organized a committee to raise the necessary additional funds. Two of his legislative friends, State Senator Ken Myers and Rep. Marshall Harris had, from the beginning, been fighting the good fight in the state legislature to keep the project afloat. At the start they had managed to eke out almost three million dollars needed to help finance the eight million cost of the replacement building.

In the 1973 session they sneaked the additional money into a bill designed to cover State overruns for construction of State buildings. An additional million and a half short, Gladstone's committee, including the two friendly legislators, worked assiduously at filling the breach.

No help from the County. Bill Hampton, Dade County's general services administrator, said this about the situation: "The County will turn the completed building over to the State. The money is a matter between the state courts and the Florida Legislature." Thanks a lot, Hampton.

Was this struggle involving the judges, the County, and the State a massive battle? Could Bill Gladstone handle it? Of course. But was the public up in arms over the delay? No way. It hardly drew any press concern, except for a few scant comments in a catch-all *Miami Herald* gossip column. That's how government works. It was a routine struggle, at least to the media and the public.

But it wasn't routine to Bill Gladstone. He had to fight the battle for construction funds, and spend more time struggling with the legislature for badly needed funds for rehab programs for children. But even before that, he had to have a juvenile court working full steam ahead. By now he had the full picture of a court totally unprepared to move into this new era where children struggling with life could at last receive the benefit of a court specially prepared to be responsive. Gladstone was ready to bring all these good things to fruition.

Completion of construction of government buildings on time was and is the bane of existence in the bureaucracy. Judge William Gladstone, now with the new title of *administrative* judge, was about to learn about patience. And so he did. The court wing, so zealously sought, was but one small hindrance, but eventually it came, and the court was prepared to move on. There were a lot bigger fish to fry. No blare of bugles upon Gladstone's first arrival, no cause yet for recognition.

At the beginning he was into the ordinary routine. Assignment of calendars for the judges, status of the mental health clinic, performance of HRS counselors, and a host of other matters mostly routine and small were in his domain. These tasks all enabled the court to function in proper fashion and had to be done.

The administrative judge also went so far as allocating parking spots for the judges in the already-overcrowded new parking lot. A newly appointed judge, Joe Durant, an old colleague of mine from the state attorney's office, had on his first day unknowingly parked his automobile in Judge Gladstone's parking spot in the sector reserved for judges. Unceremoniously, it was towed away by a deputy sheriff under the direct orders of Judge Gladstone. It took twenty-four hours before Gladstone could rescue Durant's car.

The next morning, Judge Gladstone received a proper certificate of appreciation, affixed with the Dade County Clerk's seal, an eagle emblazoned on the heading, with the following copy, tongue in cheek: "Whereas William "Bill" Gladstone has, in diligent and conscientious performance of his duties as Chief Deputy Parking Enforcer, performed his duties with distinction, this Certificate is awarded with the highest esteem."

It was signed Napoleon Durant, junior circuit court judge. His birth name was Napoleon, but he preferred the less-impressive name of Joe. Durant was then assigned a proper parking space and continued to serve as juvenile court judge.

Gladstone, amused with Durant's elegant response, kept this certificate in his files these many years. Joe Durant, a superb appeals lawyer for the prosecutor's office, was a kindly, actually beloved person who arrived in juvenile court bent on finding the best in all the youngsters appearing before him.

Durant's knowledge of the law stood him in high regard among all in the legal profession with whom he came into contact. Exacting knowledge of the law is often a secondary or tertiary requirement in juvenile court, where citizens and the media focus on the relative values of retribution as opposed to rehabilitation.

In juvenile court, unlike other courts, it is a Solomon-like decision affecting the child's well-being that counts most. Finding the appropriate program to fit the child's need consistent with the enormity of the offense is the ultimate test for the judge. No easy task.

In Durant's view, offering second and third chances, absent any punishment, satisfied a worthwhile purpose. Regrettably, in many situations it often built a "soft on crime" reputation for the judge. As a former state attorney's office colleague, I had advised Durant that the decade of the seventies was one where the courts, particularly the juvenile court, was receiving much of the blame for violent street crime.

Halfway into his term, in criminal court, *Time* magazine had labeled him with a "Let 'Em Go Joe" tag in a major crime case attracting much public attention. Amidst the public outcry, Durant was reassigned to juvenile court. There he did nothing to belie his newly acquired reputation, still willing to give defendants another chance.

I suggested he transfer to still another division where a knowledgeable judge with his legal acumen could truly be appreciated. Durant was grateful for my interest, but declined my suggestion, staying in juvenile court. He continued on with his efforts to find the most reasonable nonpunitive approach. Durant truly followed the principles social worker Jane Addams had enunciated almost nearly a century earlier.

In the next election Durant was defeated by a young lawyer who challenged him as a "Let 'Em Go Joe" jurist. It was sad to lose a man of Joe Durant's ability, but it clearly described the temper of the times. The public would no longer countenance the juvenile court as a coddler of errant youth. Did it influence the conduct of the other judges?

Perhaps so, but hardly in a significant manner. Certainly not with Bill Gladstone. He was a man driven with the goal to provide all the necessaries that would assure a child traveling through the system a positive outcome at the end. To him, incarceration was an alternative he did not turn from. In his heart, however, he felt that were the resources sufficiently available—counseling, drug rehab, psychiatric help, aftercare—then the need for incarceration could likely be seriously limited.

Early on, Gladstone established his style as a sitting judge. Firm and assertive was his approach. Shortly after taking the bench in 1973, he testified before a Florida Senate committee studying the failure of the corrections system to stem the rise of repeat offenders in Florida.

Before the committee, Gladstone bemoaned the lack of planning and resources to address children's needs once brought into the system. He denounced public school officials who refer minor problems to juvenile court as officials who are "terrified" to deal with their own responsibilities. "School principals," he said, "would rather brand a child a delinquent for a schoolyard fistfight than punish him themselves, so they dump it in my lap and ask me to declare little Johnny guilty of criminal assault and battery."

Gladstone would be assertive, demanding the state assume full responsibility for the well-being of his charges in terms of treatment. For this he saw no compromise. In 1974, in one of his first cases, dealing with an seventy-pound eleven-year-old youngster, that's exactly what happened.

Psychologists had described the child as emotionally disturbed. He had been to state school, returned to Youth Hall, had attempted to hang himself, and was under constant supervision to avoid self-inflicting injury. South Florida State Hospital was in the process of evaluating him and was unlikely to have space.

Unfortunately, the hospital served half the State, and admission for small children was limited. Gladstone, after returning the boy to Youth Hall, ruled that the child had a right to treatment, and the State must fund a private source to treat him.

Gladstone stated, "To the tragedy of these children and to the shame of the State of Florida, we have no other place." This was his opening volley, a theme he would enlarge on for the next several decades. Gladstone, from the bench, would demand that emotionally disturbed children not be left withering on the vine. By now, a year after coming on the bench, he was beginning to warm to the task. No longer the quiet pleader, from thence it was more like thunder coming from the bench.

He was, however, not reluctant to impose the maximum penalty for children charged with serious crimes. He recognized the realities of each situation, sometimes locking up a hard-core delinquent where no other resource was available, often binding him over for prosecution in criminal court as an adult.

In 1975 he had a case in which the defendant had severe character disorders. Judge Gladstone ordered a medical exam to determine if organic brain damage existed. The psychiatrist had declared the seventeen-year-old defendant so potentially dangerous that "he should not be released under any circumstances." The victim had been stabbed seventeen times in the Miami-Dade Community College parking lot.

After the medical exam, several doctors testified he knew right from wrong and was a danger to society unless treated. Gladstone bound him over to adult court for trial, agreeing with defense lawyer Gerald Kogan, later to be chief justice of the Florida Supreme Court, that his client be under observation at the South Florida Sate Hospital until trial.

Gladstone, then president of the Dade County Mental Health Association, brought those mental health concerns to the bench with him. Always, he was troubled by the inability of the State to address the problems of the psychologically damaged child before him. The system simply lacked resources to respond adequately.

One of his most serious criminal cases took place in 1977 involving three youngsters charged with armed robbery for assaulting a drifter while he dozed on a mattress under the expressway in downtown Miami. His face had been smashed with a rock, and then eighty-two dollars stolen from the helpless victim.

One, a fifteen-year-old, was a repeat offender, having committed a similar offense in a previous case before Gladstone. That had been one of the first cases Gladstone had handled. There, in a similar situation, the child had burned a man to death. Gladstone had then sent him to the state correctional school in Okeechobee for three years. Gladstone had requested he be sent to a halfway house before release home. The State Corrections officials declined to honor the judge's request, a decision within their authority.

Gladstone, following this case closely, had on four occasions unsuccessfully urged HRS Youth Services to place the boy in the State's most intensive rehab program. Now, back in court before him, Gladstone commented, "I can holler and scream like I did when he was here before. What good did that do?"

The new case, almost a repeat of the old one, and this time Gladstone transferred him to adult court to be tried there with the likelihood of long incarceration. Since adults are entitled to bond, Gladstone reluctantly set bond at $5,000. The child's mother indicated she would not post bond, preferring him to stay in Youth Hall Detention until trial. She agreed with Gladstone that for his and the safety of others he should not be allowed out in the street.

The second boy charged was a first offender, fourteen years of age, under five feet tall, weighing ninety-five pounds. After declining to send the child to adult court to be tried there, Gladstone said, "I am afraid of him and for him. In my view," Gladstone continued, indicating a tiny space between two of his fingers, "this youngster is about that far away from the death sentence—either imposed by a court or his fellow prisoners."

Gladstone asked the Division of Youth Services (HRS) what treatment the child would receive. "He'll go to state school in Okeechobee and with good behavior will be out in six months and go home," was the reply.

In an incredulous tone of voice Gladstone responded: "Six months? The psychiatrist who evaluated him recommended a long stay in state school, and then be placed in a group home." Knowing the futility of pursuing this line of inquiry and realizing he had no control over rehabilitation, Gladstone asked for progress reports and moved on to the next case.

Along with the shortage of beds, children were not accepted in state hospitals according to a new state law unless "the child is found dangerous or delinquent, or abandoned, neglected, or abused." Obviously a cost-saving decision by the state legislature.

In another court case, the child was neither delinquent nor dangerous, but the parents simply had run out of money for psychiatric care in a private hospital. They otherwise were loving parents, but the State had applied the same law rejecting the child unless the parents admitted to being neglectful or abusive. Gladstone viewed that approach as "a tragedy." Further, he angrily stated, "We, as a State, are as guilty as we can be of child abuse in its most heinous sense."

That same year, 1977, he had a case involving a seriously emotionally disturbed fourteen-year-old youth with a fascination for guns, who murdered a classmate. With his mother's approval, he had set up target practice in his family garage, taught himself sharp-shooting. The boy owned several small .22-caliber pistols and a switchblade. He had given the victim thirty-five dollars to purchase a gun for him, and during an argument over the failure to make the purchase, he had shot the victim. The State was unable to provide psychiatric care.

Gladstone, distressed over the fact that the State has only twenty-seven inpatient beds available for psychiatric therapy, and as well the high cost for private hospitalization, asked the Miami Mental Health Association to look into the shortage of beds for needy patients. These cases outlined here suggested to him the need for such inquiry.

In their response the mental health association Blue Ribbon Panel, in a scathing report, concluded that Florida has one of the worst mental health systems in the country naming as examples Dade County's Jackson Memorial Hospital and South Florida State Hospital located in Broward, but also serving Dade County.

The report described Florida State Hospital, the largest such institution in Florida, thusly: "It performs very nicely as a warehouse; it performs poorly as a hospital. Florida is violating its own law, the 1972 Baker Act, by not providing the right to treatment and the quality of treatment."

Judge Gladstone, commenting on the report, called these violations "almost criminal misconduct on the part of the State." He was beginning to hit his full stride, aggressively striking out at those he found in dereliction of their duty. Truly, he had become a powerful voice.

For so long as he served on the bench, Gladstone found the failure of the State, particularly the legislature, to properly fund this area, a battleground where only slow, very slow, progress had been made. He viewed this failure as a major contributing factor to the increase of violent behavior among delinquents.

Regularly attacking the state legislature for failing to properly provide mental health funds was appropriate. Judges ordinarily stay out of political conflict, but in this situation where an urgent public need was neglected, it was both proper and right. Someone had to speak out—promptly.

He was also highly critical of HRS's Division of Youth Services, but recognizing they were but employees carrying out the will of the state legislature, he was a bit less pointed in his assaults. Gladstone, as the administrative judge, had a leadership role to play, and he spared no individual or agency, but it was important to make certain his charges were directed at those in the highest decision-making authority

Some suggested he made a high drama out of each event, but in truth there was no playacting on his part. Gladstone meant every word uttered, and his emotions were real. He wasn't performing; rather he was living through each ordeal as it played out before him. His forthright attack was a sign of strength for the Dade Juvenile Court. Judge William Gladstone had become a worthy standard bearer.

As he became further identified with the cause, our county's juvenile court began to gain a positive image. Those early learning years on the bench set a pattern for Judge Gladstone. He was finding himself. More and more he began to realize that he had been cast for this leadership role.

It might be noted at this point that while his predecessors defended the court valiantly when necessary, Bill Gladstone was the first judge to affirmatively attack the power structure for their persistent failure to provide the means. Some of his predecessors reacted strongly in defense of the court, but Gladstone actually bearded them in their own dens, clearly branding their failure. Rarely do we see a sitting office-holder go on the direct attack with such determination.

An advocate able to focus on reform, he managed to avoid the label of being a liberal bleeding heart. He, perhaps alone, had to find ways to begin addressing the problems the State had neglected for so long. And he did.

In fact, I think his heart did bleed for these children. Each one of his cases became part of him. He took the cases home. Felt the pain of the parents, suffering with them. Whereas most other judges, I included, sympathized with the parents—at least those who meant well for their children—we did not allow these often-sordid and sad situations to engulf us. With Gladstone it was different.

To a reporter late in his career, Gladstone had explained himself,

> When I started I was in love with my job. I had enthusiasm and hope for the system. We were doing battle together to change things. I had a sense of humor. When you work in the bottom of the barrel, it's hard if you don't have a sense of humor.
>
> If you took a vote among citizens, there would be a landslide for abolishing the juvenile justice system.

Always, Gladstone has bemoaned the lack of State funding, the indifference of the community to the plight of generation after generation of criminal behavior, and as well the dependent, often-brutalized child, bit by bit turning into a violent felonious adult.

He also was concerned about how he was seen by those state probation officers and counselors who worked with and for him in court. Generally an empathetic person no matter his sometimes-strong language, he wanted to be liked by those who had to deal firsthand with these troubled children. He stated,

> I think the HRS workers view me as an ogre now, a troublemaker rather than an ally. The staff people are despondent, and I am getting cynical,

depressed, and angry. The encouragement is gone. My patience and my time are gone. The stresses are greater for all of us. Will it ever get better?

Although the state HRS leaders were often his targets, and sometimes the local workers as well, he sincerely felt for the fellows in the pits. Those were intake and field counselors who sometimes bore the brunt of his wrath. But they were not the real targets. He wished for an understanding that together they were in this with him. They were not his adversaries. Both he and they were victims.

One of the things admired most about Gladstone among the lawyers was his ability to totally adhere to the law. One might expect that his intensity and concern for the child before him might drive him to seek alternative solutions, a bit outside the governing law, but no, he persisted on a solution under the four corners of the law. Sometimes the law and the need are in conflict, but he insisted on satisfying both requirements.

A lot of that had to do with his fascination for each of the cases before him. He always delved deeply into each problem, and his answer always was designed to satisfy the integrity of the law. Never a casual jurist, always he sought the underlying reasons for any aberrant behavior. With the heavy caseloads present, the tendency existed to move fast. No short cuts for my friend.

He had this reputation around the courthouse: "If Gladstone has a hundred cases on his calendar for the day, he will sit till eight in the evening to hear them all. If he has only six cases he will delve into every aspect of each case even more and finish at six in the evening."

It is no reflection on the other judges serving with him, some long gone by four in the afternoon, but Gladstone's dogged persistence to get to the heart of each case was hard to match.

In addition to his day-to-day efforts struggling with the individual problems of those before him, Gladstone, in an assertive role, would often emerge. In his files was an unsigned note to me:

> I don't have any news clip or document on this, but I was the Judge involved in convincing the Dade County School Board to open school-based Health Clinics. It was in the early 1980's. There was a big public fight going on because of fears regarding schools providing sexual counseling, abortions, etc.
>
> I had to force my way into the Board's meeting with armed guards to get through the demonstrations outside. I must say, the clinics have been and are a success!

I remember the turmoil surrounding that school board decision, but Gladstone had never before mentioned his role, and the media had not noted his presence.

He was a guy ready to take dramatic positions, but he always avoided seeking credit. It wasn't that he was not pleased with public recognition. He wasn't that shy. He simply felt seeking credit was unseemly.

Gladstone didn't fully remember this school board incident, but Berta Blecke, our nonpareil volunteer who had accompanied him to the School Board meeting, added a few comments. She said,

> When we arrived, the mob was threatening. People cursed and spat at us. They were furious because we were there to help set up clinics to provide information for high school students as to sexual behavior. They viewed us as proabortion supporters. It was a dangerous entrance and departure for us. I thought we were in serious trouble.
>
> The background to this was that we had obtained a $600,000 grant from Johnson Pharmaceuticals to help set up these clinics for high school kids. We had made the request through the State of Florida, and after it was approved the governor of Florida turned it down. It had become a very controversial political issue.
>
> We then reapplied though the Dade County Public Health Trust. They approved it, and now we were going before the school board for final approval.
>
> Judge Gladstone so eloquently addressed the school board that they approved it and the health clinics in the schools came to pass. I was so proud of him.
>
> It seems that whenever we faced a crisis with our children, Judge Bill Gladstone came forward to our rescue.

That encounter with both the unruly mob and the more friendly school board, amid the rebuffs along the way, probably brought Gladstone to the realization that in order to realize his goals, he needed to not only speak out aggressively, but to follow up wherever necessary in order to attain the goals he sought. That health program had some preliminary use in some schools, but a lack of funds and protest groups limited its full effectiveness.

Fast forward some twenty years for the follow-up in a *Miami Herald* news clip dated January 26, 2006. David Lawrence's Children's Trust, teaming with Rudy Crew, superintendent of Dade's public schools, had designed a forty-million-dollar program to provide nurse-care practitioners and social-work teams for all 335 Dade County schools.

This new program, initiated with a six-million-dollar grant from the Children's Trust, still has a long way to go fundingwise, but Lawrence and Crew are confident donors will come forward. Both are visionaries who also are adept at raising money. Crew can account for ten million from government agencies, and Lawrence counts on public donors for the rest. Maybe so.

What is significant here is that other leadership in the community, in addition to the Gladstones and the Ledermans, are now joining the charge as advocates for children. A wonderful sign for the future.

Being the strong voice for children was a role Gladstone cherished, but he knew that developing programs was the route he had to take. Waiting for the State or County to meet the needs was not likely to happen unless a strong force was exerted. Bill Gladstone would be that force. But he couldn't do it alone.

In the period around 1980, two of his biggest scores came about as a result of teaming with community activists Berta Blecke and Nan Rich. Blecke represented the Junior League and Rich the National Council of Jewish Women (NCJW). Together they were a matchless team, and having Bill Gladstone made them unstoppable.

The programs they sought and finally attained, CHARLEE and then the Guardian ad Litem program (GAL), were two absolutely essential pieces that had been absent from the system. Both the CHARLEE and GAL programs became necessary linchpins in the dependency movement.

Back in the infancy of the child-saver days in the nineteenth century, when abused and neglected children were receiving no attention in the field and had little recourse to the courts, projects such as these were far over the horizon.

As the juvenile court movement developed over the early decades of the twentieth century, the emphasis moved to the activity of male juvenile delinquents while dependent children gained less attention. The fear of increased violent juvenile crime in the latter part of the twentieth century even further diminished interest in the plight of young dependent children.

Around the early 1980s, those in the media and in the courts became aware of numerous cases involving dependent children, mostly girls abused in day-care shelters. Criminal and civil cases abounded amid calls for attention to this problem. Charges of satanic cults committing mass sexual assaults on day-care children came forth. Cases involving the McMartins in California and Country Walk in Miami received significant media attention. The *Oprah* TV show among others brought public attention to the plight of abused dependent children.

Children testified in court as to abuses and psychologists were able to introduce memory recall that caused children to dredge up stories of horrid abuse. Convictions resulted with jail sentences. Later, many of these cases were revisited and doubt cast on the authenticity of the testimony. Though many prosecutions ensued, no satanic practices were uncovered. Other than a few cases where inappropriate touching was involved, the furor abated.

The generally accepted conclusion was that for the most part improper interview techniques had caused children to exaggerate and create situations that had not existed. The inordinate amount of publicity engendered relating to the safety of young children, along with concerns raised by what seemed an epidemic of cocaine babies, brought a great sense of public awareness in regard to dependent children. For the first time more attention was devoted to fear for the safety of dependent rather than delinquent children. From that public arousing, a much greater focus began to be placed on children in jeopardy.

The genie was out of the bottle. The plight of dependent children attracted a national concern and effort. In Dade County, improving the foster homes situation with CHARLEE became a center of attention for dependent children. Enlarging the process of the juvenile court by adding Guardians Ad Litem to represent abused and neglected children in court was also under consideration. Both huge steps forward to keep up with the times.

Things hadn't been going too well in those years finding proper placements for runaways and children difficult to place. Something had to be done. The foster homes under consideration for CHARLEE were a lot more than an individual family taking in a child. That had been the usual approach, but often the results produced a bad experience for the child. Even more negative was a large institution housing "lost" children as in orphanages of the long-ago past.

CHARLEE began at the Menninger Foundation in Topeka, Kansas, one of the most highly regarded treatment institutions in the world. This new plan for Dade County called for CHARLEE homes in residential districts housing several children living family style. It would be therapeutic treatment, with the highest-quality professionals, following the Menninger treatment mode. The CHARLEE board of local community leaders would staff these homes, monitor the operation, raise funds, and otherwise relate to State social welfare agencies.

Locally, Blecke and Rich represented their organizations as the original leaders, with the Episcopal Diocese of South Florida joining the team. They were the inside organizers. Gladstone played the role of adviser-spokesperson, the man who sold the public and the funding sources as to the credibility of this project.

When Blecke and Rich went before a private foundation or citizens group, Gladstone would accompany them. First, he would describe the children's situation along with his views on improving the system. Then Blecke and Rich would make a pitch for funds. Very carefully, Gladstone avoided the role of fundraiser, banned by the Judicial Code of Ethics.

In the courtroom he continued on as advocate for the program, now explaining to kids being sent there the benefits of going to a CHARLEE home. In his speechmaking around town, he was the tireless spokesman for CHARLEE, giving it a pedigree only a member of the bench could provide.

When Gladstone learned that I planned to include in this book all the honors and namings he had earned, he demurred, suggesting that was not important to him. I had specifically made reference to the CHARLEE honors awarded him.

He sent me a note declaring: "I was the founding Judge of CHARLEE and one of the original planners and Board members. *But . . . I had nothing to do with the founding of the Gladstone Center* which was completed while I was in D.C. for a year with Senator Graham." Thanks, Bill. I will clearly note your statement. Excess modesty will get you nowhere.

CHARLEE, today about twenty-five-years old, is one of our premier children's support agencies. Currently, it has six Family Care Therapeutic Group Homes. I remember years back, when this private group would attempt to open up homes for distressed girls in neighborhoods and were told politely by neighbors, and sometimes not so politely—NIMBY—"Not in my back yard."

From time immemorial it has always been a problem to find a comfortable, friendly, homelike atmosphere for girls who lacked sheltering and nurturing. Finding a family to provide it is often difficult. The original CHARLEE concept—meaning *Children Have All Rights: Legal, Educational, Emotional*—required single family homes with caring stand-in parents as a court resource. It was one of the earliest public citizen responses to the shortage.

Success from the beginning was due more to the advocates who envisioned it (including Bill Gladstone) than any government help provided, although all our judges supported and appreciated CHARLEE's presence. CHARLEE handled the tough cases of kids who couldn't settle into the regular foster homes available, few as they were.

Gladstone viewed Berta Blecke as the major force in creating, as well as sustaining CHARLEE, a statement we all endorse. Volunteer Berta Blecke has been a mainstay for the juvenile court these many years. In 1986 the Florida Conference of Circuit Court Judges cited her for Florida's Outstanding Individual Contribution to the Cause of Juvenile Justice. An award well-earned.

Quickly, Gladstone enlisted local community support to lobby for a spot for Dade County as a pilot program. When in 1980, the Florida Legislature appropriated money for eight pilot projects, we were first in line, ready to go. Berta Blecke and Nan Rich then created an organization to buy small suburban homes. Each home, staffed with trained individuals, was designed for kids unable to make it the old-fashioned way where little or no professional help had been available on-site for the foster parents.

Currently, Gladstone continues on their board. In 1994, the William Gladstone Center for Girls, serving severely abused girls ages three to eighteen, was built. The new center does not replace foster homes but rather addresses problems at the front-end before troubled girls are admitted to regular foster homes. The center offers an on-site school, psychological care, periodic dental care, doctors and nurses, and rape counseling. Now called the Gladstone Treatment Center, the newest addition to CHARLEE is a testament to his support.

His second big hit was the Dade County Guardian Ad Litem effort in 1980. This was also not a solo Gladstone undertaking, but his name and effort provided a major thrust. The program began rather quietly not only in Dade County but throughout the country.

It was a crucial program because it added another significant resource to the progress of the dependency movement. A court weakness had always been the lack of legal representation for the child. In addition, HRS field workers for children placed in foster homes were either in short supply or had caseloads far in excess of normal. GAL provided citizen volunteers to monitor dependent children and work with the families. In addition, GAL lawyers represented the child in court. The GAL program thereby gave the court access to a view totally objective as to the welfare of the child. In most cases the GAL lawyers and citizen volunteers joined with the State, but occasionally they took a tack differing from the State's position.

The Guardian ad Litem program was a natural outflow of events. The GAL history began in 1974 in Seattle, Washington, where it had impressed federal authorities sufficiently to offer funding for states. In 1977 the Florida Legislature provided legal status for citizen volunteers to speak in court in behalf of dependent children, and in 1979 a pilot program was established in Jacksonville, Florida. Satisfied with the potential, our legislature then funded nine pilot programs throughout Florida.

Once again at the forefront, Berta Blecke and Nan Rich, through their respective organizations, had already sprung into action, organizing a GAL movement in Miami. As one could expect, Administrative Judge William Gladstone was the front man leading the public charge.

As a lobbyist without portfolio but speaking as a judge, Gladstone sought to upgrade the court. In the early years of GAL he led the citizen group, and later continued his involvement and commitment. He provided not only the voice and the momentum, but was the spirit of this fledgling operation. Starting in two rooms in one of those small trailers adjoining the juvenile court, the GAL program, under Joni Goodman, began to progress. Goodman had joined the program in 1982 a few years after inception and is primarily responsible for the growth and development of the GAL movement to date.

One of the outstanding characteristics of Bill Gladstone's efforts was his ability to engender support from the Berta Blecke types. No matter the projects, there always seemed a large number of volunteers ready and able to join with him or to have him join their fold. This time, it was all about starting a volunteer citizen group to bring the dependency side into the twentieth century, although calendarwise we were very close to leaving that century.

Berta Blecke, as usual, was a driving force not only in organizing the GAL project but as well in the operation. Starting in the trailer section of the juvenile court complex, it has now sprawled far beyond its beginning. Training classes for volunteers, a legal staff to appear in court, a research and public relations component make this a modern live operation highly regarded by the judges and the community.

Back then, in the beginning, it was but another program that had many doubters and only a few like Gladstone, along with Blecke and Rich, who foresaw the potential for volunteers to take up the interest of dependent children.

It all had started with these three advocates. Gladstone, becoming aware of the pilot program in Jacksonville, had alerted the two women to the potential it had for Dade County. After the inception of the GAL program, through the auspices of the NCJW and the Junior League, there was a need to sell this program to the legislature and the sitting judges.

Gladstone led the way for Blecke and Rich with the state legislature to obtain the $250,000 State grant for the GAL project. Along with them, Gladstone lobbied the legislature for funding. Dade County then had an excellent legislative delegation, and Gladstone personally lobbied Senator Jack Gordon and Representatives Roberta Fox and Elaine Gordon in support of Dade County's selection. They and other members of the delegation were sympathetic.

Gladstone, recognizing these volunteers as absolutely essential, took to the stump at civic groups and sought support of the Florida Legislature. Our dependency hearings were woefully short of personnel: lawyers, social workers, and counsel for the parents. At the beginning there were no dependency courts, only hearings usually addressed at the day's end of the regular juvenile court calendar.

He also persuaded the judges to look with a less-jaundiced eye on the women volunteers. Only with sparse training at the beginning, most of their effort was in the field, meeting and knowing both the child and parent or custodian. There they performed in a credible fashion as friend, supporter, and advocate.

At dependency hearings, usually fraught with angst and fear among all the participants, the Guardian ad Litem often was the one support the lonely and distressed child might have at one of these hearings. And as well the one objective voice the judge would most hearken to. Gladstone saw all along that these volunteers were filling the breach. Looking back at the development of the GAL program, I now marvel at their absolute success. It certainly was wise of me to bypass those negative feelings I had about volunteers in the justice system.

Most judges are a bit wary of tying in with citizen volunteers. Gladstone actually relished the idea. Of course, he was wise enough to join with citizens like Blecke and Rich, who always came forward with well-conceived plans and had a cadre of eager volunteers at their beck and call.

There were some legitimate concerns among some judges back in those days over the likelihood of the GAL program ever becoming a viable asset. Volunteers can be of great assistance, but in some instances somewhat disappointing. I supported the concept, mostly because Bill Gladstone was so strong an advocate for it. This was 1980, and having volunteers (mostly women) in dependency court assisting the state in the prosecution of cases, where parents were being deprived of their children, was still something not easy to accept.

Women lawyers had just begun to make an impression in those 1980 years. Only a decade earlier, serving in the state attorney's office as administrative assistant, I had participated in hiring several new prosecutors of the female persuasion. One, Ellen Morphonios, turned out to be a gung-ho trial lawyer and, when ascending to the criminal court bench, earned the sobriquet of Hanging Morphonios with her consecutive sentencing amounting to hundreds of years. Ellen quickly dissipated the concern that the gentler sex would be too soft.

But also I recalled my experience back in the 1960s with volunteers, mostly women, in a joint project with the Greater Miami Crime Commission. I had encouraged and fostered this program in conjunction with the Crime Commission under former FBI agent Dan Sullivan. The commission had chosen to monitor prosecutors and judges as to the proper performance of their duties. Seemed like a good idea to me. Turned out to be not so great an idea.

The volunteers, with only a rudimentary understanding of how a criminal court functioned, dutifully filed in all the boxes on their score sheets with the pertinent information requested as to the performances they had observed. At best, with sophisticated legal analysts, such a review might be feasible, but with rank amateurs monitoring performance, it was a disaster. As to be expected, somehow some of these negative reports filtered out to the press. It took a long time for my boss, Dick Gerstein, to forgive my endorsing this project.

Nonetheless, in spite of my misgivings, I supported Bill Gladstone in his quixotic effort to bring volunteers into the picture of stabilizing and improving our efforts in the dependency field. For certain, having an independent intelligent volunteer to be an advocate for the child would be a major improvement in the nonsystem that then prevailed.

But knowing the pitfalls of volunteers—mostly lack of adequate training, not subject to sufficient monitoring, time constraints, and other shortcomings—I kind of held my breath. Boy, was I wrong!

Never before I had met Joni Goodman, who has run the program for these twenty-seven years. Since than I have concluded that there was no other person, regardless of gender, who could have produced this army of well-disciplined, superbly trained volunteers (yes, mostly women).

There was a strong need for an oversight group to begin to monitor the progress of dependent children in the court system. Statutory law later permitted the Guardian ad Litem to obtain access to the court files, but not until Gladstone used his clout as a judge was the problem worked out.

Today, with the presence of the Voices for Children, a fund-raising arm for GAL, those early days are celebrated as the awakening of a new dawn. The Voices for Children group comprises leading citizens who provide extensive support for GAL. As the GAL program enlarges and provides additional support for dependent children both in a supervisory capacity and in the courtroom, the costs have risen far above funding supplied by the State.

Currently (2007), sitting as a senior judge in termination of parental rights cases, I often admire the skill, knowledge, and concern shown by Guardians ad Litem testifying in these important cases. Some thirty years later, the GAL movement now has become one of the backbones of the entire dependency system. From the beginning, it was Bill Gladstone at the forefront.

Gladstone also continued to play a major role with the National Council of Juvenile Court Judges in the effort to persuade other disciplines—psychiatrists and psychologists—to form alliances with the NCJCJ in the study and planning of interdisciplinary approaches.

He also presently serves on several NCJCJ Permanency Planning Committees involved in planning for dependent children. His commitment to the NCJCJ has never diminished. Almost from the onset of assuming his judgeship in 1973, he has been a stalwart member and contributor to all their major efforts, which have been many.

Although credited highly within the NCJCJ organization, word of his national accomplishments have never yet followed him back home. Gladstone's pursuit of programs dealing with our youngest children was an approach that finally was receiving the attention warranted. He was one of the primary leaders nationally who had actually initiated this emphasis on the youngest of our children. Nonetheless, he views his efforts over the years with the NCJCJ as equally significant to his work in Florida and Dade County.

As a result, the NCJCJ pursued as part of their early intervention process the program Zero to Three. This began a trend in other communities to focus on mental health issues of the very young. Judge Cindy Lederman has also made this a major part of her advocacy efforts.

That was the time for leadership from the bench to recognize this new emphasis on dependency. Bill Gladstone, right there at the helm,. leading the advocacy, was bringing along his colleagues on the bench. This kind of new direction would be the course he would follow the rest of his days. Quietly but effectively, it all came about.

With all his surge toward the dependency issues of the day and programs to address them, Judge Gladstone wasn't giving up on his fight against delinquency. Refreshed by his progress in the dependency sector with CHARLEE and GAL, he was ready to move on his old nemesis: crime and delinquency.

He was traveling to an earlier stage to meet the enemy where he had begun. There was a lot there to be done. The opportunity arose in 1979 when State Senator Bob Graham moved to Tallahassee as governor of Florida. Although their tennis meetings were fewer and far between, Governor Graham, long subjected to his friend's harangues on the State's failures in child care, regularly called upon him for advice.

The strong outcry in Florida concerning the high rate of juvenile crime, most particularly in Dade County, called for a gubernatorial response. The new governor wanted some real progress in this area. Earlier (1978), the legislature had enacted laws designed to curb the rising juvenile violence by addressing it early on when the child made first contact with the system.

Called Community Control and described as a means to halt the revolving door of youth crime, it was mostly after-school work projects provided by local businesses. Caseloads for workers would be reduced, and long probation periods for delinquents would be replaced by work sentences. Gladstone convened community leaders to participate in the effort to lessen juvenile crime but commented, "As usual, Florida has taken a bold new approach... without providing the necessary funding."

Community Control stayed around for a long time, but it never remotely addressed the problem of preventing juvenile crime, serious or otherwise. Even at the beginning, the program moved in such a pedestrian bureaucratic manner that it neither had an impact on juvenile crime nor did it impress the public of its potential. Clearly, there was a need to move in another more forceful direction. Serious consequences for young lawbreakers needed to be blended with the softer rehabilitation approaches.

Dissatisfied with the lack of progress with the State's rehab programs, the governor thereupon invited Gladstone to Tallahassee to be the resident planning designer. The governor sought a secure rehabilitation program for serious violators of the law that responded to the public demand, yet was able to succeed in rehabilitation. Out of this grew a Gladstone creation: the Florida Environmental Institute (FEI). It all began when Gladstone broached the program to then governor Bob Graham, who thereupon ordered Florida's HRS to establish Gladstone's plan.

It was a new assignment for Gladstone, not exactly designed to provide relief from the daily firestorm but enough to provide him an opportunity to think out the problems of his chosen role and to provide new kinds of approaches for the juvenile court.

The news story of March 22, 1982, led with the headline "Ambassador Gladstone Gets a New Portfolio." Governor Graham announced that Judge Gladstone would leave his bench duties and for the next year be the governor's "ambassador," with a portfolio covering State juvenile affairs. Said the governor, "It is my desire to have Judge Gladstone step out of the case-by-case process and look at the total juvenile system for a new, fresh pragmatic approach."

This was a perfect situation for Gladstone. A man brimming to the overflow with ideas now would not only have the room to test his vision, but with the imprimatur of the governor behind him, doors would miraculously open. It took, however, some doing to accomplish this transfer.

In government there's always a bureaucracy to overcome. Since the judicial and executive branches are two distinct bodies, both wary of each other, the governor, as chief executive, cannot merely effect a judicial transfer by decree.

Supreme Court Chief Justice Allen Sundberg supported the governor's proposal, but this kind of transfer was new to Florida, and to avoid requiring Gladstone to resign his judicial office, it was necessary to create a new modus operandi. It took some good lawyering, but finally the deal was cut.

Gladstone was to be assigned to the chief justice with duties to advise the state secretary of Health and Rehabilitative Services (HRS) and the state Department of Corrections. He would be housed with HRS, be available to other state agencies, and of course, to his sponsor, Governor Bob Graham.

Hardly had the announcement been made, Gladstone was ready to move on a handful of projects. One thing about Gladstone, there's nothing petty about his proposals. He goes for the big ones. He was already floating some ambitious plans, still mostly only seeds in his mind, but you could tell he was ready to climb every mountain.

His lead plan, according to the announcement, was something similar to the 1930 Depression-era Civilian Conservation Corps (CCC) that hired the tens of thousands unemployed to virtually rebuild America's schools, roads, power-generating electrical plants, and whatever else needed a renovation or a fresh splash of paint. Gladstone noted, "I want to put violent, serious delinquents to work on projects for the State, rather than having them languish in institutions. They would earn a small salary but would pay for food, shelter and clothing."

Even before his appointment to the new post, Gladstone and the governor were at work laying plans to implement the proposal. At the 1982 legislative session, Governor Graham then requested a $569,000 allocation for a private agency to attempt to rehabilitate sixty teenagers who had committed serious crimes. This was to be a pilot program for delinquent kids from Dade and Broward counties. Not quite the magnitude of FDR's CCC, nonetheless a worthy beginning.

FEI, known as the Last Chance Ranch, was located in the swamplands of Central Florida, just west of Lake Okeechobee. No presence of civilization, as we know it, existed within twenty-five miles. The area had a formal name—Fisheating Creek. Certainly an appropriate name.

The inmates came from the Miami-Fort Lauderdale area and had been through the justice system. This was the last stop before adult criminal court and prison. Their crimes of a serious nature included homicide, robbery, and other acts of violence.

The first batch had a rapist, two boys in for attempted murder, and several for burglary. They were ghetto kids, streetwise and totally unfamiliar with living in swamplands surrounded by crocodile-infested water. No armed guards present. A bit like the French Devil's Island, where trying to escape was a lot more perilous than the camp's daily regimen.

Visiting the camp on one of my tours, I encountered two boys I had sent there. They told me of an escapade of theirs, stealing a camp vehicle and trying to escape through the wooded swampland. After a day in the woods and marshes, hearing the strange animal sounds unfamiliar to the ears of city boys losing their way, they were grateful to be captured and returned to camp.

The camp took four years of planning, and the first group of youngsters assigned to the camp came to a five-acre site that required clearing, chopping down trees, and building the camp from scratch. This was indeed a testing program.

The campers started fully aware they were being punished, and hard work was the only route at the beginning. Earning points, they moved from sleeping on a cot on a wooden floor with a bug zapper hanging overhead on a fluorescent light, to a an air-conditioned cabin with television privileges.

School work in the morning, hard labor in the afternoon. From there it was learning to cook and do laundry, then assigned to neighboring farms to learn animal husbandry. Roughing it in this fashion was designed to give these young street criminals a fresh new slant on life.

Basic schooling was also an integral part of their lives. Most had grown up ignoring education, actually looking down at it. Suddenly, books became part of their lives, and lectures beyond the basics became accepted.

In phase 3, the Associated Marine Institute, with programs in the cities where the inmates lived (mostly Dade and Broward), accepted them for skill training. After release, AMI continued to work with them, monitoring and for further instruction. Hopefully, somewhere along the way, a work ethic would become part of their lives.

A tale I heard on my first trip there, which I guess was common fodder for every newcomer, whether an inmate or a visiting judge. The story goes like this: Ernie Jones, a fifteen-year-old burglar from Miami's black Liberty City neighborhood, was at the river's edge, trying to catch some crawfish by using a net he had found at water's edge. There was a tug, and Ernie thought he had a turtle, grabbing at it with both hands. He was making slow progress when suddenly he realized it was an alligator, all eight feet of it. Ernie took off fast back to camp, screaming about his contact with this monster.

That may have actually happened, but I'm not too sure. These city kids are pretty smart. It may have been a story concocted by that forest ranger, Dan

Grizzard, who ran the camp in order to keep his charges closer to home base instead off wandering into the blue yonder.

The joint project—the FEI wilderness experience along with the AMI back-in-civilization program—started in the early 1980s and has now been operating successfully for twenty-five years. Since the beginning there has been a constant flow of national and international experts coming to examine the FEI operation. Corrections officials from all over the world visit to study the project. The reviews have been constantly favorable, and the program has been replicated in many states.

Judge Gladstone remains an active member on both FEI and AMI boards. It has been acclaimed by newspapers and TV programs nationally. The Federal Office of Juvenile Justice has often cited FEI as an outstanding program.

Gladstone, not a man to easily figure out, sought to mold children, by addressing their needs at the earliest age, yet he also supported tough programs like the Last Chance Ranch. How come?

In July 1981, Gladstone had appeared before the U.S. Senate Subcommittee on the Judiciary speaking on the violent juvenile offender. For openers, he had suggested that the government would get more bang for the buck by concentrating on the 95 percent of delinquents who are not chronically violent. He opted for a front-loaded juvenile system that intervened at an early age with meaningful diversionary programs, and constructive consequences and training.

In that presentation, he explained the dichotomy of his thinking. His two-pronged approach had been influenced by a recent Dade County research project surveying one hundred Dade County juvenile offenders and their families. It was a moral-development test determining how children's ideas of morality change as they grow older. As fashioned by the eminent Swiss psychologist Jean Piaget, it showed that as our delinquent youth grow older, unlike the great mass of children, they do not develop a sense of right and wrong. Interesting and revealing finding.

Gladstone, citing the Jean Piaget study, then went on to recommend to the senators this more strenuous activity-oriented approach rather than the more passive traditional counseling programs. In essence without naming it, he was proposing a work-oriented replication of the FEI program he was introducing in Florida.

His plan, presented to the U.S. Senate committee, somewhat mirrored the Last Chance Ranch wilderness experience, but provided for longer incarceration, more hard labor, as well as extensive development of employability skills and a basic education. His theme: kids growing up in the crime-filled ghetto streets will attain a work ethic by living it, rather than being counseled to do the right thing.

Governor Graham, impressed with Gladstone's Senate testimony, would in a few years hence, when sitting as a United States senator, gladly lend an ear and his support to Gladstone's proposal for a national effort similar to Florida's FEI project. As a social work entrepreneur, Gladstone never sat satisfied with his progress. Like the Starbucks coffee shop chain, he was always ready to open a new venture.

Since his proposal had considerably less of the social-work aspects so often criticized by legislators, his words before that U.S. Senate committee were undoubtedly well received. Little did he realize at that time that within a few years he would also have the opportunity to be part of a federal effort to establish such a program.

Gladstone's Piaget study, reflecting a lessening of conscience among delinquents toward the bad deeds they had committed, had a strong influence upon his attitude toward the rehab of violent young offenders. He appeared now to support tougher programs that could reach through the indifference that seemed to encompass these chronic youthful offenders.

At the same time Gladstone was doing his version of the Jean Piaget study, I was doing several studies of my own on our local delinquents (see Gelber chapter). His Piaget study was certainly a worthwhile one that engaged the interest of many of the major players. Together, we were beginning an emphasis on serious research that would be continued on an even higher level during Judge Lederman's administration.

The *Miami Herald* gave a big play to Gladstone's Piaget study and the tough new programs arising from it. One of their stories featured the reaction of other leaders in the field as to using more forceful techniques in rehab. Under the story heading "Experts Find Study Fascinating, but . . ." their varied comments were quite revealing.

Max Rothman, director of Dade County HRS, stated, "I don't know any program alive that can turn around the effects of learning disabilities, ghetto atmosphere, and broken families. When someone finds the cure for juvenile delinquency, he will patent it, and we will go home fat and happy."

Alan Hubanks, statewide program director of the HRS Youth Services, noted, "The old-timers at the state school at Marianna always said their woodshed was splattered with the blood of the kids who were whipped. They are still counting some of those murders those kids committed later." He added, "You have to wonder if we didn't brutalize them in the name of helping them."

Tom Petersen, Dade chief assistant state attorney, said, "We need intensive early intervention for these kids. It is incredible to believe, but we still don't know what works and what doesn't work."

Finally, Seymour Gelber, Dade County Juvenile Court judge, observed, "We see from the study that these ghetto kids aren't living in a subculture. In truth, they are living in an alien culture."

The interesting thing about the comments was that although the top leaders appeared to be disillusioned with prospects for success under the then softer approach, they were uncertain as to which way to go. That may be a problem in itself. Gladstone, moving a bit toward a sturdier, more robust program, may be a lot more realistic.

With all the problems existent in juvenile court, having Bill Gladstone as administrative judge was a great boon for his colleagues. He spoke out forcefully, represented the views of his colleagues accurately, and made a lot of sense to the general public. He also had a fine image with the press, which enhanced all who served with him.

In 1980 Mariel arrived in Miami, an invasion of 125,000 refugees from Cuba. Unlike arrivals in earlier decades, when families of some means—educated, experienced in business, professionals—had arrived, the Mariels, in great part, were escapees from oppression, some others actually released from prison to join the exodus. Most eventually became hardworking citizens and, despite the high number with criminal backgrounds, did credit to their new homeland. Among them were many children without families, with little else than high spirits to guide them.

These children quickly became classified as dependents in juvenile court. Judge Gladstone, handling the first batch, was met with a picket line formed outside the courthouse denouncing him. Local Miami Cuban radio had spread the rumor that Judge Gladstone was about to deport them. Four local attorneys representing the Cuban Bar Association were there to fight for their stay in Miami.

Gladstone handled it with aplomb, quickly disabusing them of any oppressive intention. He already had received about two hundred telephone calls from Hispanic community members offering to take the children. The twelve children before him were part of a group of forty-four he would eventually hear. In all, over one hundred comprising the first batch would go through the juvenile court system.

One of their attorneys told Gladstone the boys were worried about their future here. Gladstone, inquiring as to their concerns, reassured them. Their collective response: "We are not worried. We are glad to be here."

The three-hour hearing took on a social meeting atmosphere as Gladstone tested his Spanish, learned in Mexico as a student. They, in turn, recognizing the sight of a friendly judge, engaged him with the few English words they knew. Their Hispanic lawyers interpreted for all to understand. It was a healthy exchange for Gladstone. Something positive was happening in court. He needed that.

Gladstone's next involvement in the Mariel Boatlift crisis was a lot less pleasant. Before him was a fifteen-year-old Mariel refugee charged with aggravated assault for severely beating his aging grandmother and then, while in a State shelter, attacking a counselor. At a hearing, the judge with the HRS counselor's concurrence, offered that the child's well-being should be in the hands of the federal government.

Gladstone reasoned that the feds had welcomed the Mariel refugees and were providing support for their presence in this country. Why then shouldn't the United States assume responsibility for the education, rehab, and even incarceration of these new young guests? The state HRS spokesperson joined Gladstone's request, stating in court that the many problems facing this boy were beyond the ability of the state agency to address.

Thereupon, without hesitation or consultation, Judge Gladstone issued an order directing HRS to deliver the boy to the U.S. Immigration Services in Miami to be provided all the rights due him under the law. To make certain of the delivery, Gladstone then ordered Robert Taro, HRS director of intake, to personally accompany the boy and deliver him to the federal immigration agent in charge.

Then almost with a theatrical flourish, Judge Gladstone said, "I am releasing him to the government of the United States of America. He is their responsibility." He further stated, "I would hope the federal government would not be so reckless as to release this child. If they do, then the blood is on their hands."

Within hours, Taro reported back to Gladstone on his delivery of the child to the feds, relating his experience in detail:

> A uniformed detention guard appeared at the fourth floor Immigration reception area, taking the boy from me. He offered no conversation, placing the boy back in the elevator and going down to the first floor. I accompanied them.
>
> The guard then opened the front door of the building and told the boy he was free to go wherever he wanted to go. The boy seemed confused about the whole thing.
>
> The boy wore blue jeans and a white T-shirt. He had no other clothes or money. And of course, no home. He was all alone in this new country.

It had been a game of chess between Gladstone and the feds. The judge hoped against hope that the federal government would join in the effort. Maybe this might bring an important new player into the game. Worth a try.

To this day, Gladstone believes that had the U.S. government assumed full responsibility for that child, all the ensuing problems that Florida and Dade County encountered in the following years concerning the Cuban exodus to Miami would have been averted.

The Miami press was fascinated by Gladstone's bold move. Local state judges don't tell Uncle Sam what to do. In Washington, the INS spokesman Verne Jarvis, responding to an inquiry from a *Miami Herald* reporter, said, "I know nothing about this case. But I can say that ordinarily it is not our policy to release a fifteen-year-old, or an adult for that matter, to the street anytime that person does not have the capacity to care for himself. I will look into the matter."

Who knows? Gladstone's little ploy may be working. The feds in Washington don't quite know what to do about his order. Maybe his gall will bring some favorable action. No one before has suggested that this was totally a federal province.

The following day INS spokesman Vernon Jarvis, now fully aware of the matter and fully briefed by his superiors, stated, "We have no facilities with which to detain juveniles."

Judge Gladstone, recognizing the further futility of his endeavor, followed by issuing an order that the Mariel delinquent child be picked up by State authorities. At the hearing, Judge Gladstone resolved the impasse, declaring the child a dependent ward of our State. HRS agreed to treat him as such. Gladstone still insisted the federal government had the responsibility to care for the boy, but since HRS was now willing to address his needs, that would do for now. Diplomacy ruled.

That Gladstone was willing to tackle the federal establishment merely to make a point that these immigrant kids, literally lost in Miami streets, needed a benefactor like Uncle Sam was an amazing gesture. It is not likely Gladstone expected the INS to accede to his wishes. He probably realized he was on weak grounds legally, but he wanted to send a message to the feds that this was their problem too.

He had enough spirit in him to push the INS around, get the press and the public aroused, and generally let the world know that this mixture of Cuban, white and black kids needed America to remember them. There are some moments such as this where trying to shake up higher authority, hoping to arouse some sympathy and help, is worth a shot. Gladstone knew how far to push, yet maintaining his credibility, and still be respected as a leader.

Facing off with the feds or other higher government authority never fazed brother Bill. Nonetheless, Bill Gladstone always was a troubled man. Troubled over his children. When in that state of mind, he usually sent out a clarion call to the community—always a strong challenge

Like the time, in anger, he had reached the limit of his frustration and took George, a burglar at twelve with an IQ of fifty-nine, downtown to a Dade County Commission meeting. Barging in unannounced, he simply stated, "I ask nothing more than to share some of my outrage with you." The surprised commissioners sat there, uncertain as to what was coming.

Gladstone then described George's plight:

> He is not mentally retarded; he is socially retarded. From an impoverished family, in an impoverished community, there is no hope

for him and thousands like him. Half the delinquents in state reform school are in this category. Many will grow up to become murderers, psychopaths, and sociopath. What can we do?

The question Gladstone had asked was a rhetorical one. He expected no answer, nor did they offer one. Although several commissioners responded with the usual platitudes, mostly lauding Gladstone for his effort and urging him on. For all his setbacks, and there were many, Gladstone always maintained a valiant effort, never letting disappointment slow him down.

He always monitored the conscience of the community, testing their allegiance to the cause of children, never allowing the high and mighty to be too comfortable with themselves. So long as his children suffered, and he along with them, he wanted not one of the rest to be pleased with themselves. The guy is some kind of a saint, or a reasonable facsimile thereof.

At times Gladstone gave off the impression he was a public figure designated to be the heroic warrior chosen from above to lead the struggle for children in distress. It wasn't so much his words, which had been said before by others, but his intensity. He seemed to speak with such honest conviction that people paid attention. But he never believed or even pretended that he was some kind of chosen leader.

Some public office holders become adept politicians able to convey that special kind of sincerity (not always a genuine one). Gladstone chose not to project himself as the man in shining armor, come to rescue the troubled court system. His way instead was to challenge the most influential among us and those holding the highest public office, hoping to draw some positive response. A kind of guerrilla warfare without the Molotov cocktails.

Fortuitously, he came on the scene at the precise moment the juvenile court was in the throes of an upheaval of mass proportions caused by the U.S. Supreme Court ruling and changes in the Florida Constitution. He was there, and the process of altering the juvenile court in a dramatic way was a job that had to be done. And he set about to do it.

Was he an idealist, a showman, or merely a troublemaker? Surely he was an idealist, preaching every element of the child-saver dogma. Perhaps there was also a bit of a showman in him. He was a forceful personality, knowing full well that his dramatic statements and impressive actions were sure to leave a mark with both the public and the press. As a troublemaker he was at his best, knowing just how hard to push to get the response desired.

In totality, he was none of the above, or perhaps all of the above. He simply wanted to carry out the concept that children, our most important treasure, needed to be nurtured. In time, as with all leaders accepted by the public, his gestures were almost automatically recognized as being in the public interest.

In the courthouse he also had attained recognition as a judge who stood above the crowd. When he made that hurried walk from his chambers to the courtroom, past hundreds of seated parents and victims awaiting their call to a courtroom session, it was more than an arrival—it was a procession. Behind him followed his interns, bailiff, and lawyers each seeking a word. Led by Gladstone, they all progressed along the now-open path to his courtroom. Moving rapidly to his destination while engaged in quick conversation, all in his path—victims, defendants, prosecutors and defenders alike—felt certain of one thing: the judge was on their side.

Wisely, he never allowed the label of liberal do-gooder to be permanently attached to his efforts. All champions of children causes have that label automatically affixed to their name, but Gladstone's fathering of tough labor projects like FEI's Last Chance Ranch made it impossible to categorize him in that fashion. Requiring hard-core incorrigibles to attend camp in wooded alligator-infested swampland twenty-five miles from any sign of civilization took care of that.

He was deeply involved in creating programs to upgrade the meager services provided children of the court system. His advocacy, speaking out for children, went far beyond a routine plea. He spoke with intensity, as a pastor sermonizing his congregation, as if the world was his audience.

Lack of funding by the state legislature was the perennial problem, but mismanagement was also a factor. Whenever the call for austerity arose and budget cuts were imminent, it was social services that bore the brunt. Effective programs along with poorly operated ones felt the axe equally. Amidst all of that, though no one kept a scorecard, Gladstone probably led the way in organizing and supporting rehab programs of both the public and private sectors. At least the good ones.

One of those, perhaps the most successful private program in Florida, was the Associated Marine Institute (AMI). It wasn't created by Gladstone, but he has been a stalwart supporter for twenty-five years. One thing about Gladstone, he doesn't take the bows at ribbon-cutting and then disappear. He stays the full route, through good times and bad.

The originator of AMI was actually Frank Orlando, a juvenile court judge from neighboring Broward County. Judge Orlando probably is one of the leading juvenile court activists in the country. When the history of Broward County judicial activism is recorded, he will receive his full due.

It came about this way: Some thirty years ago, Judge Orlando visited Robert Rosof, a college chum, to console him on a difficult divorce recently completed. Rosof, a wealthy business entrepreneur, was sitting disconsolately on the deck of his yacht at a Broward County mooring.

Apparently, the divorce had resulted in heavy financial loss, and as the saying goes, Rosof was "down to his last yacht." Frank Orlando, a sympathetic old classmate, listened to the soulful plaints of his friend, and then to assuage his friend's distress, uttered the words that ultimately led to the creation of an organization that began as a small undertaking in Fort Lauderdale, followed by a successor in Miami, then all over Florida and in many other communities nationwide.

"Bob," said Juvenile Court Judge Frank Orlando, "Why don't you let me bring a few of my delinquent kids to work on your boat, give them a taste of sea life. Many of these kids from the ghetto have never even been on a boat. You can help them"

That was it. The last phrase—"you can help them"—was prophetic. Out of this grew the Associated Marine Institutes, even extending beyond the shores of this country. Rosof, the man of finance, had a new career heading the agency, serving for over two decades before retirement. He had no background or training in dealing with children, but he decided on a program that would preach morality and physical well-being, not from the pulpit, but by example. He hired as counselors a group of tow-headed, flaxen-haired college kids from Idaho and neighboring states, who looked like recruits for the Mormon Church.

Bob Rosof, as bright a man as could be found anywhere, had the loopy idea that delinquents from Liberty City with not the slightest understanding of the intricacies of boat operation or life at sea would somehow be impressed having these young WASPs from the farms of the Midwest as their counselors and models.

He was absolutely correct. Having a Jewish businessman from the North running the show, along with straight white midwestern churchgoers as models somehow worked wonders for these black southern kids. Many had not ever been on a ship or even ridden the elevator in one of our downtown skyscraper buildings. Rosof mixed some magic to get the results AMI accomplished. Don't ask me how.

Frank Orlando, no longer on the bench, now runs criminal justice programs, mostly juvenile, as a professor at Florida Atlantic University and serves as a consultant here and abroad. One of the most innovative judges ever around, Frank, now in his dotage, can be found mostly on some airplane, in the Gladstone mold, going to lecture in a faraway place on some new dazzling projects for children.

Bill Gladstone, enamored of the AMI Program, helped set up the Dade Marine Institute, recommending his colleague, newly appointed Judge Seymour Gelber, to head up the local program, an assignment gladly undertaken. Gladstone, meanwhile, became active in the development of AMI, nationally serving on the board. Thirty years later, he still energetically supports the local Dade Marine Institute (DMI) as well as the national effort.

Locally, DMI has both residential and day programs available to our courts, and has perhaps one of the best success records of any rehab program. Based on seafaring, the youngsters participate in national and international cruises, where they become not only skilled as crewmen but also learn the disciplines of work and team effort.

Bob Rosof is no longer around, succumbing to a heart attack several years ago. His and Frank Orlando's contribution for creating so outstanding a program is deserving of the highest commendation. They and Bill Gladstone also merit applause for improving and enlarging the program, both sizewise and qualitywise. Absent programs like this, courts are at a standstill in terms of providing the necessary alternatives for errant youth.

Gladstone's pleasure, if pleasure can be derived from the grind of the juvenile court, came mostly from the new programs he designed. Hardly did he enjoy a day sitting on the bench with all the despair he encountered. To Gladstone, every new program was an announcement of hope.

Gladstone also proposed turning the Okeechobee Boys Training School into a wilderness camp for ten- to fourteen-year-olds. This would be a public-private enterprise run by a foundation led by drugstore magnate who had adopted the field of juvenile delinquency as the main purpose of his foundation.

While the Okeechobee operation had been an improvement over the old one at Marianna, our judges had not been totally impressed with the progress. On visits there, both Gladstone and I were disappointed with their program to provide vocational training. Security seemed lax with too many escapees, and no follow-up on return to their home bases. Some of us also had reservations about Jack Eckerd, viewing his involvement as perhaps a public relations ploy to gain a good press for his next run for governor.

Despite my misgivings, Jack Eckerd's foundation did some yeoman work on Florida programs aimed at reducing delinquency. Included among Eckerd's successes was a excellent upgrade of program at Okeechobee. I suppose one shouldn't doubt public-minded citizens merely because they are rich and Republican.

Did our hero manage to develop these several programs he fostered into reality? In real life, there are few if any Supermen flying over the tallest buildings, wiping out evil, and saving the world. Our Bill Gladstone is a mere mortal. And certainly in this field there are no magical potions. To a great extent the answer is yes. He never quite replicated FDR's CCC in Dade and Broward, but he managed to accomplish most of his goals in one fashion or another.

Success never satisfied Bill Gladstone. He, among all the judges suffered his caseload most. Other judges were able to take the courtroom problems in stride. Not Bill. He suffered alongside every mother of a delinquent or dependent child. Some of his exasperation was vented at the social service agencies failure to carry out his orders or at the legislature for refusing to provide adequate funding.

The despair that rose from too many disappointments infected both the judge and the young people before him. A prime example was a July 1980 hearing of a youngster named Joey, who had appeared before Gladstone many times during the previous seven years. In the following scene, Judge Gladstone, only moments before, had transferred Joey to adult criminal court for trial.

One could appreciate Gladstone's frustration. Joey's first case back in 1973 involved the mother's boyfriend viciously beating him with a belt buckle. Gladstone declared the child dependent, sending both the mother and child to a psychiatric day-care program.

The daily two hour bus ride to reach the hospital for treatment wore their desire out. That didn't work. Nor did the series of programs that followed: a residential treatment program for Joey that included weekend visits home, several community-based behavior modification programs, followed by behavior restraint programs, finally State Reform School. All failed.

Poor Joey. Whatever Gladstone offered, Joey rejected. In the ensuing seven years, Joey averaged about two serious arrests a year, racking up four arrests for aggravated assault, a handful of larceny arrests, and a strong-arm robbery. Finally, the judge and the system gave up on Joey, sending him to criminal court to be tried as an adult.

At this, his final hearing in juvenile court, Judge Gladstone gave Joey an opportunity to speak out. The boy stated, "Since I've been nine years old I have been coming in front of you. You always take me away from my mama. You and the State, all you do is talk about programs, programs, programs. First you sent me to state school, then Montanari [a treatment center for teens]. I love my Momma more than anything else in the world. I want to be a boxer."

Gladstone reminded the boy that he had committed many crimes while in the custody of his mother. Gladstone asked Joey, "Don't you think a person doing this kind of stuff has to be placed where others will be safe?"

Joey responded, "I just told you I want to be a boxer. If I go to the adult system and catch some big time, I'm going to be a boxer anyway."

Judge Gladstone then tried to establish some mutual understanding with Joey, "I hope you find some way to make an honest living."

Joey answered, "No matter what you say, I'm going to be a boxer anyway."

The judge made a final effort. "You have to understand," he said, "I took you from your mother only because you were committing crimes."

Joey, shaking his head, had the last word, "Fighting ain't no crime. Everybody fights."

The Joey episode highlights the kind of futility often facing juvenile court judges. It is not true that every delinquent child can be saved. But there's no way of knowing who among those before you falls into the unsalvageable category. So, your job is to "save" all of them.

Dependency cases, are perhaps more frustrating for the judge. Here you have kids who are victims, not perpetrators of a crime. Yet in most instances they are less the beneficiaries of the State's attention. There was this case on Gladstone's calendar, a few days after Joey's appearance. It too had made its way to the *Miami Herald* pages.

A thirty-four-year-old grandmother had been evicted with her two children and a granddaughter. According to the story, her landlord said there were too many people in the tiny one-bedroom space, a violation of the occupancy law. The mother came before Gladstone asking that the three children be declared dependent so they would be entitled to have the State provide foster care housing for them.

Gladstone had to deny her request since a new law required that children be abused or neglected to be declared dependent. Poverty alone was not a valid reason. Had she beaten the children or denied them food, they would have been eligible for help. The mother earned a small salary as a bus driver and received a welfare check, none of which provided adequately for the four or enabled the rental of an apartment large enough to house them.

Abused and abandoned by her husband eight years ago, the mother couldn't make a go of it. A brother back from two years in the army in Germany had joined the family. He slept on the floor. Gladstone, aided by the social workers present, arranged for the infants to go to an emergency nursery shelter. What happens next for this family? Nobody knows for sure. The headline to the story: "JUDGE: 'I Felt Like Crying Over Plight of Family.'"

Then, in the same month of July 1980, there was the story of the eleven youths sleeping on the floor of the Dade County Youth Hall Intake Center. Due to a severe shortage of foster homes and shelter facilities, these boys, processed at the screening center as dependent children, were not allowed bed space at Youth Hall since they were not classified as delinquents. Ineligible to have a bed in Youth Hall, but sleeping in the anteroom on the floor was deemed acceptable.

Gladstone was livid at the hearing. Aware that the law properly prevented mixing of dependents and delinquents in Youth Hall, Gladstone ordered the dependents out of the Intake Center and directed HRS to find a proper placement for them. This, after these eleven dependent boys had spent almost a week being ignored, wandering around the premises, scrounging food from Youth Hall.

Marlyn Smith, HRS supervisor for direct services, stated, "The problem is we don't have enough shelter spaces for dependents. We have advertised for people to offer shelter beds and had stories in the newspapers, but we've gotten no response."

As a follow-up, Judge Gladstone instructed social workers to go before the legislature and ask them publicly, "What are you going to do with the atrocity you have created?" Frustration? Futility? Despair? All part of a day's work.

To maintain his own equilibrium, Gladstone poured it all out in his many public appearances. The U.S. Civil Rights Commission appearing in Miami that year heard from the judge in no uncertain terms.

> What do you expect a kid to grow up to be when the only successful person he knows is the pimp on the corner? A vote among our citizens would show a landslide for abolishing the juvenile justice system and simply put the offenders in jail for a long time.
>
> I don't think this community is concerned with juvenile offenders except that we dislike them and we are afraid of them. The conscience of the community is such that it simply does not want to take proper responsibility.
>
> Florida has one of the lowest funded social service systems in the country, and its citizens are among the lowest taxed people in the entire country.

That surely sounds like the proverbial angry man. Not one to mince words, William Gladstone mostly needed this outburst to appease his own soul. For a man struggling with the likes of Joey and helpless families and children with no resources, he absolutely had to let loose occasionally, telling it like it was.

The few examples cited here of a typical juvenile court calendar facing a judge probably suggests the need for frequent furloughs from the battle scene. Certainly for a judge as intense as Bill Gladstone, a cast-iron constitution, and an unflinching moral center are essentials. In 1982, when Governor Graham had drafted him for Tallahassee duty, Gladstone did receive a kind of reprieve that took him out of the battle zone. Not out of the war, but detached from the front lines.

One of the things that gnawed away at Gladstone's innards was the movement to limit the role of judges in the process of sending serious juvenile offenders to adult court for prosecution.

The movement had gained momentum in the 1970s as violent crime enveloped the nation, and as juvenile crime began to take on a more sinister turn. Prosecutors were in the forefront of gaining a new tool to properly punish these offenders despite their youth. They and a fearful community felt that the tough sanctions imposed in adult court were needed to stem the tide. The juvenile court philosophy was viewed as coddling the guilty young.

Bill Gladstone, hardly a coddler and not one averse to waiving a teenager for prosecution as an adult, was aghast at the destructive nature of the proposal. He spoke out forcefully for retention by juvenile court judges as to the decision to waive a child for trial in the criminal courts. His pleas were to no avail.

Dade County State Attorney Janet Reno, along with other prosecutors statewide, campaigned for the right to try serious offenders in criminal court, bypassing the juvenile court judge. The media editorialized, the public clamored for it, and it became the law of this State and most others.

It didn't, as Bill Gladstone had feared, "annihilate" the juvenile justice system, but it certainly did diminish the stature of the judges trying delinquency cases. Serious juvenile cases, usually committed by fifteen- to seventeen-year-olds, were quickly transferred to adult criminal court by the state attorney, leaving minor crimes of preteen-agers as the bulk of cases on the juvenile court calendar.

In one of several speeches Gladstone made on the subject, he strongly opposed this severe diminishing of judicial authority. He feared the unintended consequences and, speaking before the National College of Juvenile Justice in Phoenix, Arizona, spelled out the disastrous effect.

There he pointed out that 50 percent of juveniles transferred for adult trial were placed on probation or cases were dropped. In essence more severe punishment was provided in only few cases. Most county jails were not equipped to separate juveniles, nor did the criminal court have resources that were responsive to the rehab needs of children.

Mostly he lamented that this transfer to adult court, plus the Supreme Court *Gault* decision, had handcuffed the courts to an extent that the very purpose of a juvenile court was defeated. These and other changes had now infiltrated and weakened the court's operation in terms of addressing juvenile crime. He concluded that despite the strong movement of the court system toward a dependency model, nonetheless the delinquency concerns should not be shortchanged. This would be an ongoing debate in the years ahead.

That Bill Gladstone himself had slowly moved in the direction of the dependency side of the juvenile justice system did not diminish his concern over the delinquent side of the court. The parens patriae approach, heralded a century past, was to him still a glorious movement that encompassed all children in distress. The lessening of judicial authority in bind-over cases did not slow down or lessen his efforts.

With all of this swirling about, Gladstone maintained his sense of humor. This time in a cost-saving approach, to replace live court reporters with eight-track tape recorders. Chief Judge Gerald Wetherington chose the juvenile court for an experimental trial run. Judge Gladstone's courtroom was the designated site.

In the first trial using a tape recorder, defense lawyer Mike Gold, a supporter of live court reporters, offered a staunch defense of their cause. Gladstone, favoring the change, tartly dismissed Gold's defense saying, "The court reporters are aggrieved by the machine because it hits them right in the pocket. Had I been a blacksmith in the 1920s, I would have been awful angry about the people who invented the automobile."

Gladstone's sabbatical to Tallahassee for a year resulted in Chief Judge Gerald Wetherington naming me as his replacement as administrative judge in the Juvenile Division. Gone physically, but he was always on the phone calling about his projects, like a mother repeatedly calling the summer camp counselor about her child's well-being.

Gladstone's plan to develop closer ties between the local school boards and the juvenile justice system was not deterred by his Tallahassee sojourn. Though never gaining much public attention, this was a crucial element in addressing the totality of the problems facing a child in court system. Gladstone had no mechanism at the moment for creating this inter-relationship, but on his own he had already begun discussions with Dade County School Superintendent Leonard Britton on how to effectuate a closely knit partnership between the two most important Dade County government agencies involving the future of children.

The long time hands-off policy displayed by both was more than any rivalry or questions about privacy. Federal laws of privacy made releasing school information more onerous than disclosing the identity of a CIA undercover agent. Courts were also chary in terms of releasing information. Underneath it all was a slight distaste, and perhaps distrust, of the other's action in disciplining offenders. The result made for a total blanking out of any cooperative approach between the two systems.

Although Gladstone and I managed our respective projects so that neither interfered with the other, this was one in which we both jointly played significant roles. He had earlier initiated this project with Schools Superintendent Leonard Britton with some preliminary success. There still existed a large chasm between the two systems. For some reason, beyond the legal problems of two agencies sharing information, effective coordination had not been reached.

To resolve it, Gladstone, in a true flash of brilliance, had suggested to the Non-Group that he and Superintendent Leonard Britton be invited to one of their dinner meetings for a discussion of this problem. The Non-Group consisted of about a dozen and a half of Miami's top entrepreneurial and media elite. They ran the community; if not literally it was close. At least from their exalted view, so it seemed to them.

Although the membership names and their meeting sites as well as the subjects addressed were undisclosed to the public, theirs was not quite a secret organization. But certainly they operated behind the scenes. Their efforts were solely humanitarian of a do-gooder nature. This virtue was a kind of expiation for being so prosperous, smart, and possessing all a person could hope for in life.

An impressive group to appear before, they immediately took to Gladstone's idea for both systems opening up their resources to the other. The Non-Group offered whatever assistance necessary. Funding for new positions, lobbying for legislation, and, though unsaid, certainly relief from any critical news reporting should legal action ensue by a parent or group claiming violation of privacy rights. The involvement of these important public figures was sure to impress Superintendent Britton with the importance of this project.

Persuaded by the logic of this purpose and swayed by the power of this impressive group of Miami's finest, Britton and Gladstone thereupon agreed on setting up a pilot program covering four high schools (Miami Northwestern, Miami Central, Carol City, Southridge). These were selected for the high crime rate in those areas.

Britton immediately established the Dade County School Counseling Unit, assigning Johnny Stepherson and Gloria Burroughs as directors, the unit to function in the juvenile court building with joint consultation to aid those school children appearing for court action.

Today, virtually every child appearing in court has his or her school record included in the court file, and a school counselor available to advise the court as to how the school system can join the court to assist a delinquent or dependent child.

Stepherson and Burroughs, the two district liaison school officials, were housed in an office in the Juvenile Justice Building, and each of the four schools also supplied a contact officer on the school premises. The program purpose was to supply the court with all possible educational data on children appearing in court. Stepherson or Burroughs would appear in court with school records of defendants at the court disposition to aid the judge in decision making.

While this may not sound like some extraordinary feat, if the fact is considered that heretofore there had been absolutely no contact between the two systems, this was really a historic event. Now all other agencies dealing with children would realize that the school board and the juvenile court were a team, working hand in hand, setting an example.

It was a message worth broadcasting. Since those days all of Dade County has learned that communications between these government branches no longer is one of separation, but rather a joint community effort. At last, Gladstone's goal had been achieved.

Came Gladstone's departure for Tallahassee, the program functioned effectively during the two-year pilot period. Assistant Schools Superintendent Ludwig Gross, called Sonny, a childhood nickname that had stayed on, was assigned to oversee the project, which he did with skill and concern.

Gladstone called regularly from Tallahassee to inquire as to the progress and also wrote letters to Superintendent Britton on the subject. This had been a worthwhile and a successful program that gave juvenile court judges another weapon to determine how best to handle the myriad problems, including school concerns of children before them.

Of course, it was too good to be true, and here's where I entered the picture. Appearing before me on a case, Johnny Stepherson, the school board liaison, advised me that Assistant Schools Superintendent Gross had directed him to inform the court that the two-year pilot program had been completed and now would be terminated. "Scrap the program," had been the order from Gross, who had described it to Stepherson as a budget problem. My surmise was that perhaps the possibility of a privacy violation under federal law may have also convinced Britton to cancel.

Doing my best Gladstone imitation, I glared over my glasses at Stepherson and shouted, "What! No more school referrals? Are you mad?" Get me Sonny Gross on the phone immediately!" Gross was out of town.

Ordering Stepherson back to my chambers, I wanted a witness to my phone call to Superintendent Leonard Britton. I had no personal recollection of this conversation, but Stepherson, in a recent interview, reminded me of my end of the conversation. I had asked Britton, "What's this business about canceling our program? How can you do this?"

According to Stepherson, I was highly agitated, then calmed down, and at one point chuckled, indicating to him I was no longer angry. Finally I had said to Britton, in a quiet voice, "You can cut your budget dumb, or you can cut it smart. Why be dumb?" Then I added, "Leonard I'm going to sue the school board, so you govern yourself accordingly." End of conversation.

The next day Stepherson came into my courtroom, prepared to provide the originally requested information on the child before me. I asked why the change of heart. Gross had advised him thusly, "You do it. Let me worry about the government rules on privacy. I'll figure out a way."

One thing I had learned early as a judge, government agencies are absolutely fearful of a lawsuit threatened by a judge. Such an event automatically becomes a front-page story with the judge usually assuming the heroic role. In the bureaucracy, the official causing such action by a judge is generally looked upon with disfavor by his superiors. In this case it would be the Dade County Board of Public Instruction.

Britton, actually a fine leader of the school system, merely made some budget recalculations, and we were back in business. He followed up by enlarging the program, making it countywide, and adding four more liaison members to Stepherson's staff.

In turn, we enlarged their office space in our building, providing adequate room for their full complement. The program blossomed, becoming an integral part of the court process at every stage of a Hearing where school records were significant. Individual programs were devised using rehab resources available from both the court and the school system.

While Gladstone was still in Tallahassee, we both, at different times, traveled to the Okeechobee Training School in Central Florida to work out coordinating problems for inmates getting proper credit back in Dade County for completing classes at Okeechobee.

Transfers from one school to another always had caused accreditation problems based on the different grading systems, the number of credits earned, and hours of attendance at each school. Surprisingly, small details like this had caused great dissension among returnees who, after finally agreeing to attend classes at reform school, now upon coming home were not receiving proper credit.

Together, he and I along with the school authorities in Dade County and Okeechobee Training School worked out a system permitting the training school students to get full credit for their work while incarcerated. Only a big deal for the kids, but our reputation as Judges had been enhanced with them.

A primary effort in Tallahassee for Gladstone was creating the Governor's Constituency for Children. This was another grand-design program. Gladstone always went for the big ones. The goal was to promote and unify private and public efforts to meet the needs of children under one powerful roof. A networking process bringing together all the private civic groups and the public agencies to speak with one voice.

It would have both a grassroots representation and influential private groups along with government leaders. The state council to be headed by the governor, and the local county council selected by each county commission.

This was the predecessor to the Children Services Councils and eventually to today's Children's Trust in Dade County, now headed by David Lawrence. Counterparts exist in other parts of the state. This was the first time such a statewide effort had been made bringing together leaders of both the public and private sectors. Gladstone, with the strong arm of Governor Graham behind him, was able to make it happen.

Gladstone had also been appointed to the U.S. Commission on Accreditation for Corrections and traveled throughout the country visiting juvenile detention facilities. David Bazelon, a federal court of appeals judge, one of the eminent jurists of his day, served on the commission with Gladstone, and both had become fast friends.

Interestingly, he and Judge Bazelon had a public disagreement over Bazelon's criticizing the commission for not having a member of the public on board, and as well for cronyism—"intraprofessionalism back-scratching" as Judge Bazelon put it.

It wasn't that Gladstone totally disagreed with Bazelon, but he viewed the debate as distracting from the commission's true purpose. Our Bill Gladstone didn't seek controversy; it came to him naturally. But he didn't duck it no matter the stature of the opposition. He and Bazelon worked that one out too.

While in Tallahassee, still smarting from the new direct-file law, eliminating judge's from the process, he also instituted an HRS study to determine how sixteen- and seventeen-year youth sent directly to adult court had affected the delinquency rate. Apparently, the state attorney in District 1 (Pensacola) had been the leading supporter of bypassing the juvenile court judges.

The study found that District 1 direct files were at a rate far greater than all the other districts and several times higher than the state average rate. The study concluded that the drop in delinquency throughout the state bore no relationship to the rate of transfer to the adult criminal court.

Gladstone then copied not only the District 1 Pensacola state attorney but everyone in Florida even remotely involved in corrections and juvenile justice, including the governor. That study had made little difference on the issue, but Gladstone insisted on letting his adversaries know they were wrong. Leaving Miami for Tallahassee, Gladstone sure hadn't abandoned his feisty approach.

Also as part of his sojourn in Tallahassee, our leader was one of a group of five Dade County criminal justice experts visiting Bogotá, Colombia, in a Sister City Program to provide technical assistance and exchange information on street crime. Although these are generally junkets, Gladstone took it seriously, writing a five-page report outlining his effort.

He not only presented Bogotá leaders with many papers he had written on the subject as well as his testimony before the U.S. Senate Committee, but also put them in touch with psychologists who had designed his Jean Piaget study describing the different morality standards among delinquent youth. No matter his destination, Gladstone was ever the teacher and recruiter.

Tallahassee in early 1980s was still a slow, slow town. Obviously, Tallahassee hadn't slowed our Bill down, at all. He got around OK, making a splash with all the programs he introduced. Judge Gladstone was more than a one-man dynamo, spreading his arrows wherever he saw a need for children. He recognized that while an independent high-wire act was impressive, he needed to work through established reputable organizations to give more credibility to his findings and aims.

Early on in his career, his vehicle had been the Dade County Mental Health Association (DCMHA) in which he had served as president, and later it was the National Council of Juvenile and Family Court Judges (NCJFCJ).

For the DCMHA he had chaired a study in 1974 on "Mental Health Needs of Young Persons.". Follow-up reports were issued by that agency in 1978 and 1980. Gladstone knew whereof he spoke. As a result he campaigned vigorously against the four-year efforts of HRS and the state legislature, beginning in 1983, to separate minors from adults in state mental hospitals.

Instead, the legislature sought to place them in small homelike facilities. The problem with separating them, unlike the situation with foster children, was the lack of special mental health resources to address those specific needs. Once placed in private homes, these children needing special attention became long forgotten.

In a 1982 letter to HRS, he cited data showing the absolute need for hospital beds for the mentally disturbed children, and the failure of HRS and the state legislature to provide same. In typical Gladstone fashion, he said,

> I find it outrageous to deny residential care to children in need, in the name of separating children from adults. There are some fourteen children in Dade County who have been on the waiting list for up to six months. Some, extremely disturbed, represent a significant danger to themselves and to others.

This, of course, had been solely the sate hospital's cost-cutting measure, which among other approaches aimed at cutting down the numbers, also made admission of children more stringent. Gladstone made it clear he was not opposed to separating children and placing them in less-restrictive surroundings. But he made it clear the failure to provide adequate hospital bed space was an "abomination." As always he copied the governor, HRS director, and legislative leaders. No shrinking violet, he was ready for all responders.

The next session of the Florida Legislature (1983) indecisively neither cut more beds for children at mental hospitals nor added any, but they acted with certainty and dispatch in cutting many other HRS resources. The *Miami Herald* headline read "Cuts Imperil Gatekeepers of Child Abuse System."

In a million-and-a-half-dollar budget slicing, the legislature had eliminated as many as 23 of the 84 Dade County intake counselors. They are the first to come into contact with delinquents as well as child abuse dependency cases. There were some really stunned reactions from both Judge Gladstone and Marlyn Smith, head of the Dade Intake Section for HRS.

> JUDGE GLADSTONE: We are talking about the very heart of the system. When Intake breaks, the whole system is enormously challenged. The irony is that Intake screening works to save the State money.
>
> MARLYN SMITH: It's really upsetting. We've spent three years working to get quality service in abuse and neglect. But that's going to go down the drain if we lose all those positions.

No despair, Gladstone, still with some clout in Tallahassee, called David Pingree, state HRS head, who then cut our possible loss of intake counselors down from twenty-three to ten. Is that a victory? You bet. Beggars can't be choosers.

Gladstone and I, in the midst of our own permanent hopelessness, bordering on surrender, often came up with exchanging memos satirizing the system. Never published in the press, it was merely to provide a chuckle for our own relief. These missiles were only for our view and maybe one or two fortunate colleagues.

I liked the 1984 one Gladstone sent me in response to a request by the Criminal Justice Council (CJC) for approval of a study to determine the link between drug use and criminal conduct of juveniles.

Dr. Jeffrey Silbert, CJC executive director (I was the chair of CJC), had advised me he sought to do a sample of urine from one hundred detained youth. The data collected will be presented to the community as aggregated totals, thereby not jeopardizing the privacy of the individual youth.

Gladstone's memo response to me: "With reference to the foregoing I most observe: A. Dr. Silbert is going to need one hell of a big bottle!; B. Somehow I doubt that the community would really want the 'aggregated total' or for that matter, any part thereof, 'presented' to it.; C. I fear that the federal auditors of this research will accuse your local Council of 'P . . . ing away federal dollars.'" (I have noticed that federal agencies tend to delete or edit expletives in this fashion.)

That's a good one, Bill. Now here's mine.

HRS, in 1983, going through another one of their reorganizations, began using matrix formulations to ease the problems new counselors had in recommending sentences at disposition hearings. This was before mandatory-minimum sentencing laws were put in place.

Always having been a supporter of judicial discretion in decision making, I thought the last place for a sentencing matrix was in juvenile court. I thereupon sent a memo to my fellow judges explaining, tongue in cheek, the matrix.

> Matrix historically has an honorable lineage. During the Punic Wars, a Greek General, by name of Matrixolus, was able to overcome the siege of Athens by utilizing his far outnumbered forces in a configuration that absolutely befuddled the invading Romans.
>
> Matrix in its use here, is a very complex mathematical formulation designed to determine how many hours of public service a child on Community Control must serve.
>
> It appears to be the length of time the offense could have brought, multiplied by the number of arrests, divided by the child's age plus the number of prior adjudications.
>
> This approach while not precisely in line with the formula used by General Matrixolus is close enough. For a long time now the Court operation has been looking for some new course that can turn the system around. This may be it!

When word of my satirical memo got to the HRS counselors, embarrassed, they declined to offer the matrix in cases in my court. However, in due time, they courageously came forward with matrix in hand. And good soldier that I am, I followed their recommendations. Can't beat the system. Bureaucracy reigns, as ever. Matrix will take over the world.

In 1986 things did change. Not substantively, but a change of administration. A Republican had been elected governor, and Linda Berkowitz, past HRS administrator in Dade, was replaced. New state HRS head Gregory Coler's record showed success in the child welfare field in other jurisdictions. It made little difference, except that Gladstone's connection with Governor Graham and the HRS officials was now a thing of the past, and Republican administrations were not likely to favor heavily Democratic Dade County.

The plight of the children never left. A traveling state legislative panel came and heard Gladstone say that he is "heartsick" over having to make the same appeal for over ten years. Linda Berkowitz, deposed as local HRS head only days before, stated, "Turnover is high; half the division's caseworkers have been on the job less than a year, and they are expected to make life and death decisions for children and families in disrepair."

Ms. Berkowitz called on the legislators to give support to the new HRS administration. Positioned in the front row as an observer, the new state HRS head, Greg Coler, sat impassively. The legislators made no promises. One, speaking for all simply said, "I'm not sure more taxes is the answer." We got the message.

The new state HRS head had grand plans to improve the system. Coler's past success in the Chicago juvenile system obtaining adequate funding from the Illinois legislature had made him optimistic. His program plans were impressive: install a central state abuse hotline, introduce a new statewide computer system, improve the skimpy admission forms now in use, and keep the same counselor on each case from intake through disposition. No way a Republican administration could really have such inspiring goals. Sounded good. We'll see.

Coler's major deficit was that he had little to work with. The system was still marking time in the same posture as in the past. HRS had little credibility in producing positive results, and juvenile judges were seen by the public as coddling bad kids.

It made little difference that a U.S. Department of Justice study found that of those juveniles transferred to and found guilty in adult court of serious felony crimes, few suffered heavy punishment. Most get probation or counseling and were ordered to make restitution. Or, as happened, too many were let go. Hardly hopeful. New HRS head Greg Coler had a long way to go. Eventually, all his high hopes went to naught.

Gladstone, seeing the handwriting on the wall for delinquency in the Dade County Juvenile Court, slowly continued his move toward the dependency area. He was not the only one. Chief Judge Gerald Wetherington, also concerned over the rise of dependency, called on Gladstone to conduct a study on the plight of the dependent child.

Apparently, both the United Way and the League of Women Voters had also commissioned major studies on this situation, with their findings soon to be released. In addition, Metropolitan Dade County had recently completed its own study, and Lester Langer, a member of the Bar and a juvenile court practitioner, also had written his own analysis of the problem. The move was on.

Gladstone's study titled "A Cry For Help" had as the opening line: "Florida's system of child welfare is a disgrace." He didn't let up on his assault the rest of the way. The other studies also castigated the failure of government to take action and criticized community indifference to the problem.

The rising concern among agencies involved with children suggested that the children's dependency movement was now about to begin traveling at a high speed in a forward direction. That may be, but where there is no strong, almost irresistible force clamoring for new action, sometimes what seems like a hurricane turns out to be only a windy day.

All the reports, as well as the practitioners in the children's field, recognized the irrefutable evidence that the first step toward delinquent behavior was absolutely tied to an earlier dependency situation. The abused, neglected, abandoned child grew into the delinquent child. This new emphasis will not give up on the delinquent child, but rather go to the root causes. Approaching a dependent child early on was the best way to prevent grooming a delinquent.

Interestingly, State Attorney Janet Reno, once a leading voice for direct filing on serious juvenile delinquents in adult court, now became a strong advocate for early intervention. Advocates in the field began preaching prebirth medical involvement in terms of cocaine babies and infants suffering from other ailments. There was a bandwagon, and Reno and others were on it. The time was now.

Gladstone, always with an affinity for dependent children, now appeared to be accelerating his focus on them. It had all begun when Gladstone had ruled that HRS social workers could not process a dependency case in his court—"practicing law without a license," he had charged. That had come to the fore in the late 1980s.

Gladstone heard a case involving Rhonda, a seventeen-year-old prostitute. Rhonda's case wasn't unusual. She had been in contact with the system ten times since twelve years of age. Mostly dependency neglect cases, sexual abuse, truancy, but never any delinquent act, each time referred to an HRS agency. Then after some counseling, case closed. Only a few of the counselors knew anything about her. Her activity file had been lost along the way, only an arrest printout remaining.

The judge inquired of HRS attorney Laurie Ramsey about the lost file. "What's the problem?"

She responded, "It could have been lost anywhere along the line."

Gladstone followed up with, "Is it likely each time she was here she saw a different counselor, maybe ten altogether?"

Ramsey said, "Very likely."

"Had she had an attorney representing her each time in court?" asked the Judge.

"I don't believe so" was Ramsey's response.

That little interchange said a lot. Perhaps too much. Remember, this was years after *Gault* had provided counsel for all delinquency cases.

Five days later, Rhonda, now in lockup, was scheduled to again appear before Judge Gladstone, but hadn't been brought out. Gladstone impatient, he and his bailiff went back to get her. She came out smiling, telling two people on the way in, "My judge came to get me." For the first time Rhonda was happy. Someone cared about her. Still, no attorney present for her.

Gladstone tried to find a placement for her. First choice: a drug-treatment program, but no space. Next choice: a forty-five-day hospital rehab program. Maybe she'll be admitted. Call the next case.

The absence of lawyers to defend in dependency cases had troubled Gladstone immeasurably, but he bided his time to take action. The resolution came about in an almost routine manner. Again involved was the child Rhonda and lawyer Laurie Ramsey. Dependent child Rhonda had no lawyer since Ramsey, the only state dependency lawyer, was in another courtroom on a similar case.

Gladstone, in one of his electric moves, struck quickly. Using the Rhonda case as the basis for his move, he demanded and ordered Ramsey to appear in his court for this cases or suffer contempt charges. Obviously, as Gladstone well knew, she could only appear in one court at a time. By this act, Gladstone had decreed that dependent as well as delinquent children were entitled to counsel in court hearings. At least in Dade County.

In the past, to cover the deficiency of the absent lawyer, HRS counselors would seek waivers of consent from parents who were party to a dependency hearing. These waivers permitted the hearing to proceed without legal representation for the parent.

Surprisingly, rather than appeal Gladstone's "Lawyer Ramsey" ruling to the Third District, HRS had agreed to abide by a Florida Bar Advisory Committee decision on the issue. It may have been their timidity in taking appeals from judicial decisions, or more likely they were tired of being short of lawyers and silently supported Gladstone's concern.

Nonetheless, the HRS agency argued before the Florida Bar that a dependency did not rise to being a contested case until the parent disputed the final ruling of the court. Therefore, there was no issue requiring counsel for the parent. Gladstone's response: "There's damn well a contest when they come and take your kids away in the middle of the night. Even the best of what HRS does is inadequate."

Gladstone won that one in a walk. The Florida Bar, ruling in Gladstone's favor, forced the Florida Legislature to provide funds for lawyers in each court at dependency hearing. For dependents, the Lawyer Ramsey ruling was equivalent to the *Gault* decision in terms of providing legal counsel for parents or custodians of dependents. Gladstone, absent any serious contest or fanfare, had won a significant victory, unheralded as it was.

It signaled Gladstone's full movement to the dependent child. Gladstone had struggled mightily in the past to establish separate dependency courts and professional dependency units which slowly would now begin to develop. Before that it was akin to the situation in delinquency that the *Gault* decision had remedied. Gladstone's action fixed that for dependent children.

From this fortuitous event flowed creation of special courts for dependency and court support services (see chapter "Activists Are Many Among Us": Charles Edelstein). Now, with lawyers present at the onset, no longer would dependency cases be virtually ignored or hurried and heard at the end of the day as a poor relative of delinquency cases. To suggest that this scenario was all a well-planned effort by Gladstone, with the complicity of HRS to force the State to provide lawyers early on probably, is an overstatement. He pleads the Fifth Amendment on that, neither denying nor confirming.

Creating a dependency court was a fine accomplishment, but making it work required a structure far different than that imposed on the delinquency side. On one side are alleged violators of the criminal law, but here we have abused, neglected children who in many instances were the victims of crimes imposed upon them. The treatment process required a lot more sensitivity and care for these often-preyed-upon children.

It became evident that the State's ability to find housing for dependent children was a crucial area. Providing a foster home, however, was to be but the first step, not the final one. Someone needed to oversee the process, making certain that fairness toward the child was displayed in every step of the process and that the government overseers performed appropriately.

From this need, the Foster Care Review Project was born in 1989 as required by a federal law passed in 1980. Operating under an order from Administrative Judge Gladstone, citizen panels were established, five volunteers to a panel, meeting monthly to evaluate the foster child's current placement environment, and to make findings and recommendations to the judge.

Foster Care staff specialists collected data, recorded and examined the reasons for keeping kids in the foster care system, and wrote reports for the judges. The Foster Care Review team, consisting of staff and citizen volunteers, did the research and preparation that enabled prompt and accurate decisions to be made by the court.

The United Way spearheaded the project designed to enhance the quality of life for the 1,880 children then in foster care. Since inception, over 450 citizen volunteers have already been trained to date to review the cases of thirty-five thousand children and make recommendations to the court. Rarely has a judge rejected a Foster Care Review recommendation.

A dozen citizens were founding board members. Judge William Gladstone was the founding judge and one of the planners along with Berta Blecke, Joni Goodman, and others. Virtually unnoticed in the court operation and rarely in the media, these citizens labor tirelessly in their support of the children and the court system.

Today (2007), under the stewardship of Judge Cindy Lederman, the dependency court is a model operation. Lawyers are available, counselors are there for their role, and the judges are full-time dependency judges. No longer are dependency cases a kind of afterthought.

Judge Lederman deserves credit for later upgrading the process to an extent none of us could have predicted. Nonetheless, had it not been for Judge Gladstone's advocacy and unremitting struggles, the opportunity to further enhance would have been considerably limited. Gladstone laid the groundwork for many of the estimable accomplishments of his successor, Judge Cindy Lederman.

In fairness to all the judges, going back to our first one, Judge W. H. Penney, each of them going down the line added a piece to the development of the juvenile court. No one of them had an easy time, but none took it more to heart and absorbed the distress as did William Gladstone, nor for that matter did any add more pieces to putting together the jigsaw puzzle.

The years neither dimmed nor discouraged him. Burnout was a natural result that influenced all the judges but Gladstone always, when things seemed overwhelming, managed to dig down and find the means to revitalize himself. Always some new project seemed to energize him, and he would rise to the front. The guy doted on challenges.

In 1988 Gladstone participated in an unusual project at Harvard University, Kennedy School of Government. Sponsored by the U.S. Attorney General's Office of Juvenile Justice, some of the brightest minds in America representing all the disciplines involving children were gathered together to think. The group goal was to brainstorm the future for children in America. No way our mountain-climber Bill Gladstone would pass this one by. Dr. Mark Moore, a Harvard Law School professor, was the organizer of this project.

Included in the group of thirty-four were leading criminologists, sociologists, psychiatrists, researchers, and four juvenile court judges selected from the most prolific and wisest across the breadth of America. Just being among them was an honored position. Our Bill Gladstone was one of them. They met regularly for eighteen months. Gladstone described the sessions:

> These were some of the most creative, innovative talents in the field. Some of a conservative viewpoint, others would take contrary views.

They debated with such vigor that it became apparent no consensus would ever be reached as to the direction that might lead to resolving the plight of children. Everyone had a strong opinion and none would yield to a consensus view.

Since we were created to offer some resolution of the problem, and a book of our conclusions was to be printed, Professor Moore, our leader, resolved the problem by inviting each participant to submit an essay of his or her views. That became the lead volume.

Professor Moore then printed a volume representing his view of what he thought the consensus might or should be. An amalgam of the thought presented, as filtered through the mind of Professor Mark Moore.

Gladstone, honored at the invitation to participate found the experience mind opening. Joining in with the best minds of America was a challenge. Discovering that their views didn't vary too much from the local Miami output was in a sense reassuring.

Very wisely, our Bill declined the opportunity to pen an essay; instead he outlined his views to Professor Moore and was rather pleased when Moore's volume came out, and in prominent display were many of the ideas Gladstone had offered.

On occasion during that year and a half, I would inquire, and Bill would tell me of some of their discussions. I envied him. At the end, reading their individual conclusions, I wondered why they had spent all that time in discussion when delivering one of their classroom lectures would have sufficed.

Gladstone thought the interaction among all these bright minds was worth gathering them together. Never said it to him, but I thought—what a waste! Bringing the best minds of America on the subject to meet for a year and a half with virtually no consensus on anything sends a bad, bad message. But still it was a great experience for Bill.

There's a lesson to be learned here, but what it may be is questionable. I suppose the best way is the hard way. It takes individuals like Gladstone (and Lederman and Petersen, et al.) to go out there and struggle through the morass with new ventures, hoping for the smallest of answers. Nothing comes easy in this business of children in distress.

Though not being a politician, Gladstone was asked in 1990 to lead the Transition Task Force on Juvenile Justice for governor-elect Lawton Chiles. The report confirmed Gladstone's progression toward early intervention, dependency, and as well directions to prevent delinquency.

It was a nine-page recitation, carefully crafted on what needed to be done. Omitting rhetoric, no pontificating, it concisely introduced the problem, "The juvenile justice system, especially in Florida is so strained that it commonly fails. Cocaine babies, the drug dealing economy, violence and AIDS threaten the survival of the system."

The report focused on prevention, not punishment. It had that Gladstone touch, pointing to diverting children and their families from the court system. "Scores of thousands of Florida's children and their families are presently brought to Court—when diversionary programs would be more effective." The report urged the new administration to involve families and neighborhoods in the planning process and to de-emphasize the adversarial system in court.

Gladstone hadn't abandoned his role to fight crime by bettering the delinquency system. Instead there was full recognition on his and the task force's approach that addressing the needs of the child, long before the first arrest, was the route to take.

This was an unshrinking statement, considering that it was a political document, and both the concerns of the public and certainly the Florida Legislature were still focused on punishing miscreants. The report emphasized Gladstone's focus on the rising recognition that the juvenile court must begin to move in directions other than delinquency, most particularly toward the dependent child.

Gladstone, now as an elder statesman, continued his advisory role to heads of state government. A year later, in 1991, as a member of the State Study Commission on Child Welfare, chaired by Supreme Court Justice Rosemary Barkett, their report was a replay of Gladstone's transition-team effort of the year before. Justice Barkett summed it up in her introduction to the report:

> We do not need any more reports. Everyone knows the problems and ironically many of the solutions. We see the results of our neglect every day. Prevention is cheaper than the cure. Thus money spent now for education, prenatal, and other preventive healthcare services will save many dollars later. For example, half the beds in Jackson Memorial Hospital are filled because of our failure in this regard.

Justice Barkett said it well. A former juvenile judge in Broward County, her understanding of the situation was well-founded. Judge Gladstone, serving on that commission, surely said amen to her words.

The man never did lose his sense of humor. Later that year when selected for one of the *Miami Herald*'s Spirit of Excellence Awards, he contacted two of the other selectees, Wayne Huizenga and Armando Codina. Tongue in cheek, he offered, "Since these awards are based on a sense of community, I want to suggest we pool our incomes next year and divide up the total equally." These are two of the wealthiest entrepreneurs in Florida, with Gladstone a man of modest means. Both chuckled at Gladstone's overtures but made no commitment.

The news in November 1992 that Gladstone was retiring from the bench came as a shock to many. Twenty years of valiant struggle was over. But was it? He was bound for Washington, D.C., to work on Senator Bob Graham's staff to help develop national programs for children.

Said Gladstone, in his usual assertive pose, "I can now assist someone in a position to make a difference—a United States senator who gives a damn! He's got a lot more opportunity to make a change than I do as a judge." That was no pose. Once again, as they had been in the past, Gladstone's flags were flying, and he was raring to go.

My comment to the newspaper on his departure: "I always viewed him as the finest juvenile court judge in the country. Struggling beside him for fifteen years was a joy. He has a fertile mind for developing concepts. We may see some high-quality programs for children come out of Washington."

The *Miami Herald* also editorialized in glowing fashion. "May this estimable Juvenile Division Judge, a tireless crusader for the rights, health and well-being of children find as receptive a cheering section in Washington, D.C. as developed in Dade. His good works and clarity of decision deserve it. So do the nation's children."

He had committed for only one year, and my experience dealing with Washington (as mayor of Miami Beach at that tine) was that nothing worthwhile could emerge in that short period of time. But then again, this was Bill Gladstone.

On a trip to Washington attending a mayor's conference with wife Edith, we visited him one evening. These were the coldest, rainiest, ice-covered streets we had ever encountered. Finally able to get a cab and navigating safely through the foot-high water-logged streets, we arrived safely. Shaking myself free of the ice and seeing that Edith was safe, I asked Bill, "How can you take it here in this godforsaken place?"

His answer, "I'm doing what I love to do, and I'll stay to the finish." And that he did. He instituted the new federal Youth Environmental Program (YES) working with U.S. Attorney General Janet Reno, recently appointed to that post.

Despite my misgivings that a year was far too short to accomplish anything worthwhile in Washington, Gladstone persisted. He was the kind of guy who wed himself to a mission. He was convinced honesty and goodness are always rewarded. In his bones he really believed he could overcome both Washington politics and the bureaucracy hurdles. Also, he was a pretty smart guy, and his plan was really doable.

He tied his YES to two already-existing Florida operations—the Florida Environmental Institute's (FEI) Last Chance Ranch in Fisheating Creek and the Associated Marine Institute. In both programs he had played major roles in their creation. No dummy, this Bill Gladstone. He also enlisted his old Miami friend Attorney General Reno to personally become involved in the project.

I always had viewed Gladstone as an ideas man supreme, never the managerial type or one particularly adept at traversing the Washington bureaucracy. Creating a major program in one year? Impossible.

YES was truly a notable effort. On February 18, 1994, invitations went out for the dedication from hosts U.S. Attorney General Janet Reno, U.S. Senator Bob Graham, U.S. Secretary of the Interior Bruce Babbitt, and Florida Governor Lawton Chiles, inviting one and all to the Big Cypress National Preserve for the event. Hard to get a more impressive list of political dignitaries.

A map on the back of the invitation described the location. Somewhere between Alligator Alley and the Gulf of Mexico, off the Tamiami Trail, was this seventy-thousand-acre Big Cypress National Preserve, and within its confines was the five-acre YES site.

The program, patterned after FEI's Last Chance Ranch in Florida, also designed by Gladstone, had a hard-work approach with an added emphasis on improving the environment. Six additional sites had been selected in other national parks. Attorney General Reno, who had contributed her Office of Juvenile Justice as a partner in the venture, opened the ceremonies on the right note, stating,

> We have messed up the children of America for the last thirty or forty years. We have been too indifferent to them. We've messed up our environment. We've messed up the Everglades.
>
> We are here today to recognize that we can make a difference with our two most prized possessions.

For Reno it was a done deal. Her aide, Shay Bilchik, administrator of the Office of Juvenile Justice, had printed a handsome fifty-page booklet describing YES and the manner of support his agency would provide. Bilchik, a long time prosecutor in our Dade County Juvenile Court before joining Reno in Washington, had looked upon Gladstone as one of his mentors. No problem there.

Each of the other important speakers added to the potential of this new enterprise for children. Senator Bob Graham, the sponsor, had introduced a Senate resolution of support, adopted November 18, 1993, that would formalize this camp and the others to follow. Senator Graham, describing his interest, said, "Even young people considered serious delinquents can turn their lives around given a situation that includes hard work, education, and counseling." He added, "We have proven at FEI, that meaningful hard work along with education will change young people's values and give them greater self-confidence."

U.S. Secretary of the Interior Bruce Babbitt, administrator of our national parks offered this observation: "This reminds me of the Civilian Conservation Corps that FDR started in the 1930s. What an obvious idea. Why haven't we come to it more quickly?"

Congressman Porter Goss, the lone Republican among all the Democrat officials present, and representing his constituents in the home county of the park, congratulated this effort saying that crime is the problem foremost in the minds of Americans, and the YES offers hope for a solution.

Wally Hubbard, superintendent of Big Cypress Park, announced that after an environmental assessment and obtaining proper permits from the State, construction will begin in July, probably lasting for several months. Hubbard said the youths will help eradicate exotic plants dangerous to Florida's sensitive ecosystem, and other environmental programs will be introduced.

Each of the lead speakers made the point that this was not a traditional boot camp, modeled after the military basic infantry training. The boot-camp model, once acclaimed by the public, has recently (2006) been under considerable criticism due to lack of expected results and some harsh treatment of offenders. YES used more of a "tough love" approach that required hard work, discipline, yet with a worthy goal and a tender hand.

If ever there was a program with wheels greased for success, this was it. Funded by the State of Florida HRS, the need for such additional programs was apparent. Costwise modest, it was certain to obtain considerable support from the Clinton Democratic administration in Washington and Governor Lawton Chiles in Tallahassee. With all that weight behind it, it had to be a go.

It was, but let me tell you in Bill Gladstone's own words, in a telephone interview ten years later, how nothing goes down easy in Washington.

> The resolution establishing the program, offered by Senator Bob Graham, was in a committee chaired by Senator Herb Kohl, a Democrat from Wisconsin. He was a supporter, so I saw no problem.
>
> Sitting in Graham's office, I got a call from the Senate floor that a hold had been put on my resolution. Any senator can delay the consideration of a proposal for an indeterminate time, usually long enough to kill it.
>
> I went berserk. After working for a year on this program, and now to watch it die like this was more than I could take. I raced down to the Senate chambers, thrust open the doors, saw Kohl standing there and started to shout at him.
>
> At that moment I was excited and angry. As an aide to Bob Graham, I had floor privileges, but I suddenly realized that I had raised my voice to a high decibel in the most hallowed of halls, addressing a United States senator in a most unseemly manner.
>
> Senator Kohl recognizing my faux pas and my discomfort over my outburst, smiled, then reassured me that the hold had been removed.

YES flourished. At the end of Gladstone's one-year stay, twenty-six were on the drawing board, six were operational, including two others in Florida, one in Utah, and another in Washington, D.C. All in national parks with an environmental approach. Patterned after FEI's Last Chance Ranch, they included programs for hard-core offenders, but as well special programs for kids under age ten (Washington, D.C.).

When in recent years Gladstone had looked, the funding seemed to be evaporating. He doubted very much that it has a much longer shelf life, what with budget deficits looming and cutting of social programs sure to be a first priority. Nor did he seem particularly distressed about this likely outcome, fully realizing that political considerations often trump worthy purposes.

Gladstone understands that gaining acceptance of these kinds of programs in the federal establishment was, in itself, a substantial gain. The foothold gained would offer other opportunities in other circumstances under succeeding administrations. This was a struggle that would continue long after his day.

Continuing our conversation about the YES, I stated that in my view his work on it had been magnificent. He responded that he hoped my review of his work wouldn't become a puff piece. I assured him of my absolute objectivity.

Funny fellow, that Gladstone. He surmised I was about to paint him as some heroic figure, while he viewed himself as simply a man doing his job. A job that demanded fighting for children. He was correct in how I intended to portray him. He filled a much larger role than the traditional judge performing the duties of the bench.

We continued our discussion, going on to elaborate on those fifteen years we had worked side by side as colleagues, not only sharing the administrative responsibilities of the Juvenile Division, but also sharing the goal of activism that both of us strongly followed. He and I recounted with relish how we both took on projects, never crossing the line into the other's pursuit.

Over the years we had talked a lot about the administrative concerns dealing with other agencies, but always there had been this unsaid understanding that our individual projects never received more that a cursory comment. We each had received substantial press coverage for these individual pursuits, which ordinarily might create a competitive situation. Somehow, luckily, that never marred our relationship.

Never a cross word or evidence of annoyance or envy, always only appreciation honoring the other's effort. Our lines of demarcation were clear. The amazing part, we never had discussed or enumerated them. I don't think either one of us gave the subject a lot of thought. It was simply a mutual respect. Can't ask for anything more.

We even went so far as to avoid attending public speeches of the other or discussing op-ed pieces we each had authored. This was more than staying out of each others way. We were so familiar with the others output, and since time is always a factor, we gave each other the license of avoidance. It made our efforts a lot easier.

This longer-than-usual phone conversation (Gladstone goes in only for quick-to-the-point conversations) was the first time we ever had such a discussion in the fifteen years serving together and the subsequent years after we both had retired as full-time judges.

Like two old major-league baseball players reliving their glory days in the big leagues, he reminded me how we had struggled with the HRS bureaucracy, the failure of the Florida Legislature, and as well of some of the excellent colleagues of the past, and the few not so excellent. Mostly we doted on how supportive we had been of each other's efforts.

He pointed out how Chief Judge Gerald Wetherington had aided us extensively in furtherance of our projects. Wetherington, as chief judge and ranking Executive in charge of all the circuit court divisions, opened many doors and minds. Over the years he had gained considerable clout with both county and state officials, and his support opened up the coffers for innovative new programs. A supporter of activist judges, friendly to both of us, his weight added considerably to our offerings. Along with our own mutual support, these factors underlined, encouraged, and actually enabled whatever success attained.

Our phone chat was a lovefest long overdue. He filled me in on all the blank spots needed for his chapter in my book, again cautioning me to avoid any superlatives in describing his effort. As well he made certain to remind me not to omit the many good deeds I had performed. Mutual admiration society? You bet, but total pleasure.

Here we were, two old codgers, I, eighty-six years old; he, ten years younger. He, telling me his pacemaker was acting erratically; I, informing him I was off to the hospital for a hernia surgery in a few days. Both, fortunate indeed to have had the other close by along the difficult way.

To make progress, activist judges need considerable support from their judicial colleagues. Even if not in total agreement with the goals of the erstwhile crusader, the more traditional judges need to be, if not as cheerleaders, some form of sustaining force. The fellow taking the risk of going outside the norm deserves the opportunity, unhindered by fellow co-workers.

Power holders in the system are also essential Media support can proclaim the essence of a program to readers or impose a death knoll. Journalists of our era were quick to distinguish a public-relations effort from the real thing. I was received well at both the *Miami Herald* and the *Miami News*, but William Gladstone was the poster boy for all the media. Not only was his, at times, flamboyant style great copy for the readers, but his sincerity so genuine that many of the reporters were real-life fans of his work.

Toward the end of the conversation, I offered the observation that he sounded tired, worn-out. He replied, saying he'd been on the move attending meetings in several states, just arriving last night from Atlanta. It was typical Gladstone. Then and now always on an airplane, attending a NCJCJ meeting in some boondocks town, or appearing on a national TV show. Wherever the call came from, he was there.

I added some advice. "Slow yourself down; the juvenile justice system will make it without you or me." There was a pause, and then he said, "I'm sure of that, but I want to make sure, I have input all the way." He didn't utter those words as a challenge, just matter-of-factly. Not dispirited, only tired for the moment. That's the kind of person he is. He'll be floating ideas, recommending programs until his last breath.

Finally, setting the phone down, I told him I thought he had been the outstanding jurist of the juvenile court's eighty-five years of existence. Barely acknowledging my praise, he replied: "Wait until you write Cindy Lederman's chapter; then you'll see the real star of the century."

Later in the evening at about 9:15 p.m., I called his home to obtain a telephone number. Wife Marilynn answered, and after giving me the number said, "He's already fast asleep. He had a long tough trip." He surely has.

William Gladstone has perhaps accomplished more significant and more lasting programs than what might be expected of an activist judge in the normal course of duties. Yet to me, for a nonpolitician to be able to develop so impressive a program in so short a time is the height of accomplishment.

I had doubted he would be so successful in these one-year sprints, first in Tallahassee, then in Washington. The record shows I was wrong. Somehow, here despite all my misgivings, it all managed to work out. Or maybe he's a lot better politician than I think.

Symptomatic of the whole culture of advocacy, great ideas too often die aborning because of a lazy bureaucracy, political opposition, lack of funds, or whatever. Excellent projects and ideas come forth and simply don't get beyond first base. Here, on many occasions, Gladstone, with the help of others, put together several perfect packages, covering all the bases, and despite the likelihood that if anything can go wrong, it will, he made it.

As a close friend, I had advised him when he went off to Washington not to leave the juvenile court. Not yet of required retirement age, although not too far from it, he had this wanderlust and always a bit of a thirst for adventure. He returned to Miami, satisfied he had given Washington his best shot.

Assuming a role as a senior judge didn't cause him to miss a step. Shortly thereafter, Cindy Lederman became administrative judge. They hit it off immediately. No longer the voice of the court, Gladstone gracefully accepted his less-public role. She was wise enough to include him in her counsel, and while his influence, though less visible, was still evident.

He still carried a full load. Activity with the National Council of Juvenile and Family Judges (NCJFCJ) accelerated. Over the years he had been most active with that group, as a busy member of standing committees, participating in writing manuals and tracts, teaching at their schools, and generally being a leader among leaders in the field.

At this stage in his career, community honors began to mount up. The Associated Marine Institutes'(AMI) new delinquency facility on Key Biscayne in Miami was named the William E. Gladstone Campus. Ceremony attendees included U.S. Senator Bob Graham, Chief Justice of the Florida Supreme Court Rosemary Barkett, and head of the Office of U.S. Attorney General Janet Reno, all joined in honoring Judge Gladstone.

One thing that can be said about Gladstone's career, any event honoring him always brought out the best and the brightest of government officialdom. For a nonpolitical fellow as he was and is, that's a high salute.

Going through his papers, I came across an article he had written for the *Miami Herald*, dated June 3, 1990 titled "The Juvenile Justice System of the Future." It caught my attention because the summer 1990 issue of the *Juvenile and Family Court Journal* had published an article of mine titled "The Juvenile Justice System: Vision of the Future." I had just retired, and Gladstone was returning to Miami now as a senior judge, also retired from full-time duties on the bench.

What intrigued me was neither of us at that time had any knowledge of the others authorship. Our so-called policy of not reading the words of a colleague held true to the end. Now sixteen years later, how did our estimate of the future hold up compared to reality?

Well, the truth is neither of us hit a bull's-eye. Gladstone, still unhappy with the *Gault* decision, bemoaned considering children as little adults by imposing adult standards of due process. He wanted Guardians ad Litem to replace public defenders, thus limiting the adversarial role. He also opted to front load the intervention process at the earliest point of the child's contract with the system.

He decried the labeling of children as delinquent or dependent, preferring a less-pejorative description such as "children in need of services." He also concluded that "mediation and conciliation services to divert parties from crippling litigation would be another hallmark of the ideal court of the future."

My tone agreed with large doses of mediation and early intervention, but I foresaw dependency surpassing delinquency as the major area for concern. I also envisioned both the school and court systems working in a collaborative effort, with district juvenile courts actually located in or adjacent to public schools and their respective staffs intertwined.

We both had more complex formulations for the system than existed in the year 2000, the date for which we projected. I doubt whether he or I would make the same recommendations for the future juvenile court, say of 2050. It seems unlikely that a Supreme Court in the coming years will readdress the *Gault* decision, nor is it likely that the school system and the juvenile court system should or would tie together any closer than currently exists.

Both the Gladstone and Gelber predictions are no more valid than the sportswriter predicting the football scores for the coming Sunday. Most of what we predict is based primarily on what we hope for, not the likelihood of seeing it come to fruition.

Looking back longitudinally at the development of our juvenile court, it is plain that change is imperceptible. The first fifty years from Atkinson through Beckham saw only miniscule change. Until the *Gault* decision and the Article V changes to the Florida Constitution, H. W. Penney, our first judge, appointed in 1921, could have walked into any courtroom in the fifty years that followed him and been perfectly at home with the process and the procedures. Things had barely moved.

Having said all that, one can also see that the whole environment of the juvenile court has moved forward. Even the totally inadequate State services have improved, in that they are moving toward greater privatization. This has produced many effective groups able to attend properly to child foster care and correct other weaknesses.

The volunteer system, such as Foster Care Review, now fills huge voids heretofore virtually ignored. In addition to judges, other professionals as well as volunteers have also become the faces of the juvenile justice system, earning the respect of the community. Joni Goodman, for one, who heads the citizen volunteer Guardian Ad Litem program, and David Lawrence, who leads the Children's Trust and many other initiatives for disadvantaged children, are ideal nonjudicial models for the juvenile justice system.

Scholarly review of the system's program needs has shown marked increase, both quantitatively and qualitatively. This has been accomplished not only by an increased interest by the academic community, but juvenile judges, as exemplified by Judge Cindy Lederman and others, also have participated in this endeavor.

Change is a slow process. At this time we are going through such a development started by Gladstone and furthered by Lederman. The explosion of the Supreme Court's *Gault* decision and the changes in Article V of our state constitution has each quickened the pace considerably.

Gladstone and Lederman, along with other judges cited here, have made and are making long strides toward improving what we have. There's no telling who the next batch of leaders will be or what wondrous results will rise from their efforts.

July 13, 1995, the *Miami Herald*: "Judge William Gladstone, senior circuit court judge, was recently honored by the Children's Home Society of Florida for his advocacy efforts on behalf of children."

October 1, 1998, the *Florida Bar News*: "Florida Supreme Court Chief Justice Major B. Harding announced the creation of the annual William Gladstone Award honoring those professionals working to improve Florida's dependency system."

The year 2000 brought sad word that Derrick Thomas, a youth providing one of Gladstone's early success at Dade Marine Institute, had died in an automobile crash. Back in his early delinquency days, Gladstone loved attending forums where he could bring live examples of progress. Derrick was one of those Gladstone gladly displayed. Thomas had only one arrest for burglary to his record, but he was recalcitrant, violating all the rules while in detention, fighting and refusing to behave.

Being aggressive was his nature, as he displayed for many years as an All-Pro linebacker for the Kansas City Chiefs. Regarded as the finest linebacker in the league, he won most all the awards available. But the road hadn't been easy.

William Gladstone had been his judge. On a subsequent arrest after graduating high school, where he had been All-State, Gladstone gave him that second chance with a warning, "If ever you come back again, I'm going to give you the maximum time the law permits, plus the time I didn't give you from the time before."

He did come back. When Thomas hit the big-time big, he came back and asked Judge Gladstone how he could help other kids. With help from Judge Gladstone, Thomas founded the Third and Long Foundation to help inner-city kids improve their reading skills. He also funded programs at the Boys Club and other children's causes.

Gladstone not only gave him another chance, but instilled him the desire to help others in circumstances similar to his own. It also gave Gladstone the opportunity to dwell on the positive things coming out of juvenile court.

Gladstone prizes a letter received from Scott Brownell of Bradenton, Florida, upon his being a recipient of the William Gladstone Award. Judge Brownell had these kind words to say:

> In your time on the bench you rewrote the book on juvenile judging and created a model for the activist Judge, out of whole cloth, primarily concerned with children's welfare.
>
> I have often wished, but wish now more than ever, that I could have followed you by five years instead of fifteen and could have worked side by side with you in Miami. My learning curve would have been much shorter and the kids so much better off that much sooner.

The status of senior judge, part-time hearing cases, has hardly slowed Gladstone done. Most senior judges, recognizing their day is gone, accept their assignment as akin to a substitute teacher. They perform their duties with the same skill as offered before, but the effort is not likely to be the top priority in their lives. Sitting as a senior judge becomes a calling secondary to whatever new interest has developed. Not so with Gladstone.

Although no longer serving in an administrative capacity, Judge Gladstone has immersed himself in the furthering of the juvenile justice system. Only occasionally getting a call from the press and no longer having the bench as a pulpit to espouse his cause, he nonetheless has never faltered for a moment.

Working on "Florida's Strategic Plan for Infant Mental Health" in the year 2000, he sent me a note along with a copy of the document.

> The new science of Infant Mental Health has been my passion for the last five years or more. Working with this Strategic Plan started it.
>
> I have also worked with Cindy Lederman as co-chair of committees on the health and well-being of "Infants, Toddlers and pre-Schoolers" with the National Council of Juvenile Court Judges.
>
> Lobbying Congressmen for the "Zero to Three" organization seeking grants to teach the subject to Courts around the country was also a project of mine.

In the acknowledgement section of "Florida's Strategic Plan for Infant Mental Health" was three lines devoted to Judge William Gladstone, "our first member of the Florida Association for Infant Mental Health, for being our conscience and unwavering evangelist to bring infant mental health within the judicial system." Nice words to be remembered by.

Gladstone was among the first to actually initiate with the NCJFCJ this emphasis on the youngest of our children. Back at the beginning, before even becoming a judge, Gladstone, as president of the Dade County Mental Health Association, realized these were significant approaches that needed to be pursued as part of the early intervention process.

Through the Zero to Three Project, this began a trend in other communities to focus on this need. It was part of Gladstone's latter-day efforts to concentrate on mental health issues of the very young. Judge Cindy Lederman had also made this a major part of her advocacy efforts and enabled both of them to further this goal.

He also continued to play a major role with NCJFCJ in the effort to persuade other disciplines, psychiatrists and pediatrics, to form alliances with NCJFCJ in the study and planning of interdisciplinary approaches that could well serve juvenile court judges. In addition, Gladstone serves on several NCJFCJ Permanency Planning Committees involved in establishing standards for use in court planning

Gladstone's commitment to the NCJFCJ has never abated. Almost from the onset of his assuming his judgeship in 1973, he has been a stalwart member and contributor to all their major efforts, which have been many.

When I asked why he never held a top office in the organization, he replied,

> I served on their board for many years. At the beginning I was so busy with Miami matters, I had no time to contemplate a campaign for high office on the national council. That required a long process of going up all the chairs until being elected president.
>
> Only when I became a senior judge after retirement was I able to find enough time, and by that time they no longer encouraged retired judges to serve as officers.

I reminded him that politics had never been his strong point. Although credited highly within the organization, word of his many national accomplishments have rarely followed him back home. Nonetheless, he views his efforts over the years with the NCJFCJ as equally significant to his work in Florida and Dade County.

A year earlier he had worked on the NCJFCJ's Juvenile Court Centennial Initiative, chartering a course for the next century with the "Declaration on Juvenile Justice for the Twenty-first Century." His contribution had focused on promoting children's emotional, physical, mental, and spiritual health and well-being.

Pointing the way doesn't necessarily effectuate the results desired, but Gladstone never lessened in his purpose. Now, in the year 2006, some thirty-three years after assuming the bench, still to be toiling with the same intensity fully describes a man's objectives and dreams. His caseload in these later years may have diminished, but his vision and effort are still as steadfast as ever.

It is often said that every man has a weak spot. At least if not a weak one a soft one. With Bill Gladstone it was poetry. For a man always tied up in his emotions, he needed a private outlet for self-expression. For a long time now he had been neglecting his favorite pastime—writing poetry.

Actually, a fifty-year pause. I suppose poetry might be appropriate for a hard-nosed judge who had to spend his lifetime watching children suffer. Someone whose every emotion was bound to the kids appearing before him.

Bill Gladstone as a youth, had a penchant for writing poetry. At one point he actually had envisioned a career as a writer-poet. Sidetracked by this career, he found it emerging again, fifty years later. Even going so far as to study the new style haiku.

Haiku's lineage is traditional Japanese with formalized rules of writing. The poems style consists of simple short lines, subjects common to ordinary folks.

Two of his poems were printed in the spring 2004 issue of the *Juvenile And Family Court Journal*.

He insists that the poetry he wrote was traditional verse, not haiku, and I must defer to his knowledge. Nonetheless, both his published poems definitely have the simple people's touch so descriptive of haiku, and I will let the reader decide.

Here's one of them, commenting on the indifference of mankind.

Interruption

An urgent bell,
    Awakened.

        "Help now!
          The child may die!"

        "Yes, we hear that
          often now.
        What beast could
          do that?

        Thank you
          For telling me"

                And returned to bed,
                  And to sleep.

Reading his poetry and knowing the intensity under which this man functions, one might expect a tormented soul full of grief for his fellow man. Not so. He is a gregarious, funny fellow full of life and appreciation of all things around him. Not only the bad and the evil, but the good things and the good people who surround him.

Having a lunch appointment with Gladstone might find you with two or three others he had casually run into that morning and invited to join. With him, you are destined to have Chinese food at Em's a run-down redneck diner where the truckers and motorcycle guys congregate. He likes Em's because they offer some special vegetables like turnip greens made southern style, reminding him of his youth. But if Chinese is on the menu, that's his first choice. He gorges on it.

That only means he is a man of the people and a good ol' southern boy at heart. Em's quaint fare need not detract from his natural charm. It is a small price to pay for his company. Dining at an expensive restaurant with him, when the sommelier uncorks the wine, who else but Bill Gladstone has the savoir faire to rise above his Em's upbringing, reject the bouquet, and send the wine back. Something most of us dread doing.

Is he a complex person? You bet. There are a lot of layers to him, but he doesn't hide behind them. Mostly you get what you see. He doesn't take himself too seriously, deprecating his accomplishments. So many surprises come out of him that conversing with Bill Gladstone is like bouncing thoughts off a backboard that suddenly come back with the most startling responses. He makes you think in terms of the unexpected. An exciting man to be around.

Judge Gladstone brought judicial activism to a new level in Dade County. Some of his predecessors had taken to the stump on specific occasions, but his was an all-out devotion to establishing a moral stand for the good of all around him—particularly children. To him, allowing unfortunate children to be deprived of the opportunity to lead normal lives was the personification of evil.

Usually, our judges spoke out for more resources. Gladstone did that and more. In action, he was more like Billy Graham speaking out against ungodly forces. In behalf of his cause, he offered a demeanor, a voice, an attitude that demanded one not only listen, but that all within the sound of his voice take heed. From within his own being came the pain of the suffering of his charges. His was a powerful effort.

The programs he designed and offered did a lot more than address the trouble at hand. His programs like Last Chance Ranch in delinquency and Zero to Three in dependency, were finite solutions, not temporary relief. In essence he said, "Follow me and be delivered."

Of course, in this business there are no ultimate final answers. He knew that, but he also knew that the spirit and hope he engendered was often contagious. The Gladstone followers always voiced high levels of expectation. He and they knew for sure the next round was sure to bring some sort of salvation.

Hard to have predicted who among the judges having graced the juvenile court bench for the first fifty years of its existence would have turned out to be this oft-fiery crusader leading the march for children. Not likely the choice to be this mannerly, scholarly William E. Gladstone.

In my final interview of Gladstone, I sought to learn his future plans in terms of community service. Bill Gladstone is a tough interview. No pat answers. No full ones either. Sometimes he's high raring to go. When he's tired, he responds as if he's holding a timer on the questioner. His mind is always jumping ahead, and it's virtually impossible to keep him on track.

He said he was playing with the idea of organizing a national consortium of disciplines involved with children. This would be a formal group beyond the loose relationship currently existing. Most specifically the medical field: pediatrics, psychiatry, psychology, along with the allied disciplines of law and corrections and other related fields, to conduct research in all the areas where the those disciplines joined together.

I responded that such interdisciplinary journals already existed. He continued on ignoring my comment as if to say we need more group interface relationships, not just journal articles. I listened without further interruption. His plans were still vague, nothing in concrete. I had the impression he really liked the ideas he was offering though his thoughts hadn't yet congealed. Here we were two tired old fellows talking about tomorrow as if making long range plans for the birth of a new era.

The phone conversation began to have longer pauses, and finally as we seemed to be coming to an end, he said, "I've got to go pack some things. I have to be back in Atlanta tomorrow for a meeting," It was plain our interview was over.

No question that the next time we meet again, he likely will be in high spirits, with another plan on the front burner. One thing about Bill Gladstone, he does not know how to stop. For sure whatever he has in mind, it won't be ordinary. He, indeed, is no ordinary fellow.

Judge William Gladstone is a person of action. The telephone was always at his side in the courtroom and he frequently used it to address concerns as they arose.

Judge Lester Langer is the Associate Administrative Judge for the Juvenile Division. Having practiced law in the juvenile court, he came to the bench with a wealth of knowledge and experience. His thirst to improve the court remains unquenched. His successes for the children of Miami-Dade County and the State of Florida are many and laudable.

Tom Petersen is one of the most innovative judges in the juvenile court. He created Troy Academy, a special school for children adjudged delinquent. It operates on the premises of the juvenile court and is run cooperatively with the Miami-Dade County School Board. It offers a vocational program called, "Teen Cuisine" which trains students to operate every aspect of a restaurant.

On July 7, 1921, H.W. Penney, the first and newly appointed Dade County Juvenile Court Judge, ruled on the first case appearing in this new court. Probation officer Estelle Harris apprehended two juveniles, Irvin Hall and Laurie Johnson, and charged them with stealing mangos from Mr. Ozohu's fruit orchard. Judge Penney suspended their sentences, ordered the two children to find employment, and directed them to report their progress to him each Saturday.

—Miami Daily News Photo
INTERIOR OF DADE COUNTY JUVENILE COURT. SEATED, LEFT TO RIGHT, FACING CAMERA: MRS. NESBIT, INTERESTED IN CHILD WELFARE WORK; JUDGE EDITH M. ATKINSON AND MRS. FANNIE TULLOS, PROBATION OFFICER.

In 1925, Edith Atkinson, our second Juvenile Court Judge, presided over her court in temporary quarters—a room in a school building located just off of Biscayne Boulevard. The proceedings were informal with the unrobed judge seated at a plain table. This set up was conducive for engaging in open discussions about the child's problems. Prior to the creation of a juvenile court, authorities prosecuted and sentenced children as adults.

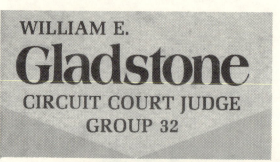

Judge William Gladstone, one of the outstanding jurists to grace the juvenile court, ran for office in 1972. His platform urged the creation of a specialized "Family Court." Under this concept, multi-family problems ordinarily heard by several different judges in several different courts, would be transferred to a singular judge and court. Upon his election, Judge Gladstone, and others ultimately achieved his goal.

Judges William Gladstone and Cindy Lederman are two of the leading advocates for children in the history of the court. Judge Gladstone began serving in 1973 and continues to serve the people of the State of Florida as a senior judge. Judge Cindy Lederman is the Administrative Judge of Juvenile Division. She is credited with modernizing the court structure and on working to meet the full needs of the "dependent" child.

In 1922, the Dade County Board of County Commissioners created the Board of Visitors consisting of leading citizens who would periodically visit sites housing delinquent and dependent children. The early board included important industrialists and winter residents who sponsored programs for delinquents in their home towns. The first board included James R. Mellon, of the Mellon family of Pennsylvania.

Seymour Gelber

Following Bill Gladstone on the bench was a tough assignment (and following him in the book was not easier). Only a year separated us when I came aboard in 1974, but he had already started to leave a strong impression. Would he be my kind of a fellow? Were we going to be in competition? How would I hold up against him? Not likely we'd have problems, but who knows?

I had just completed fifteen years as a top aide in State Attorney Dick Gerstein's office, well schooled in both local politics and the bureaucracy of public office. Prior to that, my baptism in the life of a public officeholder had been further furbished by a stint with the state attorney general in Tallahassee, and at the very beginning as legislative aide to State Senator Joe Eaton, also in Tallahassee. I had been around.

Both my mentors, Dick Gerstein and Joe Eaton, were part of the vanguard of WWII vets determined to take over public office from the old-guard prewar politicos. There was a feeling in the air, post WWII, that these young war veterans were the future leaders for the nation. No disrespect toward their elders, but it really was time to move over.

Each a highly principled man and both astute politicians, I had learned well under their tutelage. My role for both had been as a "second banana," a kind of detail man whose main purpose was to make certain that their offices were running properly for the top guy. And, if possible, to deflect any media criticism flying in their direction. Occasionally, when requested, I offered some political views to them on a situation. That was the background I brought with me as the newest recruit to the juvenile court bench.

Also, I had the benefit of an additional advantage. One of my assignments as Gerstein's administrative assistant had been to oversee the Dade County Grand Jury as legal advisor during the decade of the 1960s. Routinely, each new grand jury group, serving six month terms, would inspect, under my guidance the juvenile court and the Kendall Homes for children. Testimony was also taken, and each final grand jury report, which I helped author, had commentary on juvenile court progress or more likely lack of it.

Arriving to my new life as a judge, I felt totally equipped for what was ahead. I was the consummate bureaucrat, fully aware of the follies of government and how best to avoid the pitfalls. Also, my grand jury experience had given me special insights as to the juvenile court.

Question in my mind: Would all this equip me to be a spirited advocate for the child? Or would knowing all the ins and outs of how to function as a bureaucrat merely enable me to survive? Or better yet, did I envision myself as a spirited leader ready to take on the establishment in behalf of children? The latter was a goal I had hoped for.

Sitting with me on the bench at that time was Judge Dixie Chastain, a long time judge who, as a vestige of the past decades, had seen and been part of the struggles of stalwarts such as Judges Walter Beckham, Ben Sheppard, and Don Stone.

In that era, several others had graced the bench for short periods. As the caseloads grew, the number of judges had increased, mostly new faces in and out. Traditionally, sitting on this bench was not viewed as a prime assignment. Most judges assigned to juvenile court relished the arrival of their departure to another court division.

And then there was Bill Gladstone. Ivy League educated, confident young man, he knew exactly what he wanted to do possessing a go-get-'em attitude from the first moment. Out to change the world of the juvenile court. All of this a bit confusing for a bureaucratic status-quo guy like me. Wasn't too sure where or how I fit in with the court or with him or Dixie.

Determined that my ascent to the bench would be a lot more than a political promotion, I was still uncertain about my future role. For certain, a remake on my image as a don't-shake-the-branches person was in order. Fortunately for this high school dropout who never had obtained a college bachelor's degree, I had the advantages of the G.I. Bill that carried me through law school. Where would I have been without it?

Mostly due to political involvement, I had opportunities virtually thrust upon me resulting in a circuit court judgeship. How lucky can a guy get? Careerwise, I might have developed into a decent trial lawyer, but my experience as a prosecutor never did suggest that likelihood. Becoming a successful real estate lawyer was the goal of many of my young associates of that day, but that seemed like plodding, and my youthful ideals still held firm for me to move to higher pastures.

I had maintained these dreams of youth in law school to someday be in a position to foster the democratic ideals of my growing-up period. Serving in WWII had bolstered those patriotic views. Growing up in an immigrant family with trade-union parents, the idea of politics, in the positive sense of the word, had always been attractive to me. A liberal, I wanted to do good things for the downtrodden. Not sure how long those goals stayed with me into adulthood, but that's how I started.

Upon becoming a lawyer, it became apparent to me early on that I was not the outgoing, articulate, silver-tongued type—qualities that seemed necessary for advancement in both the legal profession and in politics.

My early activity in campaign politics had led to appointments by both Florida State Senator Joe Eaton and Dade State Attorney Richard Gerstein. My roles with them, administering their offices, had me in an important but subordinate role. Perhaps my qualities best suited me for that, but the urge to be out front leading always was present.

Now, in this exalted position as a circuit court judge, both the challenge and opportunity was there. Either do my court calendars, follow precedent, and stay in line—or jump out of the crowd and become a leader. Perhaps an activist judge?

But . . . I had never been an activist in the sense of the many who had fought for the underclass in decades past. Being sympathetic is one thing; storming the barricades is another. Neither as a quiet high school athlete nor as a WWII soldier had I leaped to the front of the pack. As a law student I spoke with pride of getting through anonymously. Time would tell.

Prepared as I was for the job, at least superficially, I had neither a plan nor a sign from above. Appointed a judge at the end of summer 1974, I was immediately involved in campaigning for the fall election only a few months away. Again luck, or more likely having Dick Gerstein in my corner, probably scared off any potential opponents. I ran unopposed.

Juvenile court hearings were then held in a discarded regional site of the County Corrections Department at 800 NW Twenty-eighth Street. Also in that building were additional court facilities, including holding cells for juveniles coming to trial. These juveniles were housed more permanently at a site distant from our premises and were transported each day by a Corrections Department bus.

The three judges then sitting—Chastain, Gladstone and I—each had a no-frills combination chambers/courtroom in this old, run-down building that formerly had housed adult county prisoners. My firmest recollection of my first day sitting as a judge was a rat running across the courtroom.

My bailiff told me not to be concerned about rats. "We'll be moving soon to new quarters," he assured me. He also cautioned me that transporting the juveniles in custody was a problem since they were housed in a distant building, and many of the delinquents tried escaping from the bus en route. Welcome to the juvenile court!

Still involved with remnants of my duties as administrative assistant to State Attorney Gerstein, my focus was there, as well as with my role with Dade County's Criminal Justice Council, which I was about to chair.

The Dick Gerstein issue at hand then was an undercover investigation of thirty government officials, mostly judges, as well as Dick Gerstein and his top assistants (including me) by the U.S. Internal Revenue Services (IRS). An IRS agent had obtained the services of a young woman who had agreed to gain proximity to these government officials and somehow learn of their extracurricular activities of a sexual nature. She reported only to her handler.

Truly an undercover agent, in every sense of the phrase, she was given the names of targets but was free to select additional persons of her choice. Unearthing unusually large expenditures by her subjects was the goal and pillow talk was the means. Possible corruption was the game.

The investigation, uncovered by the *Miami News*, drew ridicule from most sources. One of her targets, Florida Supreme Court Justice B. K. Roberts dismissed the effort with this comment in the *Miami News*: "Since I don't drink, and I'm sixty-eight years old, I am amused by it. They really flatter me about the sex stuff."

The inquiry, aimed primarily at Richard Gerstein, prompted me to pen several letters to the then U.S. Attorney General Edward Levi, demanding that I be invited to appear before the federal grand jury to protest this investigation led by a woman of the street, unmonitored and free to exert her wiles as she saw fit. When finally invited to testify, I denounced this unprofessional IRS venture. Not one question was posed to me by either the jurors or the U.S. attorney present. Boy! Did I feel good about myself after that.

Although it had received plenty of ink, this amateurish investigation proved to be no more than the proverbial tempest in a teapot. The results had embarrassed the IRS, and the inquiry was summarily disbanded. But it had kept me busy, and my indignation at being included buoyed my activist feelings.

It wasn't the direct forerunner of Gelber, the warrior for children's rights, but at least the spark was emerging. I also was getting an educated feeling about how the court functioned. This time from the inside.

The juvenile court operation apparently followed the same stilted ways, unchanged to any noticeable degree since its beginning half a century earlier. Everything was by rote, as if an original thought was denied entry. I suppose maybe all court systems are based on the status quo.

I looked and listened hard for HRS court counselors who had some degree of passion about their work. A few passed that test, but for the most part they were a passive crew. The best HRS court counselor I ever had was a young woman named Sylvia Williams. When I last looked, thirty years later, she was still there, albeit in a high supervisor capacity, still excited about the challenges of her work.

In one of my early days sitting, Ms. Williams, a tall black woman with a stately bearing came storming into my makeshift courtroom visibly agitated. Holding an eleven-year-old boy by the scruff of his collar, she shouted, "Judge, this little mother f—r ran from a wonderful placement I had found for him."

I was dumbfounded at her expletives. She froze at the realization of her own words. The courtroom was full, but silence enveloped the room. Finally, Sylvia Williams regained her composure, apologized, and we continued on with the hearing. I, ignoring her statement, made no comment as to her indiscretion.

After the hearing I called her to the bench, and now, virtually in tears, she began again to apologize. I told her it was not necessary. As she strode away. I thought to myself, "Now, there's a counselor who cares." She became my favorite ever after, and never let me down on a child.

Learning the ropes on how to be a juvenile court judge was not the easy process I had earlier envisioned. The big lesson I learned from Sylvia Williams was that the judge alone can not do it all. Knowing the rules of evidence did not accomplish the goal. Discovering who among the state counselors was trustworthy, doing his or her job, whose testimony you can rely on, was the best way to start.

The calendars each day seemed overwhelming in size. No way each child could possibly receive the attention required in the hours available. I was advised, "Move the calendar, otherwise bedlam ensues." Gladstone cautioned me otherwise, "Rushing through the calendar will prevent you from giving everyone a fair and full hearing." He was right, but somehow I managed to avoid the night sessions that identified his courtroom. Never did I reach his sitting power.

In addition to finding more Sylvia Williamses, I picked up a few other approaches. Avoid continuances and other defense lawyer tactics to delay proceedings. Witnesses will tire of coming. Case dismissed. Easier said than done, but practical measures were essential to overcome the bedlam and disarray caused by the large numbers. Court procedure improved somewhat in later years, but dealing with the masses never did come easy.

Meanwhile, juvenile court was in a continued mess, particularly Youth Hall's detention center. Never a quiet moment. Robert Taro, HRS regional detention director, stated in an article appearing in the *Miami News* on February 10, 1975, "Youth Hall is running out of money to buy food for inmates." Robert Taro, a reliable and able official, had worked with me during my earlier grand jury visits to the juvenile court. Taro added, "I just don't know where the money is going to come from. No youth has ever starved in a state facility." A shocking situation indeed.

In addition, Youth Hall faced a lack of repair money for proper maintenance, and the facility was unable to meet fire code regulations. Further, the lighting system had gone astray along with a few other mechanical problems.

In my earlier government experience, I had not come across a situation where a responsible state agency lacked the very basics for survival. Working in Dick Gerstein's state attorney's office and before that in the state senate with Joe Eaton, all the needed services had been automatic.

Becoming a judge, surely I would be in an elite circumstance where all the necessaries were provided. Who could have anticipated that meals for children in lockup would be a budget problem? Hard to believe that making certain that food was available was in fact a responsibility of the judge. Asking Taro, "What do we do?" he smiled, answering, "We have problems like this all the time. Don't worry, it will work out."

I could foresee a host of detention center problems with no quick solutions available. Although food money was eventually provided by transfer from another budget, it did indicate the sorry state of affairs within HRS, similar to the problems one read about in third-world countries.

Considering that these problems were taking place at the old West Twenty-eighth Street building, and we would be moving shortly to a completely new construction on NW Twenty-seventh Avenue, the prospects were not entirely dim. Things were bound to get better at the new place. Too often, however, the past is only introduction to the future.

My transition was still at a slow pace. Ran into a few more rats scurrying across my courtroom, but I had learned to ignore them. Colleagues Chastain and Gladstone were continuing to oversee construction of the new building at 3300 NW Twenty-seventh Avenue while I was attempting to adjust to the tempo of the juvenile court. We finally moved there, but as everything else in the bureaucracy, it took a lot longer than expected.

The new building was fine. At the end, due to budget overruns, several rooms had to be omitted, and the large patio in the center of the building with a proposed handsome glass ceiling above the rotunda finally was completed minus the glass ceiling. Budget cuts. The rotunda was to be our showpiece with the sun shining through the glass onto the palm trees and fancy seating below. Instead we got an open space.

The second floor of the building, the area designated for the judicial chambers and courtrooms, had not yet been finished. And that too was delayed for lack of funds. Thereupon, we were given temporary space in regular offices used by HRS counselors on the first floor. We remained in that posture month after month, the builders telling us to be patient.

By now I had become accustomed to my makeshift courtroom. I had longed for a judge's chambers, surrounded by shelves and shelves of law books, a kind of private retreat. This, in my vision, was the one locale that truly elevates a judge to the loftiest of positions. A safe, quiet place for reflection and away from the struggles of the day. It is the chambers that make for a judge's castle, not the courtroom. That was a dream that never came to pass.

Each morning a new crisis was on the horizon. Not unlike the atmosphere around the state attorney's office, but there we always knew we could and would find an answer to each problem. Here it was like an endless black tunnel. No way out. My early training helped a lot. Not so much in making the big decisions, but in recognizing the day-to-day operational problems. I had seen many similar situations in my prior governmental experience. Screwups and crisis scenarios become routine. Except here there seemed to be routine with no ready answers.

With the completion of our new courtrooms on the way, and things likely to get better, the day-to-day problems of running the courtroom seemed less significant. Unfortunately, things never did get better. One problem mounted after another.

Weeks before the scheduled opening of the new Youth Hall Detention Center, a grand jury report blasted the facility. The *Miami News* headline screamed, "From Cage-like Disgrace to Nine Million Dollar Extravaganza."

The grand jurors had declared it a waste to spread this new 112-bed detention area over a four-block tract of land only adequate for twenty years. They bemoaned the fact that the current detention center, built some twenty years ago to house fifty beds, now held twice as many in cagelike cells and had only this year been air-conditioned.

The report concluded, "It makes little sense to spend so much money on such an elaborate facility which will be utilized for such a brief period, and by such a very few of the children charged with a crime." Also pointed out was the fact that past grand juries have continuously deemed Youth Hall a "disgrace."

The new detention complex, opening in late 1976, turned out to be less a monument to government extravagance and more a symbol of government's inability to perform. Within a year it too was into crisis. The physical surroundings looked a lot better, but it was business as usual within the complex.

Somehow, no matter the improved physical state of a new government-run site, the failed culture of the past remained and continued to dominate performance. This is probably attributable to the same personnel running the operation and continuing all the bad habits that over the years had become accepted as part of the regular routine.

By now, I had become fully immersed in my new job. It takes time for a new judge to be able to grab the reins and move forward. Probably better to go through a longer acclimation period than to rush asserting authority. Perhaps my learning period for an activist role was a bit longer than others, but I needed to be comfortable in my own skin. Actually it was the Youth Hall crisis that really motivated me into action.

How did I go from bureaucrat to activist? It was more a happening than an epiphany. Always I had maintained these dreams of youth to someday be in a position to foster the democratic ideals. Serving in WWII had accentuated those ideals. Now that I had the forum and the power, the question remained, how well could I perform?

All my early success in politics had me in a subordinate role, never the decisive leader stepping out front on an issue, always in the background, uttering muted advice to the one in charge. Perhaps my qualities only suited me for that, but the urge to be out front leading stayed with me. It was always there.

It was that festering problem at Youth Hall's Detention Center that had been going on for years that did it. The events were kind of simple. The operation of our detention center had been an absolute disaster for a long time, but unfortunately, true change never seemed to be in the offing.

What happened and how I responded was not talked about in the halls of the juvenile court with awe in the years ahead, and landmarks do not designate the event. Only a happening, hardly remembered by any of the old timers, except for me. I had broken out of my own eggshell.

The Youth Hall Detention Center crisis actually motivated me to judicial activism. Moving up front, speaking out, taking command was a new role for me. For all my prior roles in government, interesting and challenging as they had been, I always had been the man behind the scene. Not the decision maker, not the protester, never the figure giving orders. This was to be my first venture in this unaccustomed role.

My efforts with Youth Hall, recorded by the press, were by all accounts a worthwhile undertaking, creating some awareness in the community, although hardly enough. I had moved away from the old me, now prepared to assume an activist judicial stance. This, my first test, was only one of a series of continuing challenges that periodically emerged.

The year was 1977, and the Youth Hall Detention Center had been and was now a troubled spot needing more than casual attention. A lot more. Opened January 1977, with the grand jury titling it a "nine-million-dollar extravaganza" it had a run lasting only nine months before events forced me into action. Appointing the Citizens Committee in October to take over and operate the detention center was a dramatic step.

My Citizens Committee came about in the ordinary course of business. Nothing too dramatic. Assistant Public Defender Rick Margolius had petitioned the court to close down Youth Hall. As he correctly outlined it to a *Miami News* reporter, "There were instances of rape, sodomy, overcrowding that left inmates sleeping on the floor, undertrained staff members, and emotionally disturbed youths housed with delinquents who abused them."

That the situation had deteriorated to such an extent in these few months, suggested that HRS was incapable of administering the facility. It was neither the time nor the place to begin forming study committees.

It had also been apparent in the summer months of 1977 that HRS was unable to perform in their general responsibilities to the court. One hundred and fifty of the cases being processed by HRS had to be dismissed for failure to be filed within the time limits prescribed by the law. This related directly to the overcrowding problem at Youth Hall.

At that time I told Max Rothman, district HRS administrator, he would be held in contempt of court unless the filing delay was immediately remedied. I had warned him saying, "I don't care how you get additional help. Work double shifts. Get help from the Salvation Army. Fly in counselors from other parts of the state. Just fix it!"

HRS flew in additional staff from other parts of the state, but the problem needed a lot more than a makeshift addition of new hands. Unfortunately, HRS was not only lacking in resources, but they had been so beaten down over the years that they no longer had the will to take drastic action in situations like this. Emergency situations had become normal to them, and no action the routine response. Like every other past problem, this one would go away in time. Not for this judge.

It became plainly obvious that neither the State nor the County were prepared to invest more dollars to provide adequate staffing and other resources. Closing down the detention facility was even a worse surrender. I was not prepared to accept that avenue. Too many kids left out in the street, with only additional turmoil ahead.

At the hearing, HRS director Rothman agreed with Public Defender Margolius, promising that those conditions would be corrected. Too late for additional promises. We'd been there too often. I was prepared to take extreme action. Before appointing my Citizens Committee to take over, I made this Gladstone-like statement

> There have been evils represented here in court today. Couched in gentlemanly tones, but they are still abominations, and I do not intend to be party to them in any way.
>
> It would be equivalent to malfeasance in office for me to sit quietly by. This constitutes a dire emergency, and I will treat it as a crisis.

It was questionable whether I had the authority as a judge to simply dismiss HRS and appoint my own crew to operate the detention center. In October

1977, I therefore chose instead to finesse the situation by appointing the Citizens' Committee to "oversee" the operation.

In this way I sought to avoid any suggestion that I might be formally usurping the authority vested in HRS by law. Thereupon, I notified the HRS authorities by telephone that I expected them to defer to the decisions made by my committee.

An HRS official, responding in a firm manner, advised me that I had no such authority under the law, and my ruling would be tested in the court of appeals. I responded that until so ordered by a higher court, "I was the law." High-handed on my part, but the situation called for strong action.

Since I had issued no written order, I was counting on the reluctance on the part of HRS to take legal action in face of an angry media now supporting my action. The very weakness of HRS would be my strong suit. It was a clouded course I had taken, but there was no turning back.

HRS blinked first. They declined to contest my action and agreed to cooperate with my committee. I had prevailed. Then began a year of struggle to rehabilitate the detention center. I had chosen a strong committee, each a stalwart in an allied profession involving children. They were individuals whom I had professional contact with in the past and trusted. They were to have a free hand. I would not participate in their meetings or interfere with their decision making. It was all theirs.

A risky operation, fraught with the prospect of all kinds of conflict. Would giving them carte-blanche authority prompt some of the members to run away with this new power? Shouldn't I, as the appointing authority, monitor and limit their power?

I have always believed that investigating committees appointed by government are sometimes mere political showpieces, too often held on a short leash, finding themselves hamstrung. Always in appointing such committees I have insisted on their having free rein. That way, the public and the media are more willing to accept their findings as reflecting the truth of the situation.

Fortunately, my committee members, all professionals in the field, confined themselves to action aimed at stabilizing the detention center. The extensive authority I had given them could have had unanticipated results. Bad ones, perhaps, but that was the risk I was willing to take. But my luck held out; nothing untoward resulted. Acrimony between the HRS and the Citizens' Committee had been totally avoided.

For chair of the committee I had drafted Gus Jacobson, a longtime social worker, and then executive director of the Miami Beach YMHA. I had been a volunteer worker at the Y and knew Jacobson's wealth of experience and professional demeanor was appropriate for this task. I had set the date for the completion of their task, and Jacobson and the others were raring to go. Jacobson set the tone in his opening remarks,

It is not our intention to close the facility down. We will work as long as necessary to accomplish our goal.

In our eighty-five-day management period, we want to find long-range solutions, such as creating another facility for the emotionally disturbed youngsters who presently have no overnight places to go to other than Youth Hall.

Things began to happen fast. Their first act was to request that the overcrowded Youth Hall population, with 164 youths in detention cells built to hold 112, be immediately reduced. Marlyn Smith, intake specialist for HRS, took the appropriate steps reducing the population to 103.

Next was the remaining building defects: plumbing problems, leaking roofs, malfunctioning drinking fountains, and peeling paint for a building only eight months old. Committee member Gerald Jaski, attorney for the University of Miami, along with Assistant Public Defender Norman Gerstein, filed that complaint with County Manager Merrett R. Stierheim. The manager responded that county officials would immediately comply.

After spending twelve hours touring the detention center, one Sunday, committee member Marvin Dunn, a psychologist and leader in the black community, stated, "Psychotic children are dumped into Youth Hall where no help is provided them, and there is nowhere else for them to go,"

The committee also took testimony from five HRS counselors who told of unrealistic caseloads, lack of training to deal with dependent children, and inadequate salaries. Committee member Gerald Jaski moved that the committee go into court to force HRS and the State of Florida to improve conditions.

The committee came up with a ton of proposals. Among the most important was hiring forty-eight permanent detention employees at a cost of over half a million dollars yearly. Promptly, in response, about forty-five temporary employees hired under federal and state grants were brought in to augment the detention staff if only on temporary loan. HRS added eight additional, but neither the County nor the State was willing to address the problem on a permanent basis. State Representative Roberta Fox, a member of the committee, saw no assistance coming for the state legislature. My committee wasn't hitting home runs, but they were waking up the neighborhood.

Support was sought and forthcoming from leading civic organizations such as the Crime Commission, the League of Women Voters, the Junior League, the Criminal Justice Planning Council, and others of like standing to serve in a permanent monitoring capacity. My original Citizens' Committee agreed to stay on as long as necessary. We had made an impact on the community. Was it enough?

The venture had been a long, over-one-year struggle for me but only a continuum of the problems going many years back, likely to be part of the process for a long time. The committee's presence had set a fire under HRS. Volunteer citizen groups such as this one had a limit on their energy and time, but this one became more successful by recruiting civic organizations to continue to monitor the detention center.

Problems at the Youth Hall Detention Center did not magically disappear, but we had for the moment halted the decline. Rarely are such situations resolved with finality; they mostly multiply, dissipate for the moment and then periodically creep back; sometimes finally erupting like Mt. Vesuvius. My Citizens Committee had proved that strong action can make a difference. Maybe not forever, but it's a good start.

The committee served for over a year, many months beyond their original tenure. When HRS at times disapproved of some action, I mediated the situation. Recognizing that my action had to be of a temporary nature, I accepted an HRS plan to improve conditions at the detention center: additional personnel in the next budget, cooperation with established citizen groups, and other positive changes.

We also managed to clear up the backlog of cases that the undermanned HRS had been unable to process in timely fashion, thus causing dismissal of the cases. HRS Administrator Rothman, responding to my contempt threat, had brought in twelve more workers to gain control of the speedy-file requirement. Rothman kept patching up the holes by temporarily transferring a crew from other HRS divisions under his domain, meaning only that before long the cries for help would be coming from that site.

Although long-term successes are few, small, and far between, being an activist provided me the opportunity to make strong statements of resolve. This detention-center episode shook up the court community and alerted civic groups to become more involved.

That in itself was worth the effort, but it did a lot for me personally. Never did I look backward after that, constantly on HRS to improve their situation. I also learned that their agency was more a victim than a wrongdoer.

I thanked my volunteers, relieving them of their duties. Ad hoc committees are exactly that—for a temporary specific nature to right a course gone astray. Was the detention center a model institution after that? Hardly. The juvenile court is a two-step-forward-and-one-step-backward operation. And sometimes the reverse. I think it set some good examples to follow, especially for me.

Eventually, sitting as administrative judge, my learning curve continued to grow. Routinely, new judges were assigned to juvenile court as part of the rotation system—some very effective, others only marking time until they could be assigned to a division of greater status among legal practitioners. At times it appeared that more of the less-skilled drew the juvenile court as an assignment while the class A judges gained the civil or probate divisions, more sought-after assignments.

Admittedly, all our court problems could not be attributed solely to the weak HRS social service delivery system. In my capacity as administrative judge, I broached the subject of improving the quality of juvenile court judges to our very able Chief Judge Gerald Wetherington. Not once but several times.

Getting the right judges is a difficult matter. Each, while subject to both the chief judge and the division's administrative judge, is in his own right a duly elected constitutional officer and in for the most part totally independent. Judges, therefore, aren't pushed around too easily.

Responding to my constant complaints, Judge Wetherington always reminded me in his wise and half-mocking manner, "Seymour, they were elected by the people. They have to serve somewhere." Such wisdom hard to argue with. Recognizing the realities of our situation, I chose not to press the chief judge. We were fortunate, however, to also get some high-quality jurists who stayed with us for long periods.

Judge Adele Faske, joining the court in 1976, was unique and in her own way a treasure. She brought a wise viewpoint, more as an old-fashioned parent instilling the virtues of respect and proper behavior. Not an advocate in the literal sense, she stood for all the moral standards parents in the past had envisioned in their children. She insisted that all the rules of proper conduct be enforced, more as a benevolent school teacher, than as a disciplinarian. Children didn't whisper in her courtroom nor chew gum nor speak until spoken to. Decorum, essential in every courtroom, was with her an absolute.

Profanity was an unconditional no-no with Judge Faske. A later controversial law passed on the last day of the 1981 state legislative session permitted juvenile court judges to jail children for contempt of court. Faske didn't need that added authority. The word as to appropriate behavior in her court had somehow reached all who appeared before her.

Sixteen-year-old Patrick, with only a minor criminal record, had been warned by Judge Faske not to use profanity. When the judge learned that Patrick had called his lawyer a whore during a hallway conversation, she promptly jailed him for contempt. In lockup for a few days, the buzz around the courthouse among the juveniles was "watch your mouth."

With her Victorian style, she was like a doting mother sending her child off to the first day of school. Caring was her most imposing trait, and following up on the welfare of each of "her" kids was her modus operandi. Unrelenting in the effort to obtain services, she badgered, threatened, implored those agencies offering services to do right by her charges. To Faske it was a personal thing. Cross her at your own peril.

In her earlier years she had been a strong advocate in the movement to develop a system to search out parents failing to provide child support. The first female lawyer in Dade County to be on the staff of the state attorney's office, she quickly rose to be chief of the Child Support Program. A national leader for the URESA network of states cooperating to locate these parents, she served as executive committee chairperson of the National Conference on Reciprocal Support.

Retiring in 1988, the *Miami Herald* reported the farewell breakfast in her honor. It was December 24, the day before Christmas. Specially considerate of youthful offenders during the holiday season, Judge Faske announced, "I will hear cases into the night so that families can have their problems resolved and not have a cloud (or lockup) hanging over them for the holidays." She followed with, "Unless," she warned, "anyone creating difficult problems in court will sing their 'Jingle Bells' in Youth Hall." Quite a gal, that Adele.

Judge Faske was one of those excellent judges whose duties were performed at a high level but rarely noticed in the press. She, as did many others, focused solely on each child's problems, looking for answers there rather than media recognition.

Examining the old newspaper clips for the two decades between 1959 and 1979, it had been one long cry of anguish. Starting with grand jury reports saying "Youth Hall is understaffed, overcrowded, poorly designed and a fire hazard," to calls in the 1960s for a new Youth Hall, and finally a *Miami Herald* editorial of August 1, 1979, asking again for still another new Youth Hall facility, or at least a new wing.

Those early years were part of a period in the '70s and '80s when the crime rate was spiraling and serious juvenile crime was at a peak. Not only was it my responsibility as a judge, but also serving as chair of the Dade County Criminal Justice Council (CJC), new and more stringent laws and programs were under consideration.

The direct-file law bypassing the authority of juvenile court judges to determine which cases should be prosecuted in adult court became law in October 1979. As did Gladstone, I opposed it since an already-overextended adult criminal system was neither equipped to deal with children, nor would it mete out more appropriate justice. The last of the bind-over cases I had before the law was changed supported my view that a more seasoned evaluation was necessary.

First was the *Ronnie Zamora* case involving a fourteen-year-old boy, with no priors. He had killed an elderly woman neighbor in a botched robbery. The novel defense claimed for Zamora was that he had been influenced by "television intoxication." His lawyer, Ellis Rubin, had argued that the lurid murder dramas young Zamora had been exposed to as a TV viewer had influenced him to commit the act. Although the child had no criminal past, I saw no way he could either be served or punished by the resources of the juvenile court and therefore bound him over for trial in adult court.

The other case involved a young man accused of a knife attack on Dan Paul, a highly respected lawyer in the community. Paul had met the young man earlier in the evening and invited the youngster to stay overnight at his home on Palm Island. The defense maintained that the young man was defending himself against sexual advances.

Played up strongly by the press, mostly because Dan Paul was a highly respected public figure, it might have been direct-filed by the prosecutor due perhaps to the celebrity of Dan Paul. Fortunately, at that time the juvenile judges still had preliminary hearings on such cases, and I chose to hear the case in juvenile court.

The case was resolved before me by a plea that satisfied both sides. Each of these cases had attracted considerable press attention, and in the interest of justice both warranted a preliminary hearing before a judge rather than a charging decision by some raw assistant state attorney.

My Criminal Justice Council, consisting of the heads of all major law enforcement agencies, supported tough new shock programs such as Scared Straight, requiring juvenile offenders to visit prisons and view firsthand the realities of the dehumanizing effect of prison life. Work programs were also offered in lieu of rehab programs. The press had joined wholeheartedly with a fearful public in seeking new approaches, bypassing juvenile court judges in the assessing of penalties.

In an April 15, 1979 *Miami Herald* op-ed piece bearing the headline "Juvenile Justice Doesn't Work in Florida," I came up with a radical approach. Lower the juvenile age from eighteen to sixteen, thus sending all juvenile sixteen and seventeen directly to adult court. That age groups was responsible for 60 percent of cases involving violence. Despite that the *Miami Herald* editorially endorsed my proposal, it gained little support.

In the years since then, I have, for the most part, been a supporter for the potential of the juvenile court concept although at times I have questioned the impact it offers. Always, I return to the thought that weak as it may appear at times, it is the only vehicle available to make troubled children whole again. It is also the prime avenue existent as a preventative tool against crime.

That *Miami Herald* opinion column was but one of many approaches I had used. Going back to my WWII days when I reported from overseas on my life at Guadalcanal for the *Veterans of Foreign Wars* magazine, I had always been a prolific contributor of my thoughts. As a judge, I also became aware that we lacked research data on progress, or lack of it. I was determined to use the pen to begin to educate the community as to what was gong on and possibly sway the readers in my direction.

Starting in 1977, I began issuing the "Profile of Dade County Juvenile Crime." "The Juvenile Justice System: Vision of the Future This was followed by "Profile" in 1980, and three years later another follow-up. In all, they covered nine years, enabling the reader to follow trends in juvenile crime for almost a decade. These profiles also would serve for future researchers to use as a comparison base. The data were compiled from my own caseloads carefully kept during my years on the bench.

The 1977 profile focused on juvenile crime and the schools, pointing out as the *Miami Herald* reported, that "most house burglaries are committed by youths, during school hours, but these crimes drop off drastically during Summer vacation months."

My report comment stated, "It may well be that the absence of the pressure and hostilities arising from the school environment may result in the commission of considerably less crime during the calm days of the Summer vacation period." I also opined that the school system needed to become more involved in combating juvenile crime.

Deputy School Superintendent Leonard Britton took umbrage at my suggestion that perhaps the schools should be more involved. Said Britton, "I don't believe that the school system alone can or should become involved in the correction of juvenile crime, though we can assist other community agencies."

While my research was designed more for education than challenge, I wasn't about to let my friend Leonard Britton off the hook easily. I snapped back with this response reported in the press:

> We live in a school system that is almost of the Victorian age. It is not responsive to the problems of society. Not just our Dade County school system. I am talking about nationwide.
>
> Historically, the schools have lived in a cloistered setting where their sole function has been education. But with the delinquency rising, we need to utilize the school to combat this threat.

Our juvenile judges had not been in open conflict with school authorities, but collectively the school's hands-off approach to juvenile crime had been quietly resented. It was as if they believed their area of responsibility ended with the school-dismissal bell ringing. Not only that, school principals had long had a tendency not to report crimes committed on school grounds in order to avoid the suggestion that their school was unable to maintain order.

My little verbal jousting with then Assistant Superintendent Britton put him on notice. Shortly thereafter, he became superintendent, and despite our earlier words he turned out to be a very cooperative and able head of the school system and considerably more responsive.

The data in my 1977 twenty-seven page "Profile of Dade County Juvenile Crime" also pointed out that while the large majority of crime on the streets and in the schools was committed by black youngsters, there were virtually few, if any, rehabilitative or therapeutic programs available to black children in numbers proportionate to their involvement in crime.

Also of interest, my data showed that existing rehabilitative agencies created to serve the needs of delinquent children, systematically excluded juvenile hard cores with long records of delinquency, particularly of an assaultive nature. The point being that many rehab programs preferred less-difficult clients so that they can claim greater success, thereby increasing the likelihood of obtaining federal grant funds.

Perhaps noteworthy at that time was this comment:

> The absence of significant Latin juvenile crime is probably attributable to the strong family ties and control, traditionally maintained and exercised by Latin parents.
>
> Whatever culture shock may exist between the Latin parents and their children, arising from emigration to the United States from Cuba, it is not evident as a cause for delinquent acts on the part of their children.

This information describing the minimal involvement in juvenile crime by Latin children was significant in that there was much talk in the general community about "crime waves" caused by delinquent Cuban youth.

Interestingly, in the 1980 and 1983 profiles that followed, the continued rise of Latin juvenile crime was attributed to the acculturation of Latin youth, finally fully absorbing the standards of their young Anglo and black American friends.

Although writing became my main form of communication to the community, I did not forgo the usual speechmaking before civic leaders. This one I enjoyed a lot was a drop-in at the Greater Miami Chamber of Commerce. Like good industrialists and business tycoons, they were in the midst of celebrating the promising news that Miami business revitalization was on schedule and even rising.

Throwing a bit if cold water on their celebration, I advised these Miami leaders it all might be worthless unless serious crime is curbed. I challenged them,

> You, the leaders of this community, have stayed away from the crime problem other than to bewail it. You must commit to anticrime resources for a long time ahead. We need to involve a powerful agency like the Chamber of Commerce to evaluate and recommend change for the system.

Alvah Chapman, chairman of the group and president of the Miami Herald Publishing Company, endorsed my proposal. I felt good about it, not so much for what Chapman said, but that I had laid it on the line to them. Chapman later initiated a major anticrime effort among civic leaders in Dade County.

One of the better programs I can take credit for was a joint effort with one of the leading gamblers in America. It was a confluence of four characters, each a leader in his own field but totally unrelated to each other. This wasn't some brilliant program I had dreamed up. More like a happening.

The year was 1980, and my old friend Miami Beach Police chief Rocky Pomerance had invited me for a cup of coffee. Rocky had become world-famous hosting the 1968 and 1972 national presidential nominating conventions in his city. That was part of the era when the fallout from the Vietnam War was still causing concern.

Unlike his counterpart in Chicago, where at the Democratic Party Convention in 1968 a "police riot" had occurred, Chief Rocky had managed to contain the angry protesters that same year when Miami Beach had hosted the Republican Party.

As a result of extensive media praise lavished upon him, Rocky had become a kind of rock-star celebrity. During those Miami Beach nominating conventions I had been loaned by State Attorney Dick Gerstein to serve Chief Pomerance as his legal advisor.

As we sipped coffee, Rocky's story was simple. Clifford Perlman, a former Miami Beach lawyer, now head honcho at Caesar's Palace, then the top gambling casino in Las Vegas, wanted to fight juvenile delinquency. He had asked Rocky to scout out a program for him in Dade County. Rocky wanted my input.

I had known Cliff Perlman casually way back when he was a local real-estate lawyer, and later owner of Lum's, a hole-in-the-wall hot dog stand on Forty-first Street in Miami Beach. Cliff had developed a string of Lum's across the country, and then purchased Caesar's World.

"What kind of program do you recommend?" asked Rocky. At that time I had become enamored of the local Boys Club for their fine efforts with the less-virulent kids coming into court. The Boys Club, under Executive Director Wayne Blanton, had an after-school athletic program that turned many a wayward shoplifter and car thief straight.

Cliff Perlman wanted to give something back to the community where he had started and was willing to provide a small share of the millions of Caesar's gambling casino take. He wanted a no-frills program, one solely devoted to getting dropout kids back in school again.

Perlman liked my choice. The Boys Club's Wayne Blanton was willing for a tutoring program. Chief Pomerance would lend his good name to the effort. Question: How does a strait-laced judge, priding himself on probity, take funding from the largest gambling enterprise in America?

Unquestionably, there might be some criticism. Could I bring the parties together and then step away from the operation? Chief Pomerance advised he would not participate without me in the picture. He needed my cover. Then again, I would need his.

I talked to some of my ethicist friends who saw nothing wrong in my participation. Casino gambling was frowned upon in Florida, but the proceeds from another state where it was legal could not be tainted here. Maybe some criticism from far-right moralists, but I could live with that.

It was a go. Perlman's casino chipped in about a million dollars yearly. Cliff insisted upon participating in all the decisions. He'd fly in from Las Vegas for board meetings and personally question all the group leaders on each of the students assigned. Woe unto the group leader unprepared for Cliff's grilling. It was a rigorous program, concentrating on reading and math in the morning, athletics in the afternoon, and then study time until 9:30 p.m. followed by a bus ride home. The juvenile court, through me, would recommend those youngsters eligible for the program.

Cliff was on the phone with Wayne Blanton and me regularly on all the details. He was one of those philanthropists who followed his money all the way into the program. First question he asked, "What is the salary of school teachers in Dade County?" Not even waiting for the answer, he ordered, "We'll pay 10 percent more than the going rate."

At our first meeting he announced, "I do not want any publicity on this program." This edict was scrupulously followed. The program was simply called Boys Club Aftercare Program, neither Perlman nor Caesar's Palace identified as sponsors.

The first ten graduates had 120 arrests among them before entering our program. Only one was rearrested after completing the program. Not quite as successful with succeeding graduates, but we scored considerably higher than other comparable programs. A 99+ success rate to begin with was quite a good start.

Perlman flew Blanton, me, and a number of the kids to a Caesar's Palace board meeting in Las Vegas. As financial advisors, they had President Nixon's former secretary of state William Rogers and a past governor of Nevada. There was hardly a mention of casino money. It was all stock investments worldwide.

I was the star attraction reporting on their little frolic in Miami. I told them of Perlman's personal involvement and the success of the program. They generously applauded. Nothing anyone said, but I had the feeling they were humoring their chairman of the board in this do-good venture. The million a year expended was a mere pittance to them.

Perlman, buoyed by his success, started a similar program in Los Angeles and planned to go nationwide. We suggested to him that additional donors be invited, but Cliff, so excited about the prospects, insisted that any donor offer several million in advance and be on probation for a number of years. Obviously, no takers on that.

After five years, internal problems ended this venture. Perlman made some bad business choices starting an airline for wealthy travelers that never quite got off the ground, and his application for a license to expand with another casino in Atlantic City was rejected. He was forced to sell his interest in Caesar's Palace for a paltry one hundred million, and our Aftercare program was gone.

To the credit of Wayne Blanton, the Boys Club determined to keep the program alive continued it with a smaller edition, but maintaining the original concept. Today, they still have a high-quality tutoring program though no longer connected to the juvenile court.

I tried inducing the *Miami Herald* to do an editorial lauding Cliff Perlman's generosity and the success of the program. Lord knows there were few programs around worth cheering about. They declined, no doubt viewing casino money as bad and Perlman personally not worthy of their acclaim. A small editorial of praise might have induced other moneyed people to keep the program going. Too bad.

My 1980 "Profile of Dade County Juvenile Crime" ran ten pages longer than the twenty-seven pages three years earlier. This one garnered a lot more attention than the earlier one. Both the *Miami Herald* and the *Miami News* ran stories with headlines quoting me: "Juvenile System Fails," "Judge Pessimistic about Reform," "Juvenile System Does Little to Help."

The data on criminal conduct were hard to quarrel with. Apparently, delinquency was slowly increasing, notwithstanding the efforts of the juvenile court. Despite the very low incidence of Latin crime in 1977, it had jumped up 12 percent in three years, though still below its percentage by population.

The situation among black children also continued to worsen. Ninety-four percent of black delinquents under age twelve lived in one-parent homes. In those one-parent homes with a new father-figure replacement coming into the picture, the presence of substitute father increased rather than lowered delinquent behavior.

There was little positive in this report. Female juvenile crime had actually gone down several percentage points, but in later years their crime rate would move sharply upward. No trends suggested improved prospects for the years ahead.

The most distressing news was in the recidivism area. Quoting from my report,

> At the time these juveniles appeared in my Court, in 1977, and had been referred to treatment programs over 70% had at least four prior arrests. Their subsequent record shows that while still in the juvenile system, 57% were rearrested, one third of them, as many as four times.
>
> Combining this with their rearrest records in the Adult system, 68% of the juveniles seen by that Court in 1977 had been rearrested between then and 1980. Twenty-five percent were arrested from five to twelve times in the intervening three year period.

This report, and others of its kind, might be viewed as creating a sense of hopelessness, but professionals in the field had to avoid that attitude. Much of the crime rise was cyclical due to other factors such as birth rise and other natural phenomenon. Hopefully, it would turn back in the next cycle. We were in an era of rising crime. The data were essential to create a baseline from which to operate and to assess programs.

Sound data were also important in judging the true value of programs. Many in the field, touting their rehab programs, were too quick to seek funding for programs that sounded good but had little value. Others, seeking to eliminate the juvenile system, often proffered the "no hope" doctrine rather than actual data as the basis for their belief. The situation was indeed bad, but the effort to improve need not diminish.

My reports on local Dade County and other reports providing national data on juvenile crime were only bare-bone indications of the perilous situation. Crime, particularly among juveniles, has been a scourge always with us never likely to totally disappear. Despite these low-marks, progress, programmatically and systemically, had improved the system, not by quantum leaps, but inching along. No miracles in store.

Writing opinion pieces for magazines and newspapers had enabled me to make a point to large audiences. Having columns in the *New York Times*, the *Christian Science Monitor*, and being cited in other national outlets, plus the acceptance of individual columns to newspapers statewide, became a successful technique for me.

Of course, always being in print tends to result sometimes in debating with oneself. Some months after I had been quoted with the headlines—"Juvenile System Fails" and "Judge Pessimistic About Reform," I did an op-ed column hailing the benefits of shifting more teenage hard cores into adult court. My statement "we now have a viable rehabilitation network with the potential for success among the very young delinquents" did appear contrary to positions earlier taken.

My point was that by taking the hard cores out of the juvenile judge's jurisdiction there was now room and time to do a better job with the less-violent youngsters. Most judges, including me, had opposed this lessening of their authority, but I wanted to keep spirits up by pointing to a benefit even in defeat.

So what happened next? On the basis of the direct files being removed to the adult court, HRS immediately announced a new formula for the allocation of caseworkers, cutting 25 percent of the staff. The new matrix based on caseload meant our Dade County workers would be shifted to Fort Meyers, a nice, quiet town on the west coast of Florida.

Sending off a nasty letter to HRS, I called their formula "arcane," stating, "I'm not aware of any crime wave in Ft. Meyers. Dade County juvenile crime requires staff and resources far beyond that available. Don't do it," I demanded. My letter concluded with the statement "Anytime anyone starts to run social services by formula, I know we are in deep trouble."

From there we marshaled our forces, enlisting State Senator Jack Gordon, chairman of the Senate Appropriations Committee and other legislators. Bill Gladstone, then on leave working in Tallahassee with Governor Graham, did his bit. Quite a bit. Pressure prevailed, and our staff was restored. Periodically we went through this with HRS. They had some efficiency experts in Tallahassee who, rather than going to the source to determine need, fell back on a matrix designed by some number cruncher hidden in an attic.

My op-ed piece describing how well things were going in Dade County probably wasn't the major factor in the HRS decision, but to be certain in the future I determined to be careful not too sound to optimistic about the potential of the juvenile justice system.

The Mariel Boatlift that year prompted me to do a report on the arrival of hundreds of juveniles freed from Cuban jails. The headline in the *Miami Herald* stated, "Judge Sees Crime Wave From Boatlift of Juveniles From Cuba." In Cuba, many of the teenagers had been offered the alternative of extending their jail terms or joining the boatlift. Some were in Cuban prisons as bona fide criminals, others as political prisoners protesting persecution by the Castro regime. Hard to tell who among them properly belonged in each grouping.

An estimated 1,400 juveniles came from Cuba, several hundred to Miami. Upon arrival each was required to respond to a questionnaire made available for my study. Two out of three had been released directly from a jail in Cuba. Their crimes ranged from trespassing to larceny and robbery.

Judge Gladstone, handling these first cases, attempted to persuade the federal government to take over their welfare, but that was not likely for some time to come. The immediate impact on Dade County was sharp. Nine refugee teenagers had already been sent to psychiatric hospital for treatment—estimated cost $600,000. Several had already been involved in serious criminal charges.

Ed Tutty, administrator of our mental health clinic, declared it "a very explosive situation." Our clinic was now finally fully functioning but obviously not able to handle an onslaught of new cases. This influx of potential users of our juvenile system created a burden difficult to handle. Cuban emigration to Florida at that time was a big strain on all the community resources. The Mariel Boatlift was viewed not as Cuban citizens seeking respite and safety from a cruel tyrant. Miamians, instead, saw it as an angry Castro punishing South Florida by dumping felons on to our shores.

Three years later in my 1983 profile, now extended to seventy-one pages, I had to eat a bit of crow. Reviewing the actual crime rate of the Latin juveniles arriving in the 1980 Mariel Boatlift, I had to recant on my earlier prediction. In a December 1983 *Miami Herald* column by columnist Roberto Fabrico, I was quoted eating a bit of crow. "The figures of the past three years suggest no such surge in crime by these groups, and there is no likelihood there will be a problem with them in the future."

A *New York Times* article also quoted me and in their own analysis agreed with my current position. The *Times* estimated the number of Mariel refugees who entered our public schools as high as fifteen thousand and costing the school system over sixteen million dollars.

At the onset of the 1980s, the juvenile court had been in the usual state of turmoil, but things were settling down a bit. Many of the needed programs were in place, though far from running at a high pace.

The arrival of the school board's Resource Support Program, along with the development of our mental health clinic and with some stability in Youth Hall, had us running fairly well but mostly in an uncoordinated fashion. Each of the juvenile court units ran as an independent entity, finding it difficult to mesh with each other in terms of providing a full-service coordinated program.

Administratively, I addressed the problem by Thursday morning conclaves, inviting about fifteen unit heads whose functions revolved around the court. These included prosecutors, defenders, intake counselors, school resources, detention, field workers, et al. All were intimately involved in the process, but other than an occasional exchange of memos or some conflict had little real links to each other.

Our Thursday morning gatherings were designed solely to exchange ideas and concerns. No policy established. No debates on philosophy. No conflict, no war of words. No newspaper releases. Everything said stayed there. Amazing how differences were resolved merely by being in the same room and actually talking to one another in the flesh. The press free to attend found these sessions too boring.

These weekly get-togethers also had another positive result. Some of the attendees represented small departments. Others led units that though large in size had little influence on decision making. Participating here, where everyone's comment had equal status, gave a sense of importance to all. As chairman, I avoided dominating the meeting or preaching to the folks in attendance. These meetings were an unnoticed but valuable addition in stabilizing and coordinating the process.

No other court setting has the potential explosiveness of the juvenile court. The many disciplines involved are in a kind of tinderbox always waiting to explode. The participants, always under the gun, crisis after crisis facing them, don't have time to calmly assess each situation—except on these peaceful Thursday mornings over a cup of coffee.

I recall an incident where an HRS supervisor, promoted to deputy administrator, immediately sought to impress his subordinates by exercising his authority far in excess of what was necessary. Reports had come to me urging my intercession. As the administrative judge, I had no direct authority over his conduct. Nonetheless, I sent him this private memo:

> To: John James (not real name)
> From: Seymour Gelber
> Power: *In governance, the greater power one possesses, the less it need be exercised.*
>
> —*Anon.*

I then added this little made-up allegory to impress upon him the proper use of power.

> As the tumbrel rumbled slowly through the crowd toward the guillotine, King Louis XVI espied Robespierre, his former Prime Minister, now heading the Committee to Avenge the Revolution.
> 'You know,' he said to Marie Antoinette, standing alongside him, 'He used to be such a nice, quiet boy when he worked for us.'

My memo worked a lot better than had I pulled rank and admonished him for his behavior. He thenceforth calmed down and performed in a more reasoned and subdued fashion.

Back in 1982 I delivered a speech, unrelated directly to children, more to the lack of community leadership, titled, "Where Have Our Heroes Gone?" My words then described an earlier era of the 1950s when civil rights and school integration had captured America. Relatively new then in the community and still a pure liberal, I had been enchanted by my Miami heroes, each having played so dramatic a role in the struggle for equality.

There were the black heroes, two clergymen, Ed Graham and Theodore Gibson, who struggled valiantly leading sit-ins and speaking out as the voices of the depressed minority.

There was Jack Orr, a Florida state legislator from Dade County who was the lone voice standing on the House floor, stating boldly to his colleagues that segregation was immoral. His was the only vote against segregation. And yes, it cost him his House seat in the next election.

And Dick Gerstein, though aware he was personally a target of a racist group bent on assassinating newspaper editors and prominent Jews, he refused to make arrests until sufficient evidence was gathered, enabling all the top conspirators to also be charged.

I asked that question about leadership—"Where Have Our Heroes Gone?"—using as an example those events of yet twenty-five years earlier.

My underlying theme, then and now, is still the same, and it does relate to the condition of children.

The lack of community leadership always has been the nub of our problem. The community indifference to the plight of our underprivileged, wayward youth is reflected in the failure of our state legislature to be responsive to the need. Where are our civic leaders now?

It's not often that a judge can claim a coup, but back in 1983 I took credit for masterminding this one. It all came about over the Gladview Center, a drab-looking discarded public school in Liberty City. Viewed as excess property by the school system and now used as a center for three programs for abused and delinquent children, it was in dismal shape. No funds available. Total community indifference. No prospects in sight. What do I do?

Challenged by some parents, I took the problem home to our dinner table to Edith and our three kids. Something I rarely do. The answers were quick and varied. Start a fund-raising drive? A raffle? How about a carwash? None of the above.

Now Judy, the new lawyer. Then Daniel, the first-year law student. And Barbara, the college undergraduate—all were really vying with idea.

A walkathon? Write to President Reagan? On and on. Daniel finally hit it. "Why not a classified ad? Half the things we have in the house Mom got at garage sales out of *Miami Herald* ads. Why don't you run a classified ad challenging the community?"

It was the best forty-one dollars ever invested in children: "Want a piece of Liberty City action? Social agencies need help for kids in trouble. Talk or deeds?" (plus my home telephone number).

I was confident some reporter would pick up the ad perusing the paper, and sure enough, a nice story followed with a good follow-up of contributions. But that was only the beginning.

Shortly thereafter, the *Miami Herald* Classified Advertising Department ran a contest inviting classified ad users to compete for the most successful want ad printed in the paper. No way I could lose that one. I wrote a piece describing the need and how my own children had provided the approach. The *Herald* prize was printing my description in a full page ad, reprinted weekly for months after.

The outpouring was continuous. First, a foundation offering to build a baseball stadium on the rock-filled lot adjoining the building. A Sun Bank president donated a ping-pong table. The Boys Club offered the use of a swimming pool. Jobs came from restaurants and other businesses. Best of all, leaders in the neighborhood who had been unhappy with the presence of the programs, now organized a community board to look after the interests of the forgotten children.

No, none of the kids' problems were solved permanently, but for one brief stretch of time, things came together, and hope was theirs. At least they could see that people in the community cared about them.

The classified ad caper was a heartening experience, but only a sidebar to what really troubled all those who practice in this field. Why can't we do better for children is the question always asked? The answer is usually the same: We don't have enough resources. Our programs are inadequate. There's insufficient aftercare for delinquents. The public refuses to invest sufficient funds for treatment programs. And a few others, all part of the responses judges deliver for their Rotary Club luncheon speeches.

Hearing these plaints for years and uttering a few of them myself, I decided to do something about testing the "not enough resources" theory propounded by all the professionals.

After all, don't I have an entire rehab system at my disposal? As the administrative judge, I can order whatever I deem appropriate in the best interest of a child. So, why not select a handful of the worse delinquents we have and devise a program that offers everything the experts believe can make over a serious delinquent? And presto! The good deed is done.

Thereupon I did exactly that. For my research experiment I selected a handful of recently convicted hard-core delinquents, each with a long rap sheet, at least ten arrests. Sentenced to the harshest punishment in the juvenile system, namely putting them on the next bus to the State Reformatory, they became the targets for my study.

Meanwhile, I obtained a streetwise master counselor (Cornelius Foster) and had him literally remove the boys from the bus. He told them they not only are free, but also that every need of theirs and their families will be attended to in the coming year. Jobs, schooling, counseling, housing, and clothing to be provided through the auspices of the master counselor. And besides, they had a judge looking out for them.

Throw in a college-trained supervisor who followed the book and knew all the bureaucratic ropes to assist the master counselor. Add the idealistic judge to open doors and guarantee access to every available program no matter the cost. Initially planned as a one year experiment, instead it ran for four years.

Was it really the lack of rehab programs and other resources that caused repeat delinquent behavior? Did the court have the bottom-line answer to make the family whole again? We would find out soon enough. Wouldn't we?

Here's how each of these kids turned out (names have been changed):

Lester Burrows, "the Runner." Black male, fifteen, twelve arrests. Last arrest: burglary. Discarded by mother at early age. Grew up in streets. Placed in more than twenty shelter homes. Pleasant, likeable, devious. Survived by hustling homosexuals and occasional burglary. Rejected offers of jobs, schooling, and housing. No matter the plan offered, he ran. Trusted no one in authority. In final interview before disappearing again, he admitted he had a job selling drugs and therefore unable to abide by rules.

Marco Zargula, "the Charmer." Latin male, fifteen. Last conviction: armed robbery. Twelve arrests. Broken family. Sent to several quality, expensive drug programs. Talented, bright. Thrives in institution, always cited as "most likely to succeed," then back to drugs. Visited with him in Fort Pierce, Florida, lockup after escape from Last Chance Ranch. Now a forlorn, broken figure. Last contact in adult prison.

Lawrence Samuels, "the Fighter." Black, male, fifteen. Eighteen arrests, eleven including violence. Six foot four, tough, powerful, and violent. Parents caring, hardworking government employees. Master Counselor Foster arranged for high-school basketball scholarship. Skipped first day of practice; instead arrested same day for robbery of motorist in stalled car on expressway. Assaultive, starts fires, attacks counselors. Last contact in adult prison.

Andy Sills, "the Drinker." White male, fifteen, eight arrests, plus nine family neglect charges. Broken family, father alcoholic. Mother moves from city to city, man to man. Andy gets drunk, then remorseful. Sent to trade school, then relapsed. Can't hold job. Weak. Last contact working as pizza delivery boy. Last seen—. Sober, no arrests but questionable future.

Dwight Anderson, "the Migrant." Youngest in group. Black, male, age twelve, fifteen arrests. Large family of migrant workers. Low IQ. Lives in overcrowded hovel with countless relatives. Will not ride school bus. Mother refuses to wake him for school. No one in charge. No one cares. Determined to be a disc jockey and buy house for mother, whom he loves very much. Last contact, rejects schooling. Working at odd jobs. No recent arrests. Stable, but likelihood of success doubtful, at best.

Our program was a highly intense day-to-day, almost hour-to-hour program with Cornelius Foster, our master counselor, in constant contact with his charges. In some instances he was virtually a family member, visiting family early in the morning to make certain the child was on the school bus.

Foster grew up in Liberty City, a Vietnam War veteran who returned to Miami unable to adjust and went on crime spree. He was sentenced to two fifteen-year terms for liquor store robberies, served five years in Raiford State Prison, attended junior college classes in prison, and upon release earned a bachelor's degree at Florida A&M. Employed for eight years by HRS as counselor with excellent performance record.

Full medical and psychological profile was done on each child. Each in the group was fully tested before acceptance to the program. None determined to be intellectually incapable of performing, nor was any illness or disease discovered that would prevent decent performance.

Regular conferences that included the judge were held with parents and child. Clients were sent to both public and private programs, all expenses covered. Several were sent to private summer camps, cost covered from fines for lawyers late coming to court. The program obtained decent housing for families and jobs for family members—no stones unturned.

Two of the five held their own. The other three were abject failures, or perhaps we were. Other definitive studies showed that two out of five delinquents avoid further arrests where no program help is offered. Convinced that no matter the perfect program, there is no one fit that automatically does the trick.

The book *Hard-Core Delinquents: Reaching out through the Miami Experiment* was published by the University of Alabama Press in 1988. Interestingly, several major publishing houses had expressed an interest, but candidly advised that had the experiment proved successful, they would have deemed it publishable.

From my own professional point of view, I thought that rejecting this widely held theory among field professionals was a worthwhile finding. Perhaps our high failure rate was due to other causes, not alone the lack of resources and tools necessary. But I do understand the publishers. Who wants to read a "how to do it" book that fails in telling how to do it?

The poor results of this four-year experience dampened my spirits for a while. However, working directly with this group did give me a close-up view and perhaps a more caring one. In time, reflecting on the overall picture, I realized there was no point in being dejected. I was only the custodian of their stories. They were the ones who had to bear their own lives.

Moving on. Occasionally, I'd visit our detention center school lockup during one of the regular classes for the student inmates. These were kids either waiting for trial or transfer to a more permanent program. On one of my visits, a *Miami Herald* reporter came along and recited these exchanges in his newspaper story:

> Teacher: Everybody met Judge Gelber?
> Elroy (A cynical seventeen year old awaiting trial as adult for Armed Robbery): Yeah, longtime ago in Court. He didn't speak to me in the courtroom. Just looked at my file. It's a big change to have a Judge sitting here in front of you and talking to you.
> Harry (A fast taking, fifteen year old awaiting trial for Robbery in Juvenile Court): If they withhold Adjudication in my case, I'm going to become something in life. Probably be a lawyer. Can I become a lawyer?
> Gelber: Maybe. But first you had better stay in school and learn to read and write.
> Pedro (A youth facing a four year armed Robbery sentence in Adult Court): Can you express some thoughts about how we can go about changing our lives?

> Gelber: You've heard enough lectures. The problem is you. You are the problem. Not the Judge, or the world out there. It's you. When you go out and commit a burglary, it's because you choose to do it.

Mostly what you have to do is to talk to yourself, about how you are going to govern yourself to become a better person. I can't give you a formula. If I had a formula, I'd package it and sell it at Walgreens.

Pedro wasn't too impressed with my blunt response, later telling the reporter that my answer was a "dodge."

> Pedro: Society has to share the blame for my condition. Somebody should have taken me aside when I was thirteen and warned me.

When I had these talks with these young inmates I usually varied my approach. Sometimes the kind, caring, fatherly figure; other times the blunt "tell it like it is" guy. I preferred the latter. Hard to tell what works, if anything. I'm not sure how much the kids benefited from my talks.

At least, I always came away learning something. This time it was Elroy's comment suggesting I was more interested in reading his file than in looking at him. That was a good pointer for me. I tried to do better.

Always I had cautioned new judges assigned to our court, "Don't take these cases home with you. If you do, you'll burn-out quicker than a two-inch candle." But that's no excuse to avoid personal contact. An extra few minutes conversing with these kids can only help.

Every once in awhile, some kid comes along you can't escape. With me it was J who wanted to shoot all the Porsches, Trans-Ams, and Camaros. Also kill his parents and blow out his own brains.

His heroes, he announced, were serial killers David Berkowitz, "Son of Sam," and Carl Brown, a local man who had killed eight people, here in Dade County, in a welding shop massacre for no apparent reason.

J, a sixteen-year-old, came before me after an arrest one night breaking into Hialeah Junior High School. Dressed all in black, he had in his possession a .45-caliber Colt Automatic pistol with ammunition in his glove and a four-inch dagger hidden in one of his socks. When asked by the police officer why he chose to break into a school, he calmly replied, "If I were to go into a house, someone might be there, and I would have to kill that person."

In all my conversations with J he was pleasant, smiling, presenting a normal demeanor. Examination had shown him to be a paranoid schizophrenic, with a high IQ, living in a twisted reality. His parents made light of his behavior wanting him to be returned home to them. His mother stated, "J has never threatened any of us." His father, a former military officer in Cuba, always had chided him on his lack of manliness.

Placed in several treatment programs, all pronounced him in need of long-term specialized treatment. There were only few places to send kids with these delusionary problems. Mostly as a favor to me, he was seen by several competent physicians, all agreeing he was dangerous and in need of long-term treatment. Only short-term treatment was available to the court. Besides, J was of an age where he would soon be out of the jurisdiction of the juvenile court. What do we do with kids like J? And there are many.

I took the problem to a meeting of the Florida Bar, attended by about two hundred lawyers, mostly handling matrimonial case, and outlined some of the recommendations made by Bill Gladstone, who had struggled for years with this fearful mental health concern. I was sharply critical of the Bar's failure to arouse excitement over this issue. "Professionally," I told these matrimonial lawyers "you deal with children, but are concerned with only how they affect your fees."

After the session, one of the lawyers confronted me, "I take offense with what you said." My response: "I intended to shake you up. I didn't come here to attack matrimonial lawyers, but you are a member of the community and should be concerned about things beyond your fees."

My flip response was probably uncalled for, but lawyers at times do tend to focus on self-interest, rather than public interest. With a lot of urging by Judge Gladstone, the Florida Bar has moved forward on the serious mental health problems of children like J.

What happened to J? He visited several more doctors, but no serious treatment was available. No longer living with his parents, nor under my jurisdiction, he had not shot up any Porsches. At age twenty he came back to visit me and seemed in decent shape. He had a job but wanted to join the marines. The recruiting officer required that he obtain a letter of endorsement from his juvenile court judge.

With a smile, he asked for my support. In return, I smiled back, saying. "Not on your life. Not anyone's life." That's the last I heard from or about J. In a short time, he was sure to become a marine officer, and with all that weaponry around I'd be responsible for his action. No thanks.

Life never gets any easier dealing with HRS and the state legislature. A rash of child molestation cases produced legislation prohibiting State youth counselors with criminal records to work with children. A splendid safety concern quickly approved by the state legislature.

Problem: Some of our best drug therapists are former addicts with criminal records. In addition, field counselors, including Cornelius Foster, my own master counselor who had directed my experiment with those five kids, will be summarily dismissed. I petitioned and begged to make exemptions for those HRS workers in these essential categories. The legislators sponsoring the Bill declined.

About forty fit into the discharged group, and despite efforts by their union as well as individual judges, the sponsoring legislators were adamant, claiming any weakening of the legislation would open the door for violators. To me it appeared that they had received such good press on introducing the legislation; they were fearful some of the luster would disappear by making exceptions.

Entering into a protracted volley of public exchanges with them, I was making only small progress, but I sensed the press was shifting to my side. Fortunately, one of the discharged employees took the case to court and won. The jobs of the forty were saved. The next session of the legislature would make the necessary alterations. It feels good to win one every so often.

The year 1985 also brought a few other problems to solve. Although other metropolitan areas—Los Angeles, New York, and Detroit—were overrun by street gangs we had been more fortunate. At least until this year. Apparently some of the large more dangerous gangs were branching out to Miami.

My position as chair of the Criminal Justice Council led me to join with Metro-Dade Police major Doug Hughes in organizing a countywide task force. The police were focused on identifying the culprits and their activity. My aim was to involve the gang leaders in an effort to divert their energies in other more positive directions. I was chosen as the nominal head of the group by virtue of my office.

Many of these gang kids were now patrons of the juvenile court. Together our task force set up joint forums aimed at finding employment and recreational avenues for the gang members. Gang control officers went into schools and jails contacting gang members with an eye toward solutions. Our major pursuit was to involve these youngsters in the decision making. In the past it had been preaching or the strong hand of the law.

Too often these efforts are one sided with the authorities making all the decisions. State Attorney Janet Reno, school board chairman Janet McAliley, and I decided to have face-to-face discussions responding to the needs and wishes of the gang leaders. We also contacted local business leaders for employment opportunities, followed with grant applications to institutionalize our effort.

Major Hughes and I met frequently with the gang leaders to set up joint action. The opportunity for input changed their attitudes considerably. Comprising about eight hundred members among forty gangs, they were believed to have been responsible for a dozen murders as well as robberies and aggravated battery.

One night, the gangs decided to hold a midnight dance session at a Miami Beach movie house on Washington Avenue. The site was identified as featuring risqué shows and wild dancing. A few police officers and I were invited. The dances consisted of the newest dance fad, throwing participants from the stage, bouncing them off the cement floor. After a few of the participants started showing ill effects, we conferred with the organizers. I suggested that the number of ambulances available at night was limited.

The leaders laughed and abided by our suggestion. Would they have complied so easily had we not established a trusting relationship, limited as it was? Probably not. I thought some of those kids actually liked me. A good word here and there can go a long way . . . sometimes.

As chairman of the group it was my responsibility to keep the project together. This joint effort—involving personnel from law enforcement, the court and school officials—provided an opportunity in all the aspects of controlling delinquency. Unaccustomed to a nonpunitive effort by the very authority sworn to eliminate them, I sensed a positive reaction from the gang leaders.

Never before had they had so much constructive attention turned in their direction. The police personnel involved also were heartened with the possibility of gang control without the need for actual hand-to-hand struggle. Gangs, once organized, are difficult to dislodge, but this was a good beginning. We will see.

Another big problem came my way at the tail end of the 1980s. AIDS had become a major concern in the country. At first it was designated as a disease limited to homosexuals; later it found a way into the black community and eventually struck all classes. AIDS had a frightening impact. How to halt the spread was a major concern among health officials.

Without consulting with either health officials or HRS, I determined to take a lead in attacking AIDS among teenagers. The data showed only a small number of incidents among the teenage group. However, since AIDS had a five to ten year incubation period, teenagers most likely were catching and then transmitting the virus even before it surfaced in their own bodies.

Our detention center, with four thousand youngsters passing through it yearly, seemed an appropriate place to intercept the virus. Kids arrested and placed in Detention awaiting trial constituted a population with a greater likelihood of having had sexual encounters. Certainly, some belonged to one or more of the high-risk groups. As administrative judge, with authority to control the detention center operation, I could install this program.

Prior to my effort, AIDS tests had been provided in our detention center only when some symptoms appeared. Thus far only fifteen detainees had been tested for AIDS in the past two years. Two, both prostitutes, tested positive. My goal was not to wait until AIDS was apparent, but to detect it early to aid the child and avoid transmittal. Prevention is always the aim of the juvenile court, and what better way than my proposed plan to examine those most likely to be infected coming through our detention center?

Joyner Sims, the HRS AIDS program administrator, supported my reasoning saying, "We can't ignore the fact that we may have a very significant problem that we don't learn about until years later, when it is too late." A spokesman for Greg Coler, HRS secretary in Tallahassee, said, "We put a lot of weight in what Judge Gelber has to say."

Our program would be voluntary, offering testing to detainees in several AIDS high-risk categories: intravenous drug users, homosexual or bisexual males, prostitutes, and those with multiple sex partners. Proper follow-up medical care were to be provided through Dade County's Jackson Memorial Hospital.

The *Miami Herald* news story quoted me,

> The proposal would be part of a comprehensive program aimed at a segment of the population that has been ignored in efforts to stop the spread of AIDS. These are the kinds of people who are most likely to become victims and transmitters.
>
> Many of these kids are into drugs. They are into easy sex and they are alienated from society. These are the kids most vulnerable to AIDS.

I further announced that the testing program would be designed with careful consideration of issues such as privacy and confidentiality, and would be carried out in conjunction with extensive counseling.

Though the inherent power of a judge is a powerful weapon, it is not absolute. Lacking direct authority over personnel in the detention center, I nonetheless felt confident all the bases needed to make a go for this project had been covered.

This would be the first detention center in the country to institute such a program, and treading carefully was essential. To gain support outside of Dade County, a report, prepared by me, carefully detailing the purpose and the procedures was sent to other jurisdictions and organizations. I was ready to move out as a trailblazer.

Dr. Margaret Fischl, director of the Jackson Memorial Hospital AIDS Clinic and a national expert on the subject, had met with me and recommended a list of questions to be added to the standard Youth Hall medical interview. A tentative date for screening to begin on the first week in November had been set. We were really moving—fast.

Then some rumblings began. HRS had some reservations as voiced by District Administrator Linda Berkowitz, who said, "I have concerns about what the court's expectation of us will be. I also have concerns about the population at the detention center backing up while tests are run."

Steve Levine, head of the Juvenile Public Defender's Office and a skeptic about many of my projects, added his doubts on the subject saying, "Ideally, HRS should have plenty of money to handle this problem. But the fact is, we're great at identifying problems while not having anything we can do about them."

These were shots across the bow but hardly insurmountable. Next, it was some defense lawyers claiming that since the Youth Hall only held juveniles before going to trial, the court had no authority until after sentencing to impose testing. Didn't argue with that one since I welcomed a law suit.

Then came the ACLU contending that the privacy question required parental consent. They also questioned the manner the test results would be used. Finally, the State Health Department nixed the proposal completely. This was their domain, and any act by a Judge would be unacceptable. And that was that.

I was disappointed over losing the opportunity to launch what was sure to be a national project. Upon reflection I realized I had been too eager. My behavior was way out of character for me. Ordinarily, with projects of this magnitude, moving cautiously taking in partners would have been more my approach. Probably best had I referred it to the state Health Department for them to take the lead. And properly that is where it belonged.

I learned an important lesson. Don't rush headlong into the unknown until the land is properly surveyed. Being an activist, even with all the power of a judge, only means that moving forward often calls for stepping on the brake. Pausing in order to take careful cognizance of what lies ahead made more sense.

One year ahead for the end of my term. It was September 1988. Next year at this time the glory days are over. Reaching the age of seventy was the compulsory retirement age for judges in Florida.

In years past, I had viewed seventy as dotage years, but now I was just warming up to the fray. I had a fifteen-year run, enjoying every minute of it. Pleased with myself over having shed my "second banana" posture and had moved into conflict with confidence and certainty. Although my sense is that I messed up my AIDS project by going headlong into the project.

Still one more important contest ahead. Hopefully, this one would be better managed. On September 6, 1988, Dade voters gave initial approval to a nine-member Juvenile Welfare Board (JWB) to administer youth programs, teen pregnancy, and child abuse. This was a project I had initiated along with State Attorney Janet Reno and school board chairman Janet McAliley.

Our county attorney had ruled that the proviso for providing funds with an added tax on property needed to be on a separate ballot, two months later. We disagreed with the county attorney preferring both issues on the same ballot, but realizing a lawsuit would be too time consuming, deferred to his opinion. In the first balloting we had prevailed by a sixty-to-forty vote advantage with wide win margins in the Anglo, black and Hispanic communities.

Since both Pinellas County and Palm Beach County had already succeeded in establishing a JWB and some other Florida counties were also so disposed, we were confident in the next go-round of voting.

Our group began by meeting weekly, raising some funds, but our early strategy was to low-key the proposal. No advertising until the day before election. Reno, McAliley, and I would meanwhile cover all the civic groups urging their support. Martin Fine, a leading lawyer in the community offered to be our fund-raiser. In the first half successful campaign we had raised only $10,000, viewing this amount as adequate.

A wide range of organizations backed our referendum. These included the Greater Miami Chamber of Commerce, the Urban League, the League of Women Voters, and the Latin Builder's Association. Any candidate for public office would be a cinch for election with this kind of backing. To say the least, we were confident.

Thus far the strategy to low-key the campaign had worked. Sometimes these under-the-radar campaigns, involving an additional tax, are more likely to succeed without arousing the "no tax" legions. For the second go-round imposing an actual tax, our board members at first opted for a highly visible campaign with a goal to raise $100,000 for advertising. However, since no organized opposition had yet appeared, we chose not to emphasize fund-raising.

Reno, McAliley, and I made the rounds of all the civic groups, espousing our cause, receiving welcome receptions. I recall running into Reno in a bowling alley out near the airport at 7:00 a.m. Our scheduler had messed up, but we were both glad for each other's presence. Everything looked good.

The November 8 second ballot asked the voters to give taxing authority to impose a property tax of a maximum 50¢ per $1,000 of taxable property value. We had calculated about an average of $25-$30 dollars annual cost per property owner. The newspapers endorsed our proposal, and I arose on election day, November 8, certain of victory. I decided to skip the planned victory celebration, preferring instead to watch the TV results at home.

After the first-round victory, I announced to the press, "The real test will come November 8. Since people will be voting on the actual tax, there will be some who will raise questions whether they want to pay for the programs."

I had never given those words a second thought since they were made merely to keep our troops working steadily and not be overconfident. Home that evening, tuned to the TV results, I awaited the final tally. Sure enough, it was the same as the first go-round, sixty to forty in our favor.

I called to wife Edith in the kitchen, "Come in and see. We won." A moment later Edith looked at the screen and said, "Seymour, you have that upside down. You lost." Grabbing for the phone I called the TV station to tell them of their reporting error. Really couldn't believe we had lost. It wasn't possible. It was.

Not a total loss. McAliley, Reno, and I went before the Dade County Commission and sold them on this proposition. "Even though the voters refused to fund a Juvenile Welfare Board in November 1988," I said, "they had voted by a large margin two months earlier to establish such a board. So, you have a moral obligation to create such an entity by ordinance."

Surprisingly, they acceded to our wishes by authorizing the Children's Service Council but provided no program funding. Even without adequate funding, the council functioned fairly well under Chairman Modesto Abety. Four years later in 2002, David Lawrence, then heading the Children's Trust, placed the subject on the ballot again, and this time won handily.

Modesto Abety was again chosen head of the now fully funded new entity, titled the Children's Services Council. Obviously, Lawrence, the former publisher of the *Miami Herald*, did a better job promoting his cause. It is still hard for me to believe he was more politically adept than three veteran campaigners who among us had won at least a dozen elections.

To me it was more likely that requiring us to go on the ballot twice, the second time the ballot issue clearly focusing on the tax, was our death knoll. I'll never understand why the county attorney insisted on that two-ballot approach for us, and that a few years later only one ballot was required. Undoubtedly, our efforts back in 1988 opened the door and led the way for Lawrence's successful 2002 campaign.

Sometimes developing new programs are will-of-the-wisp projects that fall into your hands and prosper. Other times they suddenly disappear like our failed Juvenile Welfare Board proposal. Hard to predict what makes the difference.

Badly in need of an additional county drug treatment program more accessible to youngsters in need, had been a concern for some time. The few private programs available were located in areas far distant from the neighborhoods where the drug blight was greatest. I enlisted Marty Steinberg, a mentor of son Dan at the Holland & Knight law firm. Both the firm and Steinberg personally had been long involved in communal activities for children.

I advised Steinberg that the site needed to be proximate to a neighborhood with easy access to offenders. Steinberg, a former federal prosecutor, immediately contacted U.S. Attorney Leon Kellner to learn if any large homes had been seized by the federal government for possible use as a drug center. Federal law enforcement had the authority to take title to property illegally used for criminal enterprises.

"What a great idea," responded Kellner. "How about the Palace?" The Palace happened to be a sprawling compound owned by the largest supplier of cocaine in North Dade. The government had seized it and sent the owner to prison for 137 years. What an opportunity. How did we get so lucky?

Steinberg, Kellner, and Dade County officials immediately began to make plans to obtain and convert the Palace into a drug rehab center. This was a two-story house, three-car garage, cabana, swimming pool, surrounded by an electric fence and guarded by Dobermans. Closed-circuit cameras also guarded the premises.

Steinberg, along with his Holland & Knight law firm, volunteered hundreds of hours working out the details. I gave moral support and whatever prestige my office offered to further this project. This could be an important addition to our rehab programs as well as a boost to the neighborhood.

In order to comply with federal requirements, the Palace would also be used as a mini-police station, further enhancing its value to the adjoining neighborhood. Steinberg pressed county officials to meet with leaders of the black community and to begin making application for a zoning variance.

County officials advised a wait for a more appropriate time. Steinberg and I deferred to their judgment. Finally the neighbors caught wind of the plan and called a meeting, suspecting this would be a residential treatment center for hard-core criminals.

County officials chose not to attend. Neither Steinberg nor I were advised of the meeting. Had we been invited, we would have told that the plan envisioned only a day program for first-offender juveniles.

Seventy-five residents showed up, twenty making impassioned speeches about powerful forces from outside the neighborhood hurting their property values and bringing criminals to their neighborhood. It had now become a racial thing and a rich-vs.-poor conflict. A week later the county withdrew their support for the project.

Poor Marty Steinberg, flabbergasted at being left out in the cold, was in a state of shock. All that effort to no avail. U.S. Attorney Leon Kellner quietly made other plans for the the Palace.

I was greatly disappointed at losing a drug treatment program. The neighborhood had done a NIMBY—not in my back yard—but no one on our side had bothered to talk to the residents about the project until word had leaked out.

Who to blame? Probably timid county officials who had tiptoed around the subject, likely knowing the neighbors might rebel, and for political reasons avoiding a testy issue. As the president of the Little Rivers Neighborhood Association had said, "In a black neighborhood, they think they can come in and tell you what's good for you."

I hated my final effort as an advocate for children to fail this way. We were so close; if only we had handled it a bit better. Had Marty Steinberg, since then a top administrator of several major law firms in Dade County, been free of all the bureaucrats involved, he probably could have found a way. Certainly, he and I together would have had a chance, but what's that about too many cooks spoiling the broth?

I suppose the story of the Palace and other similar incidents illustrate how difficult some of these ventures can be. Interestingly, not one of our judicial advocates going way back to Edith Atkinson ever was deterred by not reaching a goal. Disappointment and defeat are part and parcel of this business but surrender is not. All our activists always moved forward, no matter the obstacles.

Writing my own chapter may leave the reader a bit short. Self-appraisal rarely tells the full story. Fortunately, back in 1985, Ted Rubin, a former Denver Juvenile Court judge, and today a well-regarded consultant on the field, authored a book describing the judicial style of five judges. Selected nationally, each was chosen as best representing one of these traits—leadership, dignity, realism, literalism, responsibility. I was Rubin's choice as the prototype for judicial realism.

Several paragraphs from his book (*Behind the Black Robes*, Sage Publications 1985) have been excerpted here to offer perhaps a more insightful look at the subject of this chapter:

> [Quoting Gelber] Sometimes nothing in the system provides for the kid. Absolutely nothing and you know it. A Judge then must realize that in all likelihood he's not going to be able to cause any basic changes in a child's circumstances.
>
> Then you have a choice. Punish the community because it fails to offer adequate social services. Or protect the community from the child?
>
> Clearly, my decision is in favor of protecting the community. This is a marked departure from my philosophy when I first came on the bench . . . .
>
> There is little rhetoric or child-saving zeal in most of Gelber's commentaries. His initial enthusiasms for more rehabilitation and intervention faded away early in his judicial career, replaced by the sober recognition that good intentions do not necessarily make for good results. (p. 106)

* * *

> Hearing after Hearing may transpire without any questions or conversations between Gelber and the juveniles before him. Communication efforts are just not his style.
>
> [Gelber quote] I don't think it makes a damn bit of difference if you lecture these kids. They've had lectures in school, from the police, from their parents from everyone. If I do the same thing all the others do, then it tells them this guy isn't much different.
>
> I want them to know they are in a Court and not in a library. I want their level of apprehension to be high and stay high. The kids have to believe this proceeding is not cut and dried. That it is fair, that they have a chance in this setting, and that something good might happen . . . .

It is doubtful he is the favorite judge of the youngsters who appear before him. They refer to him as "iron balls," hardly a flattering reference, but one that draws a smile from Gelber. Nor is he the favorite of HRS social agency workers who have mixed feelings about him.

Their top-level administrators often acknowledge even less affection for him. They admire his intellect and astute political sense, but have trouble handling both his bluntness and his humor. The steady flow of sharp Gelber newspaper and magazine articles circulated statewide that critiques them are not to their liking. (p.107)

* * *

Somewhat unusual among juvenile court judges, Gelber does not need or seek the affection and plaudits of the courtroom crowd. Rather, he obtains his strokes by working at a few more hopeful rehabilitative enterprises, and by his barrage of carefully designed media reports and commentaries.

His hard line on crime endeared him to the public, though insiders do not deem him unduly harsh. He is a favorite of the media because he understands the nature of the enterprise and of the public pulse. (p. 108)

* * *

Gelber, the writer, has come a long way from his earlier days, before ascending to the bench. Then his words came only as a commentator on the scene, not too sure of his power or his voice.

Now, he frames the issues, buttresses each of his position with data, communicates knowledge, educates the community to what is happening, and challenges his readership and the power structure to take action on his recommendations.

He debunks popular mythologies about crime, and worries publicly that crime-control panaceas not only may diminish our liberty but too often don't really work. Gelber offers panoramic visions, but is really a piecemeal engineer, seeking to do things that can be implemented now. (p. 109)

* * *

[Quoting fellow Judge Charles Edelstein] Seymour is one of the most complex people I have ever known. He doesn't reveal himself to too many. Unlike most Juvenile Judges, he has realistic expectations as to what can be accomplished.

He doesn't have impractical ideas about the government's ability to change behavior. He knows that kids see through a lot of Judges with their father role efforts, so he doesn't work for a relationship. That's his realism.

Gelber, in Court is impatient with empty formalism. He wants to get to the point. He applies due process the way an English Magistrate might. But when he wants to use a big case to change institutional practices, he gives a clear message for very heavy-duty lawyering. He is a practical intellectual. (p. 115)

* * *

In Gelber's view, monitoring is the Judge's most important role. A Judge must insure that intervention and rehabilitation programs are taking place. Though he lacks direct authority over State agencies; Gelber often asserts such authority, shrugging off charges of judicial imperialism. (p. 126)

* * *

Seymour Gelber expresses and implements the belief that a Judge has the responsibility to cause change. This catalyst role applies both within the internal Court setting and outside with the broad community.

[Quoting Gelber] I go for the soft underbelly of the State support agencies hoping to find muscle. I push and push until the muscle shows. Force them to see and use their own strength. (p. 128)

* * *

Gelber looks upon the Juvenile Court judgeship as superior to other judicial assignments. The other Courts keep things in order while the litigants flail each other about.

According to his view, the Juvenile Court Judge is the main actor. Judges in other Divisions have supporting roles or are bit players. Absent the Juvenile Court Judge, there is no part of the system able or willing to assume the leadership role. (p. 136)

Ted Rubin did an excellent analysis catching all the nuances of my personality, some of which I tried to conceal or hadn't even been aware of their existence. I had carefully designed my image to portray what I deemed essential to further my role as an activist judge and as well to survive politically.

How did I view myself? In a *Miami Herald* interview not too long before I retired, responding to a series of questions on "How to Fight Crime," I answered that question,

> I came in as a big liberal, and then upon becoming a prosecutor and a Judge, I swung over to a stricter stance. Now, I'm moving back to rehabilitation. Locking up people and throwing the key away has very little long-range potential.
>
> That's not my idea of what this country is about. We have to start helping kids at an early age. The citizenry and the resources of the private sector, not the Judges, will have to carry the main burden.

I suppose the *Miami Herald* story headline on September 2, 1989, was the commentary most appreciated—"Troubled Kids Lose an Old Friend." Those are words for every juvenile court judge to treasure upon retirement.

In response to a reporter asking me what message I had for my colleagues on departing the bench, I recited this incident, recalling attendance some years back at a judicial seminar. The question had been raised as to how best to handle social workers voicing sharp objection to the recommendations of the judge.

One of the judges present leaped up saying pointedly, "Only the judge cares for the child." He followed with advice, "I tell them in no uncertain terms, 'I am the boss!'" I thought his statement somewhat foolish and ignored it. Suddenly I realized that most of the other judges present were applauding his bravado statement. I was shocked at their reaction. I should have responded but didn't.

My message to my fellows: Judges are not prescient. Unquestionably holding certain command authority, they nonetheless need to exercise it with care. The welfare service agencies are not the enemy. And judges aren't licensed to presume that social workers are indifferent to the task. Humility coming from the bench is a worthwhile endeavor.

Few, if any, books have been written on Florida's juvenile courts. One of the purposes of this book is to encourage historians, social planners and practitioners to record for history the role each of the participating groups have played. Describing the process through the eyes of other partners will add immeasurably to the knowledge necessary to assure the continued growth and development of the juvenile court.

From my view, the last quarter of the twentieth century has been the period when judicial activism flowered in the Dade County juvenile justice system. Most of it powered by judges beginning with Bill Gladstone and reaching new heights with Cindy Lederman.

In that period, I worked alongside Gladstone. We had common goals with different styles and different projects. Both of us ready and eager to take on the world. Following me was Tom Petersen, a throwback to the old time child savers, willing to go anywhere and do anything in behalf of justice. An inspiring fellow.

Following Petersen is the Cindy Lederman chapter. She is the current occupant as administrative judge, easily the finest, most able systems designer ever to assemble so disparate an institution as the juvenile court. More about her later.

Then, the final chapter is devoted to a host of other judges, some not serving in the juvenile court, but all with roles as activists developing programs for children in need, and also taking strong positions in the community. Again, as noted in the book's introduction, being a warrior for children is not limited to juvenile court judges.

Countless other citizens of the Berta Blecke and Janet McAliley mode have been in the forefront. Names that come to mind: Karen Gievers, who has pursued many lawsuits successfully in behalf of the cause for children. Gievers, working out of Tallahassee, has been a one-person crusade relentlessly taking state agencies to court in behalf of children. And with an excellent win record.

David Lawrence, currently the lead public spokesperson for children with the Children's Trust and the Children's Service Council. Lawrence has morphed from his ivory tower life as the *Miami Herald*'s publisher to the nitty-gritty, difficult ways to aid needy children. Hard to expect so strong an advocate to rise from the executive boardroom of Knight Ridder. Good to know that democracy also works from the top down.

Daniella Levine, a lifetime activist currently heading Dade County's Human Services Coalition (HSC) who is into everything. She has organized coalitions in behalf of the elderly, the poor, and the children. The HSC has helped more than two hundred thousand children apply for the State's child healthcare program.

She is a visionary applying practical solutions. Her latest (*Miami Herald* 1/6/06) is a project called Imagine Miami. "I envision a City that works for everyone." She's signed up two hundred civic leaders ready to join the effort. Don't bet against her.

Shay Bilchick, starting as a state attorney juvenile prosecutor going to the U.S. Justice Department to head the Juvenile Section and now executive director of the National Children's Welfare Bureau. One of our local boys who made good on the national scene.

And the indefatigable Georgia Jones Ayers leading the Alternative Program, finding jobs for released inmates. Above that, Georgia has risen to every cause in behalf of the poor black child running afoul of the law. For decades now, every Dade County law enforcement official has had to face the entreaties of Georgia Ayers, in behalf of one of her constituents, numbering every black child in trouble. Georgia is not to be denied.

And State Representative Gus Barreiro (Miami Beach) has been a great asset in Tallahassee supporting worthwhile ventures for children. As a Republican, he has often receded from the party line of his colleagues to lead the way for important and needed legislation, along with investigations as to the inadequacies of the system. Most of all, Barreiro is always willing to speak out.

Also Hank Adorno who had led the new surge of privatization with the Our Kids program. Adorno, with his leadership board of community leaders, has set a new trend of independence in dealing with the State. He has been and will be a strong voice of the future.

These and other citizen volunteers have been to the barricades, some in the past, some now, and surely many in the future—all deserving of full recognition. Hopefully, they too will have pages afforded them in any subsequent recounting of this noble venture in behalf of children.

Leaving the bench in 1989, I saw no great prospects for the juvenile court. Gladstone already was talking about going to Washington, D.C., to join U.S. Senator Bob Graham, and while newly arrived Judge Tom Petersen was a positive addition, the likelihood of achieving the massive change necessary seemed dim. Was there anything out there to pick up the momentum Gladstone had initiated?

Tom Petersen

Six months before his March 1989 appointment to the circuit court bench, Chief Assistant State Attorney Thomas K. Petersen received a bouquet from *Miami Herald* feature writer Liz Balmaseda, carrying this headline: "Tom Petersen—The Last of the Great Idealists." Ordinarily, this kind of accolade comes at the end of an illustrious career. Here, Tom Petersen, the soon to be juvenile court judge, had already won the acclaim activist judges yearn for to cap their careers.

The story described a younger Tom Petersen.

> Tom Petersen began his career as a social activist with the wind at his back in the late '60s, when the issues seemed clearer and it was easy to find young, idealistic volunteers to work in the country's poor neighborhoods.
>
> He has been called crazy, a hopeless bleeding heart, but Petersen points to his once controversial projects that are functioning, however painfully. In three Dade County public housing projects—Larchmont Gardens, Modello and Liberty Square—he has opened grocery stores, set-up day-care centers, new parks and Little League baseball teams.

A paragraph in that article also quoted me.

> "He's a hands-on pioneer," says Juvenile Judge Seymour Gelber, who had hired Petersen as an Assistant State Attorney seventeen years ago.
> While the rest of us give speeches, Tom's out there in the street doing things. He is the last of the great idealists. I have often been revitalized by the unflagging spirit he displays.

Eight months later, September 1, 1989, upon reaching the mandatory retirement age of seventy, I retired. Thomas Petersen, appointed a circuit court judge by Governor Bob Martinez to fill a vacancy, was assigned to replace me as a juvenile court judge.

For the last forty years Petersen has been allied with the plight of children in Dade County. Some of those years serving as a judge or assistant state attorney, others with the school system, some with the private sector. Wherever he has been as an adult, he has been in the midst of doing good for the public.

Most of our activist judges have had those roles thrust upon them. Petersen appears to have been born to it. No matter the point of his career or the job assigned to him, always he has focused on helping deprived children and has maintained a close relationship with those who live in Dade's pockets of poverty.

Although he already had a praiseworthy career, earning the plaudits of a grateful community, his arrival on the bench enabled him to use that office to further enlarge many of his projects. Tom Petersen, no matter the office held, always had usually innovative new programs to offer. Never projects easy to bring to completion, always he faced a struggle. But then he almost always prevailed.

Judging Tom Petersen's efforts, one must recognize that in the years of the 1990s, his era as a judge, and a few years prior, the social service delivery system was in a shambles. *Miami Herald* reporter Andres Vigilucci (in an April 24, 1990, story) recounted incidents portraying conditions as that decade was ushered in.

According to writer Vigilucci, losing kids in the bureaucratic shuffle was almost the rule, not the exception. In Dade County, probation field counselors handled twice the number of clients according to national averages. Some as many as ninety to one hundred fifty cases. Juvenile court judges, rather than the agencies they worked for, had become the monitors of the field counselors' performance.

In Vigilucci's article, Petersen recalled calling in a field counselor to explain to the judge why he had not seen the boy in question even once in seven months. The counselor responded, "I am responsible for one hundred kids, and frankly, Judge, I don't even know who this kid is."

That same day, Petersen had interviewed seven other counselors from a busy Liberty City district. Their kids had been rearrested, and the court had received no notice of their status. Four admitted they had not seen their clients even once. With one exception, the counselors said their caseloads ranged from 120-200 cases.

The State provided no residential programs for girls, no programs for emotionally disturbed delinquents, none for drug abusers even though 75 percent of delinquents committed to halfway houses were involved in drugs.

In Dade, only 111 beds were available for juveniles spread among seven residential centers. Normally, each center housed about forty, leaving many without beds. But even that shortage was exacerbated by what Judge Petersen called an "absurd" policy.

Since the shortage extended statewide, the authorities in Tallahassee had ruled that bed distribution was to be done statewide on a first-come-first-served basis, resulting in half the beds in Dade being occupied by kids from outside Dade County.

Thus the few beds we had were not always available for Dade County kids, and similarly others of ours ended up at different sites in the state. This confusing situation made it difficult for judges in terms of following up on progress of those under their charge.

Some Judges issued contempt citations against HRS counselors for shoddy handling of this situation. Prosecutor Leon Botkin, commenting on the confused situation described it thusly: "That the contempt petitions were actually filed reflects growing frustration with HRS and the delinquency system. If all the Judges wanted to push contempt every time they could, HRS would be in Court every day."

Tom Petersen, the new judge, trying to get a handle on the overall problem, visited two halfway houses. There he found little to satisfy his concerns. He met many overwhelmed, underpaid, disgruntled HRS staffers. Long vacant positions for social workers and psychologists at the halfway homes were unfilled because HRS couldn't find anyone to take the low-paying jobs. Petersen's quote in the news article: "The children go there and nothing happens. They just sit and watch television."

The situation described in Vigilucci's *Miami Herald* story was a sad picture. Social services, never a big plus in the delivery system, had even worsened during those years surrounding the beginning of the '90s. Improvement arrived before the end of the decade but never did reach a comfortable level.

Judge Tom Petersen quickly determined that targeting HRS for the ills of the system was a useless endeavor. Attacking the weak HRS and the profligate, indifferent legislature was not his mode. Developing positive programs with education as the centerpiece made a lot more sense to him. And why not?

Petersen came along at the right time. From inception, the Dade County social services delivery system had never truly righted itself. The community, however, demanded new approaches to address delinquency and dependency problems. Petersen saw himself as a vehicle for this change.

Change was indeed in the offing. In the decade of the '90s, the courts, now with a more cooperative public school system were open for badly needed ways to together address the plight of children. Petersen didn't need a shake-down cruise to familiarize himself with the issues or the solutions at hand. His coming aboard was akin to the Miami Heat basketball team acquiring Shaquille O'Neal and becoming an immediate play-off contender.

One of the continuing court problems arose from the placing of our troubled delinquents back in the school system after adjudication. Only in recent years, with the arrival of the school's Court Support Program, had we begun to move together to address the problem. The Support Program, pushed hard for by Judge Gladstone, had opened the door to provide judges with up-to-date school info on the progress of court delinquents.

Still lacking were school facilities specifically designed to handle the more difficult criminally prone delinquent youngsters. Many of these delinquents with several arrests were close to incorrigible, totally rejecting schooling. The then-existing Alternative Schools designed for recalcitrant students who rejected authority were not adequate for this task with these hard-cores.

The school system's Alternative Schools program, designed for classroom troublemakers and worst, had in the past reluctantly included our more difficult Court delinquents. Unfortunately, the latter group, highly disruptive, made discipline in the Alternative Schools hard to maintain. The school system was ready for another Tom Petersen initiative.

Petersen, new on the bench, had brought with him a strong philosophy concerning the delinquent child and the school system. He believed most of them were still workable, and the way back from delinquency began on the path to the schoolroom. Among all his disposition considerations in court, returning the delinquent to a strong school regimen ranked the highest. Regrettably, the now fully cooperating school system had found that adding our court delinquents to the Alternative Schools rosters had been too disruptive for their classrooms.

What to do? Petersen didn't waste a moment. Rather than call a conclave of all concerned agencies and spend months and perhaps years studying the problem, he reacted in true Tom Petersen fashion. He determined the answer to be a school specifically planned for those court delinquents unable to properly perform in a public school setting. Cooperative as the school system was, the likelihood of constructing a special school at the whim of a judge was at that time most unlikely.

Petersen, bypassing that approach, found a shortcut. Adjoining the juvenile court structure were half a dozen large trailers, leftovers from the days when the juvenile court was being built on its present site. Used for storage, extra office space, and short-term programs, they were managed by George LaMont, our juvenile court administrator.

LaMont's job as top aide to the administrative judge, was as a combined property manager, security coordinator, and overseer of the daily court calendars. He had been an invaluable asset in that capacity. Years back he had been an HRS counselor during the period Petersen had been a lawyer in the court, and still had a strong personal relationship with Tom Petersen.

Petersen obtained a commitment from LaMont for two trailers, and describing his effort as an experiment for his court alone, then proceeded to move ahead. Since it was a project solely for his court, neither the chief judge nor the juvenile administrative judge chose to be involved.

Next Petersen approached Octavio Visiedo, superintendent of schools, with his plan to relieve the Alternative Schools of some of the delinquents ordered there by the court. The plan sought to place the children in Petersen's proposed new school called TROY (Teaching and Rehabilitating Our Youth).

Considering that the school system, up until the recent arrival of the Court Support Program, had the reputation of being totally insular, rejecting any alliances beyond its own stilted bureaucracy, approval was indeed doubtful.

Schools Superintendent Visiedo surprised many by quickly buying into Petersen's plan. Whereas most superintendents in the past had been wary of a relationship with the court, Visiedo, new on the job and anxious to show an innovative approach, readily agreed. He also assisted Petersen by expediting accreditation, selecting a teaching staff, creating a curriculum, and other fine points usually taking years to accomplish.

In addition to obtaining a line in the Board of Public Instruction budget, Petersen set about gaining public support and private funding for this new project. Taking a low-key approach, Petersen drew little media attention to the growth of TROY. This was a highly innovative effort, and excessive publicity was sure to bring out detractors. Hatched from a small idea, growth to a full potential could fill a serious shortcoming in the court's attempt to rehabilitate youngsters.

Over the long haul, the program flourished. Now (2007), fifteen years after inception, it has proven to be a highly effective means to keep the hard-core kids within a school setting. Wisely, Petersen did not rush to enlarge it beyond the then capacity of forty-five kids. Too often, successful programs are quickly mass-produced, and somehow benefits are lost in the process.

From opening day, TROY was no easy task. Petersen recalls the opening ceremonies well. The press had been invited, and it was a kind of gala mini-event outside the two trailers. Judge Petersen, being interviewed by a TV reporter was extolling the prospects for TROY for the TV audience's benefit. During a slight pause, the TV reporter nudged him, whispering, "One of your students was just halted by a security guard for having a gun in his possession. Do you want to comment on that?"

Petersen, nonplussed for the moment, signaled for a break and then implored the reporter to save that news for a less damaging moment. Few elected officials had the goodwill credits Petersen had earned over the years with the media, to expect such a request to be honored. For Petersen, the interviewer, name long forgotten, relented and passed over the news of the gun-toting TROY student. Opening-day celebration went by without further incident.

Truth was, many of the students sent by Petersen to TROY were hardly ideal citizens. The location of the TROY trailers, directly in the path used by others, was an area sometimes best avoided by social workers and court employees somewhat fearful of encountering tough TROY attendees. But then again, choir boys did not need the benefits TROY provided.

Jennifer Schuster has served as director of TROY since its inception in 1992, and as of this writing she still holds that post. Adopting the more impressive title, Troy Community Academy (TCA), the first Annual TCA Report (1993-1994) described the beginning years progress in the development of the program.

Troy was conceived in 1991 after Petersen and Schuster visited Glen Mills Academy in Philadelphia, a residential program for 750 highly at-risk urban youth. The Glen Mills philosophy that the primary culprit for their troubled students was the inability to function in a normal social setting. In addition, the extreme educational deficits these students brought with them made playing catch-up very difficult. The visitors from Miami impressed with what they saw, the plan for their new school began to take form.

After three visits to Glen Mills, Petersen and Schuster, while not attempting to replicate Glen Mills, adopted a strategy for TROY to remediate educational deficits and to introduce a positive peer culture. Students at TROY had grown up in neighborhoods where the delinquent subculture did not prize education, and models other than recidivist delinquents were in short supply. The TROY strategy would be sorely tested.

Of their first-year class, 88 percent had either dropped out of public school or had failed all classes and had an excessive number of absences. After a year at TROY, the results showed all the students who had dropped out of school in the past or had F averages were now maintaining passing grades. There was also an 80 percent reduction in the arrest rate. As for attendance, the average number in the past public school year had been fifty-three absences, whereas at TROY the average dropped down to eight absences.

One of the unique aspects of TROY was the creation of a restaurant in the juvenile court courtyard run totally by TROY students, providing an on-site vocational work experience. Started with a $5,000 contribution from American Express and a donation of patio furniture and a barbecue from Home Depot, other contributions followed. Petersen was not only an innovative program designer and a skilled grants writer, but he was also adept at gaining community support in terms of money and resources.

For Teen Cuisine, the aptly named eatery, students were divided into teams of ten, each working one day a week. With the advice of a volunteer dietician, the students selected the daily menu, purchased the food, and served and cleaned the area. All city and state laws pertaining to restaurants were followed. Amazing how quickly they took to their roles as new neighborhood entrepreneurs.

Located within the confines of the juvenile court, a palm-treed courtyard adjoining the Teen Cuisine diner with artistically adorned stone tables and benches topped with handsome umbrellas was the dining area. This site became a pleasant respite area for the juvenile court staffers during lunch break. Upon my retirement, Petersen was kind enough to name the site Gelber Gardens, but one of the hurricanes that frequently visit tore the nameplate down.

Still operating today, the diner now has a fully refrigerated new facility with up-to-date equipment. There's always a line of customers, mostly court lawyers and social workers, including a sprinkling of neighbors. The *New Times*, a weekly Miami newspaper in its "Best of . . . Selections" chose Teen Cuisine as the "Best Buy in Town." Teen Cuisine also offers a catering service and has been hired for local public and private events.

In discussing the success of Teen Cuisine before civic groups, Petersen always talked about the vocational aspects of the project: kids learning how to be productive, obtaining a skill leading to a job in the employment market. One day, I asked him what makes for a successful program. His reply:

> Telling kids, particularly street kids, about the value of the work ethic gets you nowhere. You need a hook that appeals to them that got these kids to stay in school. Teen Cuisine was it.
>
> They want immediate gratification. The prospect for the future is to far away for them to grasp. With Teen Cuisine, each of them went to school four days, worked one day, getting twenty dollars pay and tips usually about three dollars. That did it.

Recently, November 24, 2005, the *Miami Herald* section Tropical Life ran a four-page spread titled "Teen Cuisine." As a Thanksgiving holiday story, it recounted the history of the project, detailed the fulsome menu, and most of all the excitement generated by the student restaurateurs and their customers. Getting paid for a days hard work made each of them a satisfied student. They vied for the job having to accumulate points daily for classroom work.

Said Nakeil Jackson, a slight and shy 12th grader who was in "the wrong place at the wrong time," having in the past spent three years at the Okeechobee

Corrections Center for Delinquents, "I really wanted to be in this program. I think I set a record getting points to make it. Right now I am chopping cucumbers, tomatoes, and crab. I chop fast, and you know what else? I chop beautifully."

The *Herald* story also pointed out that they feed a lot of satisfied customers. "I'm there every day," said Jenny Leyva, a legal secretary. "I could not survive without them."

Vanessa Chavez, a legal secretary, said, "For breakfast I'll go for an egg, white omelet or toast and sausage. Then at lunch, I'll go for a green salad and some of those French fries." She then adds, "OK I realize my lunch is not a well-balanced diet by anybody's standards, but there's something crazy good about those fries. Let's not even talk about the lasagna."

Petersen was real proud of the feature story even though the writer had somehow managed through all the copy and photos not to mention Tom Petersen as the founder of both Troy Academy and Teen Cuisine. Nevertheless, Tom proudly said, "Listen, a father does not need to be mentioned when his son scores the winning touchdown for his high school team. Seeing those kids avoid arrest and many of them going on to college is satisfaction enough."

One significant quality about Tom Petersen was his refusal to sit on an accomplishment enjoying the praise. Already with long experience in the state attorney's office dealing with federal grants and foundations, he knew the success of TROY would enable him to approach federal and State funding as well as private foundations for additional support.

Most importantly perhaps was the need for a TROY-like school within the school system to handle the large number of difficult cases beyond the capacity of TROY. Petersen was also ready for that.

Hardly was TROY off the ground than the Petersen-Schuster duo approached the Dade County Public Schools system, proposing that the juvenile justice system and the public education system jointly initiate such a school for high-risk delinquent youth. This one aimed at a much larger capacity to further relieve the public schools of difficult-to-handle hard-core youngsters.

Emboldened by Petersen's success, the Dade County School Board in July 1992 voted to fund such a school for 150-200 students, additionally allocating five and a half million dollars for construction costs. The school to be named for a revered black poet, Langston Hughes Academy. Public school administrators on Superintendent Visiedo's staff were directed to "launch a nationwide search for a revolutionary educational program aimed at turning round the lives of these troubled youth."

Said Juvenile Judge Tom Petersen, who had spearheaded the effort and was aiding as a consultant, "We will unite the best teachers, counselors, and social workers under the same roof." Modeled after TROY, the new school will be home base to students selected from our juvenile court system, but not limited to hard-cores.

Superintendent Visiedo, truly excited about the prospect of creating this major effort at salvaging troubled youth, was publicly touting this as a full-service campus staffed by the criminal justice system, the state HRS, and as well the school district. A pleasing enough statement but far reaching when one considers the standoff approach of past school system leaders.

This new initiative to save juvenile offenders was underway before the end of the summer with a pilot program for 150 students in temporary quarters. Said Petersen at that time, "This pilot program shows a lot of promise. They have a 95 percent attendance rate, and the students seem to be staying out of trouble,"

Still riding the momentum of immediate success, Petersen and Schuster, while awaiting the construction of Langston Hughes Academy, had applied for a three-year grant for TROY from the U.S. Department of Education. This grant was to develop curriculum and educational planning appropriate for youth who had failed in both the existing traditional schools and as well as in the alternative public schools.

Awarded $200,000 for each of the next three years for planning, these funds also permitted enlarging their original TROY vocational training program into a full-service vocational school for their forty-five students. The Dade County school system provided four teaching positions with the new federal funding enabling TROY to add an additional four more to their staff.

Tom Petersen's effort for this kind of schooling as part and parcel of the juvenile court was a venture never before undertaken by any of our judicial advocates and unheard of throughout the country. His prior experience dealing with funding sources was so extensive and his initiative so impressive, along with his endless energy that a whole new vista had been opened.

Petersen and Schuster were like two proud and pleased parents watching their offspring grow. They had built an institution from the ground up solely on desire and struggle. Unlike most government agencies, they had no grant specialist on staff, nor a leading citizen advisory committee to open doors for private fund-raising. Petersen was the outside partner dealing with planning and the bureaucracy; Schuster exerted all her professional teaching skills running the school.

Petersen did not seek the advice or approval of his colleagues on the bench. Nothing personal. He was a man so centered on his mission he feared too much outside advice might slow him down. If Petersen had a weakness, it was his desire to see his missions completed as soon as possible, almost as if he wanted to be up and running before the naysayers had a chance to react.

Dave Lawrence, publisher of the *Miami Herald*, a big supporter of both TROY and Judge Petersen personally, featured those efforts in many of his newspaper columns. Lawrence, long with an affinity for the plight of children, currently as a private citizen heads the Children's Trust, the agency disbursing state program funds to groups aiding children in need.

Back then, Lawrence, so impressed with Petersen's TROY program, wrote a letter to one of the TROY students, Israel Joyce, offering a personal commitment of $5,000 toward his third year of college should he complete the first two years. He completed the letter with these encouraging words: "Like others, I believe in you. You can do it, I know."

In Israel's last year in public school, he had amassed sixty-six absences and Fs in all four of his subjects. In his first year at TROY, he had only nine absences and averaged a B on his grades. That's an excellent recovery by any measure.

Did he make it through the first two years of college? I asked Dave Lawrence. His response: "Unfortunately, I never heard from Israel. I would have been happy to contribute to his college education."

A 1995 independent program evaluation concluded that the rearrest rate of TROY students was less than half of their prior arrest numbers. Rearrest is considered a realistic indicator of progress. Here, cutting the crime rate by more than half suggests positive steps.

With respect to school attendance, TROY students who in the past had dropped out of school or were absent more than half the school days, now at TROY demonstrated an 80 percent attendance rate. Further, with respect to academic performance, the evaluator found statistically significant improvement in both reading and math.

TROY, after almost fifteen years, still maintains the same quality sought by its founders. The success rate moves up and down, but it always far surpasses the low marks attained prior to entry.

The Langston Hughes Academy, built on a dream even larger than TROY Academy, would have literally created a marriage of juvenile court and the school system. It provided for HRS counselors to be housed on the premises of the school, able to meet with their clients at a moment's notice. Bringing the court to the school and vice versa had been a dream of many.

Tom Petersen's credentials had brought him many supporters. Large among them was Dr. Paul Bell, who had served the school system as both assistant superintendent and later as superintendent. Tom Petersen had years earlier as an assistant state attorney persuaded Paul Bell to set up preschool programs within the low-cost housing projects alongside the grocery stores Petersen had developed.

Preschool programs had always in the past only been housed on the site of a public school, never in a housing project. A risky proposition, but Paul Bell had confidence in this young activist. When Petersen became a circuit court judge, Superintendent Bell congratulated him saying, "I want to work with you and support your school projects to help delinquent kids."

That was a message echoed by many of the other top public school leadership. Under Bell, with Petersen as a consultant, the school system moved ahead on the

Langston Hughes Academy project. Unlike TROY with forty to fifty students on the juvenile court grounds, Langston High would be a full-fledged high school with hundreds of students.

Too good to be true, fate stepped in. Paul Bell suffered a heart attack and death caused a whirlpool of change in the administration. Everything was off the drawing board as new leaders appeared with their own new plans. The idea of Langston Hughes as the forerunner of a true merger of the schools and the social work system became lost in the shuffle. Instead Langston Hughes was added to the existing number of Alternative Schools where disciplinary problem children were housed. Nothing special or innovative about it. That was mostly a storaging process to keep troublesome kids out of the regular schools.

Any new project fostered in the bureaucracy needs a power figure's strong hand among other ingredients such as media support, adequate funding, minimal-to-none detractors, and most of all the planets above aligned in a prophetic order. With the new change of school board administration, it just wasn't to be.

Currently, Tom Petersen, no longer a judge, is still chairman of the board, actively involved in the decision making at TROY. Jennifer Schuster continues to run the operation. Teen Cuisine remains a fine vocational project.

Langston Hughes had a career of its own. After serving as one of the receiving schools for maladjusted youth coming from both the regular school system and the juvenile court, it became the home of a project fostered by Dade County senator Fredericka Wilson called the Five Hundred Model Citizens. This program aims at enlisting leading black citizens as volunteers to serve as mentors and models for school children. An excellent program in its own right—but not quite what had been envisioned.

That these Petersen projects earned a high batting average from the onset comes as no surprise. Tom Petersen had been an activist long before becoming a judge. As a bona fide liberal with the urge to change the world, he was on that path early on. Asked where and how this approach to life came upon him, he smiled saying, "I don't know. I was the child of two loving parents, both voting the straight Republican ticket. Never heard much talk in the house about politics. I gained adulthood during the Vietnam War, a war I strongly opposed.

"Those days at Columbia University Law School probably influenced me the most. By the time I graduated in 1966, I knew had to do things to assist others in need. I figured that as a lawyer the opportunity was there for me."

A wise planner even back then as a new lawyer, he realized that to make a serious impact he needed to work through a public agency where his hopes along with his skills could be put to test. Entering private practice, catering to business clients, and the legal skirmishing that made for a successful law practice were never in his cards.

Fresh out of law school, starting as a VISTA member—the home-front Peace Corps—he later found his niche in 1971 when added to State Attorney Richard Gerstein's staff to run the Pretrial Intervention Program in adult criminal court. Instead of requiring inmates to produce a bond in order to be released, Petersen's program placed good risks in release programs where they could be monitored assuring their return to court.

In those days, the traditional DA was pictured as a hard-fighting, lock-up-the-bad-guys crusader, never ever thinking of releasing suspects. Gerstein's program was a highly unusual approach and considered risky for a prosecutor. Moving from demanding high bonds to offering rehab programs was a sure sign to attract an opponent. A social—worker prosecutor in those high crime days was not likely for reelection to office. Gerstein, a highly effective, popular prosecutor with five elective terms under his belt bought into Petersen's project to relieve the overcrowded Jail.

He recognized Petersen as a man able to provide the skilled handling necessary for this assignment. Gerstein was right. The program succeeded. Few of those placed in the program failed to appear for trial, and none of those were serious violent offenders. Many went directly to rehab programs, thus avoiding the cost of trials for the State.

On the day he took charge of that program, Petersen was met by a bondsman, who, angry that Petersen might be taking away business, threatened him with, "Get out of town by nightfall, or you are dead." Welcome to Miami of the sixties. Thus began Peterson's entrance as an administrator handling nontraditional programs.

This was one of the earliest of such programs nationwide initiated in a state attorney's office. Prosecutors until then viewed their roles as solely to indict, prosecute, and jail offenders. The idea that some criminal types might avoid prosecution, instead going straight to a rehab program, was not viewed as politically correct for a prosecutor.

Years later in 1985, then as chief assistant state attorney under Janet Reno, the full fruit of his early endeavors as a do-gooder were put to a test. In an effort to fight poverty, State Attorney Janet Reno had organized a consortium to address the plight of black women in housing projects and the high incidence of inner-city juvenile delinquency.

Tom Petersen was chosen as the coordinator. The consortium included heads of the offices of the county manager, the superintendent of schools, and the Dade Women's Welfare Coalition. The latter organization consisted mostly of women directly involved in welfare dependency and welfare reform.

Newly named the Schools and Neighborhood Consortium, the project began with no capital and had no staff. As coordinator, Tom Petersen had complete control of planning and implementation, subject only to the consortium board.

It was a kind of skeleton operation placing the full burden on the coordinator. Rise or fall it was all his.

This venture could easily have followed the usual time-consuming approaches. Feel-good speeches by elected officeholders, endless follow-up meetings with those needing guidance, and finally reports describing the goals. All the good intentions duly reported in the press. Result: a year gone and the first shovel not yet lifted. Petersen nixed all of that. He, as did the welfare recipients, wanted action. Promptly.

The board, at Petersen's behest, decreed that the first project would involve going into housing projects and there create employment opportunities for women on welfare who wanted to work. Added to that goal was a secondary project to address the related problem of the disproportionately large school failure rate among young blacks.

This was no easy task even for a chief assistant state attorney out to save the world. It was clear to Petersen he could not approach this task from the safe confines of the state attorney's office in the Metro Justice Building. Petersen promptly took a leave of absence from his chief assistant duties and for the next three years virtually lived in three housing projects located in neighborhoods with a predominately poor black population.

His becoming a field commander rather than a desk-bound leader separated him from many activists. In later years, as a juvenile court judge, he made a point of frequently visiting not only programs he had initiated, but as well drop-in visits on programs servicing delinquents he had committed. Truly a hands-on activist.

Funding for his housing project activity was limited to monies provided by the three participating government entities. This amounted to a total of $100,000 for their start-up operating budget. Later several private foundations contributed additional operational funds. It was a three-year project with the goal to enter three inner-city neighborhoods and create new opportunities for the residents.

The underlying theme was a self-help project to improve economic conditions, heighten self-esteem, and to create an environment where serious problems of a depressed community, such as school failure, teen pregnancy, and welfare dependency could be addressed in an holistic manner.

The whole ball of wax was in Petersen's hands. This was the kind of idealism that hearkened back to FDR's Great Depression days of the 1930s when Harry Hopkins and other radical planners of that era came up with the WPA (Works Projects Administration), the CCC (Civilian Conservation Corps), and other alphabet agencies that literally influenced the course of this nation for the remaining decades into the twenty-first century.

The first neighborhood selected by Petersen was Larchmont Gardens, a 440-unit public housing project in Northwest Dade. Ninety percent of the household heads were single women, eight of ten on welfare, and a median resident age of sixteen. Their teen pregnancy and delinquency rate among the highest in Dade County.

Petersen had his work cut out for him. First on the agenda—a request to the Dade County School Board to place a preschool program for three- and four-year-olds in the empty community center at the Larchmont site. A low priority for a long time, this would be evidence of the willingness of the establishment to provide equal resources to those in the lower economic strata.

Without hesitation the preschool program was established. Petersen was on his way, heartened by the knowledge that the playing field was now even. His project would now get the attention it warranted. He found this a full-time endeavor, spending most of his working hours and a lot of nights in the Larchmont Housing Project.

This was his start. Finding viable yet not too costly programs was his goal. Scouting the neighborhood he was aware of the lack of activity; neither children nor adults milled about the hot unsafe streets. Only when the ice cream vendor rang his bell signaling the arrival of his truck did people materialize. Suddenly, it was a eureka! moment. How about a food store to bring people together? The old-fashioned grocery store always was where neighbors ran into each other.

Thus came about the opening of a small convenience store labeled Larch-Mart in the center of the project. The United Way subsidized it until it became self-sufficient. Residents, mostly welfare women, would run the store on a salary. The store stocked food, ice cream, disposable diapers, and other family items residents now had to walk a half mile to buy.

Operating a grocery store became the focal point of Petersen's efforts. "The whole idea," stated Petersen, "is to provide an alternative for women on welfare. Larch-Mart was an attempt to break the cycle of poverty, and to produce a blueprint for projects in similar communities. Not only was a grocery store a natural site for women to congregate, but actually running a grocery store as a business would heighten self-esteem."

To celebrate the formal opening of Larch-Mart and the renovated recreation center, a festival featuring the school bands of Horace Mann Jr. High and Miami Edison High led a parade that included the Larchmont Garden mothers and the preschoolers as well as applauding neighbors.

One, a nineteen-year resident at Larchmont Gardens, was heard to comment, "It's a great thing. It means a lot. It makes you feel like they want to do something for children. If anybody had told me they would come this far, I wouldn't have believed it."

Organizing a fully chartered Little League baseball operation was next with six teams, all uniformed, courtesy of business sponsors. A job-training program for eighteen- to nineteen-year-old school dropouts was organized to develop vocational skills and provide employment as maintenance workers at the complex.

Major repairs on 250 deteriorating apartments followed. Larchmont Gardens was finally waking up.

A *Miami Herald* article dated December 1, 1985, authored by Heath Merriwether, described the teenage pregnancy problem at Larchmont and Petersen's efforts to address them.

> The problem of teen-age pregnancy is difficult to overstate. In one family the mother had her first child at age eleven, and that child now seventeen had four children, the first of which she also had at age eleven.
>
> In Dade schools, the topic of contraceptives surfaces briefly in the tenth grade, much too late for the Larchmont mothers.
>
> Petersen has pulled together experts on sexuality and teen-age pregnancy to advise and assist School Principals at public schools in the neighborhood.

A year later, Larchmont Gardens was making more than satisfactory progress. Now the recipient of a health clinic housed in Larchmont's community center alongside the thriving grocery store and the fully functioning preschool, Petersen was ready to focus on phase 2, the next site of the Consortium Project.

Liberty Square was next. Located in Northwest Miami, it was a housing project in straits even poorer than Larchmont Gardens. Within six months of the opening of Larch-Mart, a grocery store had risen at Liberty Square compliments of Petersen's consortium. Liberty Square is unique in that it is the oldest public housing project in Miami, and the third oldest in the country. Petersen personally traveled to Washington, D.C., and researched archives to locate documents attesting to Liberty Square's longevity.

In 1989, in one of the worst civil disturbances in Miami's history, Liberty Square Mart was burned down by an angry mob protesting the shooting of a black motorcyclist by a Miami police officer.

Three years later in 1992—through the efforts of now Judge Tom Petersen, HUD officials, and the tenants of Liberty Square—the convenience store was rebuilt. The Black Lawyer's Association, the Cuban American Bar, along with the Jack and Ruth Admire Foundation also contributed toward the $100,000 rebuilding cost for a bigger and better market.

Petersen stayed with each of the projects, attempting to improve the lot of the tenants. In 1995, Judge Petersen attended a graduation of inner-city parents who had completed courses in parenting, conflict resolution, and self-esteem. The program, another Petersen brainchild, was sponsored by Metro's Youth and Family Development Agency.

Parents had attended once-a-week classes. They also met once a month at their children's school for lunch with both the children and their teachers to discuss grades and progress. One thing for sure about Petersen, no matter the stated major purpose, he always managed to tie all his programs into his main goal—schooling for children.

The final target of the three-pronged Consortium Project was the Modello Housing Project. This one, a small isolated community of 120 units, population 550. As with Larchmont and Liberty Square, the neighborhood was in desperate straits, perhaps even worse than the others.

Whereas the median age in Larchmont Gardens was sixteen, in Modello it was eleven. No playground existed despite half the Modello population being under age eleven. It was a housing project with rampant crack addiction, crime, and teen pregnancy—all adding to despair.

As a result of a report to United Way by Tom Petersen, a special task force was organized, bringing a rush of support to rescue Modello. Funds and assistance were provided by foundation sources, Southeast Bank, and the Greater Miami Junior League among many others. A Housing and Urban Development (HUD) official subsequently labeled the Modello store the most successful of all three HUD-backed convenience stores operating in Dade County.

Tom Petersen's work with the housing projects carried over in his efforts with TROY and other school projects. He never deviated from his plan to better the life of the underprivileged, and always proper schooling was in the forefront of his programs.

Petersen, obviously both a thinker and doer, had a philosophy about how to treat juvenile delinquency. All the activist judges before him had struggled with this problem with little success. How do we turn around kids gone bad?

The target for failure of both the media and the judges was mostly the social service agencies' inability to stem the tide of delinquency and the state legislature for failing to enact legislation and fund adequate resources. The war among the judges, social service agencies, and the Florida Legislature had now gone on for seven decades with no appreciable solution.

Petersen, unlike some of his predecessors on the bench, declined to engage in sometimes harsh critiques of those agencies and bodies that neither authorized adequate funding nor properly implemented the programs that did exist. He couldn't revise the existing status quo, but he could revive the flagging hopes of these disheartened communities.

His approach was simple and more of a positive nature. He avoided going into the basic theories that led a child to delinquent behavior. Psychological? Genetic? Environment? Dysfunctional family? Was it all of the above? Some? Or still another cause?

Admittedly, he reasoned, the experts are uncertain as to the cause. Too often, he added, rehab programs, designed around improving conditions of one or more of the above causes, failed to hit the mark. He saw punishment only as a last resort to protect the community.

Petersen's somber *Miami Herald* article of May 25, 1991, entitled "Rethinking Juvenile Justice," summed up his conclusions about the system in two short sentences: "Juvenile justice today, in any large city in America is about race, poverty and alienation. And no Judge, and no 'rehabilitation program,' if indeed there is such a thing, is going to solve that or wish it away."

He was as strong an advocate for children as has appeared on the scene, but he was also a powerful critic of the process. "Why focus," he asked, "on theories based on the uncertainty of the cause of delinquency?" Instead, he preached, "We know with certainty that adequate schooling will better prepare a child for life ahead, no matter the difficulties of life before."

Programmatically, he rejected the traditional choice of counseling and the whole galaxy of new programs, such as tough love and boot camp, designed to make-over the child. He opted for improving the child's status in the world by making schooling more available for the needs of troubled children.

"Give a youngster the tools by which he can advance in the world . . . and he will advance," he said repeatedly. Perhaps an overly simple answer, but why not? Every program he has put forth that included schooling as a major element has had some degree of success. "What other kind of program can claim that achievement?" he asked.

Petersen laid no claim to being a wiser, kindlier person than his colleagues. Yet he was not a one-prong, one-direction activist. In addition to his focus on schooling, he always ordered a follow-up component requiring close counselor supervision and as well reports of progress to the judge. But in his heart and mind was this total commitment to emphasizing schooling as the means to make a significant difference for the errant child's future.

I recall a case in my court that suggested that Petersen's singular approach was meritorious. There was a youngster on whom I had extended great effort to maintain him in public school. I saw a glimmer in him worth the attempt. No matter, however, my urging or threats, he found school so distasteful that he rejected both my entreaties and my penalties. Somehow we failed to communicate. Most likely, my message simply did not reach him.

Finally, I sent him to a Dade Marine Institute residential program. DMI, a private program, takes kids out of the ghetto, most of whom have never been on a ship, and teaches them the seaman's craft. Visiting DMI one day, I spotted him sitting in a class studying undersea diving. Physics was the subject at the moment. The teacher was explaining Boyle's law.

Listening carefully, neither the instructor's recitation nor the formula that student's were writing on the blackboard made too much sense to me. Boyle's law relates to the pressure placed on divers undersea. Knowledge of it often means survival. To the students, Boyle's law, complicated as it may have been, was an essential piece of information. Eventually, my young man was called upon. Confidently, he strode to the blackboard, recited the proper diving procedure to the class, and then outlined on the board the physics formula, clearly explaining the implications.

I sat there dumbfounded. Here was this young man who had refused my order to attend school, to learn basic reading and writing skills. Now suddenly he was explaining the complexities of Boyle's law.

Afterwards, I asked what brought about his change of attitude. Matter-of-factly, he replied, "Teachers only tell you what they want you to know. Here, I'm learning what I have to know." For the first time, he made sense to me.

Petersen's schooling efforts seemed more in-line with what the youngster had said to me. The TROY school programs involved first creating a feeling of self-satisfaction, then peer recognition, and above all a full understanding that the student was there for his own benefit, not because of duress by the judge. Petersen's programs have an underlying approach that encourages youngsters to take on the spirit of the institution and accept those goals as their own.

No easy task and not always successful, but unlike other character-building and personality changing programs, his provided immediate satisfaction where the participant saw positive results. Offering those tools may well be the practical route to go. That's Petersen's lifestyle.

Early in 1995, Judge Petersen., and former Miami mayor Maurice Ferré came up with the idea of the Juvenile Assessment Center (JAC). Here all the agencies involved with a child's first contact with the law together addressed the child's problems and made an early and sensible referral choice. This involved choosing among a rehab agency, court prosecution, or perhaps a return home to parents without government intervention. It was a proposal already operating successfully in Tampa and Orlando.

Mayor Ferré was the lead advocate with Petersen arranging for many of the local contacts, particularly school officials. Petersen made certain that one of the goals of this new assessment center would be the tracking of truancy. Somehow, no matter the project, Petersen maintained a singular approach to his most important antidelinquency facet—adequate schooling.

Ferré met with local and state officials while Petersen scheduled a meeting in Washington with U.S. Attorney General Janet Reno, his former boss in the Dade State Attorney's Office. Adequate funding was their goal. Reno was cooperative and encouraging, but the line was already long for communities applying. Miami would have to wait its turn.

Eventually, the State and County, working in cooperation with Juvenile Judge Lester Langer (see Lederman chapter) and the many agencies concerned with the welfare of the child, joined to establish an effective Juvenile Assessment Center. Petersen and Ferré played important roles by first recommending the project.

Petersen never stopped with innovative ideas. He established an open-door policy in his court, permitting parents with problems to come before him for assistance without the need to have a formal court action filed. This had been one of Judge Lindsey's approaches back at the beginning of the century in his Denver courtroom. Apparently, no other juvenile judge in a major metropolis in the country had attempted so simple and novel an approach until here about a hundred years later.

The idea of a truancy court presided over by retired judges was his next bid. This would require the state legislature's approval. Instead of creating this special court, the legislature enacted a law permitting the sitting judges to detain chronic truants for up to five days. Not satisfied with that, Petersen came up with the Truancy Alternatives Program (TAP).

Since only five percent of juveniles arrested three or more times graduate from high school, why not break the cycle by keeping them in school? Like his other offerings, TAP had a simple concept—trade detention for attendance at school.

For starters, Petersen talked the Dade Schools superintendent's office into installing a computer on his courtroom desk that linked him directly to the school databases so truancy info could instantly be gathered. In addition, the number of classes a child skipped was provided.

For ten months, in 1996, Petersen ran a voluntary TAP pilot program in his court involving several thousand kids accused of nonviolent crimes. Only two hundred, less than 7 percent, chose the lockup in the detention center instead of school.

Support by the other judges was unanimous, the three other juvenile court judges agreeing to adopt the program. Said Russell Wheatley, associate superintendent for Dade County Schools, "Any time you have the courts behind you—it's a powerful motivator for school kids."

Echoed Juvenile Court Administrative Judge Bruce Levy, "We have to be partners with the school system because truancy leads to delinquency, which means we are otherwise funneling kids from court to delinquency." He added, "Kids don't need psychotherapy; they need success in school and self-esteem."

Judge Levy's last statement exactly summed up Judge Petersen's approach. Unsaid in the discussion was the benefit to the always-overcrowded detention center by making additional beds available. Under TAP, all the judges would have immediate access to school information on truancy, thus aiding immeasurably in their decision-making process.

Petersen, a man who loses no time to follow-up on his program ideas, moved quickly to take care of the TAP program needs. He immediately applied for a grant to the newly established Florida Commission on Community Service enabling Miami-Dade College instructors to train housing project welfare recipients to track truant students for the court and the school system. By learning to use computers to record home visits and other follow-up contact, the project workers also freed up HRS counselors to focus on their field responsibilities.

His primary focus on schooling as an antidote to juvenile crime did not deter Petersen's concern over other inadequate conditions in the system. Present always was the overcrowded Youth Hall Detention Center as well as other shortcomings of the social service delivery system throughout the state.

In his early days on the bench, Petersen had declined to assume the role of the HRS scold. Fully aware of the many HRS shortcomings, much of which could be attributed to lack of State funding, he nonetheless determined to follow a less contentious approach. His goal was to be schooling. There were times, however, that required and warranted a strong critical approach on what he perceived as official wrongdoing.

Holding a sixteen-year-old Liberty City youngster improperly for forty-six days in a Dade Youth Hall Detention Center solitary cell drew his wrath. Said an angry Petersen, "It is inhumane and illegal. I am offended by the idea that a kid can be locked up for forty-six days without anyone telling a judge, his lawyer, or his father."

On three occasions the detention authorities had stripped the young man to his underwear and removed a mattress from his cell. He was allowed out only once a day to shower, fed leftovers, and given no opportunity to exercise.

In response the authorities stated that the boy had a serious crime record, had escaped the year before from detention center, and therefore was held in a special holding area. "Nonetheless, the rules," Petersen pointed out, "require a prompt hearing and notice to the court, his family, and a lawyer."

Petersen ended the debate with the comment, "You can't expect a detention center to be a pristine drawing room, but too many officials knew about the boy's situation, and no one did anything about it." The detention center manager recognized the failure to notify the appropriate parties and offered to investigate the mistreatment charges. Though no serious injury had occurred, it alerted Petersen and the community to the likelihood of a recurrence.

This was not be the first nor the last allegation of mistreatment in a juvenile lockup. Holding children in a secure detention is a difficult situation leading to both allegations and, at times, serious mistreatment. The significance here was that Tom Petersen was perhaps moving into another arena. Was his next role to be that of crusader against the inequities of the system?

Not really. Others of the judges had taken that stance. Petersen moved back to his more natural posture working to improve the school situation of those coming before him. But for a man with his moral beliefs, the issue of inhumane treatment was bound to find him. When it happened again, it wasn't even in Dade County. The small town of Pahokee in western Palm Beach County was the site of the aberration that propelled Judge Petersen into action.

The official name of the fenced compound on the shores of Lake Okeechobee was the Pahokee Youth Development Center, originally built as an adult prison. The state Department of Juvenile Justice had then used the Pahokee facility to house moderate-risk juveniles. It held 350 teenagers, about thirty-five from Dade County; others from across the state. Delinquents were to serve the maximum for level 6 moderate-risk offenders—six-month sentences. Many had committed property crimes; a small number violent crimes like strong-arm robbery.

Pahokee was no barrel of laughs for the young inmates. The compound was double fenced, topped by rolls of razor wire. Allowed weekly family visits and one five-minute phone call, the children slept in cells with narrow cots and stainless steel toilets.

As recounted by reporters Amy Driscoll and Gail Epstein in the August 27, 1997, edition of the *Miami Herald*, freely quoted here, Judge Tom Petersen viewed that the center was inappropriately severe for children considered only level 6 moderate risks.

Said Petersen, "Neither I nor anyone else critical of this place is saying we don't need a prison for juveniles, but these are the wrong juveniles to be put there. Level 6 programs don't call for a prison term more fit for adults."

Considering that 1997 was still in the era of escalating crime, with citizen's angry and fearful of hard-core juveniles, the State was not about to back down. Officials there denied mistreatment of these youthful offenders, defending against the accusation that Pahokee was too harsh for potentially serious offenders.

The conflict had begun during a routine hearing when Judge Petersen asked two returning juveniles about conditions at Pahokee. Petersen was taken aback when the boys complained of overly harsh conditions, including solitary confinement, cold water, inedible food, and shaved heads.

Judge Petersen, along with Public Defender Marie Osborne, quickly visited the Pahokee Center and were shocked with what they saw. Petersen, angry as he had ever been with the Juvenile Justice Department treatment of children, wrote a scathing letter enclosing photos denouncing the department, circulating it statewide to other judges and officials. Assistant Public Defender Osborne called the place a "sham facility appropriate only for maximum-security adult criminals."

Then the fun began. State officials maintained that neither the judge nor the public defender could tell them how to run their facilities. Judge Petersen threatened to resign over abuse of power by correctional officials.

Pahokee was 120 miles away, but word had already reached the inmates and the buzz around their cafeteria was all about this judge fighting for them in Miami. No news as to the results, but the battle continued in Miami. All the young inmates were hopeful.

The mistreatment issue apparently had serious implications. The State Juvenile Justice Department had recently started to privatize many of their operations, and Pahokee was now run by a private corporation under contract to the State. Was Petersen about to attack the continued privatization of juvenile corrections facilities?

The department also couched the issue in terms of judicial interference likely to decimate all the programs run by the State. "Should this kind of interference be permitted here, then Judges could control all department programs" was their lament.

This was a rerun to the early days of Judges Edith Atkinson and Walter Beckham, back in the 1920s and thereafter, when both the County and later the State vied with the judges over who had full control of the programs for delinquent children.

As had happened in all similar such conflicts of the past, it was worked out peacefully. Judge Tom Petersen wisely withdrew from the contest, allowing other juvenile judges to resolve the differences. The Juvenile Justice Department agreed to review and improve conditions at Pahokee, putting the private corporation on notice someone was actually watching their performance.

In the interest of harmony, Petersen had stepped aside, still questioning the operation of the Pahokee institution. Other juvenile judges continued to assert their inherent judicial authority in terms of control over delinquents sent to the custody of the State. This, notwithstanding that the legislature was slowly eroding this authority

After several fruitless hearings, an assistant public defender arguing the case seemed to sum it up best, "Time is of the essence here. By the time this issue between these warring parties is resolved, these kids will be old enough to have voted in several elections."

This issue "can a judge still maintain control over what happens after sentencing?" reappears from time to time. The legislature vacillates from side to side, with the judges always maintaining their inherent authority. Usually some band-aids come into play, and the issue fades for the time being. Absent a Tom Petersen, it is more likely to quietly vegetate until the next media exposure of prison mistreatment comes along. And it surely will.

Interestingly, ten years later in 2006, Petersen, long retired, hadn't lost his fire when a similar incident occurred in a Bay County boot camp run by the sheriff's office. A fourteen-year-old sent there for joyriding in his grandmother's car died after maltreatment by staff instructors for his refusal to continue to run laps.

Petersen, called for a comment by a newspaper reporter, denounced the weak explanation offered by the staffers in no uncertain terms. "This was a plain-out mugging that can't be couched in euphemisms," he stated, then adding, "Such brutal action is an insult to anyone who ever worked in the juvenile justice system." The boot camp was closed down, followed by a governor-appointed state attorney criminal investigation. Petersen continued to be the man to speak out against injustice.

Tom Petersen's long career working for children going back to his days as a VISTA member in the public defender's office some fifty years ago has earned him a reputation as a tireless, fearless advocate for children. In every capacity as a defender, prosecutor, and judge he has met every test.

Most public officials earn a wall full of plaques and other testimonials attesting to their high quality performance. Petersen is probably most proud of two: Three days before his resignation from the circuit court on March 27, 1998, Congresswoman Carrie Meek, Judge Petersen's old and dear friend, paid tribute in the *Congressional Record* calling him "one of Dade's unsung heroes." Excerpts of the tribute follow:

> Having dedicated a major portion of his life to making the system work on behalf of our wayward youth, he was relentless in the development of many innovative programs that have helped turn them around.
>
> He was virtually the lone voice in the wilderness exposing his righteous indignation over the many irrelevant programs that had siphoned off funds from the public good, instead of eradicating the symptoms of juvenile delinquency.
>
> In his stint on the Dade Circuit bench, Judge Petersen truly represented an exemplary public servant who abided by the dictum that those who have less in life through no fault of their own, should somehow be lifted by those blessed with life's great amenities.
>
> As one of those hardy spirits who chose to reach out to the at-risk youth living in public-housing projects, Judge Petersen thoroughly understood the accouterments of power and leadership and sagely exercised them.
>
> Judge Petersen truly exemplified a one-of-a-kind leader-ship. His courage and wisdom appealed to those of our noblest instincts. His compassionate and resilient spirit has genuinely dignified the role of a true public servant.

The second of his awards that most pleased him was the *Miami Herald*'s Spirit of Excellence Award presented to him in 1988. Each year a panel of leading citizens chose five persons for this honor. Probably the most esteemed award offered in the community, receiving it represented the finest in accomplishment.

Interestingly, in all the years of this presentation, only three elected officials were among those chosen. Significantly, all three were juvenile court judges—Seymour Gelber, William Gladstone, and now Thomas Petersen. Who dares to say that Juvenile court judges who speak out for children are not given their due?

I asked him why he had retired at least ten years before he reached retirement age. He thought for a few moments and then said,

> Frankly, the pace was too slow for me. When I worked to set up those programs at Larchmont Gardens and the others, I was totally free to move at my own pace. There were several agencies involved, but they were almost glad to have me carry the ball. I virtually lived in Liberty City and enjoyed every moment of it.
>
> Setting up TROY was also an effort of love. Seeing those kids begin to blossom made me a happy man. Having Jennifer Schuster there as school principal took a lot of pressure off me.
>
> After that the bureaucracy seemed to take over. I know I was an individualist, but it wasn't because I wanted the credit. I only wanted good things to happen.
>
> My fellow judges were fine with me. Supportive, but I sensed I was traveling on a different spaceship. A change of atmosphere was needed. I'm still active in the community. I'm in the phone book available for another go-round when any new exciting venture appears on the horizon.

Upon retiring, Petersen became an adjunct professor at the University of Miami teaching a sociology course featuring juvenile justice. And therein lies another tale of Petersen and the rest of the world, this time the college sports world.

For the most part college scholarship, athletes tend to take soft courses like sports management or criminal justice that don't require heavy academic exercise. Instructors of these courses were aware that varsity team participation requires extensive use of energy, and time usually give these students a bit of leeway. Not so Professor Tom Petersen.

Petersen's teaching style was to introduce a series of historical events and extract from them a better understanding of how the past often foretells the future. Interesting approach. A term paper and a final exam followed. Students showing up and satisfying the requirements passed without any problems.

One of the football players, an All-American no less, chose to be less than cooperative, cheating on the final exam and then plagiarizing his term paper. Petersen dropped him from the course, and the student honor court suspended him for two semesters, thus denying him eligibility for the next football season.

A furor broke out: Which is more important: U of Miami's academic stature or the standing in the national football ratings? Embarrassing to the University of

Miami president and the alumni? You bet. Petersen was adamant. The integrity of scholarship is more important than a national football title.

Not only that, but Petersen then advised UM by letter that theirs and the whole national college football structure needed to be revised in terms of student athlete participation. The media picked up the debate, and Petersen single-handedly seemed to be tackling this sensitive national problem at football schools. College administrators and influential alumni would just as soon have had the subject disappear from the press and the public mind.

This was a no-win situation all around. Petersen, though a UM football fan, stood his ground. The university relying on the federal statute that protects the privacy of a student's records, declined further comment. Finally, the erring football star was permitted to take a makeup summer course protecting his football eligibility.

The university agreed to tighten up scholarship rules, actually enforcing class attendance; the football student went on to become a star in the NFL earning millions of dollars. Although the university offered Petersen a contract renewal, he respectfully declined.

This little tale is not about the athlete scholar or the University of Miami (my law school). It's about Tom Petersen.

I personally had advised him on this matter. My advice had been to work out a nonadversarial solution. Reciting a similar experience of mine many years ago at Florida State University teaching a group of basketball players, one, who eventually became an All-Star NBA player, fell behind in his work. I stretched it a bit, helping him prepare for the final essay exam. Should I have not given him an edge? Probably not, but I figured no harm done, no foul.

My friend and colleague Tom Petersen is a man of huge principle. Doing the right thing for him had no exceptions. He ruled from the bench, designed programs, and treated his fellow beings of all castes and status the same way. Yes, he was an advocate ready to speak out for children, but more than that he was, if not a saintly figure, at least a symbol of one rising above the rest of us by simply doing the right thing. Good and true man that Tom Petersen.

When suddenly he had resigned from the bench in March 1998, after nine years of service, it came as a shock to his friends and those in the juvenile justice system. The *Miami Herald* headline said "Juvenile Justice Loses Caring Judge." At age fifty-eight, twelve years before mandatory retirement age, there was still a lot to be done. And not too many around of Petersen's quality and courage to do it.

He had been a controversial judge. Somehow conflict always followed him; he never turned away from it. As *Youth Today*, a national newspaper on youth work described it, "State officials didn't like him because it's their policies he's trying to change. Some say he's too soft on juvenile criminals. Others say he oversteps his boundaries. Petersen has been an opponent of building more prisons."

Petersen would be the first to agree with his critics. He strongly opposes following the more popular punishment model, instead favoring the sending of delinquents to school and rehab programs. As to overstepping bureaucratic boundaries, that's something he does with relish. There have been few delinquency judges anywhere with his courage and ability willing to test the waters with new creative approaches, ridding the system of outmoded ineffectual programs of the past.

Why did he leave the post? He said he was burned out, somewhat disillusioned with the system. Probably true. He had been in the criminal justice system in several important positions for about thirty years. Starting as a VISTA member with the public defender, then introducing one of the first trial intervention programs in the country as an assistant state attorney, and as well his exemplary housing projects. And finally these nine productive years on the bench. A worthy record indeed.

From my own view as a longtime observer of the criminal justice system and as his friend and colleague, it wasn't fatigue that caused him to leave. Tom Petersen is a free spirit. In his other positions before becoming a judge, he was given freewheeling authority to fix what wasn't fixable. The judiciary, fortunately or not, is rather a hidebound institution. Advocates, within bounds have freedom, but the Canons of Ethics and institutional mores do establish limitations.

Petersen was a man of ideas, not one to merely fine-tune a system having huge structural deficits. He was a loner who focused on adequate schooling as a solution, and by that concentration had made a strong contribution. Personally, I think he could have stayed and performed wondrous things during the remaining twelve years before mandatory retirement. But I'm no Tom Petersen. He felt shackled, and without that true feeling of being a legendary knight in armor striking down evil, he was somewhat at sea.

Upon his retirement he immediately announced plans to investigate federally subsidized housing in Miami's inner city and write a book on alternative history with the working title *What If Oswald Had Missed?* (forthcoming).

He's probably still dreaming of getting out in the field again, starting neighborhood projects anew in the depressed areas of Miami. Tom Petersen is gone, but he has not forgotten. Whenever we talk about the old days, I see that glint in his eyes. It's a clear message—he will be back.

Meanwhile, Administrative Judge Cindy Lederman had been struggling with a system that at times has shown promise; other times a disaster. Unlike Petersen, she worked totally within the established system. He was a person always ready to bypass what existed; she, a structural engineer type fitting the old pieces together to be fresh and new.

Apparently, among advocates there is room for many approaches. None before her had been able to really pull all those disparate entities together, but then again the past had no Cindy Lederman around to lead the way.

Cindy Lederman

Quiet, dignified, cultured—a true lady. So why then do they talk about her in whispers in the hallways of the juvenile court? Well, for one thing she is a tough, demanding taskmaster. She's also not one for too much small talk. All her adult life, her main focus, other than her family, has been on public service—more precisely children. Totally committed to it. She may not subscribe to the idea that everyone in her orbit must follow her, but she sure expects those who have chosen this path to hew to her line. Perform. Perform. That's the signal she sends out.

Suddenly, after meandering along and making very slow incremental gains, the juvenile justice system has jumped into the forefront. Hard to tell what propels a movement. Sometimes a series of horrific events. Sometimes the time has arrived. Maybe even a dynamic leader. All of the above were here, present and accounted for.

Judge Cindy Lederman, the architect of the juvenile court's dependency system, has earned a well-deserved reputation, locally and nationally, as an efficient and skilled draftsman. Her projects are purposeful, directly addressing the concerns, and totally lacking in frills.

Preparing her proposals, she avoids flowery and emotional language to gain the necessary support. She gets to the point quickly. Is she tough-minded enough? Is she a woman intent on showing a hard side in the environment of this male-dominated criminal justice system?

Her first project with the juvenile court in 1996 best described her innate qualities. Attempting to probe the psyche of her new charges, she asked herself, "How can we get abused and neglected children to better express the hidden feelings about their own condition?"

"Certainly," she mused, "kids in these circumstances need an outlet to examine themselves and appraise their situation."

Do we appoint a panel of psychologists to study them? Should they be writing essays describing their reaction to life? Lederman came up with an approach not only novel but also, in a way, tender and warm hearted. Called the Picturing Ourselves Project, she enlisted *Miami Herald* photographer Marice Cohn Band and photo artist Sharon Gurman Socol.

At lunch, meeting with photographers Band and Socol, they discussed how to use art as a form of therapy. Judge Lederman voiced concern about the daily struggle these kids have in terms of self-expression. What better form than photography to display both the condition and the response?

The plan was hatched: eight teenagers, survivors of abuse and neglect, were to join them to spend two hours together every Wednesday learning both the art of photography and something more about themselves. A simple idea, but in the hands of provocative minds it could evoke many untouched personal areas.

Donors were quick to supply cameras, equipment, film, and cover other costs. The children were interviewed for the program and participants identified. With professional advisors to consult with and seeing the finished result of their efforts, the eight young photographers soon became a proud and self-assured group.

Their photos included shots with their foster parents, the homes and rooms where they stayed, events attended, and routine home activity like mealtime and TV watching. Captions were attached to the photos describing the events.

Samika, a fourteen-year-old, did portraits of herself and the neighborhood. A shot of the sun shining out from behind a couple of puffy white clouds, she titled "Heavenly Father." It was her favorite. Samika said, "For the first time, I finally got a chance to tell people about my dreams and goals in life. The Lord has watched over me all my life. He knows what I have been through, and he knows where I am going."

Daniel, age thirteen, had included his therapist among snaps of his foster father and one taken alongside his foster mother. He said, "We learned to express our feelings."

Norma said, "When I first came here I was shy and scared. Now I don't feel that way. This class has helped me out a lot."

The public exhibition of the art work had all the trappings of a New York Metropolitan Museum grand opening. The who's who of the juvenile justice system were in attendance, as well as the press interviewing the artists and taking photos of the photos. Attending the exhibit, I realized how easy it was to feel the warmth these eight foster kids had engendered. And how each of them now glowed in appreciation.

Although at times, "hard" and "tough" have been words used by some in describing Judge Cindy Lederman, I always look back at her Picturing Ourselves Project and say, "There's a lot more to that woman than may appear on the surface."

In an article in the *Judge's Journal*, co-authors Cindy Lederman and Sharon Gurman Socol described the origin of the project. Ms. Socol, a professional photographer, had been aware of the Literacy through Photography program in use for the Houston Independent School District and had broached the possibility to her friend Cindy Lederman. Thus came the idea for Picturing Ourselves as a tool to encourage self-expression, discover self-awareness, and develop greater self-esteem.

The program was designed to benefit adolescent children who had experienced neglect and abuse. The coauthors stated the purpose,

> Our experience shows that beyond the excitement of taking pictures, these children can reveal feelings, clarify relationships, demonstrate humor and pride, and give us honest portraits of their world in words and photographs.
>
> We also hoped that by singling out children for a positive, one-on-one experience with someone they could work, trust and respect, they might reap the benefits of a stable, healthy and honest relationship with an adult, something quite rare in their lives.

Sharon Socol began the curriculum by acquainting the eight participants with the photographic process. This included exercises on the properties of film, the chemistry of photography, how to frame shots, and finally the actual use of the camera. Then they added language lessons, teaching descriptive adjectives that enabled the children to properly describe their responses.

Polaroid Corporation provided cameras, and the weekly assignments covered photo portraits of themselves, their surroundings, and their families. Roundtable discussions then followed as they sought to verbalize their emotions about the camera subjects and finally express their feelings in writing.

In their magazine article, authors Sokol and Lederman described their reaction.

> We discovered how much the children thrived on mentoring and individual attention. We learned how comparatively easy it was to instill a sense of dignity in these children, who often live in an environment of constant uncertainty and fear.
>
> The self-portrait assignment encouraged them to explore how they felt about themselves, while the family photos showed how they felt about biological or foster families.

These children were accustomed to being shy and reluctant; but their participation in group projects encouraged interaction and spawned spontaneous, creative ideas.

This unquestionably had to be a most rewarding program for both Socol and Lederman, as well as other instructors involved. Perhaps the intimacy of having only eight students added to the satisfaction. Certainly, a worthwhile project for all involved.

With the dawn of the twenty-first century, Judge Lederman faced some daunting challenges. We all can recall how the date of January 1, 2000, had brought us face-to-face with fears that our computers had been programmed improperly, thus causing all the electrical systems worldwide to go asunder. Visions of planes falling out of the sky and other calamities were projected in the media.

Fortunately, computers were properly adjusted, and no such fate befell the world. However, with the arrival of the new century, the fate of the juvenile justice system was, while not about to fall from the sky, still was up for grabs. Would it vanish like other institutions that no longer serve a purpose? Do we finally have a direction? Can Cindy Lederman lead the way?

After Judge Gladstone had retired to join Senator Bob Graham in Washington in 1992, things slowed down a bit. With Cindy Lederman's ascent to the circuit court in 1994 and becoming administrative judge shortly thereafter, the hiatus was over. Things began to heat up.

The system still was in a precarious position. Not the end of the world, but still no signs of deliverance. Our new leader for the twenty-first century had the makings of one to guide us out of the wilderness. That marine recruiting poster proudly heralds, One Man Can Make a Difference. There's a slight gender gap there, but the thought is perfectly applicable. Can new leader Cindy Lederman make the juvenile justice system what it was intended to be?

Bill Gladstone had laid the groundwork, and Cindy Lederman began to transform it into a functional, viable reality. Were the planets in proper orbit for her to succeed? They hadn't been for a good part of the preceding century, so why now? One thing in her favor was the move to give dependency the priority it warranted. Operating in the shadow of delinquency, it was now about to flower. Early on, dependency had been mostly an afterthought struggling for attention. Would this trend change the focus of the juvenile court?

Upon becoming administrative judge in 1998, she wisely supported separating the two, placing herself in charge of dependency, and Judge Lester Langer as delinquency boss. When Eleventh Judicial Circuit Chief Judge Joseph Farina had appointed her, she had asked for Judge Langer to be named associate administrator to head the Delinquency Section.

That was a move showing good judgment. Years before becoming a judge, Langer, long involved as an activist lawyer in the juvenile court, was well equipped for that assignment. He had a wealth of knowledge and experience and yet had the same enthusiasm and thirst for improvement as she possessed.

Respecting each other, both had the good sense to avoid petty differences. Sometimes judges differ over miniscule points that impede the progress of their greater purpose. Besides, her presence immediately gave the Dependency Section added stature and gave her more time to concentrate on an area in great need.

Since serving in the juvenile court is not considered a plum, most assuredly serving in the dependency unit is viewed as the least favorable post. Generally, judges prefer assignment to higher-status divisions, such as civil or criminal, where the top law firms function. Only on rare occasions are juvenile court judges promoted to higher courts or recruited by the top quality law firms.

Dependency court has the further imprint that these cases often involve wrenching tales of child abuse, decisions to terminate parental rights, and other family struggles that make a judge's involvement a most trying and stressful event.

When the strife involving the destiny of an innocent child finally reaches the court system, all the participants suffer the agonies. It might be the damage done to a child by quarreling parents on the eve of a divorce. Or the trauma caused by forcing a potentially adoptive parent to surrender the child when the birth parent suddenly appears. Not only judges but down the line to the field counselors, the clinicians, and all the players en route, these situations are distressful. Invariably, cases appear that educate and harden the job for all involved.

Every juvenile court judge somewhere along the way runs into career cases that not only attract the media and public attention but seem to run on interminably. The tendency of the judge is to move quickly to remediate a bad situation. The tempo of juvenile court usually requires fast action since the lives of children before them are at stake, and a prompt response can avoid a disaster.

Judge Cindy Lederman had several cases that plod along, month after month, and even year after year. Her longest and best known was the *Rilya Wilson* case. But before that, at the onset of her juvenile court term, she had another case that fully initiated her to the travails of dependency actions both for the families and the Judge. One of her first cases sorely put her to the test. The case occupied the newspapers and TV for well over a year.

It involved an infant abandoned for three months and then placed in foster care for over two years. Ideally, with custodial parents ready to adopt, a year is the time expected to complete the adoption process. Such a couple had been available. This couple had another previously adopted child and, from all appearances, had both the temperament and means to serve appropriately as adopting parents. For one reason or another, the State had failed to complete the adoption in the one-year designated period.

The birth mother, a cocaine addict, had now for the second time voluntarily surrendered her parental rights, leaving the child up for adoption. Suddenly, she appeared with cousin relatives, requesting the child be placed with her relatives who, according to the caseworkers, previously had rejected the proposal to take custody.

The custodial (adopting) mother resisted, claiming that HRS had given her assurances that adoption would soon be forthcoming. Two psychologists also had reported that moving this cocaine-infected child now would likely cause permanent psychological damage.

The custodial mother, a college administrator, was also an elected officeholder in a Dade County town. She had resigned her political post, and along with her husband had sold their apartment and bought a house in Broward County for their now larger family, which included a previously adopted severely medically abused child. HRS caseworkers had written glowing reports as to the progress, for the past five years, this formerly abused child had made in the care of his new adoptive parents.

Judge Lederman, following the law that gave priority to family members, ordered the child placed in the custody of the cousin relatives. Obviously a hard decision for the judge. In dependency court there are few easy ones. The custodial mother promptly took off for parts unknown with the two children.

Newspaper stories recounted the story many times. After hiding in Central Florida for three weeks, she reappeared, surrendering the child to the Children's Home Society, the agency handling adoptions. A caseworker thereupon delivered the little girl to her cousins.

The custodial mother had acted in panic. As she gave up the child, she said simply, "This is my baby." The U.S. Attorney thereupon filed unlawful flight charges, only later dropped because she had not left the state. She still faced court action for violating Judge Lederman's order and other criminal charges in Broward County arising from these circumstances.

She defended her action accusing HRS of misleading her into believing the adoption was a certainty. Also, that HRS failed to file promptly for adoption under the required federal guidelines. Further, she added HRS had been able only to locate a grandmother and uncle as family relatives, neither in a position to adopt.

With charges facing her in both Broward County and Dade County, friends and sympathizers began collecting funds for her defense. Dozens of letters to the press and to her personally urged her to fight on. This case became a cause célèbre.

After spending three days in jail, the custodial mother said, "The thought of spending more time in jail horrifies me, but I made a commitment to both of my children. This baby is the light of my life. We are going to fight this all the way to the supreme court. I'm willing to risk anything."

The struggle continued. Her lawyer accused the judge of bias, asking her to recuse herself, a request Judge Lederman denied. The *Miami Herald* ran a poll, "Who should get custody of the baby?" The case had the kind of human interest that made it fodder for discussion among legal circles, at the breakfast table, and on talk shows.

HRS Dade County administrator Anita Bock, in an unguarded moment, admitted that "HRS knew or should have known that the baby's extended family may present suitable placement possibilities." This after a *Herald* reporter uncovered a report by an HRS caseworker showing that months earlier the cousins had been available and had purchased a crib for their young cousin. The counselor's report stated the following in regard his assessment of the cousins: "In my four years of doing home studies, rarely have I witnessed such enthusiasm, motivation, and determination demonstrated in gaining custody of a child."

Unfortunately, this report had been mislaid, never seeing the light of day. The cousins also contended that as soon as they had learned of the situation, they began phoning HRS, even attending many of the hearings, but somehow they were lost in the shuffle.

The custodial mother, vowing to continue her efforts to regain the baby, filed for adoption. New evidence appeared showing plans by the custodial mother to disappear with the two children long before Judge Lederman had awarded temporary custody to the cousins. Her plan was to go to New Zealand since that country had no extradition treaty with the United States. She had gone so far as to scan obituaries to obtain a new identity. At a subsequent hearing before Judge Lederman, her request for visitation was denied.

Judge Lederman, in support of her decision, quoted a psychologist's report that "such visits would be confusing to the child, threaten her sense of security, and as well jeopardize her psychological well-being." The Guardian ad Litem had testified that the child had adjusted smoothly with the cousins, "It is truly rewarding to see how well the baby continues to do and how happy she is with the cousins."

When last heard from two years later, the custodial mother was still pursuing a legal remedy. Had HRS properly pursued this matter in a timely fashion at the onset, the presence of the cousins would have been disclosed early on, and the custodial parent might have relinquished the child without a struggle, although at times foster parents gain so strong an attachment that resistance continues no matter what.

Was the birth mother a sympathetic figure, though an addict who had failed three drug treatment programs? Yes, to some extent. No matter the adverse conditions, having to surrender a child is still a wrenching experience.

How about the custodial parent? Surely, HRS had botched the case and misled her. Yes, but does that legally entitle her to custody of the child when family members are available?

Should Judge Lederman have given her more consideration because she and her husband had already successfully adopted an abused child and might prove to be better parents for the child? I think not. The judge clearly followed the law, giving first priority to next of kin.

The point of reciting this case is to illustrate the tough decisions that are commonplace at dependency hearings. Most involve separation of a child from a custodial or a birth parent. One of the contestants generally find the decision destructive. The hurt never goes away.

Too often a war ensues with family members at sword's point with each other. The state regulatory agency is frequently at sea, uncertain as to what to do; the media report the tragedy mostly for its sensationalism value, and a judge in the middle is expected to make a Solomon-like decision resolving the conflict. A dependency judge needs but one of these cases for a proper baptism. Trouble is they are there every day.

The full recognition of the importance of the dependency system became most apparent in the decade of the 1990s under the aegis of Judge Cindy Lederman. It didn't suddenly appear. It grew slowly but surely. Before, hidden in the backwash of the court's calendar, it only emerged when a case with all the dramatic elements of the one cited here became known to the public.

Judge Gladstone had kick-started the move toward full recognition earlier, but it needed more substance added to the skeletal structure. It also needed a leader totally committed to making the crisis of dependent children the paramount issue of the juvenile court structure.

The delinquency side of the court, heretofore more prominent, had changed mostly by U.S. Supreme Court decree. Also, public fear over the rise of violent juvenile crime had diminished much of the early child-saving fervor. Despite these changes, the delinquency side had long been viewed as having many systemic shortcomings and had never come close to satisfying its critics.

Many experts unquestionably now view the dependency side as more crucial to the child's well-being and certainly a much more difficult task for all those involved. Organizing the dependency operation as a productive system would become a major part of Judge Lederman's career, leading into the early years of the twenty-first century.

One must glance at the setting in the Miami-Dade community to appreciate the task ahead. It had a signature appeal as a pleasure town—sin city, fun city. Miami, the most populous city, is also one of the poorest cities in the country, one where government was often identified by the media as inept and corrupt. The large influx of Cubans escaping the tyranny of Fidel Castro, as well as others seeking haven here, has caused considerable dislocation despite the positive impact much of this immigration has provided.

We also have a politically conservative state legislature that provides minimal services for the basic needs of our less fortunate. Consistently it has failed to fund an adequate social services network, thus resulting in a negative impact on our children. In this kind of setting, the juvenile court has struggled to make do with what we have. Difficult but not insurmountable.

That was the environment facing Judge Lederman. She realized that storming the Legislature and chastising the shortcomings of the social agencies, while perhaps necessary at times, were not the most successful or appropriate approaches. First, she needed to make the system work, establishing both its credibility as well as her own.

No easy task since an administrative judge's powerful voice was but one part of a complex system. Speaking out for children was not enough. More importantly, proving to the legislature and the public that the system was capable of working was the key. Making the system functional was the first step. That would be the slow but sure route, one step at a time.

A good example was the simple problem of getting the many reports of a child's progress assembled and presented to the court in a professional manner. Just think of all the individuals involved in assessing a child appearing in dependency court: school personnel, health clinicians, probation staffers, psychologists, police, medical, and many others. Some of these may appear in court; others provide written reports. In totality, the process of apprising the judge constitutes reams of paper and days of testimony. Reasoned Lederman, "There must be an easier, more efficient way to make this information available."

Lederman's solution, so obvious, was mind boggling. Called a comprehensive assessment, it involved a trained therapist to review all the reports, interview the parties, and then write a summary of all the information available in a case. This doesn't necessarily eliminate the essential testimony, but in one fell swoop the judge now has guidance at his or her fingertips pointing to decisions that can expedite the proceedings.

The assessment provided a road map for what should happen. Considering the complexity of these cases and the often divergence of opinion, this was a tool of immeasurable assistance to the court. It insured with certainty that all significant factors were available in the decision-making process. The coordinating therapist was a licensed mental health counselor with a master's degree. These court-ordered assessments were paid for by Medicaid $48.50 hourly, twenty hours maximum per case. Who said federal government bureaucracy doesn't work?

Judge Lederman and Judge Gladstone, both leaders of national and state task forces addressing mental health problems, had learned to deal with these so-called minor problems. This approach was one of many proposed systemic alterations. Although Lederman would move to more encompassing programs as her career progressed, she remained constantly aware of the piece-meal approach in correcting "minor" deficiencies.

Another such problem was the inability of mothers to obtain child support ordered by the juvenile court. The general public might expect that such a judicial order could be implemented promptly. Unfortunately, our bureaucracy oftentimes overwhelms the good intentions. In a response to the problem, Judge Lederman had advised the Child Support Division of the delay in enforcement of such orders by the juvenile court judges.

The Division of Child Support Enforcement, manned by the state attorney's office, functioned independently of the juvenile court. In fact these two courts were located miles apart both physically and operationally. Thus, orders to pay child support emanating from the juvenile court did not necessarily have some priority with the enforcement clerks in Child Support.

Apparently in the past, the Child Support clerks had followed the then-accepted practice to merely issue verbal warnings or at most a letter to the nonpaying fathers advising of the failure to pay. The word that Judge Lederman now sought to enforce these orders had, for some unknown reason, not yet filtered down to the proper sources. When one hundred of these new juvenile court orders languished on the desk of Child Support clerks for eight months, it became a crisis.

Lederman convened a meeting with the offices of the clerk and the state attorney to restructure the process for enforcing her court's child support orders.

No big deal you think, but absent someone covering all the loopholes in the system, things can and will go awry. Better known for her systemwide enhancements, Lederman was also a stickler for the falling-through-the-cracks problems. Often, it is the less-publicized acts that are most beneficial to citizens in need. Ask the mother waiting eight months for child support relief.

Lederman, like all her predecessor administrative judges, was in a constant struggle with the social service agencies. Collectively, the judges were often critical of the agencies' performance lapses, while the agencies regularly contested the extent of judicial authority. It was an ongoing dispute not easily settled.

Usually the judges prevailed in these differences. That is, unless the administration in Tallahassee had a political philosophy more in the direction of cutting budgets of social service agencies. Regrettably, prevention programs take longer to be effective and are more expensive, thus making them easier to target for budget cuts. This occurs mostly when a conservative Republican sits in the governor's office, as exemplified by Jeb Bush, governor from 1998 to 2006. Then it becomes open warfare.

During his term of office, Governor Jeb Bush reorganized the Health and Rehabilitative Services, giving the Division of Youth Services (DYS) new personnel and more fiscal controls. Under new management, the DYS aggressively resisted the large social services net that the juvenile judges and HRS had preferred in the past. The struggle with HRS in the olden days (Democrats in power) had been more a family squabble, while with Governor Bush's DYS there existed sharp philosophical differences.

Determined to balance the state budget as required by state law, the Bush administration focused on social service cuts sorely impinging on programs affecting the juvenile court. Under the Bush administration, the changes imposed were more negative than positive, at least in terms of the wishes of the judges.

Fairness, however, dictates the recognition that the juvenile justice system, despite earlier efforts by more social-minded administrations (Democrats), had never found a formula or funds able to give sufficient comfort to children in distress or to satisfy the safety concerns of our citizenry.

Issues between Lederman and the Department of Children and Families (DCF) constantly erupted. There was a recent one involving Lederman's efforts to extend her authority over foster care children after they turn eighteen, when the court presumably loses jurisdiction over the child. The problem was a real one.

Do we turn these now young adults loose on the streets? With no resources or place to live and limited employment skills, will they end up homeless, unemployed, or incarcerated? What to do?

Addressing the problem, Judge Lederman appointed the Independent Living Advisory Panel. She had included a former DCF district administrator and heads of various agencies involved with this group of children. Since eighty such teenagers at that time were preparing to exit the foster care program, their recommendations would be important.

This indeed was a sad situation facing children whom the State had sheltered for several years. Meanwhile, a Broward County delegation, calling on state legislators, joined in asking state lawmakers to allow foster children to stay under the jurisdiction of juvenile judges for at least one year after turning eighteen. Support for Lederman's position was increasing.

In the past, the legislature had provided financial and medical support until age twenty-three. However, the legislature, in one of their fits of wisdom, decided that only eighteen-year-olds who are finishing high school and already enrolled in college can continue to get State support. Apparently, the change was aimed at those who either choose not to go to college or for some reason had delayed their application. For foster care children, with college not always a priority, it meant facing the perils of the street homeless and adrift.

The Lederman-appointed panel wrote a report urging changes in the law, which earned a favorable editorial in the *Miami Herald*. The *Herald* praised the report as compelling evidence. Earlier, Dade Circuit Court Judge Sarah Zabel, sitting in the Juvenile Division, had also ordered DCF to continue a seventeen-year-old foster girl in the State's custody for her coming release upon reaching eighteen. After repeated hearings, with DCF refusing to provide further funds for the child, Zabel threatened contempt action. The court-appointed lawyer for the child said, "I am afraid DCF officials are simply biding their time, waiting for the child to turn eighteen and then release her to the street."

Judge Lederman, in a similar case, responded to the problem by ordering DCF welfare administrators to provide assistance to over-eighteen foster children. DCF declined to follow the court order, appealing to the Third District Court of Appeal. Lederman lost that one, but on her appeal, the Florida Supreme Court clearly vindicated her position that judges do play a major role in all aspects of the child's treatment.

That some sort of deep black hole in the earth's surface exists in which foster children turning eighteen fall into may be shocking to the casual observer. But there are probably many other deep crevices where unfortunate children totally lack a support system to sustain them. The struggle over the plight of the eighteen-year-old foster children would continue on.

With it all, Judge Lederman furthered her efforts to institute new programs to bolster the still unsteady dependency operation. The time was just about right. Slowly over the century, our judges had only inched along. Until the Gladstone era beginning in the midseventies, it had been a defensive struggle to hold on, mostly hand-to-hand combat with the government social welfare agencies.

With the advent of Gladstone, he and his successors, became more positive, promoting a whole variety of programs. Thus they began to reinforce the court with adjunct programs on the premises, such as a mental health clinic, and also the trend toward a joint effort with the school system as advanced by both Judges Gladstone and Petersen.

The judges also introduced research and grantsmanship into the equation. Gladstone, with his Jean Piaget study, examined the differences between delinquent and conventional children. Gelber produced an almost four-year experiment to determine the effectiveness of the present system, and along with Petersen both collected yearly data on the progress of children appearing before them. All three sought grants for new programs. Perhaps unnoticed at the time, these qualitative efforts brought, if not a totally new approach, certainly a more pronounced one to the Dade County Juvenile Court.

Lederman's aim has taken the court one huge step forward to a yet higher strata. The earlier research efforts, while of singular importance and impressive, did not carry the imprimatur of professional academic research. She introduced an analytical examination of each problem as if preparing a dissertation for a PhD exam. Research became her important tool along with publishing her findings in quality professional journals.

Every one of her programs was thoroughly researched in preparation for a sure-to-follow grant request. Follow-up articles appeared in professional periodicals. She looked for other experts in complementary fields to join her as coauthors. As a result, Lederman was publishing far beyond the op-ed pieces of her predecessors and in more prestigious periodicals. The appearance in recognized and respected law and medical journals gave her a special cachet, adding considerably to her reputation and that of our juvenile courts.

Her simultaneous effort to examine each problem through an interdisciplinary approach also opened new avenues. Involving other related disciplines such as medicine, psychiatry, psychology, and sociology gave a fuller dimension and understanding to the problems at hand. Her academic approach was not only scholarly but practical as well. Examining a project through several prisms provided more depth and perhaps a broader appreciation.

Defining Cindy Lederman's judicial style, one would have to admit it was eclectic in the sense that her intellectualism covered every aspect: legal, social, and political. Her proposed programs arrived as finished products. Though far from being a practiced politician, she had an unerring sense of making the right moves at the right time.

She also had the added protection of looking and sounding like the girl next door who only sought one's good graces in return. Instead there was a woman fully poised to defend her position with skill and force. Some have even commented that she is known to occasionally have raised her voice. This is a leader in full command. She may not win every battle, but adversaries will surely bear testament to the fact that she is not an opponent to be taken lightly. Yes, indeed.

Prior to becoming a circuit court judge, Lederman had been a strong advocate as a county court judge addressing domestic violence Appointed to the county court in 1989, she had helped organize the domestic violence court, serving as the first judge of that county court. She had attacked the problem as a true academician. This work in county court would serve as much of the underpinning for her major efforts upon her 1994 rise to the circuit court.

In developing the dependency system in circuit court, she considered one of her main concepts to be the fact that social scientists had identified domestic violence as closely associated with child abuse. Data showed one going with the other as though guided by some magnetic pull.

Researchers had observed that wherever severe violence existed between parents, on at least half the occasions, children were present to observe and were influenced by it. In less violent altercations, there was a strong likelihood that children heard, saw, or were certainly aware of parents torn apart. These scenes would have serious psychological implications for the child.

In 1997 she organized a thirty-six-month federally-funded program called Dependency Court Intervention Program, designed to study the correlation between battered women and abused children. The program's purpose: to assess the relationship between these conditions in order to find ways to protect children from the negative impact of domestic violence. First, determining the level of danger children face in these situations, and then exploring for positive techniques that could resolve the crisis in the best interest of the child.

To buttress her grant request and to further the significance of the ongoing results, she enlisted the aid of several PhDs in the field and other experts to join her in having national journals publish her articles on the subject. This grant was funded by the U.S. Department of Justice and viewed as the first grant nationally to recognize the important role the judiciary can play in terms of situations involving the total family.

Prior to her approach, there had been a tendency in many courts to assume, almost automatically, that the mother was a willing participant in the domestic violence, and thereby the child was taken into State custody. Judge Lederman opened the door for a fuller understanding of all the implications of domestic abuse.

This project grew into an interdisciplinary field involving many agencies. Her aim was to include schools, law enforcement, welfare agencies, citizen assistance, and other groups. The goal was to create a cross-pollination process, each agency setting up a warning system as well as a preventive program, possibly eliminating the need to call on the courts for relief.

By tying all these groups together, the troubled area of domestic abuse no longer remained a single-thread operation involving only spousal abuse. Both the implications and the manner to redress the situation took on much more significance.

The grant proposal had several important components, not always addressed in domestic violence court proceedings. Besides screening for domestic violence, these additional approaches included outreach advocacy services, evaluation of children as well as the adults, a victims' services intervention program for mothers and children, and a program evaluation component.

Initiating the grant request, Judge Lederman stated, "It is extremely frustrating knowing that no system is in place for victims of domestic abuse within our juvenile court proceedings. We feel that recognizing the high occurrence of domestic violence in child-abuse cases suggests that by helping the mother be safe from violence will make the child safer too."

In the three years since the program began, more than nineteen thousand Miami-Dade women had been screened; about seventy-five percent screened positive as victims of domestic violence. Said project director Christine O'Reilly, "The State's fatality review teams have found that domestic violence was a factor in 55 percent of the child deaths."

Where maltreatment of a child appeared to be a factor among battered women, a screening tool was developed that enabled child protective workers to introduce an advocacy program for the mothers. Theses intervention services increased the safety and self-efficacy of the mother. This program showed the screening tool as four times as effective as previously had been determined for mothers and their children in need of assistance.

Judge Lederman's primary thrust was to develop relationships between the child protective service system, the battered women's advocates, the judiciary and mental health and victim service providers. Specially trained advocates were provided as well as counseling, finding job opportunities, and even bus tokens. Making the mother self-sufficient was the ultimate purpose.

This program, by accentuating its interdisciplinary purpose, was viewed as a major step by the federal-funding agency and as well by practitioners in the field. It portrayed Judge Lederman's leadership in examining areas of concern in a more holistic manner. Focusing on all the relationships provided a full picture beyond the domestic violence between the two partners.

Lederman's Dependency Intervention Program didn't quite rank with Madam Curie's discovery, but it raised the professionalism of approaches in the dependency field several notches. Rarely, if ever before, had a program been so carefully validated prior to inception. Her efforts slowly but surely attracted national attention.

In 1999, one of her early op-ed pieces expressed her goals and views on the meaning and opportunity of the juvenile court, referring this time mostly to delinquent children. Describing the celebration to take place honoring the first century of the establishment of the juvenile court in America, she decried Florida's low ranking among states in regard the well-being of children—an embarrassing forty-fourth. She noted as well that in the last decade the reaction to the hard-core delinquent had become more punitive. She warned, "We must not create a one-dimensional system with rules, laws, goals, and practices designed to adjudicate Billy the Kid, when most juvenile delinquents, now remaining in the system more closely resemble Dennis the Menace."

Lederman was referring to the trend in those years to more easily place jurisdiction of violent offenders, like the legendary gunslinger Billy the Kid in adult court, leaving only the child prankster Dennis the Menace for juvenile court. Her point being that under recent legislation and court rulings, currently those violent offenders of yore were now in adult court, no longer in juvenile court.

The clientele on the delinquent side of the court had become not much different from those on the dependent side. She proposed to treat the younger delinquent children with the same kind of care as directed toward dependent children. In her article, she suggested a strong emphasis on research. She noted, "We must learn more about collective efforts, how neighborhoods can intervene to protect and control children. We must learn all the mental health needs of our youngest children. We need to have a rational, measured, scientific approach to the problems of crime."

Looking at her words and her accomplishments today, we note how she has carefully followed her credo.

In another 1999 article, this one in the *Juvenile Justice* magazine, she described her version of "Tomorrow's Juvenile Court." Featured is her pointed "Commandments" to judges on how to perform:

1. Knowing the law is not enough. Judges should be aware of available diagnostic tools, sensitive to the developmental needs of children.
2. Juvenile Court Judges need to take the lead in promoting program evaluation as an integral part of each new intervention.
3. Judges should be willing to collaborate across disciplines and with Juvenile Court practitioners to answer the questions of what works empirically.
4. Juvenile Court should stress its non-adversarial nature, keeping the best interest of the child in mind. And avoid duplicating the criminal court model.
5. Adjudications should provide individualized dispositions and, as well, adequate monitoring as the cornerstone of the Court's work.

That's quite a plateful for judges. Most would accept those concepts, although complying with these commandments might be a more difficult task. It would take strong leadership such as Lederman exemplifies to bring about the approach she recommends. Unfortunately, judges assigned under the rotation system come in different shapes and sizes and not necessarily with similar goals.

In the year 2000 she followed up with a program directed at our very young children. The Miami Safe Start Initiative was for infants and toddlers who, though under care of the State, still lacked special medical and developmental assessments. A *Miami Herald* editorial lauded the effort.

> Safe Start coordinators were appalled at the official neglect that infants and toddlers in State care were experiencing. There is little or no comprehensive medical assessment until these children are at age six.
>
> Also many of these young children in State care had not yet been immunized, had speech problems and other cognitive delays.

A concurrent program with Safe Start was her Infant and Young Children's Mental Health Project (IMHPP). The pilot program included parents and toddlers who participate in a weekly evaluation and therapy program with trained clinicians. The University of Miami's Linda Ray Center, serving as intervention partner, helped parents learn new ways to respond sensitively and play reciprocally with their young children, understanding the children's nonverbal clues.

Prior to these programs, as part of the Intervention Program for Family Violence, a component called PREVENT focused on evaluating the reciprocal bonding and attachment of infants and toddlers to their caregivers. All three of these programs with the very youngest of children have been part of her attempts to design a way to break the hold that child abuse has in our families.

Judge Lederman has become the patron saint for dependency, a role she gladly fills. Although Assistant Administrative Judge Lester Langer more than adequately has headed the delinquency side, she had not foreclosed on participation on that side of the building. This time it was the Girls' Advocacy Project (GAP)—titled by some advocates as Girls Are People. These were girls charged as delinquents, although in Lederman's view a closer examination would show the more likely need for treatment as a dependent.

Back in the earlier days in the juvenile court of 1970, the rate of female juvenile delinquency had held steadily at about 10 percent, mostly crimes of a nonviolent nature. In the '80s and '90s, the numbers began to rise steadily until currently girls number close to 30 percent, and violent crime has increased among them.

Census data (2000) from the Department of Juvenile Justice showed a 67-percent increase statewide (Florida) in the number of girls arrested over the prior decade. The number of boys rose only 25 percent during the same period.

This meant that in the past our detention center, mostly housing a handful of runaway girls, continued to face a steady increase hosting a much larger number, including some for more serious crimes. On any given day, in the year 1999 for example, as many as sixty girls were held in Dade's Juvenile Detention cells.

Lederman began her campaign to improve conditions for girls with articles published in the *University of Buffalo Law Review* and the *Child Law Practice*, a magazine for lawyers practicing in the field.

According to Judge Lederman, data show that of the many girls accused of minor offenses, 80 percent had been victims of physical abuse and 70 percent sexually abused or assaulted. Our Miami Detention Center officials provided no special attention to the needs of these youngsters. GAP was created in 2000 to make certain a support system was in place for the special needs of girls.

Visiting the detention center, Lederman was highly critical of the manner in which the detention center handled these children. Many girls were staying longer than the average eleven-day stay for boys in detention. Waiting for a bed in a residential treatment program, some stayed for months before an opening appeared.

Her article in the *Buffalo Law Review* expressed her basis for challenging the then current system. She wrote,

> Girls entering the juvenile justice system are not receiving the help they need. They rarely seek help, and help is rarely offered. Juvenile justice professionals have failed to recognize the desperate situation that many of these girls are in.
>
> Girls have different health needs, yet the system continues to place them in programs originally designed for boys.

She was highly critical of the handling of young prostitutes, citing a 1990 study of the Florida Supreme Court Gender Bias Study Commission that charged that, "A direct casual link appears to exist between the treatment of runaway girls by the juvenile justice system and their future recruitment as prostitutes. The impact of prostitution upon runaway girls cannot be minimized."

According to Lederman, most juvenile judges are remiss, usually sending runaway girls home, failing to inquire as to abuse or causes for their action. "It is essential," she offered, "that Judges focus our resources on examining and addressing these difficult and pressing issues of girls with broad strokes and greater depth."

The *Law Review* article noted that the physical conditions of the modules housing the girls were bleak at best and unconscionable at worst. The girls slept on concrete slabs with thin blankets, although the temperature was very cold. When overcrowded, which was often, two girls shared a cell. Entering the cell area was heart wrenching to see girls' noses pressed against the glass cell doors like caged baby animals.

Lederman's GAP project, funded by the Florida Department of Juvenile Justice, provided gender-specific programming for girls and advocacy to link them with services upon release from detention.

Girls voluntarily admitted to the GAP were offered, among other choices, an educational component of five intensive group talks for two hours every other day. Most of the girls had failed in school, and these group sessions intended to revive an interest in school attendance. Other programs included substance abuse, conflict resolution, sexual education, and contact with alcohol and drugs anonymous programs. In addition a GAP journal existed for contributions of poetry, stories and artwork.

Instead of sitting idly in the cells, the girls now had books to read, and a phone was available to call relatives. Special therapy, long ignored, became a part of their daily regimen as provided by GAP.

In strong terms, Judge Lederman described the situation,

> My obligation is to punish but also to rehabilitate. I cannot do this if these girls are treated like animals. If we take them, and only lock them up, how are they going to learn to nurture, to feel safe, and to be a parent to their child?
>
> Girls have much greater needs that are not being met. The pathway to their delinquency is very different than boys. They have a horrific history of victimization. All have the same stories of lack of both role models and guidance. They have grown up in an environment of neglect and abuse.

The GAP Advisory Board, consisting of thirty-five high-profile women, visited and mentored the girls. Their great concern was the lack of amenities. These girls did have a television set available, but little else in the way of ordinary comforts. No books, no therapy sessions, no washing machine and dryer to do their clothes, no female doctor. They sat in small one-room cells and received three pairs of recycled underwear they hand-washed. Not much of anything. It was as if girl inmates didn't exist.

Destiny, a sixteen-year-old, became the poster girl of GAP. This was her third trip to the detention center, all involving fights at school. She had attempted suicide in the past. In her most recent fracas, defending herself, she beat a girl over the head with an iron and now faced charges as an adult for aggravated battery with a deadly weapon. She had spent more than three months in the Adult Women's Annex before transferring back to the juvenile detention center.

Describing her stay at the detention center, she stated, "There are 164 bricks in my cell. All I did was count the bricks in my cell. The GAP counselors were the only ones who made me feel worthwhile."

She had nothing else to recall. Eight months later she was out of jail. She credited GAP counselors with giving her a new lease on life as she announced her intentions to enroll at Barry University.

Said Mary Larrea, GAP director, "What we are trying to do is give the girls a sense of hope and provide them with something to let them know there are people out there who care about them."

Three years later, celebrating the progress of GAP, participants from government, business, and volunteers gathered to receive awards for providing first-step intervention for girls in detention awaiting further processing.

Included in the celebration was a resolution from Governor Jeb Bush in recognition of GAP's efforts. Also present was State Representative Gus Barreiro, chairman of the House Juvenile Justice Committee, without whose efforts to gain the original State grant of $150,000, this project might never have survived.

Four years later (2004), Judge Lederman published a study paper in the *International Journal of Law and Psychiatry* titled "Characteristics of Adolescent Females in Juvenile Detention." Her coauthor was a senior research professor at the Department of Epidemiology at the University of Miami School of Medicine.

In the introduction to the study the authors cited the problem.

> The long term consequences for arrested and incarcerated girls are daunting. They are at high-risk for drug addiction, psychiatric problems, delivering substance-abuse newborns, and losing custody of their children.

> There can be no doubt that female adolescent delinquency constitutes an extremely serious public health, child welfare and juvenile justice problem.

The Lederman study conducted at the Dade County Detention Center concluded,

> It is evident that detained girls can best be characterized not by one or two unique features, but rather by having multiple related social and psychological problems. There is no single isolated feature to characterizes these girls. Instead they are typified by having many problems in several of the domains.

Further, the authors offered this in summation:

> Addressing the problems of detained girls in the here and now by immediately engaging each of them in comprehensive, developmentally appropriate intervention programs has the potential to not only improve their current functioning but also to prevent recidivism and an overall further decline of these very vulnerable and engaging girls.

The study provided several things in addition to describing the characteristics of the study population and offering some avenues of assistance. For one, and perhaps most importantly, these girls will not be forgotten, and for certain Judge Cindy Lederman will continue to be there for them. The research paper itself will also keep these concerns alive among other advocates and researchers.

Lawyers, as a class, are more prone to deliver heavily cited research papers. That is their trade. Having a multi-dimensional administrative juvenile court judge ready to address social issues with a scholarly, research approach is a major step forward. Although readership in learned journals may be considerably less, than say, an op-ed piece in the *Miami Herald*, nonetheless this select readership may in the long run be more influential, and for certain will have the grant-funding agencies a lot more responsive to the need. Equally important, however, is the ability to communicate with the larger public audience concerned primarily with the positive results rather than the means to achieve.

Judge Lederman satisfies at both levels. In addition to her extensive authorship, she spends a large amount of time explaining the purposes and programs of the juvenile court to whatever assembled group may be available. She has a considerable following among civic groups she addresses. Besides the educational purpose, meeting with citizen groups heightens the opportunity to recruit volunteers.

Programs such as GAP, Guardian ad Litem, and others always need citizen volunteers to carry out the mission. Most successful programs involve citizen volunteers who are there to let the children know that the community cares and who also in a sense monitor staff performance. Professionals, including field workers and the judges, automatically perform at their best when the citizen volunteer is about.

Citizen volunteers are often available, but to fully indoctrinate them into the program can prove difficult. Initially great enthusiasm may be expressed by volunteers, but staying the course is another matter. This, not because of lost desire, but rather the difficulty in following the regimen required to deal with the problems of both delinquent and dependent children. This is understandable and volunteer involvement programs are designed with this expectation.

The role of the judge in regard the volunteer is important. Citizen volunteers giving their time and energy have high expectation of the person they see as the highest authority in the court setting. Similarly, the manner in which the judge affords respect to the performance of these volunteer, impartial participants does play a large role in maintaining a continued and enlightened number of volunteers.

Recruiters, such as Judge Cindy Lederman, who always have a basket of new programs at hand, utilize these volunteers to their maximum, giving them responsible tasks and being rewarded with high quality performance. The Guardian ad Litem Program and Foster Care Review are two prime examples. Most of these volunteers are women, but lawyers including many men, by virtue of their professional involvement along with a community spirit, are often a strong source of volunteers. Every hand helps.

At about the same time as she had pursued women leaders of the community to form GAP to assist delinquent girls, Judge Lederman sought lawyers to aid in dependency cases. This time it was a national group—Lawyers for Children in America. Their purpose was to provide a safety net of legal professionals to work in the best interest of the child. Said the national director of the group, "We want to get lawyers involved with tough cases where children and parents have no one to turn to for help.

Many of Miami's heavyweight legal firms answered the call. These included Holland & Knight, Greenberg Traurig, Broad & Cassel, and Blizin Sumberg to name a few. Addressing them and urging their participation, Judge Cindy Lederman said, "The juvenile system is a chaotic and frustrating world. No one is there to fight and scream for these children. You are the only ones that can help. This should be your inspiration."

In addition to taking on pro bono clients, the program sought to send these volunteer lawyers to lecture in our public schools on resolving conflict through mediation and other kinds of effort to assist school youngsters with their day-to-day concern.

The children in these programs generally have a long history of a dysfunctional family, or poverty, or mental health concerns that usually have not been tended to promptly. Yet these successes, as long as they take to materialize, sometimes unexpectedly are a huge gift not only to the child but to the volunteer—and of course to the Cindy Ledermans of the world.

In the midst of the many worthwhile projects initiated by Judge Lederman, differences with DCF were ever present. In 2003, officials in Tallahassee had dreamed up a new plan to allocate funds for each of the state districts. Instead of the existing formula based on population, funding would be steered to regions with the highest number of hotline abuse and neglect reports.

A perfectly sounding, fair approach, except that Miami-Dade and Broward counties, with large numbers of immigrants who often don't report child abuse, would suffer deep cuts. Many relocated residents in Miami-Dade, fearful of their immigrant status and mistrustful of government, avoid formal contact with government agencies though using the medical clinics. Experts who had studied migrant relationships with government estimated a loss of almost thirty-eight million dollars for the two counties with this new plan based solely on hotline calls.

Judge Lederman, as chairwoman of the district's Community-based Care Alliance, stated, "We are very unhappy about this. Our county has the most poverty in America. The new funding formula is very dangerous for our children." Other leaders and groups joined in protest. DCF secretary Jerry Regier agreed to reconsider the proposal.

Attending a meeting in Miami of Lederman's Community-based Care Alliance, Secretary Regier, despite the pleas of several, including former DCF administrators, stated he was reluctant to tinker with the base of the new funding formula because it tied money to something that can be counted objectively.

Judge Lederman responded, "In the past quite frankly, we have failed these children. We have failed in our duty to protect them." Unmoved, Regier replied that he was only willing to consider supplementing budgets of certain areas "if they were beset with unique challenges." He indicated Dade County might be one of those but offered no assurances.

It had been a relatively cordial meeting, both sides realizing that antagonizing the other would only aggravate existing wounds. But that was only for surface appearances. It was apparent to Lederman and the other South Florida officials that this was a bureaucratic and political response to the dissatisfaction voiced by our local officials.

The adversarial situation between Cindy Lederman and DCF head Jerry Regier would continue. However, within a year, Jerry Regier, involved with a purchasing scandal by some of his associates, quietly resigned.

The persistence of budget cuts emanating from Tallahassee led to a call for privatization. Our local leaders, including Judge Lederman, sought this as a means to wrest control from DCF, while DCF and the governor, anxious to deflect the strong criticism surrounding DCF's failures, also sought the change.

Apparently, state DCF officials hoped that another layer of performance by an outside private agency might somewhat insulate them from the torrent of criticism they had faced for what many considered as negligent performance on their part.

This criticism reached a height with the revelations in the *Rilya Wilson* case, a matter first appearing in juvenile court on November 9, 1996. Judge Lederman had inherited the case upon assuming the circuit court bench in 1998. It had continued in her jurisdiction, currently as of this date, for seven years. This indeed was her career case.

Some cases become important enough because a significant issue of law may be resolved. Not this one. It was pure negligence. But whose? Beyond the disappearance of a child, great public concern had been aroused by what appeared to be the gross inadequacy of the DCF. In great part the disappearance of the child Rilya Wilson accelerated the move toward privatization.

Rilya was a five-year-old girl whose whereabouts became unknown about fifteen months after she disappeared from her grandmother's house while under the supervision of DCF. It was clear that after Rilya's mother, Gloria Wilson, a chronic drug user, had her rights terminated, Rilya had been placed with her grandmother, Geralyn Graham, and her great-aunt, Pamela Graham. After that everything was cloudy.

DCF field counselors, working on a custody matter involving Rilya's sister Rodericka, also placed with the two Grahams, could not account for the absence of Rilya. Grandma Graham told police investigating the child's disappearance that in January 2001 a DCF employee had taken Rilya from her home for a further placement.

No record of such act existed, and no DCF counselor was identified as having made the contact. And, of course, DCF had not the slightest idea of Rilya's whereabouts.

In September of that year, eight months after the sisters had been placed in custody of the Grahams, an internal DCF memo had sounded the alarm that something was amiss with Rilya and her sister Rodericka. The memo raised questions asking "Why haven't they been placed for adoption? Why does their long-term goal state 'Independent Living' for the children?"

The memo concluded, "Find Counselor. Need effort to adopt." Nothing happened, and no answers were provided.

It took another seven months before the agency discovered it couldn't find Rilya at all. She seemed to have vanished into thin air. A nationwide search followed. Miami-Dade police scoured the house of the Graham sisters with cadaver dogs. Miami-Dade State Attorney Katherine Rundle announced her office would begin a full investigation for foul play. The Florida Department of Law Enforcement also joined the hunt.

Police went to Cleveland where the mother, Gloria Wilson, lived to get a DNA sample. They then followed a report of a child found decapitated in Kansas City, but that was a dead end, as were many other sightings.

By now the case had attracted national attention, the focus shifting to the manner in which DCF had kept tabs on Rilya's stay with her grandmother. Had DCF properly monitored the child's stay with her grandmother? Apparently not too well. In fact, the supervision to which the child was entitled and that DCF was bound by law to deliver turned out to be nil. Responses from DCF were unsatisfactory.

The *Miami Herald*, determined to get to the bottom with their own investigation, obtained 2,500 pages of DCF reports. These reports were mostly on efforts sixteen months after her disappearance when the authorities first became involved. Reports covering the early months of her disappearance were skimpy at best.

Excerpted here, the *Miami Herald* inquiry was a very thorough one. According to both state law and procedure, Rilya was to be visited once a month, and brought before a dependency court judge every six months. Also an adoptions counselor was required to review the case immediately after her parent's rights were terminated. As a child with special needs, Rilya also would have been eligible for other services. In addition, Rilya should have been enrolled in school upon the termination of her mother's rights. None of the above had occurred.

Rilya's caseworker was accused of falsifying records to cover up the failure to provide the services required. Things never did get any better. Grandmother Graham continued cashing checks sent to her from the State for Rilya's care long after the child was no longer living with her.

Graham had notified a DCF supervisor of receiving these checks but was told, "Continue keeping the checks, because when Rilya is located it will be difficult to reapply for these subsidies." The supervisor, assuming Rilya was on runaway status and likely to return, had neglected to alert any other DCF official as to Rilya's situation.

Meanwhile, Governor Jeb Bush sprang into action, organizing a citizens' panel led by David Lawrence, the former publisher of the *Miami Herald*, to look into the matter. The governor also asked for legislation creating criminal penalties for caseworkers who falsified documents.

He also met privately with Kathleen Kearny, secretary of the state Department of Children and Families (DCF). Secretary Kearney immediately took full responsibility for the mess, calling the Department's work "abysmal." She added, "The ineptness in this case by the worker and the supervisor was appalling."

The *Herald* investigation of the court docket sheets showed hearings scheduled at least five times during Rilya's fifteen-month disappearance. All reflected the child safe and sound at the grandmother's house, and no request had been made for a pickup order that is required for a missing child. Only two days before DCF finally revealed that the child was missing was a pickup order requested. By then the cry already had been out assailing the negligence of DCF.

After the resignation of several counselors responsible for mishandling the case, possibly falsification of documents, certainly negligence, a DCF representative came before the court, finally notifying Judge Lederman that the child was no longer with the grandmother, and asking for a pickup order.

In an effort at self-rehabilitation, DCF immediately removed Rodericka, Rilya's sibling, then still living with and still in the custody of the grandmother. Appearing before Judge Lederman for approval on this sudden removal action of the sister, this exchange occurred between Judge Lederman and the DCF attorney:

> JUDGE LEDERMAN: Why after everything that has happened in this case, after I have been kept in the dark about the status, well-being, and placement of this child for one year, why would you think I now would allow the department to remove this child's sibling without my consent? What is the department hiding now?
>
> DCF LAWYER: The department isn't hiding anything, Your Honor. We had a child who had disappeared from a foster home. We simply didn't know it either. We didn't hide that from you.
>
> As soon as we learned that this child (Rilya) was no longer in our physical custody, that she had disappeared, and we further realized that another child in our custody was in that home at risk, we wanted to get that child out of there immediately.

Judge Lederman, a picture of judicial restraint, refused to further engage DCF counsel in the exchange. This was a replay of the long-held DCF position that that they resist any effort on the part of the court to exercise authority over the determination of action to be taken once the child had been placed in the custody of DCF. Ironically, had DCF accepted the court's monitoring of the case, the Rilya fiasco might well have been averted.

The matter of who is in charge? had been a longtime issue with both DCF and HRS, its predecessor agency, which also had resisted the Court's strong role but rarely made it a contentious issue. DCF, with the support of the governor, was now more willing to tackle what was viewed in conservative political circles as an overreaching judiciary.

DCF, by accident or design, regularly failed to notify the court of the current status of children in custody. This occurred almost as if not providing information was a payback for the judges assuming authority that DCF believed was theirs alone.

In the *Rilya* case, not only had DCF failed to provide adequate supervision, but had they kept the court properly informed, there is a strong likelihood that the court in its monitoring capacity would have spotted the failings of the DCF counselors, thereupon remedying the problem before it became a national scandal bringing shame on DCF.

The *Herald* inquiry discovered other discrepancies. According to internal DCF e-mails, the local DCF brass spent six days searching for Rilya through hospitals and other social service agencies before notifying the police or the judge. And this only when a high-ranking administrator in Tallahassee wrote the Miami district chief, "When are you going to notify law enforcement that this child is missing?" The department's own rules required notification within three days to state and federal centers for missing children.

On May 2, 2002, a hearing was held before Judge Lederman as to the placement of Rilya's younger sister, Rodericka, who had been taken from the home of the Graham relatives (Grandmother Geralyn Graham and Aunt Pamela Graham). Since the police were now investigating Rilya's disappearance as a possible criminal act, DCF, without the approval of Judge Lederman, had removed the younger sister.

The old battle was renewed. When DCF's most senior lawyer refused to divulge to the court the whereabouts of Rodericka, challenging the judge with "You have no authority to scrutinize the Department's decision over where Rodericka lives." Responded Judge Lederman, "I have ultimate responsibility for this child. I need to know what is happening with this child. I need to know why this child was removed. I need to know where the child is.

"I take my responsibility very seriously. I will do all that is necessary to find out where she is, why she was removed, was she in danger, and is she in danger now?"

Though talking about younger sister Rodericka, it was clear that the judge was claiming "ultimate" responsibility for all children appearing in her court. Lawyers for DCF responded, as in the past, that DCF had the sole authority over the placement of foster children when their parents' rights have been terminated.

A comment heard during the hearing was that state DCF secretary Kathleen Kearney, a former Broward County juvenile court judge, had routinely voiced the same position during her judicial tenure as Judge Lederman now asserted.

Criticism continued to mount over DCF's performance. Florida's Child Abuse Death Review Team, claiming lack of DCF cooperation, sought to subpoena records of children who have died of abuse and neglect. Judge Lederman, clearly frustrated, found DCF in contempt of court for hiding details over Rilya's disappearance, this included giving false information about other foster children in another case.

Further it was learned that DCF had 721 Florida children placed in their custody by the court, living outside of Florida in institutions or with relatives, without benefit of the interstate compact. This compact required the receiving state to provide supervision of the child. Not one child from either Miami-Dade or Broward County now living in another state was the subject of an interstate compact request by our DCF, thereby under no supervision by the receiving state.

The Third District Court of Appeal settled at least for now one of the issues, ruling that Judge Lederman had a right to know where DCF had placed Rilya's sister Rodericka. This ruling may have far-reaching implications in the Lederman-DCF imbroglio, although prospects for a peaceful settlement are not likely.

Lederman then ordered a medical evaluation as to the extent of the developmental delay incurred by Rodericka and as well testing for a serious eye ailment she appeared to have. The judge had ordered these tests two years ago, but the department had never carried out her order at that time.

Meanwhile Rilya had made Saturday night TV's *Most Wanted* program with a flurry of tips, none locating her. Wal-Mart displayed photos of Rilya at its 3,200 stores and on billboards. DCF accelerated its search through all the custodial institutions in Florida where foster children might be lodged. Someone finally suggested that Rilya's Medicaid billing be tracked, a sure way to have followed her. Nothing there.

An August 2001 DCF report filed with the court by the worker assigned to the case stated in regard Rilya's placement with her grandmother: "At this time, this is the best placement. Since the last Hearing there has not been any educational disruptions."

In truth, Rilya had not been in school, and in fact, she had not even been seen by that case worker for at least seven months. Thus far, at least eleven DCF caseworkers and several supervisors have been fired or allowed to resign arising from the heightened internal security generated by this case.

While the search for the lost Rilya continued, new issues arose in court. Are the Graham sisters actually related to the children? And are they really sisters? Suddenly their role as half-sisters was being questioned by other witnesses. Both also showed signs of some deception on a lie-detector test. Each gave conflicting testimony before Judge Lederman as to these relationships.

In court, Judge Lederman chastised Geralyn Graham. "You can't just stand up and say, 'I'm the grandmother,'" Lederman intently inquired. "Do you have proof? How did you get custody of the child? I never gave you custody, and you never signed your name to the custody form."

The judge thereupon denied the Graham sisters visitation rights to Rodericka. The documents examined by the *Herald* also showed that apparently DCF officials had not seen their own records showing Grandmother Graham suffering from a form of dementia that produces hallucinations and paranoia, facts which might have precluded the grandmother from obtaining custody of the children in the first place.

An earlier neuropsychological evaluation dated May 1977 of Mrs. Graham also concluded, "This patient is clearly in need of psychiatric medical management. She has suffered from dementia due to a head trauma, and an organic personality disorder as a result of a car wreck." Considering these conditions, how could DCF have placed the children in her custody?

The mishaps in the *Rilya* case caused grave concern among Governor Bush and his DCF minions. DCF state secretary Kathleen Kearny had at the onset lashed out at the failure of DCF staff and field workers, using strong descriptive terms like "abysmal" and "appalling." Later, becoming defensive, she repeatedly stated that Rilya's case was only an "isolated incident that does not point to systemic problems."

A reading today of the *Herald* documents depicts a department that does not communicate, often fails to distribute routine paperwork properly, and tolerates field counselors who are slack or indifferent to their duties.

Governor Jeb Bush's budget cuts for important Dade County programs has visibly upset the Dade County Juvenile Court judges and other advocates in the child-care community. He has, on the other hand, taken a strong position against DCF laxity, demanding that every one of the 46,000 children under the supervision of the State be visited by a field counselor. Rilya has made life difficult for both the governor and DCF.

Following up, Governor Jeb Bush's newly appointed Blue Ribbon Panel met for the first time. Charged by the governor to investigate the *Rilya* case with all its implications, the members included David Lawrence, former publisher of the *Miami Herald* who since his retirement has headed several community projects involving the welfare of children; Sara Herald, an expert in child welfare; Carol Licko, former legal counsel to the governor; and Sister Jeanne O'Laughlin, president of Barry College.

There were some murmurings of protest about the composition of the panel, considering that Ms. Licko was the governor's former legal counsel, and Ms. Herald had been part of his transition team when he took office. Knowledgeable people, however, recognized that these were four competent and intelligent folk who would do a careful and fair survey.

The general public and others in the field were outraged by the *Rilya* case. "This is horrible," said Karen Gievers, a children's advocate who is spearheading a class-action lawsuit that alleges children in foster care are unsafe. "How can they keep taking kids away when they can't do right by the ones they have?"

"What we need most now is a sense of confidence that children in the department's care are safe," said Jack Levine, president of the private Center for

Florida Children. "The confidence in the community seems to be eroding more and more," he added.

By April of the year 2003, state DCF secretary Kathleen Kearney had resigned, followed by the departure of Charles Auslander, DCF district administrator in Miami-Dade County. But things hadn't changed much. Jerry Regier, succeeding Kearney (also to soon resign), was now using the *Rilya* case as the basis to recentralize control in Tallahassee, meaning local control, a measure long sought for Dade County, would now shift back to Tallahassee.

With the police still pursuing a criminal investigation of Rilya's disappearance, the fireworks had abated for the time being. Judge Lederman could find little solace despite the almost universal criticism of DCF's performance. The power was still in Tallahassee, and somehow the bad press managed to include the judges. A few lawyers, critical of the tight ship that Lederman ran, did not hesitate to publicly state their views. For the judges, this added spotlight meant it was time to act like jurists: stay cool. Judge Lederman was the coolest of all.

Major media—newspaper, TV and radio—recognizing the difficulties in handling controversial cases, afforded her the respect to which she was entitled. No more, no less. The *Miami New Times*, a weekly muckraker, chose to take her on, printing a devastating article ("Courting Disaster"). describing her as "draconian." A former child-welfare professional with eighteen years of experience in the South Florida area responded in a letter to *New Times* in Lederman's behalf writing, "I know Judge Lederman from personal experience in her courtroom and also through her reputation among my child-welfare colleagues. Her courtroom is the model of fairness. She listens to everyone and evaluates carefully before rendering a decision. She is always respectful of all the parties involved."

The *New Times* article in question ran several pages, quoting unhappy lawyers venting. It is not unusual for members of the Bar to show displeasure with judges. As a matter of fact it is a healthy gesture. For the most part lawyers appreciate a judge consistent in rulings, showing no favoritism, knowing the law, and one who moves the calendar. Judge Cindy Lederman gets high scores in all those areas by her fellow judges and by most practitioners appearing before her.

Media criticism comes with the job, but it didn't cut down on her own literary output. A 2004 article titled "Infant Mental Health Interventions in Juvenile Court" appeared in the *Journal of the American Psychological Association*. Written with Joy Osofsky of the Louisiana State University Departments of Public Health and Psychiatry, it presented the current approaches earlier introduced by Judge Lederman.

The article noted that back in 1997, responding to a significant change in dependency law, the federal government had mandated that the safety and well-being of the child to be the paramount consideration of the court in dependency decision making. Reunification with the parent no longer was to be the primary goal. Adoption would take precedence where it served the best interest of the child.

As such, the federal government had imposed a one year deadline for judicial decisions, clearly favoring the option of adoption. No longer were children to be held hostage for long periods of time awaiting a reunification that might be neither practical nor possible. Though not attracting much media attention, this was to be a major change in treatment of children in distress.

To respond to this new status, Judge Lederman added a special cadre of senior judges devoted solely to hearing termination of parental rights (TPR) cases. This became an important part of the dependency picture, not only for judicial efficiency, but to hasten a resolution to a family crisis not responsive to ordinary means.

It related to situations where birth parents have reached what appears to be the end of the line in court. Usually the child had already been removed from the home, case plans had been offered and violated, and last chance had been to no avail. At this point the state agency (Division of Youth Services [DYS]) filed a termination of parental rights case before the division judge hearing the case.

This kind of case involved depriving the parents of all rights to the child and eventual adoption. No other event in the history of that family was more important to their lives. These cases often took days of trial, as they should, thereby tying up the remainder of the division judge's calendar. Regular calendars were heavy, and these cases were often continued on and on to get the attention they deserve.

In addition, the federal mandate governing adoption provided strict deadlines; the failure to observe meant a substantial monetary penalty against those states for non-compliance. Recognizing that juvenile court judges have always had overloaded calendars, Judge Lederman established this Senior Judge Division to hear the TPR cases. Many of these TPR cases require not only heavy lawyering, but also intensive planning for the child.

Thus came about Judge Lederman's special calendar utilizing senior judges (Gladstone, Gelber, Rivkind, and Edelstein currently make up that roster). Each sits a week at a time, hearing cases referred by the division judges. All their rulings are subject to review by the Third District Court of Appeal. Data show the federal time limits are being met more consistently.

From my own experience having served as a division judge and currently sitting as a TPR senior judge, the system provides the division judge with more time to attend to regular calendar duties, and as well gives the offending parent another opportunity to present the case before a fresh officer of the court looking anew at the case. In addition, it enables the State to comply with federal guidelines. No small matter.

As Lederman notes in her *Journal of the American Psychological Association* article,

The federal ASFA Act (1997) recognized an important departure from the previous law, that reunification may not always be possible. For almost two decades, the law mandated reasonable efforts to reunify families.

The emphasis on reunification was a legislative response to the concern about the increasing length of stay of children in foster care. While many of the tenets of the earlier law were unchanged, ASFA shifted the emphasis away from reunification to the health and safety of the child.

"How," she asked in the same article, "can the Juvenile Court fulfill its legal mandate, especially in an adversarial system with the limitations of huge caseload and inadequate services?" She suggested the court focus on intervention with the youngest and largest cohort of children: babies and toddlers under age six, who make up one third of the child welfare population entering the jurisdiction of the court. Twenty-five percent of this group are under age two, and twenty percent under one year of age.

Judge Lederman's efforts to approach the problem through research and education is a formidable one. Operating within the bounds of a court and the legal limitations therein is a tremendous challenge. There's a long way to go before her research bears full fruit, but for certain she is providing a body of work that offers those who follow a line of vision. She, however, will go forward not only as a visionary leading the way for others but also in the full expectation that here visions will become real.

Judge Lederman, like the juggler at the circus, seems to have innumerable projects simultaneously flying through the air. One wonders how she cam maintain control over all the action flying about. As one who had preceded her as an administrative juvenile court judge, about a decade earlier when things were no better or easier, I can only marvel at her dexterity.

The delinquency side of the court, with Associate Administrative Judge Lester Langer at the head, has had its share of public attention. Sharing equal billing with the dependency court, it has undergone significant change. No longer the major focus due to the legislative change granting the state attorney authority to direct-file serious cases to adult criminal court, nonetheless there is enough on Langer's plate dealing with younger delinquents.

As a matter of fact, it provides an opportunity for child advocates to focus on first and second offenders at the onset of problems, rather than concentrate on the violent older repeat offender requiring extensive rehabilitation services. Despite this statement, it is fairly clear that replacing preliminary hearings before a juvenile court judge with a prosecutor's direct-file action has had no positive impact on reducing the crime rate for these more trouble-prone older juveniles sentenced in adult court.

A truly significant forward movement on the delinquency side has been the development of the Miami-Dade County Juvenile Assessment Center (JAC). Proposed at the onset in 1995 by Judge Tom Petersen and former City of Miami mayor Maurice Ferré, it came to the forefront again in 1998. The idea had been around for some time but had never gained any real traction.

In the past, the arrest process for juveniles had been haphazard at best, not having changed since 1921. Over the years it had been a bone of contention, breeding dissatisfaction among all the components of the juvenile justice system. A time-consuming hit-and-miss situation, mostly miss. The changeover when it came brought a sigh of relief from all concerned.

The various agencies involved—police departments, clerk's offices, prosecutors, defense lawyers, Department of Human Services, and the judges—had all been hard-pressed to keep up with the whereabouts or status of those in the arrest process. Records were scanty and scattered, and an awesome amount of time wasted.

Police officers spent long hours requiring repeat visits to the juvenile court to perform their end. With the current Juvenile Assessment Center (JAC), it is all accomplished within two hours. This included a pretrial conference with the state attorney and LiveScan fingerprinting. In addition, a complete record of the juvenile became available for the judge at trial.

As part of their function, JAC also recommended pretrial diversion programs where appropriate. Judge Langer, vice-chair of the JAC program, had this to say about JAC: "JAC's accurate record-keeping is a tool for prevention. It also enables early intervention. Our goal is to keep kids out of the system." In 2002, JAC was made into an independent county department. Progress indeed, though a long time in coming.

The delinquency court, focusing on younger children, became an important tool in addressing the problems of truancy. In the past, burdened with large caseloads of serious crime by sixteen- and seventeen-year-olds, crimes such as truancy, shoplifting, and other minor transgressions had been virtually brushed aside. Perhaps these offenses were less important in the broader scheme of violent offenses, but in terms of preventing delinquency, this was where it all began.

Now, with the legislature making truancy a priority, the state attorney became an enforcer. In 2005, Rudy Crew, the new superintendent of schools, began his own crusade to wipe out truancy. It all began, advised Superintendent Crew, when his chief of the school police stopped a child trying to climb into a school warehouse. "Why are you skipping school?" asked the police officer. The kid replied, "I went yesterday." Smart-aleck comment, but it reflected the attitude of many youngsters.

Superintendent Crew offered an all-out program to combat truancy. He asked the juvenile court judges to create a pilot truancy court staffed by volunteer judges who could order chronic truants to social service programs, tutoring, community service hours. In extreme cases Crew recommended sixty or ninety days in a secure residential program.

He also requested that Dade County social agencies investigate family situations in regard cause of truancy. In addition, Crew set up a hotline to report suspected truancy. He and Judge Lester Langer then requested that police departments institute a more proactive role in apprehending truants. The Dade County Association of Chiefs of Police approved a partnership among the county police departments with assurances that truancy will become a police priority.

Rudy Crew has also brought the Dade school system fully into the law enforcement fold with a Zero Tolerance program. Students committing crimes are now funneled into the juvenile justice system with regularity.

Ironically, a recent report (*Miami Herald*, 4/20/06) studying the impact of Zero Tolerance accused school authorities of "overreacting" by arrests for minor offenses rather than offering in-school counseling and furthering parental involvement. This is a far cry from several decades earlier when school authorities were pushing crime under the rug despite Gladstone and I urging the school superintendents to become more proactive in crime control.

Prior to the arrival of the Rudy Crew Zero Tolerance program, the juvenile court judges and the state attorney had already been involved in a program targeting parents for failing to send their children to school. In addition, a recent state law permitted lockup for several days for excessive truancies. Judge Langer had been consulted by legislators as to the efficacy of such legislation. Langer's personality and style suggest he's a good man to have around when tough decisions like that need to be made.

That Superintendent Crew was taking strong steps to address truancy was surely a positive sign. That Judge Lester Langer was there to counsel him was also a good portent. It is too early to talk of success for a new program, but with this quality leadership, the promise is there.

Lester Langer is an old hand in juvenile court. Before appointment by Governor Lawton Chiles to the circuit court bench in 1997, he had served as a county court judge working in domestic violence court, the ideal place to prepare oneself for the juvenile court.

He had also earned his spurs working for many years as a private lawyer, handling both delinquency and dependency cases in juvenile court. Those of us on the bench, before whom he had appeared, recognized Langer as a lawyer with extensive expertise in the field and a person with exceedingly good judgment.

Despite the major changes in jurisdiction and the new focus on younger children, the same problems that had existed for years continued to thwart the efforts of judges and others seeking to help children in trouble.

Hardly had Langer assumed the juvenile court bench, then the perennial issues of the past came before him. First was the budget cuts proposed by new governor

Jeb Bush. These included slicing funds from the Dade Marine Institute (DMI)). Though recognized statewide as one of the few effective rehab programs in the state, the DMI program, along with other day treatment programs, suffered a sharp cut when Governor Bush caused a meltdown trimming their funding by almost three million dollars. Judge Langer was troubled because the youngsters he had sent to (DMI) would now be deprived of the benefits.

The governor had suggested to the House Juvenile Justice Committee that hiring more probation officers to check on these kids, and also hiring psychologists to talk to them as being more productive than the DMI program. Judge Langer waited for his testimony before the House Juvenile Justice Committee to respond.

In his quiet way, Langer voiced agreement with the governor in regard hiring more probation officers and psychologists, and then in an aside Langer quipped, "How many psychologists are going to work at the State's rate of thirty-two dollars a day?" Langer got the audience laughter but didn't sway the governor.

Budget cuts for treatment programs as well as mistreatment of children in state custody continued to plague delinquency programs. The same wars and woes that had encompassed both the dependency and delinquency systems in the past continued to be present. In his 2004 budget, Governor Jeb Bush even cut funds for electronic bracelets to track a child placed at home instead of lockup in detention.

Judge Langer estimated that on any given day, 110 kids were being monitored with electronic devices on their ankles. Complained Langer, "The cuts put the court in a position of either detention or outright release." A spokesperson for Governor Bush called the cut "a realignment in judicial costs that does not prevent counties from coming up with their own method of home detention." Thanks for the advice, Governor.

Maltreatment of children in the custody of the State never has really been halted. On occasion it appears to have receded, but then the ugliness reappears. One of the worst occurred as this very chapter was being written in October 2005. This one was a horror tale.

The first paragraph of the *Miami Herald* story told it all.

> A Florida Juvenile Justice Lieutenant was fired and a lock-up Supervisor was suspended after these Detention Center officials allegedly ignored reports of a juvenile sex offender raping a mentally retarded boy he was supposed to wash and diaper-change while in a State jail. The boy was fifteen with a thirty-two IQ.

Fortunately for the local system, it happened in Tallahassee, not in Miami. The case was four months old, and only when the *Miami Herald* had reported the event did state officials take actions against the alleged offenders. And so the struggle continued on all fronts for juveniles.

Next was the Department of Juvenile Justice's decision to build a treatment center for Miami youths on a fifteen-acre site on Krome Avenue, leased to them by Dade County for one dollar a year. Despite the agreement, instead of a treatment center the State built a twelve-million-dollar jail with institutional gray-cinder-block walls, small cells, concrete slab beds, metal latrines, razor-wire fencing, and virtually no natural light.

Dade County officials refused to accept the structure, and children advocates were furious. Said Representative Gus Barreiro in the *Miami Herald* account, "This place is not fit for any kid. I favor turning it over to the state Department of Corrections. It should be an adult prison for the harshest prisoners."

A professor at the University of Miami Medical School added that original plans had called for a therapeutic center for children having drug abuse problems. Concluded Judge Langer, who had been a member of the county partnership formed to develop the project, "The community as a whole is showing increasing frustration and distrust of the State Department of Juvenile Justice." Yes, indeed. Yes, indeed.

Judge Langer had been more successful setting up a long-sought program years ago when plans were made for a unified family court. Hearing all matters involving a troubled child in one court before the same judge had long been a vision for many.

As noted in other chapters of this book, it was a mission that had only limited success, but Judge Langer, along with Judge Sandy Karlan, managed to put together a workable program that enabled a kind of cross-pollination in many of these areas of concern. Under the new system fostered by the two judges, cases in several courts involving one family can now be heard by one judge (see chapter "Activists are Many Among Us": Judge Sandy Karlan).

Judge Langer is of the kind that keeps the system working. He's been part of and has survived all the deficiencies and as well enjoyed the moments of success. Hardworking, avoiding the limelight, he sets an example of consistency and support for all others in the system. He and Judge Lederman are a matchless team in their ability to get things done.

His has been no easy task. Delinquency matters at an earlier historical point had been the major purpose of the juvenile court. Dependency was an adjunct coming at the end of the calendar, receiving what little energy remained among the court participants.

Beginning with Judge Gladstone, this change began and was accentuated by Judge Lederman. Awareness was beginning to set in so that the relationship between these two units of the courts was really indivisible, one directly hinged to the other. The national attention given to the dependency work produced by

Gladstone and Lederman also heightened the importance of dependency back home in Dade County.

Perhaps the link binding dependency and delinquency was the decision by the Florida Legislature to permit the state attorney to direct-file serious violent crime to the adult criminal court. This, a long-held province of the juvenile court, effectively eliminated serious crime committed by sixteen- and seventeen-year-old delinquents from the province of juvenile court judges.

Probably a wrong decision, but it completely changed the complexion of delinquency court. Now the number of violent, destructive, dangerous teenagers, while not a rarity, has considerably diminished. Delinquency court has become the home of mostly minor offenses: shoplifting, truancy, petty larceny—many below the age of thirteen. Often the judge looking down from that high perch on the bench barely could see the head of the pint-sized youngster standing before him.

Fortunately, Judge Lederman and Judge Langer understood well that this circumstance provided, nay required, a joining of forces, dimming the line between the two parts of the court. The very concerns that controlled the course of the child in Dependency Court are directly related to the problems that befell the preteen-age child later to appear before a delinquency judge.

That both judges had early in their judicial careers served in the Domestic Violence Division of the county court sharpened their awareness and made a joint effort more feasible for both.

They worked as a team. Judge Lederman promulgated programs designed to focus on the very young child, and partner Judge Langer adapted those principles to those older children becoming part of the delinquency caseload. Of course, there was no perfect symmetry between the two, but the awareness of the relationship enabled the delinquency court to follow patterns established in dependency.

Patterning delinquency programs for Judge Langer's court population to fit the dependency model required an experience and skill he fortunately possessed. He tackled some hard ones, for example, the problem of young children committing domestic violence against their parents and siblings.

First, Langer commissioned a study (year 2000) and found that annually there were over 1,000 juvenile domestic violence cases in juvenile court. Further, at that time there were no community-based organizations trained in either multisystemic therapy nor family functional therapy. True, some social agencies had caseworkers properly trained to address domestic violence in proper context, but more training was needed. Langer persuaded several social service agencies to examine the problem in terms of the entire family, and now those services are available.

And as well, for example, for the Zero to Three program that he and Lederman had introduced to Miami aimed at helping maltreated infants and toddlers, he developed a comprehensive program to meet the abused and neglected young children coming into his delinquency court. This very year, a *Miami Herald* feature story (7/2/06) described a new Langer parenting program for teenage mothers who have committed crimes.

Another program he and Lederman worked on was a federally funded court coordination project arising out of the U.S. Attorney's Weed and Seed sites. W&S involves buildings and money confiscated by the U.S. Attorney from drug arrest convictions. The proceeds are made available to police agencies, cities, and community agencies for the betterment of work in behalf of the community.

Both graduate fellows of the Zero to Three Center Program, Judges Lederman and Langer applied for Weed and Seed grants to assist child development agencies and mental health organizations to organize better responses to abused and neglected infants as well as young children. How successful are these many programs that have crossed the scene during the Lederman-Langer era?

Judges Lederman and Langer don't keep score on who gets credit for what. They are truly professional in their approach. Many of their projects are lasting; some have a short shelf life. This is apparent with any individual or group that constantly looks to improve a situation.

At times, even the highly successful innovations often outlive their usefulness. The point is that every step forward leaves an imprint for a successor to follow. Much of the work of the Lederman-Langer duo involves step-by-step progress hardly noticed by even regular court observers.

Rilya is back with us. The tale continues. Back in November 1996, the first court hearing was held to determine Rilya's custody status. Nine years later, at this writing (November 2005), the Rilya story is never ending. Unquestionably, *Rilya* has been the longest front-page running saga in the history of the Dade Juvenile Court.

Currently, Rilya's whereabouts are still reported unknown, and grandmother Geralyn Graham has been indicted on charges of first-degree murder, kidnapping, and aggravated child abuse in connection with Rilya's disappearance. Apparently the press intends to publish reports regularly on the *Rilya* case progress.

The governor's Blue Ribbon Panel, headed by David Lawrence, did an excellent analysis of both Rilya's case and the underlying problems causing the breakdown of the system. Their report to the governor properly showed that "DCF is underfunded, understaffed, underappreciated and overworked." Unquestionably true.

Also, the report states, "The search for the culprit, rightly, should not point only toward DCF. It should also point toward the Florida Legislature which does not give—and never has given DCF the resources needed to cope with the enormous burden that it faces." Amen to that also.

Then the report goes on to cover two pages with frequent defenses of the top administrators—Florida state secretary Kathleen Kearney and Dade County DCF administrator Charles Auslander.

> We see no constructive purpose in changing DCF's leadership, either in Tallahassee or Miami, despite this awful, and still potentially tragic lapse in its performance.
>
> Rilya Wilson did not disappear because of top-level misfeasance by Secretary Kearney, or District 11 (Dade County) Administrator Auslander.
>
> Rilya Wilson disappeared because of in-the-trenches malfeasance by her DCF caseworker, misfeasance by that caseworker's Supervisor, and the malfeasance by the caregivers.

"In the trenches malfeasance" indeed! Of course, the culprits are the "trench" people, but where were the higher-ups monitoring the operations? Every large organization—be it military, government or big business—has a chain of command, and the top man takes not only the credit but the blame as well—at least some of it.

It is almost ingenuous to say, in their behalf, as the report suggests, "Secretary Kearney and Mr. Auslander have been wholly forthcoming and cooperative. All that we have asked them to do or provide they have done or provided." Really? One might ask, how does their cooperation absolve them of their responsibility?

Not a line in the report questions the steps taken by the top administrators to avoid this fiasco. Not a line to learn what knowledge they had of the goings-on or explanation of their failure to be aware. And most interesting, not a line about Governor Bush's responsibility. Sure the legislature has been remiss, but mostly this Republican-controlled legislature has approved the governor's budget priorities.

There are other suggestions in the report that similarly fail to address underlying causes for failure. With due respect to the members of the panel and to the governor, this panel sorely needed some diversity in membership, views other than those supportive of the governor to fairly and accurately represent the situation.

As to the findings of the panel, part 1. "Immediate Priorities," this section offers excellent basic day-to-day needs that can have an immediate impact. The committee further suggests a willingness to reconvene to assist in furthering these proposals. With this in mind, it recommends that the governor add people to the panel to reflect more diversity. That's fine, but unless court practitioners involved in the court process and critics such as public defenders and yes, even Judge Lederman, are included, it will all be a futile gesture.

Part 11, "Longer-term Priorities." The idea of a DCF Children's Summit calling together representatives from all the disciplines involved in the process, as well as related groups, is somewhat premature. A tremendous amount of preliminary preparatory work needs to be done so that such a Summit does not become a forum for all the disparate groups speaking out but accomplishing little or nothing. Most of these all-encompassing summits, like those international conclaves of political leaders, are only showpieces unless some heavy preparation and plans precede the event.

The other items in part II are for the most part systemic efforts that must begin internally in DCF. The suggestion that "the Governor use his White House connections to make DCF a national model program" borders on the ludicrous. Our DCF is held in such low repute nationally that using it as a model for anything would be exceedingly embarrassing to this state.

As to part III, "Priorities for the Legislature," the wish list of what laws the legislature need enact is fine, but we all know this starts with the governor, then gaining media along with public support. Currently, most positive change for children comes not from the legislature but through constitutional petitions and public vote, such as the Children's Trust and several statewide school amendments. Civic-minded bodies of advocates for children do exist, but their efforts to educate and influence the legislature have had minimal results. That takes strong participation from elected officials, starting with the governor.

The section in the report, titled "Rationales" offers compelling and positive recommendations, particularly as to Guardians ad Litem and Foster Care Review These are programs that have stood the test of time and are worthy of maintaining and improving. The panel endorsements help, but every legislative session brings a governor's budget ignoring social needs and an indifferent legislature that forces these programs and others of worth to struggle merely to survive.

The community-based care concept—meaning that independent, private groups would do the field work—fostered by the report sounds like the future. However, privatization doesn't always work. The Our Kids program in Dade County seems to be a project that can make it. However, already there are rumbles and challenges about funding. Will this go the way of all the many failed reorganizations of the past?

For sure, this hastily thrown together panel has done yeomen's work and come up with many solid suggestions. No matter what happens with their report, they deserve high commendation for their effort.

Panels, such as this governor's panel, are only temporary palliatives to provide the public with some assurance that government cares. Lacking any machinery to follow through on these recommendations or a monitoring capacity to at least report on progress, the effort, while worthwhile, raises hope, but further expectations are illusory.

Some good will yet come out of the *Rilya* case, which brought about the existence of this Panel, but more likely, if remembered at all, *Rilya* will be recalled as one of the gross miscarriages of our system.

The year 2005, particularly the date April 15, may yet be one of the most important dates in the history of the Dade County Juvenile Court. No bands playing and no fireworks display, but the following paragraph in the *Miami Herald* may usher in a new beginning for the court:

> The Florida Department of Children and Families (DCF) signed a seventy-five million dollar contract Friday to turn over all foster care and adoption programs in Miami-Dade County to private-care administrators, initiating what may become the largest child-welfare privatization project in the nation.

Responded Judge Lederman in a burst of enthusiasm not normally associated with her usually serious expression, "Hallelujah! We believe this will be the new standard for the provision of child-services quality. This new standard will no longer be how many children are served or how quickly or how inexpensively. Quality is the new bellwether of the system."

Judge Lederman is chairperson of the Community-based Alliance, a group that has aggressively lobbied both Governor Bush and the state legislature for funds to make possible this contract with Our Kids. As recently as this is being written, she has been in Tallahassee seeking support from legislators and from the governor's aides.

For the past two years, officials of the state DCF and Henry Adorno, president of Our Kids, have been in heavy negotiation over the contract agreement. Adorno, one of Miami's leading attorneys, had at first rejected the DCF funding formula as being insufficient. He sought funding adequate to the task of dramatically improving a foster care system often described as one of the worst in the country.

Mr. Adorno, generally known as Hank, heads a large law firm in Dade County and formerly was chief assistant to State Attorney Janet Reno. He has a long record of achievement with United Way and other civic enterprises. A man of principle, he will keep DCF to their commitment.

Said Hank Adorno, "We negotiated hard, that's for sure. Our board made it very clear to DCF that we will not take direct services away from existing kids in the program in order to take in new kids."

Little progress had been made on that issue. State contracts with other Florida counties had already been signed for as much as three-year periods. Adorno insisted on a shorter fourteen-month period so that any financial adjustment found necessary could be corrected within a reasonable period of time.

Completing this agreement, every county in Florida will now become part of a Community-based Care network of private foster care providers. This project is perhaps the only time Governor Bush and Judge Lederman have been together on the same page.

After *Rilya*, Governor Bush, realizing the shortcomings of DCF and unhappy with the bad press, began to seriously consider another course. Privatization became his cornerstone solution. One of the selling points made by the state administration was that privatization saved the State money by eliminating pension and medical costs. Budget cuts always have been a primary aim of the governor.

The governor, for the most part, is regarded favorably by his Florida constituents, and having blame attributed to his stewardship (as in the Rilya case) was not acceptable to him. Never a supporter of government providing layers of social service benefits, his turning this troublesome children's service endeavor over to private interests made good political sense.

Presently, about five thousand children receive services. Should the number of children in care rise by more than 3 percent, the Our Kids contract provided for additional funding. This provision is not present in the twenty-three other such contracts statewide. One agency in Pinellas County already has been deemed a failure due to higher-than-anticipated caseloads—with no extra funding.

The Our Kids contract in this area also is the first one statewide to forbid vendors who service the program from serving on the board of directors. Adorno insisted on this clause to avoid the kinds of conflicts that sometimes surround public service agencies.

During the summer of 2005, the program started first in May in Monroe County, and then in each successive month another program was initiated in other geographical areas of Dade County. Staffwise, Our Kids sought to retain the best of the DCF field counselors available.

Although the legislature has borne much of the blame for the State's foster care failure, it should be recorded that years earlier the legislature had mandated that the foster care services statewide be contracted to private community-based organizations with a 2003 year deadline.

The new plan called for each child to have only one primary-care manager, replacing current practice that often sees a child shuffled among many overseers resulting in a disorganized effort and a disservice to the child. This disarray in DCF service has caused frequent protest from the bench. Pleaded Judge Lederman in a critical memo to DCF district head Auslander,

> We have 8,000 children under Court supervision as a result of abuse, neglect or abandonment. These children are at risk in our community. They have been beaten, raped, assaulted, neglected and abandoned by people who are supposed to love them the most.

If DCF is the Pinto, and the CHARLEE program the Cadillac, then the children deserve the Cadillac. CHARLEE (a highly regarded private foster program) does not have twelve different case managers involved in one case.

We could easily have designed a Pinto based on our present budget. But these children deserve a Cadillac. We want the Cadillac.

Unfortunately, a Cadillac costs lots more than a Pinto. For these purposes, the costs estimates would be over 100 million dollars more than the State currently allocates for Miami-Dade and Monroe counties. The Our Kids program expects to do private fund-raising to augment the State's share.

Finding a replacement for DCF holds a lot more promise than improving DCF. For over thirty years since the State's entry into the field with the Division of Health and Rehabilitative Services (HRS) and its successor DCF, virtually no progress has been made. The only game left remains the private sector. Although many private welfare providers have done well, too many, for whatever the reason, have failed.

Our Kids is still a dicey situation. Progress in Dade County will be observed throughout the state and beyond with great interest. Failures of the State in many areas of criminal justice have created a cottage industry of private entrepreneurs setting up correction programs to replace State-run prisons, as well as many private rehab programs for juveniles in drug treatment and other treatment modes.

Some have been disappointing since too many are established solely as profit enterprises where too frequently the therapeutic advantages take a secondary role. Often they are modeled after corporate structures that promote efficiency and economy but lose sight of the rehab purpose. At times, a high quality staff is also difficult to attain, due to the minimal wages offered and the lack of pension opportunity usually provided by a government program. The jury will be out for a while with Our Kids and a cost-cutting legislature. We'll wait and see.

One year after the momentous contract signing between DCF and private providers that had elicited a hallelujah! from Judge Lederman, we learned that privatization is not a magic word that automatically solves an eternal problem. In a *Miami Herald* article dated April 4, 2006, Mark Fontaine, executive director of the Florida Juvenile Justice Association, again raises the plaint that a shortage of funds is about to force the private providers over the cliff's edge.

Mr. Fontaine cries that although private providers successfully treat 80 percent of the youth in the juvenile justice system, the system is in serious trouble. Costs have far exceeded State funding. "Of the most recent twenty-two RFP's (requests for bids) for residential and detention programs, eighteen had either no bidders or only one. Three proposals for moderate to high-risk males in Dade County had no bidders."

As in the past during legislative sessions, the governor may yet prompt corrective action by reluctant legislators, but this regression, falling back on the underfunding of the past, forcing agencies to live on the precipice is a bad omen.

Being an activist judge has many perils. Sometimes the disappointments are less when one goes along with the tide. Judge Lederman, like others of her proactive colleagues, has learned to handle setbacks and continues to move forward.

After the glow of the 2005 legislative session saw State Rep. Gus Barreiro, a Miami Republican and chair of the Justice Appropriations Committee, steer to passage a proposal expanding her Girls' Advocacy Project (GAP) into a statewide program with a one-million-dollar grant, Governor Bush not only vetoed Barreiro's bill but killed the entire statewide GAP program.

Lederman, aghast at this onslaught, spoke out, "We are just beside ourselves. This program changed the culture of the juvenile detention center for girls. It is tragic for this program to disappear.

"Supporters of the program will begin the difficult task of seeking money to keep GAP operating. We will never let the governor do this to our girls."

Said a disappointed State Rep. Gus Barreiro, "It's very disheartening. It took three months to balance this budget on a pin, and they just took away a program that has been effective."

Governor Bush, in his own defense, commented, "Many of the projects vetoed are well-intentioned, but they did not follow the criteria established by this office and by the legislature." That statement, of course, is Tallahassee speak—a technique all governors use in rejecting budget proposals of which they disapprove.

There was a suggestion by some that State Rep. Barreiro had earned Governor Bush's disfavor by stepping out of line in an internal Republican Party dispute. From my observation, that is unlikely. This governor tends to be more doctrinaire than vindictive.

Shortly thereafter, Judge Lederman and a group of GAP supporters went before the Dade County Youth Crime Task Force seeking a replacement for the lost funding. Thereupon, every penny was restored for the Dade County GAP. Going statewide for these funds as Rep. Barreiro had envisioned would have to wait for another time and probably another governor.

The Adorno-Lederman team is a powerful duo for Our Kids. Although DCF holds the purse strings for funding, Governor Bush can't claim his effort at statewide privatization a success, absent the inclusion of Dade County, the largest, most populous county in the state.

Hank Adorno has taken a firm stand: he will not back off in resisting DCF efforts to cut funding. In fact, he has rejected the DCF request that Our Kids raise that sum by cutting corners in its own budget. Instead, in a recent letter, he has demanded eight million dollars from the State to support the over-eighteen-age foster children.

The Adorno vs. DCF toe-to-toe struggle over funding goes on. New DCF district administrator Charles Hood declined to discuss the dispute in detail, other than charging that Adorno's letter was a misstatement of the facts.

Judge Lederman, head of the Community-based Alliance supporting Our Kids, stated, "It is absolutely disgraceful if true that Mr. Hood had encouraged Our Kids to cut corners in its foster care program to cover the underfunded Independent Living Program for foster children over eighteen."

Hank Adorno responded to Hood with "You say the only alternative now is to spread the pain by reducing services to our population. My board has said from day one—they will not do that." And that impasse was where the struggle stood. At least until the next volley. Both Adorno and Lederman's Community-based Alliance are forthright in demanding the funds necessary for top-quality service.

A day hadn't passed before Hank Adorno was before the *Miami Herald* editorial board blasting DCF once again. Still on the "aged-out" children, Adorno repeated that the new Miami DCF administrator Charles Hood had insisted that Our Kids cut services for children in State care to cover the eight-million-dollar cost.

According to Adorno, State records show child welfare officials asked for less than half the amount necessary to keep former foster children from slipping into homelessness upon reaching eighteen. This, despite the fact that this program is funded mostly by the federal government.

DCF then threatened to institute an audit examining Our Kids' records. Adorno questioned DCF's motives for the audit, pointing out that the program is but four months in operation, and no concerns had been expressed about their financial stability. Judge Lederman declared the audit "retaliatory."

On December 4, 2005, the *Miami Herald* pitched in with a lead editorial fully supporting Our Kids. The newspaper stated, "DCF should stop stonewalling and deliver the eight million dollars needed to fully fund the Independent Living program for young adults who have aged out of the foster care system. It should not abandon them at age eighteen."

The newspaper pointed out that Our Kids had accomplished the job that DCF had set for them, namely to determine the eligibility of former foster children who qualify for assistance while they attend school and mature into independent adults. Apparently, Our Kids had qualified 650 young adults whereas DCF had asked for funding only for their predicted 400.

The threat by DCF district administrator Charles Hood to conduct an audit of Our Kids' books brought no backing down from Adorno. In addition to his proposed lawsuit, he raised the prospect of returning the whole package of foster care and adoption back to the State. No easy target that Adorno fellow.

Eight million dollars is the deficit amount. It is hardly likely that Governor Bush will allow privatization, one of his most cherished concepts, to whither away over that relatively small amount. Small, at least in terms of the size of State budgets. And that's where it stands, at least for the day.

Will the privatization effort go the way of all the other child-saving projects introduced over the years? Perhaps, but this one has all the parties supposedly joining in the effort to make it work. This time the project is supported by the governor, and if the State is able to coalesce all the counties, Jeb Bush is likely to receive national recognition for this accomplishment.

In addition, Judge Lederman's Community-based Alliance had strong, assertive citizen leadership who also displayed a vested interest in making Our Kids work for the best interest of the Dade County community. Maybe we'll get lucky in the months and years ahead.

This is the first time in juvenile court history that a program provider, who must rely on the State bureaucrats for referrals, has openly blasted State authorities in so direct a manner as chosen by Adorno. Since the program provider is subject to the wishes and whims of the State, any such criticism is usually muted. In most instances, the judges will carry the ball for the program providers. That Adorno is willing to bite the hand that foots the bill may mean a new era is forthcoming. Or it may be just a passing moment. We will see.

It was no more than ten weeks later (2/18/06) that the next shot was heard. Charles Hood, DCF's Dade County welfare administrator resigned. Hood had taken over that job May 2003 from Charles Auslander as a result of the fallout from the *Rilya Wilson* disaster. Hood had been credited with bringing some stability to the local DCF, but apparently the overall situation was such that not only he, but the DCF district chief in Palm Beach as well, had resigned. Management disarray seemed the order of the day for DCF.

Hood had strongly opposed the State providing any additional dollars to fund the 850 just-turned-eighteen-year-olds under State care. Both Cindy Lederman, head of the Community-Based Care Alliance, and Hank Adorno, leader of Our Kids, were adamant in the belief that this was a State responsibility. Neither side seemed inclined to compromise. Despite this difference, Judge Lederman lauded Hood on his departure from office, "He worked on their behalf at an impossible task."

Although local judges and community activists are able to make great steps forward, it is the powers that be in Tallahassee that ultimately must enact, fund, and manage the process to make it work. That has yet to happen. Absent Governor Bush and his minions getting their act together, progress is doomed to be slow. Very slow.

After having scanned all the Cindy Lederman news clips in the *Miami Herald* archives and read all her well-cited articles in learned journals, I decided to interview her to get a better glimpse of what really constituted her makeup.

From my few meetings with her since my becoming a senior judge, I surmised she was an easy conversationalist with a warm, friendly approach. But I had the feeling that a lot more was there than appeared on the surface. Whatever are those depths she possesses, they are controlled. I wondered how her early years had influenced her. Family? School?

She had to have been an activist in her early years. No one comes full blown into a life of zeal, ready to take on all comers, without a history or at least some hidden motivations that have welled in her being for a long, long time.

Our conversation went smoothly. Growing up in her family, she was in the midst of a clan that rejected the ordinary; they thought taking risks was the only way, and they questioned almost every proposition accepted on faith by the general populace. A family just dysfunctional enough to be exciting and fun.

In high school she had been a debater and had learned to express herself in forceful fashion. Learning how to organize a cogent argument and being ready to handle both sides of an issue with equal skill had prepared her for the internecine warfare existing among the several agencies that comprised the juvenile justice family.

College life brought her out as a feminist, not one brandishing picket signs or demanding faculty resignations, but rather hers was more a middle-of-the-road approach, studying the legal implications, writing articles, recruiting the passive, and convincing the doubtful.

For openers I led off with the question, "What or who motivated you the most, in terms of your advocacy for children?" I expected her answer to be Bill Gladstone, her colleague and good friend whom she viewed as a mentor, or some old college professor who had inspired her, or even an untoward incident of her early years.

It was none of the above. Almost before the question was uttered, she blurted out the word "anger." She went on to say,

> Upon arriving on the juvenile court bench, I was shocked and then angry at what I saw. It was like the hurry-up treatment at an emergency room in a crowded public hospital.
>
> Moving the calendar seemed the only goal to get through the day. One or two of the judges were responsive to what was before them, but for the most part it was disarray. Parents and witnesses milled about outside in the large waiting room, as if it were a flea market.
>
> It was standing room only in the courtroom. Field counselors often were tied-up in other courts and their substitutes, unaware of the facts, usually asked for a continuance.

She realized also that as head of this court it would be a lot wiser to introduce the new approaches she sought in a conciliatory rather than a hostile manner.

"Anger has its place, but rebuilding this court will be a long learning process for all, including me," Judge Lederman went on to say.

Thinking that a sensible and perceptive response, I nodded approvingly, omitting the comments made to me recently by two DCF caseworkers that they still feared her rebukes, though admitting they had diminished somewhat.

Before I could ask the next question, she continued on,

> What perhaps concerned me even more than the disarray was the lack of disciplined research utilized in our court. I had become aware of a research center concerned with the very problems that perplexed us here.
>
> This was the National Research Council and the Institute of Medicine that had a sector called the Board on Children, Youth and Families. Becoming a part of it changed all of my attitudes and my professional life.
>
> Their research unit was a part of a large international network that had studied and designed programs in the very areas of our concern. No longer would we have to grope for a plan of action.

Fascinated by her excitement over the discovery of this research group and a bit abashed that it had been unknown to me, I checked the group out on the Internet. The Board on Children, Youth and Families (BCYF), organized in 1993, stated as its goal "To serve as the focal point for authoritative, nonpartisan analysis of child and family issues relevant to policy decisions. The board brings the collective knowledge and analytical tools of the behavioral, social, health and medical sciences to bear . . ."

Apparently some members questioned the goals statement as a bit pretentious, and currently the goals are in the process of being stated in less lofty terms. As proposed, the new goals statement read, "The BCYF mission is to provide a national source and forum for timely, independent, and objective scientific research on issues that can improve the health and well-being of children, youth and families." A more modest agenda that appeared realistic.

The BCYF, as are the other units of the National Research Council, is non-partisan and relates to a loosely allied network of national and international organizations similarly concerned with children issues.

Their research goes from the esoteric to everyday concerns, covering heavy-thinking research to practical solutions. Lederman supports the proposition that there is a science to modifying human behavior, and it requires the most learned professional approach. Considering that I had always prided myself on my own research, I asked myself where had I been all those years, muddling along on my own, ignoring the larger academic world outside.

The Lederman interview went on as she reported the research of the board as it related to programs she had introduced or was contemplating. Also, she named the experts who had been made available to her and other assistance provided. As she described some of the pre- and posttests essential to establish an effective program, I sensed the extent of her dissatisfaction with the manner of our past operation.

She spoke with fervor in her voice describing the tight scholarly disciplines required in program development. As one who had always been a mite skeptical of relying too much on academic answers, relying more on my own practical experience, I came away from this interview, not necessarily convinced, but with a fresh open look.

After all, this woman has not only moved dependency to the front burner, but she impresses a listener as someone who, at last, can follow through and bring the changes to make our system workable. Most gung ho new judicial projects in the juvenile court usually result from someone detecting a flaw in the process and immediately trying to patch it up with scotch tape, sometimes with a bit of success. Usually, the imperfect system swallows up the effort, and that's that.

Judge Cindy Lederman avoids any pretext of shoot-from-the-hip solutions. Bringing her scientific approach with tested procedures to the picture increases considerably the likelihood of a measured improvement. In the past we have reacted to each crisis only to avoid an immediate catastrophe. Lederman tries to anticipate the crisis and forestall it with some permanence. Her approach is a lot more than a finger in the dike.

Judges, particularly juvenile court judges, receive community honors in great number. Lederman probably reaped the most, although Gladstone is right up there. His has been a much longer tenure, but Cindy is likely to one day surpass him. Her twenty-page résumé lists not only countless awards from important organizations but a significant list of journal articles, participation in Bar association projects, and respected chairmanships of worthwhile legal and community endeavors.

Impressive is her work with the National Council of Juvenile and Family Court Judges. Serving on their board of trustees, she chairs the Mental Health/Medical-Legal Issues Committee and is a faculty member at their judicial college. Looking only at a sampling of her current travels during the first six months of 2005, one can see the depth of her involvement.

January 26   Training Institute, Mesa, Arizona. "Building Community Capacity to Meet the Needs of Infants and Toddlers"
March 3-5   Traumatic Stress Network, Alexandria, Virginia. "Transforming Care for America's Children"
March 30-31   Surgeon General's Conference, Bethesda, Maryland. "Parent and Family Innovations for Prevention"

May 3-5	"Building Mental Health and Judicial Partnerships to Help Traumatized Young Children"
July 6	Workshop, Brisbane, Queensland, Australia. "Healing the Young in the Court System"
July 7-9	Workshop, Brisbane, Queensland, Australia. "Violence Through the Eyes of a Young Child," "How to Talk about Mental Health"
August 5-6	Bellevue, Washington, "The Need for a Systemwide Focus on Infant Mental Health"

She has made a point of not isolating herself from the local community, always available for a forum, debate, or information session. Unlike many elected officials, she does not shy away from the media. Her door is always open, and the press has free access.

Outside of one story accompanied by a quarter-page photo of the judge, mouth agape in an agitated pose, the media response has been excellent. Never having had an opponent for office and unlikely to get one, she neither curries favor nor rejects the press.

Regrettably, few of the problems with the recalcitrant DCF agency were resolved by the year 2005, nor in 2006, though large steps forward were advanced.

Somehow, whatever progress made in the last decades, the struggle between the judiciary and the state welfare agencies has continued, perhaps a bit more pronounced during the Jeb Bush administration. The years ahead may see a change, but no one is counting on it.

In May 2005, Lederman's long-fought struggle to attain benefits for the over-eighteen-year-old youngsters finally found a positive response in the state legislature. Nicknamed by a Republican wag the Cindy Lederman Relief Act, it provided an extra year of relief for 4,400 foster youths leaving State care until they turn nineteen. Senator Nan Rich, a Democrat from Weston in Broward County and longtime advocate for children, sponsored the legislation. Said Rich, "The bill will make a real difference in the lives of children aging out of foster care."

No sooner had the legislature resolved the problems of foster kids turning nineteen than a report by a study team commissioned by the DCF brought some more heartburn. On June 7, 2005, a *Miami Herald* story reported a dramatic reduction in the number of Miami families receiving State services.

This study had come about from a request by Judge Lederman's Community-based Care Alliance for an outside consultant team to learn why the court filings in these cases had decreased in spite of the increased number of calls to the Abuse Hotline. While the hotline had brought a 25 percent increase in calls, the number of cases brought to court had decreased by a like percentage. How come?

The *Herald* story, citing the consultant, concluded that apparently DCF did virtually nothing to help children and families unless the family situations became grave, thereby lessening the number. The consultant suspected that the reduction may have left hundreds of children in harm's way.

Other agencies involved in foster care became concerned. Child advocate Berta Blecke, a leader with Our Kids, said, "This confirms my worst fears. This may be an effort to cut the State's share of allocation for foster kids, since that amount is based on the number of children in care."

In a telephone interview with one of the consultants, the *Herald* reporter was told, "DCF is working only with families who are in the most severe, egregious circumstances. Children are harmed when child-welfare officials are called over and over again before they eventually take action."

Alerted by the consultants about an original draft of their report, the *Miami Herald*, using the Public Records Law, also obtained a copy of the first draft. This contained several passages missing later in the final version submitted by DCF to the press. The *Herald* story a week earlier had been based on the altered version. In its second story covering the incident (June 14, 2005), the lead paragraph corrected the earlier version by proclaiming, "Miami Child Abuse Investigators said that they were strongly discouraged by top administrators from taking the abused and the neglected into State care, even though they (the investigators) thought it was necessary to protect children."

This earlier draft by the consultants, omitted from the final report, had also described three cases where the families had been the subject of numerous phone calls to the hotline. In one case fifteen calls; in the others nine and six. This inaction bolstered the consultants' claim that investigators often closed abuse cases by doing little more than handling out brochures for services.

The local DCF administrator responded that the editing of the report was for the purpose of providing for feedback, clarification, and accuracy. Said Judge Cindy Lederman in response, "I'm absolutely shocked that the department (DCF) would remove pertinent parts from a report that respond directly to our inquiry. I'm now even more concerned than before for the safety of children in this community."

From my own courtroom experience, I can attest to the fact that although a good many field counselors do shoddy work, most make a decent effort. Also, unquestionably many of the hotline calls are of dubious quality. However, this DCF approach can be likened to the wartime triage effort by doctors who often had so few resources available they were forced to chose the one of the three wounded soldiers who had the most likely expectation to survive. That our social service net in Florida selects aid recipients through a triage system is a horrible thought.

The State is assuredly not free to ignore the less needy. The problem lies with the lack of monitoring by DCF supervisors. Just as the military has learned to treat all their wounded, the State must adapt the same procedures. What is also distressing here is the manner in which the agency took the work of independent consultants, critical as it was of them, and still attempted to doctor the final report.

Other problems constantly arise. The month of July 2005 had produced a technical failure for DCF. Apparently, a fax machine broke down, and the machine's electrical alert failed. Staffers, apparently unaware or negligent, allowed the glitch to go unnoticed for two months.

According to a follow-up report from DCF, the fax had finally been replaced and a quality assurance review was under way. No indication any of the children have been harmed by the delay. DCF received about 32,000 calls and about 2,300 faxes monthly reporting possible child abuses. No comment necessary.

In August 2005, DCF finally won another one over Judge Lederman. The judge had threatened to hold the Agency for Persons with Disabilities (APD) in contempt unless they provided services so that this fifteen-year-old girl didn't end up homeless at age eighteen. The APD agency is associated with the state DCF. Both have vigorously fought efforts by juvenile court judges to provide State-paid services for disabled children in foster care.

The Third District Court of Appeal ruled that Judge Lederman had exceeded her authority by threatening contempt or even ordering the agency to appear in court to explain their action. Advocacy groups were in a fury. Andrea Moore, director of Children First, said, "I am incensed that APD officials have refused to help this foster child while leaving a sixty-three million dollars surplus, unspent from the last budget year."

The fifteen-year-old child in question had, according to medical reports, a thinking ability of an eight-year-old and was raped throughout much of her childhood by her mother's boyfriend. In his report, psychologist Michael Di Tomasso said the teen was reading at the level of a first grader, had the writing skills of a seven-year-old, and the coping skills of a six-year-old. The decision of the Third District Court of Appeal said that the trial judge lacked the constitutional authority to interfere with what is wholly within the purview of the executive branch, namely agencies such as APD and DCF.

Fast-forwarding to almost a year later, this APD ruling is currently under appeal before the Florida Supreme Court. The Bush administration, in anticipation of a possible unfavorable ruling by the high court, has introduced legislation during the current session (April 13, 2006) to strip judges of authority to order services for disabled children in State care.

Why the governor, a man ordinarily of reason and intelligence, would insist that judges be denied the opportunity to monitor services for these defenseless children makes no sense. The abysmal performance record of APD and DCF over recent years suggests the absolute need for judicial intervention. Said Judge Lester Langer, handling one of these cases, "My fear is that under this new bill, all we will be doing is setting up some of our most vulnerable children for failure."

As this book moved to completion, the DCF continued its money-saving plan by temporarily halting monthly visits by field counselors to children under State care. This involved some fifty thousand children statewide. The decision arose from a shortage of gasoline fuel resulting from Hurricane Katrina. DCF, responding to the crisis, had on its own suspended visits to kids in foster homes for ninety days.

There was some irony in the situation. As exemplified by the *Rilya* case, Governor Bush's own panel, the one headed by David Lawrence, recognizing the poor supervision record of field counselors, had recommended more frequent counselor visitation to foster kids. Now, but a short time later, DCF was bypassing on its own that urgent request.

Democratic Party leaders attacked Bush with glee pointing out that when Katrina hit, they had urged him to suspend the State gas tax by executive order, which he had declined to do. The private foster care agencies, Our Kids in Dade County and ChildNet in Broward County, had both received the DCF memo cutting out visits to foster homes, and both had declared their intent to ignore it.

An angry and embarrassed Governor Bush, advised by a *Miami Herald* reporter of the DCF decision, immediately countermanded it. He was highly critical of the *Miami Herald*'s constant and critical coverage of DCF, but relented enough to say, "This one happened to be true. It was a DCF decision that needed to be changed."

On December 16, 2005, the Rilya case came up before Judge Lederman for the final review of the case for the year. Nothing much had changed. The criminal homicide case against Geralyn Graham, Rilya's caregiver, still was under further investigation. The state attorney's office advised the judge they expect to try it sometime in 2006. Though DCF promised to improve the tracking system for missing children, the number reported missing (537) hadn't decreased.

The Our Kids duel is back in the newspapers. This time good news. The sword-rattling is over. At least for now. Dated March 3, 2006, the story described Governor Bush pledging an additional three million to close the budget shortfall for the over-eighteen-year-old former foster children still attending school.

Not quite the eight million demanded by Hank Adorno and Judge Lederman's Community-based Care Alliance, but it will do for now. The governor stated, "This valuable program helps foster children assimilate into adult life. It gives them the funds necessary to make that transition and lead to a productive life." Adorno responded with an equally gracious note thanking Governor Bush for his leadership in reaching a solution to the contractual dispute.

Is this a sign of better times ahead for rehab agencies? No, not really, but it will do until something better arrives. I suppose beating up on the governor and his cost-cutting allies in the legislature isn't the answer. They have a philosophy that needs to be understood and maybe even respected. For sure, however, that constant drumbeat by Hank Adorno and Cindy Lederman kept this issue alive.

Although Governor Jeb Bush is responsible for the top DCF hires and their policies, it would not be fair to place the failings of our welfare system squarely on his shoulders. Florida is a truly conservative state, particularly in the northern regions. Occasionally a "moderate" administration is elected, and a flurry of social welfare programs emerge. That never lasts too long. The budget-cutters too often take over. And that's that.

What does all this add up to? Do we need better, stronger judicial advocates like Cindy Lederman? She is as good as we can get. Then again so was Gladstone. And in his fashion Petersen carried the wand as well. I suppose the Cindy Ledermans of the world can only stem the tide. And at that, only for a short time. Somehow the system always remains an immovable obstacle.

But then again, despite it all, we have made dramatic changes for the better in the years beginning with Gladstone and Lederman, probably more so than in all the years past. There's no marker to denote it, but the process has moved further toward a higher professional standard.

Cindy Lederman has a great reputation among serious observers of the court. Judge William Gladstone, the dean of all juvenile judges, still sitting as a senior judge, views her with almost awe as the finest ever to have come to the juvenile court.

I suppose the best accolade given her was offered by Governor Jeb Bush. Although the two have been on opposite sides of many of the more serious differences involving the welfare of our children, they have never ever met or even conversed. Philosophically and practically they are eons apart.

Whenever controversy arises, Lederman deals with whoever is the highest rank below the governor made available to her. This is normal procedure, not a designed snub by the governor. Their debate usually takes place the following morning in the *Miami Herald*, where their conflicting views are presented side by side for all to see.

Governor Bush, in making judicial appointments particularly at the highest level, personally interviews applicants who have survived the nomination process. I have it on good authority, if one can call thirdhand good authority, that interviewing applicants for the Third District Court of Appeal (Miami-Dade area) he has asked half jokingly of the candidates, "You are not going to be a judicial advocate like Judge Lederman, are you?" That's a rhetorical question. The governor doesn't expect an answer to that one.

When reporting this exchange to Judge Lederman, she smiled, saying, "What greater compliment could I ask for?"

It has been difficult to fairly outline in one chapter the efforts and the impact of Judge Cindy Lederman. She has accomplished so much for a process that since birth always has been on a life-support system.

Her goal to create a systemic approach to child care rather than a piecemeal, ad hoc response has been frustrated by countless impediments. Undaunted—that word is not used lightly here—she has struggled against all the obstacles, sometimes successfully, at times otherwise. For all those battles she has provided a reasoned, cogent construct to improve the juvenile court process so that the lives of our children are made better and safer.

Her message has been heard not only in Dade County, but in the halls of Tallahassee, Washington, D.C., at conferences throughout the country and as far away as Beijing, China, and Queensland, Australia.

Addressing social welfare problems of mostly underclass children will never provide a vehicle for public acclaim. Too many things can and do go wrong. That's the nature of this cause. Cindy Lederman accepts and understands her role. It is one of commitment. No matter the day-to-day disappointments, she'll always be in the forefront for positive change. What more can a community ask for?

Activists Are Many Among Us

Selecting seven juvenile judges as leaders in judicial advocacy since the advent of the court in 1921 was not a difficult task. Much of their individual efforts had been reported in the local media of their day, and the *Miami Herald* archives made my research efforts a lot easier. Nonetheless, it has struck me over the years that their efforts have never been properly memorialized, hence this book.

Those seven featured here epitomized traits that brought credit to the entire justice system. Each served for many years at the task and faced many hurdles to overcome. Some in the early part of the twentieth century faced long odds to establish the credibility of the juvenile court. More recently, the interagency conflict testing the court's authority made refining the judicial role one of serious difficulty.

Others, however, more recent among the judiciary deserve notice not only for their performance as advocates but also for their potential for future leadership. Of significant note is the fact that in recent times there has been a marked increase in the number of judges involved in behalf of children's causes.

Some, no longer serving in the Juvenile Court Division, and others never having been in that division, have also instituted programs of importance for the well-being of children. In terms of the judiciary, the welfare of children is not the sole province of the juvenile court judges. Responsibility goes far beyond any one division of the court system.

In the introduction and in other references, I have noted the equal importance of citizen volunteers and many other individuals and groups who have made enormous contribution to maintaining both the substance and the integrity of the juvenile court. This includes court personnel, public defenders, state attorney prosecutors, and field caseworkers. Though rarely attaining credit or positive media exposure, they also have been strong advocates for the juvenile justice system.

Most particularly, I refer to the public defenders, a valiant corps of lawyers who soldier in the court, protecting the legal rights of their young clients and monitoring the judges, making certain that the guardians of the law stay within the law. No easy task. Two fine examples of assistant PDs are Marie Osborne and Steve Harper, who for many years have kept the flame of fairness for children burning.

This, as far as the records show, is but the first book about the juvenile court (or for that matter any court in Dade County). I believe the juvenile court is unique among all the courts, but each division has a history, a pulse, and a story worth telling. I would hope that local historians take on the project of more fully describing the courts of Dade County so that those following will at least have some idea of what has preceded them.

And perhaps some curious citizens might even espy such a book on a library shelf and learn that the courts operating under the rigid rules of law are also made up of flesh-and-blood people who, while doing their duty, have a care for those before them.

Unquestionably, I have for lack of space or by oversight omitted some judicial colleagues, and as well have failed to describe other advocates worthy of recognition. For this my regrets.

Ellen Sue Venzer

Ellen Sue Venzer, a juvenile court judge for the past several years, has blossomed into a strong advocate, Lederman style. Whereas in past decades, judicial advocates have been limited in numbers, currently there are many, mostly in juvenile court, who speak out freely in behalf of children causes.

An examination of Judge Venzer's courtroom demeanor suggests a judge who reaches far out beyond the ordinary. For her, dependency cases demand full performance from DCF, the lawyers, and all who provide services for the benefit of the children. Similarly, she makes the same demands on her own performance. In her court, there are no routine cases. Where a child has been dealt short, she is willing to explore a full-fledged inquiry of a questionable DCF policy or inadequate performance.

In a series of recent year 2005 cases, she clearly took command. In April of that year she challenged DCF over their failure to locate runaway children. This had been an ongoing problem since 2002 when five-year-old foster child Rilya had disappeared, and a special panel selected by Governor Jeb Bush had described the State as "mired in a swamp of scandal over the DCF failure to report and locate runaways."

Judge Venzer, concerned over the five hundred runaways listed by DCF and dissatisfied with DCF efforts, appointed her own special panel to recommend reforms in the way social service and law enforcement search for runaways and missing kids. She said, "I have a number of missing kids in my division for whom I am responsible. These kids are basically unprotected, and they have no ability to protect themselves. We need to do something and do it fast."

Judge Venzer and other child advocates are insistent that despite the promises of the governor and DCF, the situation is still perilous.

An official of the Dade County Guardian ad Litem program serving on one of the governor's panels opined, "The situation has not been fixed."

Lawyer Karen Gievers, a Tallahassee children's advocate, agreed, saying that one of her clients, a sixteen-year-old Miami foster child, has been missing for a week, and her name was not included among the over 514 listed on DCF's website.

A missing child specialist for CHARLEE, a private foster care agency, told Judge Venzer he had tried for three days to enter a girl's name in the DCF database for missing children but was denied entrance. Until a child's name is entered into the database, state and national agencies cannot begin their efforts to locate the child.

Judge Cindy Lederman joined in with one of her own cases involving a thirteen-year-old runway from foster care. Lederman said, "My concerns are that vulnerable children, many with psychiatric and emotional problems, are living on the streets of Miami. What could be more dangerous than that?"

The point here is not that Judge Venzer's own panel might resolve the runaway-from-foster-home problem, but that she, on her own initiative, absent a crisis case (like *Rilya*), chose to take positive action. That's high-quality advocacy.

Three months later in August 2005, Venzer's battle with DCF over their failure to locate runaways took another turn. This one involved two cases the same morning. One involved a emotionally troubled, diabetic seventeen-year-old girl who ran away from a foster home. The girl, insulin dependent, had spent much of her adolescence in a locked psychiatric hospital.

She ended up in a hospital in a diabetic coma, where she remained in a semiconscious state. DCF had made no effort to locate her, claiming a long-standing computer glitch prevented any action. Judge Venzer, restraining her anger and hoping a softer approach might do more, implored the field counselor saying, "I want you to think about your own kids. If any of your children had an emotional problem, and you knew they needed insulin, don't you think you'd do more? She added, "This is disturbing. Without anyone looking for her, I can't imagine any other predictable outcome."

Earlier that morning, Judge Venzer had blasted DCF for making no effort to find another seventeen-year-old in State care. This one, the mother of an eighteen-month-old child. "You must assume," she cautioned the DCF counselor in court, "that a seventeen-year-old who is a runaway, is in harm's way, and her one-and-a-half-year-old child with her is in harm's way as well."

The judge was told by DCF that a month ago DCF had disbanded its unit for tracking missing kids. Venzer's reaction was one of distress. "It's disturbing to say the least. Dozens of children may be missing but have not been reported on the computer. How can you allow that?" This led Judge Cindy Lederman, head of the Community-based Care Alliance, to call an emergency meeting over the breakdown.

In September 2005, Judge Venzer held a hearing with state officials to review runaway cases to enable the panel she had appointed to better examine the situation. The judge wanted to learn how hard state officials were really looking for missing children. Dade County had a hundred runaway kids missing for whom the Judge had issued pickup orders. She now wanted information as to the efforts by DCF and the police to locate these children.

On September 10, 2005, the *Miami Herald* described the response. "As the hearings unfolded," the article read, "Venzer took testimony concerning about half of the one hundred missing children before closing for the day. It became abundantly clear that the mere existence of a pickup order did not guarantee anyone would actually search for a missing kid."

Witness after witness described reasons why a particular child was not sought, mostly bureaucratic rules. Others testified that if a child is not already in a State program, locating the child becomes too difficult. Some State caseworkers cited lack of time, understaffing, other priorities, failure to share info with other agencies, and on and on.

That Judge Ellen Venzer had selected runaways as her area of significance to devote special attention to, tells a lot about her determination. Locating runaways comes as close to being a dead-end in the dependency area as any other such issue. A judge with that kind of grit and the willingness to stay on that route must be labeled a star in the making.

That Ellen Sue Venzer was and is a go-getter is apparent by only a cursory examination of her résumé. Graduating from U of Miami Law School in May 1987, now a twenty-year lawyer, she hasn't wasted a minute. Never any doubt in her mind that the bench was her ultimate destination. She devoted the first eight years in private practice working with five different law firms, getting her feet wet, learning about the full dimensions of the law business.

Next was election to the county court, where she handled thousands of nonjury trials and over sixty jury trials. To augment her credentials she became adjunct professor at both the University of Miami Law School and Florida International University, teaching law and criminal justice courses. After nine years in the pits, she earned appointment by Governor Jeb Bush (January 2004) to the circuit court and assignment to the Juvenile Court Division.

She was ready, her learning curve complete. But that wasn't enough for this ambitious young woman. While in county court, the advocacy that would later define her became evident. She brought a high-intensity civic endeavor effort to the fore, namely an educational program designed to warn students of the perils of drinking and driving.

It is called Courtrooms in the Classrooms, designed to prevent underage drinking. She was a guest speaker at many public forums and appeared on TV panels. In 1998, Mothers Against Drunk Driving (MADD) gave her their Award of Distinction. Currently, now sitting in the circuit court Juvenile Division she heads the dependency drug court, where the problems of drugs and alcohol are addressed as to their negative impact on children and parents.

Ellen Sue Venzer represents perhaps still another trend that lies ahead. It may be that a Gladstone and a Lederman, each driven by the challenge, will be followed by a breed of juvenile court judges who recognize that merely by virtue of their judicial assignment, advocacy is imperative and perhaps the way, the only way, to bring this court to the height of its original destiny. The best interest of the child demands that kind of performance. Ellen Sue Venzer stands for that kind of leadership.

Jeri Beth Cohen

Back in 1989, Judge Herbert Klein, then Deputy Chief Judge of the Eleventh Judicial Circuit, designed a drug court program, the first of its kind in the nation. Historically, specialty courts had been utilized in the past. Similar efforts in the mid-nineteenth century, then called narcotics courts, had been introduced in this country, but those were not designed for rehab. Rather, they were established merely to separate drug users from the regular prison population. As a matter of fact, the juvenile court itself, in its infancy, had been designated as a specialty court.

Judge Klein developed a program designed to create a nonpunitive process by which drug offenders would have an opportunity to correct their drug problems. Avoiding criminal court trial and the prospect of heavy jail time, these hearings focused on rehabilitation. Jail time was the last alternative. Without fanfare, the program caught on, quickly being replicated in jurisdictions throughout the country.

Judge Herbert Klein, the founder, and Judge Stanley Goldstein, the first drug court judge handling referrals from the criminal court, became sought-after figures in the criminal justice talk circuit throughout the nation. The success rate was impressive. Miami had the honor of being the home site for this new approach, and Herb Klein had the satisfaction in knowing he had successfully introduced a therapeutic form to the criminal justice system.

The drug court concept traveled far and wide throughout the nation, including our own Dade County. Ten years after the Klein experiment had started for adults charged with a drug crime, it traveled some thirty blocks north to the juvenile court. There, in 1999, Judge Jeri Beth Cohen began the dependency drug court (DDC).

Hers was not a direct offshoot of the adult drug court but obviously was influenced by that success. Judge Cohen, prior to coming to juvenile court, had spent four years handling DUI cases in county criminal court. There she had an informal drug court supported by a grant from the Florida Department of Transportation for a program that monitored repeat DUI offenders.

Her work in county DUI court brought her in contact with community mental health and substance abuse treatment providers. Upon her elevation to the circuit court and assignment to juvenile court, she was the logical and the ideal person to start a full-fledged dependency drug court.

Because substance-addicted parents are so often the cause of children becoming dependent, Judge Cohen recognized that in order to reunite families, intensive monitoring was essential as well as a treatment program that emphasized the whole gamut of programs designed to make a family whole again. This would require specially trained counselors and other skilled caseworkers to properly guide their charges out of the addiction disorder engulfing them. In addition, Miami, as a multicultural community, required staffers conversant and sensitive to those diverse needs.

Judge Cohen thereupon negotiated agreements with the regional DCF office to dedicate three caseworkers along with obtaining funding from the Florida state legislature to support three addiction specialists. Three other staff members were also added to serve as a link between the court, parents, and treatment providers.

Under court procedures, Judge Cohen made referrals to the program based on space availability and the complexity of the case. Participation by the parents was voluntary. Clients signed a contract accepting the court requirements. Legal counsel was provided at all phases. Sanctions for failure to perform were clearly enumerated. These included community service hours to short periods of incarceration.

Success of the program was predicated on the client buying in to the goals. The expectations of both Judge Cohen and the client had to run parallel. Since clients involved in this program were subject to termination of their parental rights, there was a strong effort to avoid sanctions. Similarly with drug addiction, a difficult situation to overcome, it was important for those in control to be sensitive to the treatment mode imposed. In her first year with the program, Judge Cohen invoked a jail sanction only five times.

In terms of funding, though the state court system traditionally viewed specialty courts such as the drug court with some reluctance, Judge Cohen sought and received grants from a variety of sources.

Judge Cohen also worked out a strong collaboration with the University of Miami's Linda Ray Center, an early-intervention center for substance-exposed newborns between the ages zero to three. Together they obtained a grant for a multicultural interactive parenting skill program for substance-addicted parents and their children. The program offered effective parenting strategies to decrease substance abuse by improving parent-child interactions.

The Linda Ray Center also prepared genealogies on each child's family tree, thus providing a family history of value as medical background information. Their staff appeared at all court hearings and were an integral part of the dependency drug court team. In May 2000, DDC graduated its first class. As of October 2003, seventy parents with 234 children had graduated the program.

Judge Cohen has written several articles on the drug dependency court for the *Journal of the National Council of Juvenile Court Judges* and also has spoken extensively before civic and law groups as to the operation of the DDC. Rotation to other divisions of the court had Judge Cohen sitting in the General Jurisdiction Division of the circuit court. As of January 2006, she returned to the juvenile court division and now, among her other duties, participates in the unified family court.

Her legal career began in Washington, D.C., where she was a trial attorney for the U.S. Securities and Exchange Commission. In the early 1990s, upon arriving in Miami she organized a network seeking to uphold *Roe v. Wade* and other women's rights issues. In the few short years prior to ascending to the bench, Jeri Beth Cohen had gained a reputation as a progressive force in politically activist circles.

Always an outspoken advocate for many causes, Jeri Beth Cohen brought that dynamism to the bench. Her work in spearheading the drug dependency court was a high point, but she has the drive and commitment to pursue other civic goals and challenges that come her way. Those efforts likely will be displayed as she performs her duties as a circuit court judge. Those who know her suggest there is no telling in what venue she will perform. Whatever she does, wherever she goes, this is one advocate who will never relinquish that title.

WILLIAM JOHNSON

Little did Judge Herbert Klein realize when he introduced the drug court for adults back in 1989 that close to eight hundred courts here and abroad would replicate his program. Today, throughout the country, specialty courts, like the drug court, are springing up in other jurisdictions, such as mental health, sex offenders, domestic violence, and for the homeless. Some are here in Dade County; New York City has several, and others flourish in other communities as well.

There is a trend, a small one at best, that searches for problem-solving courts with therapeutic responses rather than incarceration. Old-line purists in the criminal justice system view these courts as oddities, while modern-day progressives see them as the courts of the future.

There is no real fear this trend will overcome the criminal justice system. Security from criminal activity is too strong in the public mind for this trend to cause a change of attitude. And rightly so. Incarceration and other forms of punishment are here to stay. And so will specialty courts. They fill an important need.

Judge Klein, whose name has been all but lost as the creator of the specialty drug court as an alternative to criminal prosecution, had this to say about his claim to fame:

> I am proud to have been instrumental in designing this court. It is not comparable to the Salk vaccine or other important advances in medicine, but it has moved the criminal justice system forward.

> I know my role, and that is enough to make me feel that somewhere along the way I made a significant contribution in my field.

Modest man that fellow Klein. Along the way, William Johnson picked up on Klein's beginning. In 2001, two years after Judge Jeri Cohen started the dependency drug court, Judge Johnson introduced the juvenile drug court for use among delinquent children. The alternative among dependent children was the possibility of the parent losing custody of the child. Here with Judge Johnson's program, the penalty was likely incarceration of the child or transfer for trial to adult court. Neither pleasant possibilities.

The delinquency drug program lacked the large number of controls exercised by the dependency program. The latter usually focused on parents who had failed to avoid substance abuse and the damage thereupon wrought upon the child. The delinquency drug court centers mostly on the child's behavior.

The client is usually a fourteen- to seventeen-year-old adolescent in need of corrective behavior. The program was founded on the premise that arrest and court involvement provided an ideal opportunity for the juvenile justice system and treatment providers to work together to intervene in the child's behalf. In this fashion, this intervention program carried out the juvenile court concept, the best interest of the child.

The court regimen required regular court appearances, urine analysis, linkage to community treatment service providers, ongoing case management, family intervention, and educational/vocational referral. In some cases when the parents are the drug abusers, family involvement also became significant.

A full story in the *Miami Herald* (8/5/04) described the travels and travails through the delinquency drug court, of a seventeen-year-old arrested for burglary. His public defender had persuaded Judge Johnson to put the youngster into the juvenile drug court (JDC) rather than trying him in adult court. In his final appearance before Judge Johnson, the boy received a certificate, a T-shirt, and medal for successfully completing the program's four levels of treatment, drug testing, and probation.

This once-surly boy who used to hang out on street corners all night, as reported in the article, had earned a college scholarship and regained the trust of his family because he was now drug free. Judge Johnson had placed him in the Dade Marine Institute, an alternative school where he learned to scuba dive, had risen to the rank of captain, and won a two-year scholarship to Miami-Dade College.

This court, like the Dade County Adult Drug Court, was created in response to a growing body of research suggesting that focused treatment, not jail time, helped combat a child's substance abuse. A study by the University of Miami's Center for Treatment Research on Adolescent Drug Users found their rearrest rate was only 13 percent compared to 74 percent for a matched group of offenders who did not receive the intensive treatment provided by the JDC. That is a astounding result.

While observers focus on the subsequent behavior of the defendants to count improvements, one must also judge their progress by what those who deal with them say. Said his lawyer, Assistant Public Defender Robin Faber, "When the kids buy into the fact that that you give a damn about them as people, they buy into you and your programs."

Judge William Johnson gave credit to the closely monitored progress by a team of probation officers, treatment specialists, school representatives and attorneys who tracked each teen's progress throughout the yearlong program. Judge Johnson stated, "These requirements make children accountable. Once they accept responsibility, the battle is halfway won. When the kids get better, the parents often become aware of their own shortcomings and try to improve."

Judge Johnson, six foot three, in the vicinity of three hundred pounds, looks like one of those massive Miami Dolphin linemen out to terrorize enemy quarterbacks. Personally, he is an easygoing, friendly hulk of a man who likes kids, and they like him.

The headline to the *Miami Herald* story describing Judge Johnson's court read,

"Teenage Drug Abusers Earn a New Start in a Caring Court." Certainly an accurate description of Judge William Johnson and his goals.

Steve Leifman

Among the judiciary, Dade County Court Judge Steve Leifman is probably as good a choice that can be made for a judge who exemplifies advocacy at its best. A former Dade County public defender, his primary focus has been in mental health, developing programs that recognize the need for the police and the courts to give special attention to those who by virtue of a mental incapacity become defendants in criminal cases.

Though not a juvenile court judge, he has designed programs to aid children in need. His first project, back in 1989, was putting together a mentor program for seventh graders at Booker T. Washington. He enlisted volunteer mentors from Temple Beth Shalom, his synagogue in Miami Beach. These volunteers committed until the child graduated high school.

Twenty volunteers joined, mostly professionals, determined to keep these kids out of trouble and in school. Dropout kids were their targets. At that time juvenile judge Tom Petersen was putting together a new kind of countywide school program designed for delinquent kids coming out of juvenile court. He invited Leifman to develop a mentor's program for this new venture, an assignment Leifman gladly accepted.

Today, Leifman's focus is on mental health. Along with other county officials, they have been beneficiary of a twenty-two-million-dollar bond issue to outfit a new mental hospital with beds, both short-term and long-term, for inmates with a diagnosed mental illness.

In the past, mentally ill inmates were usually detained in the same lockup status as other criminals. They slept in metal bunks, given food through a bolted slot, and allowed out of cells twice a week to be sprayed by a hose attached to a concrete wall.

This new structure, unlike regular jails, will be built specifically for inmates with chronic and severe mental illness. Housing includes a secure building several floors high with 150 beds, and dorm-style living. Not your typical jail, but not a country club either. Located near the Richard Gerstein Criminal Court building and the county jail complex on Seventeenth Street in Miami. it will be called the South Florida Evaluation and Treatment Center.

The upper floor will resemble a hospital emergency room where inmates committed under the Baker Act will be treated with psychiatric drugs and therapy. On treatment floors, care will be provided by mental health professionals, mostly paid for by Medicare, rather than prison guards.

Leifman views his focus to be on those committing minor crimes involving trespassing, disorderly conduct, and domestic valence. His goal is to obtain medication and prompt attention to their ills. He views the cost for such hospital care for these mentally ill patients, left unaided, will far exceed the cost of this new institution. Training the police, jail officers, and prosecutors to provide intervention services so they can recognize symptoms is the underpinning of this project.

A Leifman quote in a *Miami Herald* editorial warned, "We have a mental health crisis in this county. The lack of resources to treat the mentally ill have turned the Miami-Dade jail into the largest psychiatric institution in the State. On any given day there are between 800 to 1,200 people with mental illness in jail."

In 2005, Miami-Dade County mayor Carlos Alvarez appointed Judge Leifman to lead a task force aimed at studying and making recommendations to improve conditions for the homeless and others with mental health problems in terms of their relationship with the justice system.

One of the items noted in the announcement was a statement by the State Department of Children and Families that Miami-Dade County has the highest number of mentally ill people per capita in the country, three times higher than the national average.

In addition to his regular assignment in the Domestic Violence Division of the county court, Leifman heads the Eleventh Judicial Circuit Special Mental Health Program established by Chief Judge Joseph Farina.

Judge Leifman's commitment and his experience in resolving concerns as to mental health treatment for inmates suggests that he will be a strong voice in rectifying problems that have arisen and may arise in this important field. How well a community treats mentally ill inmates, both adult and children, is probably a true standard to judge the humanity of that community.

The United Way of Dade County selected Steve Leifman as the winner of the 2005 Public Leadership Award, saying he exemplified volunteerism by working tirelessly for reform in the mental health system.

Steve is an impressive person. On two occasions, running for a judicial post, he was targeted as being politically "too liberal" and was defeated for election. His current interest, seeking a more humane approach for the mentally ill who become involved with the criminal justice system, may well attract hard-liners to oppose him at the polls again.

Though not relishing it, Steve Leifman expects that kind of opposition. Since judicial contests are nonpartisan, rarely does the issue of liberal or conservative enter into consideration. Besides, Leifman has never been a banner-waving crusader for any political cause. How or why he was targeted is unclear.

In the 2006 election, he again drew an opponent, probably now because he may be viewed as an easy mark. Win or lose he will doggedly pursue his goal to decriminalize people with mental illness. (He won his election handily.)

Although his major focus is not now in the children's field, a man of his breadth and spirit is sure to come back to our fold. We welcome an advocate of his stature.

Steve, let me point to an October 15, 2006, story in the *Miami Herald* describing an order by Circuit Court Judge Julio Jimenez, directing DCF to find a bed for a mentally ill patient who had gouged his own eyes out. DCF refused, their lawyer stating that the judge lacked the constitutional authority to order the State to place this individual. Judge Jimenez responded, "I remember twenty-five years ago as a lawyer in Juvenile Court hearing that same argument from your department. I'm sure your department has emergency funds." The response by Judge Jimenez shows why we really need you.

BONNIE RIPPINGILLE

Not all our judges described in this chapter are new shining lights on the horizon. Some have been around awhile and have been performing good deeds all these many years. Judge Bonnie Rippingille spent twenty years in private practice and now has nine years behind her as a county court judge. Presently, she sits in the Domestic Violence Division, a court that brings her intimately close to the problems of children.

The program that makes her service noteworthy is a solo creation. She conceived it, developed and brought it to life, and in a sense is the sole proprietor. I refer, of course, to the Sisters of the Heart, a project that links delinquent girls with mentors. Organized in 1999 and replicated in 2001 in Palm Beach, it flourishes here and in other Florida sites.

The concept of the program was a simple one: introduce wayward girls to a better way of life, and by such association their goals and attitude will improve along with their self-esteem. These were not girls with serious criminal problems or necessarily dysfunctional families. Judge Rippingille's program addressed a group of girls on the fringes of delinquency, engaging in shop-lifting, truancy, and becoming involved with gangs.

The program started with attending court sessions, usually Judge Rippingille's, followed by anger management classes, and finally sitting in on mediation sessions. They were there as observers, no need to participate with their own stories, or undergo examination by a mental health professional. Listening can often be a very therapeutic approach.

Judge Rippingille did not believe in force-feeding. She wanted these girls to begin building up in their own minds the consequence of crimes, to learn how to curb violent tendencies, and to see how problems can be addressed peacefully by negotiation and meaningful resolution.

The girls also were placed in a position to develop their aesthetic values by attendance at the ballet, concerts, and the theatre. All were cultural influences never before encountered. Judge Bonnie Rippingille said, "It was surprising to see how impressed each of them was with these performances. They were in awe of the ballet dancers who seemed to fly around as if on strings. One girl at the opera thought it unusual that so many elderly people were in attendance."

From culture they proceeded to power lunches with influential women—legislators, lawyers, business leaders, political aides, and probation officers. This provided a full network of role models and mentors. These lunches were head-to-head meetings, no speeches, just girl talk, the kind these kids would long remember.

This simple formula worked. Rippingille had no national sponsor, no full-time staff, no regular grants, no dedicated source of State support. She scrounged around for financial help, usually footing most of the bill on her own.

Her project does have cooperating relationships with the Dade County Public Schools system, the Women's Fund of Miami-Dade County (a partial funder), the Miami-Dade Police Department, and other governmental bodies. Once established, word got around and benefactors sought her out.

Professionals in the child-care field have been extreme in their praise. Jennifer Schuster, director of Tom Petersen's TROY Academy said, "The girls in my program participate in the Sister of the Heart program. It offered them a much wider opportunity of experiences than TROY.

"The experience of networking with mature, successful women was especially wonderful. I think it made them feel better about themselves, more intrinsically valuable as human beings."

One of the girl graduates of the program said, "I was having a hard time, but my mentor, a retired nurse, gave me a strong shoulder to lean on and a willing ear that carried me through. It was the one thing that got me through my juvenile court sentence."

Judge Rippingille gave her own estimate of her program, "I started this because there seemed to be a shortage of places a young girl in trouble cold find some solace and direction. It gives them a sense of belonging and something to look forward to.

"Along the way the girls learn how to build a resume, how to balance a checkbook, how to open a bank account. And other day-to-day practical things."

Judge Rippingille hasn't sought applause, but some has come her way. In 2001 the state Department of Juvenile Justice recognized her as Florida's Statewide Juvenile Justice Volunteer of the Year. The members of the Miami-Dade County Commission also dedicated the Women's Park Gallery Rotunda in her name for her work as founding chair of a project designed to honor the role of women in society.

Impressive about Judge Rippingille is her ability to go it alone. She supports the theory held by many (especially me) that true advocates don't wait around for grants to arrive. Looking back at Edith Atkinson almost a century ago, she barely knew anything about juvenile court, yet she immediately set about selling the need for public support.

Among more recent leaders—Gladstone, Petersen, and Lederman—they hardly have paused to reflect on how hard the road ahead looked. They all went out and did it, whatever it was that had to be done. That's what makes a real advocate, and that approach best personifies Judge Bonnie Rippingille.

Charles Edelstein

Known as Chuck throughout the Dade County criminal justice system, and as well nationally, Charles Edelstein is an uncommon person. A man of superior ability, his recognition has never quite caught up to his talent.

Edelstein's area of expertise is court management. Recognized nationally, he is a teacher, program designer, and evaluator who has traveled the country and the world for both his pleasure and for his craft. He has spent twenty years in and out of the University of Southern California, heading their master's degree program in the Department of Judicial Administration. He had a Ford fellowship to serve as dean at the Court Management Institute at Denver, Colorado, and was director of Trial Advocacy at the University of Miami Law School. His home base is Miami, where for many years he served as an assistant state attorney, heading the Criminal Appeals Division.

Serving as a county judge, never having risen to the circuit court, he nevertheless was often chosen by Chief Judge Gerald Wetherington to try some of the most difficult cases in circuit court. A really good judge is sometimes hard to find.

He had one great asset that Judge Wetherington recognized, as well did other members of the judiciary; Chuck was a brilliant lawyer. Unfortunately, Chuck was an iconoclast, refusing to go along with the norms of commonly accepted legal practice, at least in terms of showing proper respect to his betters. He was his own man, totally independent, a radical naysayer.

There is a certain homage offered to the high-powered downtown law firms that Judge Edelstein, in his intransigence, refused to adopt. He treated them as ordinary mortals. This lifetime trait, his inability to defer to the barons of the Dade County Bar, held his judicial career back, but didn't hold Chuck back.

In his court, no continuances unless warranted, no filing of meaningless motions to wear out the opposition, and other such big-boy tactics often practiced with impunity by the powerful. As a result, every time the name of Charles Edelstein came up for promotion to circuit court, somehow his influential critics prevailed. He wears this as a badge of honor.

Judge Wetherington, however, did use Edelstein for many special assignments in his area of expertise. In that capacity he played a significant role in the development of the dependency movement in juvenile court. Back in 1989, the National Center for State Courts conducted a study of our juvenile court. Edelstein served as part of that study team.

Judge Wetherington thereafter appointed Judge Edelstein to follow up on their recommendations. As indicated in earlier commentary, the dependency side of the juvenile court had always been an area of omission, never getting the attention warranted until Judges William Gladstone and Cindy Lederman began that movement. It had been Edelstein's specific recommendations that hastened the changes.

Edelstein's follow-up on the National Center's study was the turning point in opening the door for dramatic change in the area of dependency. The first priority Edelstein offered was to split the dependency caseload from the delinquency side.

According to Edelstein, "This allowed the social service agencies to more adequately staff the Court and provide better accountability." That idea had been broached before but with this formal recommendation, it now had leaped to the top of Chief Judge Wetherington's priority list.

Next was the problem of the unduly length of stay in shelter care. Often children were kept there for weeks rather than days. This failure was attributed to the lack of lawyers to represent the parents in court. As well, additional social workers and paralegal were required to properly process the flow. Never before, budgetwise had this request for these funds ever gotten out of the starting box.

When advised by Edelstein that this was essential to the juvenile court's well-being, Wetherington asked for the cost for such an addition. When Edelstein replied, "In the neighborhood of two million dollars," Judge Wetherington promptly picked up the phone, and made that request to the Dade County budget director. Two days later the money was allocated. Wetherington had a powerful influence with the Dade County Commission (as did Edelstein's advice with the chief judge).

For openers, four lawyers, two paralegals, and two secretaries were hired. Later the County came across with fourteen senior caseworkers. The result was the average length of stay in shelter care was cut by seventeen days, saving the State over a million dollars a year and most importantly moving children in shelter closer to adoption.

In addition, Edelstein organized what was called the Working Group, consisting of senior managers from the involved agencies. The group studied many aspects on the delinquency side. They addressed the excessive number of continuances using time and motion studies, the effect on judicial time, and other aspects of court waste. Edelstein, in a no-nonsense report, concluded, "The problems were caused by poor case coordination, the adversary nature of the system and just plain indifference. Since all the agencies represented by The Working Group were part of the problem, their proposed solutions protected their own agencies and therefore made little progress."

At a later date Edelstein was also asked to look into the detention center problem. He labeled the center grossly overcrowded, poorly staffed, and ineptly managed. He tartly concluded, "One of the juvenile justice system's most visible problems is their lack of care for the kids." As a result of his proposals, the population was lowered, but the next crisis brought it back to the old way.

Edelstein investigated and also made recommendation in terms of the lack of space for the several agencies located in the present juvenile justice complex. He was put off by being told that a new juvenile court building would attend to that problem. His response: "That new building has been coming for ten years, but the first bit of mortar has yet too appear." Today, in the year 2006, the "new" juvenile court building continues to be on and off the drawing board (target date now 2010).

Legal scholar that he surely was, he still recognized the practical limitations of progress. His was a voice ready to contest the bureaucracy, but in this instance he realized the so-called lack of a new building was a means to delay prompt action in terms of correcting deficiencies. Never fearful of "fighting the system," he nonetheless was fully aware that the stone wall that often appeared was both impassable and impenetrable.

Not adequately recognized for his talent in his hometown (other than by the chief judge) he continued his professional court management efforts in other jurisdictions throughout out the country, occasionally earning an assignment in Dade County. Through his formalistic studies, he brought a greater acceptance of system analysis research to the fore. Too often in the past, structural decisions had been made mostly on subjective reaction.

No longer as demanding a taskmaster, and more accepting of his fellow lawyers, he today sits as a senior judge, filling in for judges unavailable for their calendars. Occasionally, he is called upon for advice as to court management, to which he gladly obliges. Respectfully he is listened to, his advice given the due that younger practitioners offer—which isn't too much.

His most recent words, "I'm just happy having made a little bit of difference in juvenile court, even if only for the moment."

Edelstein, not only a criminal justice colleague of the author but a career-long close friend, has always been a valued source of information. Not only in our field of endeavor but as well in other areas. Somewhere and somehow he is a virtual encyclopedia of medicine. Whether by his own maladies or by devouring the Internet, you name the ailment and "Doctor" Edelstein will immediately bring you up to date on the medical profession progress to date.

He is an awesome example of a man who through his lifetime has remained faithful to his principles. He shrugs off friendly taunts of being a liberal, even called a radical. Some view him as a protégé of mine. Truth is, I've learned more from him.

Where has all that early-on aggressive energy gone? Don't despair. Chuck spends six months a year fording rivers in the Amazon, visiting the ruins of Inca tribes, taking photo shoots in the African veldt, examining turtles in the Galapagos Islands and building a summer home in Colorado. Suddenly, he will descend on Miami in those alternate months, announcing his presence. Watch out! That radical spirit is sure to rise again.

Norman Gerstein

Back in 1970, as a young assistant public defender, Norman Gerstein galvanized strong media and public support for his crusade over the mistreatment of children at Sunland Training Center. Sunland, a state residential treatment center for mentally handicapped people, housed four hundred, mostly youth, and operated under the State Health and Rehabilitative Services (HRS).

At Sunland, activist public defender Gerstein snapped photos of kids drinking from toilets, children sleeping in cagelike cribs with locked tops, and some people not even retarded who didn't belong there. Outraged at what he found, Gerstein denounced HRS, "This is like the Dark Ages. No one would ever believe that such a cold place exists in the country, in this state, in this year." As a result of his efforts, the Florida Legislature passed the Bill of Rights for Retarded Persons.

Ten years later, in 1980, when I was already a veteran judge in juvenile court, and Norman Gerstein was still a flaming public defender with his Sunland Center victory and other noteworthy ventures in the public's behalf under his belt, he and I had this exchange. It came about upon word arriving that Governor Bob Graham was considering Gerstein's appointment to the county court bench.

I am not now, and was not then, particularly enthralled with public defenders. Some of them I admired and applauded for their fervor carrying the banner for the rights of kids in our court. Others were much too overwhelmed with their own virtue and viewed judges disagreeing with them as un-American and vipers of the lowest class. Gerstein fit into the first group.

He was gung ho, challenging the court and the world, always ready to mix it up with the bad guys. He didn't always agree with me, but there was something in his true sincerity and his grit that made me admire him.

I had that bad reputation with the PDs because of my tendency to lockup kids overnight to improve their character. Too many of the PD's young clients thought juvenile crime was an entitlement of their generation and therefore viewed the juvenile court with disdain. The general feeling among them described juvenile court as a place where "nothing happens." An overnight stay in detention sometimes gave some of them a fresh new look at the system, at least so I thought back then.

This is the short colloquy Gerstein and I engaged in.

> GERSTEIN: I've applied for a county court seat and think I've got a good shot at getting the appointment. What do you think?
>
> GELBER: You are only thirty-two years old, still wet behind the ears. Why waste the best years of your life so early? Never again will you be able to attack all these evil monsters who deprive children of their rights.
>
> Sitting on the bench you will become an automaton following stare decisis. Wait a bit. Enjoy life. Shake up the establishment. I waited till I was fifty before applying for a judgeship.

Gerstein, gave me a perplexed smile, as if not sure of my seriousness and thanked me. I am not certain as to how serious I had been. Being a judge isn't that bad. And Norm Gerstein as a judge hasn't lost all those juices that made him a standout as a young man. As a matter of fact, he is still an activist in terms of children's causes.

First assigned to criminal court, he had opted out, then doing one short stint as a judge in the juvenile court. In a *Miami Herald* article (11/1/1988), the reporter described the reason for his quick departure from the Criminal Court Division and his short stay on the Juvenile Division bench. Apparently, a death penalty imposed by Gerstein while sitting in criminal court was the reason he had asked for transfer to juvenile court.

Judge Gerstein personally opposed capital punishment and the death penalty decision, according to the reported story, "personally devastated him." Transferred to juvenile court, hearing both delinquency and dependency cases, Gerstein tangled again with HRS over their inability to properly track children held in

Youth Hall's Detention Center. Operating under an antiquated card-file system, HRS managed to regularly "lose" inmates, making it difficult for the PDs to seek release of their clients. Judge Gerstein held HRS in contempt but lifted it when HRS installed a computer system in the detention center.

The newspaper reporter, quoting the judge, had hinted in his article the reasons for Gerstein's departure from the juvenile court, stating, "The constant flow of misery through that courtroom takes its toll on everyone. Some days it overwhelms your emotions. Either the hardship or the depression just destroys you."

Recently, I interviewed Judge Gerstein, currently sitting in the Probate Division, asking how he viewed the scene today in terms of his days sitting in juvenile court. Gerstein preferred discussing today rather than the past. He spoke little of his circuit court career, quickly moving the focus to his camp for needy children.

Judge Norman Gerstein runs a camp for children that began in 1999 when he and wife Jackie, a practicing lawyer, organized a summer camp for ten abused or abandoned four- to five-year-olds. This was a ten-day outing on the grounds of Temple Judea. In the best tradition of their religion, it was called Mitzvah Camp. *Mitzvah* meaning good deed. The Gersteins personally funded and operated the camp.

The response from temple members and the community was so overwhelming that in a few years the camp population exploded. Renamed Summer Fun for Kids, the camp went from two weeks to a full summer, from ten to two hundred population, and from one campsite to three. The children are no longer four- and five-year-olds, instead now from age five to sixteen.

The kids are provided by CHARLEE and the Children's Home Society, two of the most reputable private welfare agencies in Dade County, who advise and provide social work assistance to the camp. Grants from foundations have augmented the programs. Long-range plans call for another camp in the Orlando area, and opening one for developmentally disabled children, tutoring and mentoring to be an important part of each program—eventually with expansion into year-round operation.

He has received many honors for this work. The Dade County Bar Association named him for the Outstanding Community Service Award. The Greater Miami Jewish Federation Community Services Award was tendered for his work in behalf of children. Judge Gerstein doesn't tout his performance. He realizes these are community efforts that constantly need to be replicated.

Unquestionably, wherever Norman Gerstein functions, in whatever court, in whatever capacity, he will always be an advocate for children. There is that innate feeling he possesses that insures solidarity with those who are oppressed, particularly children.

Some judges have accepted the challenge for their lifetime pursuit. Other look at it as but one in a long line of mountains to climb. Norman Gerstein had it when I first knew him some thirty years ago, and it still flourishes today. A truly independent personality. How, I ask, do we rekindle that flame and get him back into juvenile court?

Sandy Karlan

Judge Gladstone's dream of a unified family court, which prompted him to seek election to office back in 1973, is beginning to fly in the Eleventh Judicial Circuit. It took a lot of lifting to get it airborne. It began with the opinion from the Florida Supreme Court, "In re Report of the Family Court Steering Committee," establishing directions for creating a unified family court.

Judge Sandy Karlan did much of the piloting along with support from other advocates. Not that it totally resembles Gladstone's youthful vision, or that of the Supreme Court, but the machine is in place and running. It's called Division 48, also known as the Complex Litigation Division.

Judge Karlan, who has served as a circuit court judge since 1995, was first assigned to the Juvenile Division, Dependency Section, and then rotated to the Domestic Relations Division, where she now sits as associate administrative judge.

In the past she had observed many cases involving the problems of one family assigned to two or more divisions of the court. This piecemeal resolution sometimes resulted in the appointment of two Guardians ad Litem or two psychological evaluations for the same child, and often conflicting orders by each of the Judges. It hardly made for either efficient or substantial justice.

As Karlan described the problem, "Florida's family courts are disjointed.

The judges handling divorce, dependency, and delinquency cases too often operate in separate worlds. Cases involving the same family too often are assigned to judges in different courts. Each of these judges are likely to issue conflicting orders. Children and their families more often than not are summoned to needless and confusing multiple court appearances on the same issue."

The new Division 48 was created so that families with cases in more than one of these several divisions (Juvenile, Family, Criminal, Domestic Violence, Child Support) are handled in one court before one judge. As a result, these multicourt actions can be heard in one forum.

Recent reports to the Florida Supreme Court reflect that Division 48 has handled the matters of over 120 families representing over 300 individual cases. These matters addressed in a coordinated manner have resulted in timely resolution of all cases and have limited needless postjudgment litigation. This is due in large part to the model's reliance on alternative dispute resolution and active case management by the judge.

Opposition to the implementation of this unified family court approach has been limited and stems largely from human resistance to change. However, as Judge Karlan points out, "Although having separate divisions for areas involving the family may be administratively convenient for calendaring purposes, it promotes only piecemeal resolution for many family issues and almost certainly insures that the families will continue to return to court over the years."

Judge Joel Brown, Administrative Judge of the Family Division, and a strong proponent of a unified family court, has reported that lawyers participating in these unified cases offer praise over the accomplishments for the total family.

Division 48 has a history of over a thirty-year gestation period in Dade County. Back in the mid-1970s, then Chief Judge Ed Cowart, with support from Bill Gladstone and others, set up a division to hear multifamily cases. Among other reasons, the several judges assigned full time found the assignment unmanageable, and after a short span the venture was disbanded.

In 1991 the concept reemerged with a supreme court directive requiring each circuit in the state to develop a local rule establishing such a family court. Little progress was made at that time in Dade County, perhaps due to the ill-fated earlier experiment. Ten years later (2001), Chief Judge Farina issued his administrative order for Dade County titled "Reaffirmation of United Family Court Plan."

By the time Sandy Karlan had arrived on the bench (1995), the Chief Judge Ed Cowart-Bill Gladstone proposal of a bygone day had long ago met a stillbirth. But it kept coming back to life. During Karlan's two-year stint in the juvenile division, she and Judge Scott Bernstein, under direction of Administrative Judge Cindy Lederman, had been assigned to a Division 48 pilot program that developed into the process later performed by Judge Sandy Karlan and Judge Lester Langer.

Sandy Karlan currently serves in the Family Division, sitting as associate administrative judge. Consistent with her commitment to children and families in our court system, Sandy Karlan was appointed in 1999 to head the Florida Bar Commission on the Legal Needs of Children. Karlan's advocacy for a court dealing with multifamily problems once again had come to the fore. She has been the driving force in establishing and maintaining the current posture of this project.

The Florida Bar commission included judges from courts throughout the state as well as representatives from the offices of the state attorney, public defender, GAL, as well as Supreme Court Justices Fred Lewis and Barbara Pariente. Also included were nonlegal advocates.

The commission spent three years studying these complex issues. The American Bar Association acknowledged their effort, characterizing it as the first state bar association to undertake so comprehensive a look at the legal needs of children in our courts. Judge Karlan steered the project, encouraging the members to be thoughtful, practical, and creative in their recommendations.

In 2002 the commission issued its report including the establishment of a permanent Florida Bar committee to work on implementation of the multiple recommendations. In addition to the proposal for a unified family court, the commission proposed and the supreme court adopted a rule for juvenile procedure, requiring lawyers to be appointed for children in foster care in certain mental health matters. The state legislature followed by funding costs for these lawyers.

Many other recommendations for strengthening standards for GAL attorneys and providing more access to records were also included in their recommendations. The commission's work resulted in an official and permanent commitment by the bench and bar to guarantee a voice for children in our courts.

The report also laid out many technology concerns. The Florida Bar thereupon provided a $25,000 grant to identify technical areas in need of further research. In addition, the report cited the wide use of paper as the primary medium for the transfer of information, as an obstacle to upgrading technology. Also of importance was "the lack of a governance structure to facilitate a continuing dialogue regarding strategies to address the immediate and long term-opportunities for children in need."

Following the report, Judge Karlan and the others noted here, intensified their efforts, and Division 48 came to life. Sandy Karlan and Lester Langer, respectively associate administrative judges of the Family Division and the Juvenile Division, in addition to their regular duties, were appointed to preside over the new Division 48, described as the Unitary Family Division.

Whereas the earlier Chief Judge Ed Cowart project of the 1970s era came on with huge fanfare, Division 48 functioned in quiet solitude. There's a director of the project and a case coordinator. The coordinator digs potential cases out of the daily computer listings and also receives referrals from judges of other divisions.

Judges Sandy Karlan and Lester Langer use case managers, and other specialists as are available in their respective divisions.

Division 48, already beyond the pilot project mode, has been operational since January 2002. Of Judge Karlan's caseload, she reports only two families needing further court intervention. Supportive of the project, she said, "This really works for meeting the needs of a family in trouble." As she described the operation in more detail, her enthusiasm grew. Her final estimate was voiced with one word—"magnificent!"

Had Gladstone's vision finally become a reality? Too early to tell, although Karlan already ultimately sees the division enlarged to four to six judges. I suppose so long as Judges Karlan and Langer stay with it, chances are good. But the problems are numerous, with no clear avenue for success ahead.

For one, these kinds of cases cry for case managers to follow up and untangle the cross wires sure to emerge. Not only is court staffing essential, but the flow of information needs to be constant, accurate and easily available. Conflict resolution techniques such as mediation are also important tools. All of the above require State funding for the project, which has been in short supply. Very short.

Will the unified family court finally find a permanent home in the Dade County judicial firmament? Chances are excellent for both survival and success, though questions are occasionally raised. Judge Langer, a supporter, sitting with Judge Karlan in Division 48, has been optimistic but uncertain how the program will fare over the long haul. He observed, "It has the ability to work. It would be more workable if we had dedicated case managers and the technology to identify cases." He added, "The Juvenile and Family divisions, each in separate buildings, make the personal communication difficult. I'm just not sure that at this time we are accomplishing the supreme court mandates."

One might ask, why does it take over thirty years for a perfectly obvious solution to a complex problem to get off the ground? I suppose it's the nature of the beast. Dealing with the problems of people intertwined with the bureaucracy just isn't easy. Even though the concept dawdled along for decades, Judge Karlan, along with Judge Langer, have kept the project alive in the Eleventh Circuit. History will show that worthwhile efforts usually manage to stay afloat, no matter the last rites administered.

Because of her extensive work on this commission in support of families and children, Judge Karlan received the 2002 Florida Bar Judge Hugh Glickstein Child Advocate of the Year Award. In 2004 she was again recognized by the Greater Miami Jewish Federation with their Community Service Award.

When the model family court in the form of Division 48 brings speedier and more complete resolution to families in trouble, and legal protection for children becomes commonplace, it will be due to systemic alterations that leaders like

Judge Karlan and many of her colleagues will have designed. Nothing radical, just plain common sense.

Just as all significant changes in the juvenile justice system have been a long and difficult trials, so has the progress been for a unified family court. Time here is the ally. The slow, sometimes-uncertain progress made over the last half century suggests better prospects for this and the many others on the drawing board. Judges, like Sandy Karlan, have always risen to lead the vanguard. Thanks, Sandy.

Afterthoughts

This book started out as a kind of history of the role of the judges in the development of the court from its birth to adulthood. A simple-enough task to recite the many programs initiated by judges through the years. Over three hundred pages later, it turns out to be more than such a recitation. The activism described in this book validates the need for creation of such a court, separate and apart, for children. It affirms the original child-saver mode, though now clothed in far-different attire.

Here, in Dade County, and nationally, the juvenile court has crawled from idealism to reality. All the child-saver concepts remain, but more restrictive elements introduced into the process have added new dimensions. Progress is often measured by half steps. Looking at the Dade County Juvenile Court longitudinally, as recounted here, the test has been met.

Sitting as a judge is no picnic, particularly in the juvenile court. Dealing with family tragedy on a daily basis, with dysfunctional parents and too often no good end in sight, makes for trying days and sometimes sleepless nights. However, all who serve in social agencies addressing the needy, less fortunate, the clinically retarded, and others similarly situated, suffer these same circumstances.

There's no need to cry for the plight of juvenile court judges. Judges may make the final decisions that enhance or shatter lives, but their psyches are no more damaged than other professionals in the public service field. Doing this hour to hour, day to day leaves a mark, a discomfort many undergo in all walks of life. So, the bell does not toll for us.

Rather than personal regrets or deserving of sympathy, I believe those who undertook the juvenile court as life's main work have a special pride in their contribution. Some judges, talented lawyers as they were, like Walter Beckham and Bill Gladstone, who could have gained fame and fortune as esteemed legal practitioners, made the choice to stay in the pits for the long struggle, a voluntary one. To them it was almost as a patriotic duty to their country.

Others like Cindy Lederman and Jeri Beth Cohen came forward at first for equality, the desire to overcome injustice in the women's movement, and stayed to mount the cause for children. Some like Lester Langer, Adele Faske, Don Stone, and Dixie Chastain had already come up through the ranks of the juvenile court system and well knew the uncertainties ahead. Dr. Ben Sheppard and Tom Petersen made their marks for children before assuming a judgeship, continued their contribution on the bench, and then went on to further the lives of children in other venues. A disparate group, all were there to answer the call.

I have this feeling that while juvenile court judges may refer to the daily despair they face and the hopeless clientele they seem encumbered with, underneath is this fierce pride in what is accomplished. A result not always measured as a success, but in the effort itself worthy of prideful moments.

Progress has come mostly from incremental steps sometimes barely visible. The forward movement, measured in inches, between Judge Edith Atkinson in the 1920s and Judge Cindy Lederman eighty years later, shows Judge Atkinson vouching for many worthwhile programs that slowly moved forward without gaining fuller acceptance until many decades later.

In the early years of this twenty-first century, there are additional positive signs that portray signs of movement forward. The arrival of Division 48, titled the Complex Litigation Division, where one judge hears all the problems of a family, is a prime example. What better ideal than placing all the dilemmas of a family in one basket? Yet the bureaucratic and structural problems have made it a daunting task for many years. Nonetheless forward movement is evident. That has to be a healthy sign.

Another significant sight is the emergence of the Children's Trust. Created by a self-imposed citizen tax, it has since its inception in 2002 excelled in aiding the growth of privatization. Headed by David Lawrence, the trust has in three years leveraged over a million dollars annually primarily with private child-care community organizations. More than 35,000 students have been enriched in summer and after-school programs. Dave Lawrence not only created the trust but has personally given it a credibility and vigor long needed in the community of citizen advocacy.

Problem is that service agencies, public and private, must in the end primarily rely on State funding. A March 2006 report by the Florida Juvenile Justice Association warned, "Florida's Juvenile Justice System has reached the breaking point. Providers can no longer safely provide services at the existing reimbursement rate."

Clearly, unless Governor Bush and the legislature respond, our resurgent private service agencies may face the same fate as in the past has befallen our state agencies.

Still another sign that children's advocacy is alive and full of hope was the impressive turnout at the Children's Legislative Summit held in Miami. This was an informal brainstorming session on Friday, January 27, 2006, called by State Rep. J. C. Planas, a Miami Republican attempting to generate ideas for new laws.

Maybe only a vote-getting idea for the next election, but six hundred judges, prosecutors, public defenders, teachers, agency officials, citizens, and lawmakers showed up, not only with proposals for the next legislative session but with angry words directed at the Republican administration for failing to fund the needs.

Said Judge Lester Langer, with a touch of sarcasm, "It is wonderful to have the ability to make referrals to private agencies for services, but if there are no services, aren't we really just sending people to waiting lists, this accomplishing nothing?"

Supporting Langer was Florida Supreme Court Chief Justice Barbara Pariente, also in attendance. She observed, "This summit's best ideas and proposals will be falling on deaf ears unless lawmakers beef up spending for the programs."

The really noteworthy aspect of this gathering was that six hundred important leaders showed up to spend a full day on that Friday to dwell on these needs. By this appearance at only an informal session called by one legislator, a strong message emerged. Advocacy for children is growing far beyond the shrill voices of juvenile court judges despairing of community and government support. A momentum never before seen may be rising, involving the total community.

Another significant sign was the March 8, 2006, U.S. Justice Department "Report on Juvenile Offender and Victims" as front-paged in the *Miami Herald* of that date. The headline read, "U.S. Has Sharp Decline in Teenage Crime Rate." The subhead explained, "Despite experts' predictions a decade ago that juvenile crime would soar, Americans have experienced the sharpest decline in teen crime in modern history."

Criminologists, cited in the article, looking to determine what works, offered many reasons for the turnaround, but their answers offered no sure formula for the future. Some sociologists suggested that the decrease in juvenile crime and the improved safety in our streets and schools was attributed to the sound economic times.

> Older teens, neither in school nor at full-time jobs, are most likely to commit crimes. That number had dropped by nearly a third according to the U.S. Bureau of Labor Statistics. Prosperity gave teens more and better options than crime.

Unlike mayors and chiefs of police, our juvenile court judges cannot and do not claim credit whenever the juvenile crime numbers go down. Most likely, the decline or rise is cyclical, either from changes in the economy or a larger birth cohort reaching puberty and young manhood.

Whatever the cause of the decline, what bodes well for both the courts and the community is that the fear of savage juvenile crime sprees will be considerably lessened. Hopefully, this will result in the citizenry looking more favorably upon the courts introduction of long-range rehabilitation. Time will tell.

The juvenile justice system, often ignored and regularly maligned, has weathered many storms and has seen many leaders rise to the occasion. Some early grandiose cure-alls of yesteryear (boot camps) have withered away, and some continue to plod along.

Those situations have defined our juvenile justice system since birth. But who is to say that this new century, with intense new advocates from both the judicial and private sector, that our twenty-first century will not produce even finer, better-defined systems than now exist?

The juvenile court may never be a perfect vehicle for children, for perfection is not in the nature of things affecting humankind. But through the efforts of those who serve and those who care, the system, hopefully, will continue to move forward inch by inch, step by step. Both our children and our community will be better for it.

—S. G.

Index

A

Abety, Modesto 273
Abuse Hotline 355
ACLU. *See* American Civil Liberties Union
activist judge 14, 16, 20, 55, 61, 76, 81, 98, 110, 127, 152, 160, 197, 222, 223, 226, 230, 240, 245, 277, 278, 281, 282, 296, 349
Acts of 1911 32
Addams, Jane 20, 22, 28, 71, 127
Adorno, Hank 280, 346, 349, 350, 358
Adorno, Henry. *See* Adorno, Hank
Advisory Council of Judges 87
Agency for Persons with Disabilities 357
Allegheny, Pennsylvania 49
Allen, Mel 167
Allen's Drug Store 146
Alternative Program 279
Alternative Schools 284, 291
Alvarez, Carlos 374
American Association of University Women 58
American Bar Association 164, 389
American Civil Liberties Union 127, 128, 129, 141, 147, 271
American Express 286
American Legion Auxiliary Women's Group 79
AMI. *See* Associated Marine Institute
Anderson, Dwight, the Migrant 264
Andrew, Dorothy 79
Anna (Bill Gladstone's grandmother) 167
Annual TCA Report 286
APD. *See* Agency for Persons with Disabilities
Appalachia 168
ASFA (Adoption and Safe Families Act) 337
Associated Marine Institute 190, 191, 197, 198, 218, 224
Associated Press 144
Atkinson (Boys Club head) 50
Atkinson, Edith (née Meserve) 14, 15, 33, 36, 62
 appointment 36
 election 42, 43
 electoral defeat (judgeship) 59, 60, 67, 68, 69, 70, 71, 72, 73

electoral defeat (National Youth Administration) 61
juvenile court judge 37, 39, 41, 42, 45, 47, 48, 50, 51, 55, 56, 57, 59, 63, 65, 66, 76, 78, 89, 96, 103, 116, 143, 302, 378, 394
law school 36
marriage 36
reelection 56
relocation 35
Atkinson, Henry 36, 37, 39, 41, 42, 48, 61, 65, 66
August, Nimkoff & Gladstone 165
Auslander, Charles 335, 344, 347, 351
automobile crime 53
Aviation Building 154
Ayers, Georgia 279

B

Babbitt, Bruce 219
Baker Act 177, 374
Balaban, Henry 128
Balkin, Revy 163
Balmaseda, Liz 281
Band, Marice 308
Bangladesh 168
Bankers' Ticket 46
Barco, S. J. 61
Barkett, Rosemary 217, 224
Barreiro, Gus 280, 325, 341, 349
Barry College (old name).
    See Barry University
Barry University 325, 334
Bartle, A. H. 70
Bay County Sheriff's Office 302
Bayfront Park 69
Bazelon, David 207
BCYF. *See* Board on Children, Youth and Families
Beckham, Robert 82
Beckham, Walter
  death 105, 110
  early years and education 73
  election 58, 59, 62, 66, 72, 73

juvenile court judge 14, 15, 48, 50, 63, 74, 83, 84, 85, 89, 91, 93, 94, 97, 100, 102, 103, 106, 109, 123, 126, 139, 153, 158
pre-Miami 64
private lawyer 66
relocation 64
Behind the Black Robes (Rubin) 275
Bell, Marjorie 51
Bell, Paul 290
Berkowitz, David 266
Berkowitz, Linda 211, 270
Berlin, Germany 73
best interest of the child 48, 119, 128, 130, 141, 145, 154
Big Blow. *See* 1926 hurricane
Big Cypress National Preserve 219
Bilchik, Shay 219, 279
Bilikes, John 164
Bill of Rights for Retarded Persons 383
Billy the Kid 321
Bird, Preston 80
Birmingham, Alabama 167
Black Lawyer's Association 295
Blackwell, Walker & Gray 146
Blanton, Jack 95, 97, 98, 102, 103, 110, 126, 139, 150, 158
Blanton, W. F. 28, 58, 84
Blanton, Wayne 255, 257
Blecke, Berta 180, 181, 182, 184, 215, 279, 356
Blizin Sumberg 327
Blockton, Alabama 167
Blue Ribbon Panel 334, 343
Board of Visitors 49, 103, 123
Board on Children, Youth and Families 353
Bock, Anita 313
Bogotá 208
Booker T. Washington High School 44
Botkin, Leon 283
Boyle's law 297
Boys Club Aftercare Program 256, 257
Boys' Work, Inc. 49
Bradenton, Florida 226

Brief History of National Council of Juvenile Judges, A (Whitlach) 88
Britton, Leonard 170, 204, 205, 206, 253
Broad & Cassel 327
Bromley's Men's Wear 70
Brooklyn College Law School 115
Brooklyn Dodgers 167
Brown v. Board of Education 78
Brown, Carl 266
Brownell, Scott 226
Burdine's Department Store 52
Burns, Haydon 109, 131, 152, 153, 164
Burroughs, Gloria 205
Burrows, Lester, the Runner 263
Burwell, William 69
Bush, Jeb 316, 325, 330, 334, 340, 351, 355, 359, 363, 365

C

Caesar's Palace 255, 256
Caesar's World 255
Caldwell, Millard 61
Campbell, O. W. 99, 104, 120, 123
Cape Canaveral, Florida 65
capital punishment 384
Carol City High School 205
Carver Village 125
Castro, Fidel 112
Catholic Service Bureau 143
Catholic Welfare Bureau 143
CCC (Civilian Conservation Corps) 61, 189, 219, 293
Center for Florida Children 335
Central Florida 30, 46, 49, 189, 206, 312
Cermak, Anton 152
Chapman, Alvah 254
Chapter 8663 30
Characteristics of Adolescent Females in Juvenile Detention (Lederman) 325
CHARLEE 181, 182, 183, 187, 348, 385
  Family Care Therapeutic Group Homes 183
Charleston Naval Base 47
Chase, Henry 37

Chastain, Dixie (née Herlong) 109, 114, 129, 132, 151, 153, 154, 158, 171, 239, 240, 243
Chastain, R. B. 59
Chavez, Vanessa 288
Chicago, Illinois 13, 20, 21, 22, 23, 24, 26, 30, 31, 47, 48, 60, 74, 127, 152, 157, 160, 170, 211, 255
  Chicago Circuit Court 20
  Chicago Juvenile Court 20, 23, 25
Chiefs. *See* Kansas City Chiefs
Child Law Practice 323
Child Runaway Act. *See* Interstate Compact for the Return of Runaway Children
Child Support Program. *See* Dade State Attorney's Office:Division of Child Support Enforcement
Child Welfare Board 51
Child Welfare Committee of America 51
ChildNet 358
Children First 357
Children Services Councils 207
Children's Home Society 40, 51, 225, 312, 385
Children's Legislative Summit 395
Children's Service Council 273, 279
Children's Trust 124, 180, 207, 225, 273, 279, 289, 345, 394
Chiles, Lawton 216, 219, 220, 339
Christian Science Monitor 258
Cindy Lederman Relief Act 355
Citizens' Committee 247, 248
City of Miami Recreation Department 50
Civitan Club 29, 30
CJC. *See* Criminal Justice Council
Codina, Armando 217
Cohen, Jeri Beth 367, 371, 394
cold war 78
Coler, Gregory 211, 270
Collins, Leroy 84, 92, 93, 94
Colorado Supreme Court 25
Columbia Law School 148, 291
Columbus Hotel 54
Combs, J. J. 28

Commandments (Lederman) 322
Community Control 188, 210
Community-based Care Alliance 328, 346, 347, 350, 351, 355, 358, 365
Complex Litigation Division. *See* Division 48
comprehensive assessment 315
Congress for Racial Equality 125
Congressional Record 303
Connors, Tom 136
Consortium Project. *See* Petersen, Tom: Schools and Neighborhood Consortium
Cook County, Illinois 19, 22
Coral Gables 27, 40, 43, 54, 70, 105
  Methodist Church 85
CORE. *See* Congress for Racial Equality
Court Dependency Unit.
  See Dade County Juvnile Court: Dependency Section
Court Management Institute 379
Court Support Program 284, 285
Courtrooms in the Classrooms 366
Cowart, Ed 162, 388, 389
Crandon, C. H. 29
crash of 1929 42, 57
Crew, Rudy 180, 338
criminal court 13, 23, 30, 33, 37, 39, 59, 69, 84, 127, 133, 154, 174, 175, 186, 189, 200, 202, 203, 208, 292, 322, 337, 342, 367, 374, 384
Criminal Justice Council 210, 241, 248, 251, 252, 268
Criswell, Walter 87, 105
Cry For Help, A (Gladstone) 212
Cuba 31, 111, 157, 193
Cuban American Bar 295
Cuban Bar Association 193
Cuban Missile Crisis 111
Culbreath, William (Bill) 84, 85, 92, 93, 95, 96, 100, 107, 109, 110, 111, 124, 139, 142, 158
Cummins, Albert 21

D

D'Alemberte, Sandy 164
Dade County (now Miami-Dade) 13, 15, 16, 27, 28, 29, 30, 31, 32, 33, 37, 40, 48, 49, 53, 57, 58, 63, 73, 74, 79, 80, 81, 84, 85, 88, 92, 97, 99, 101, 103, 107, 108, 111, 114, 115, 117, 120, 121, 124, 125, 126, 132, 135, 137, 138, 140, 143, 150, 154, 156, 157, 159, 160, 161, 162, 164, 171, 173, 177, 180, 182, 183, 185, 187, 188, 191, 194, 202, 204, 205, 206, 208, 209, 213, 228, 230, 250, 253, 254, 255, 256, 257, 258, 259, 266, 270, 273, 274, 278, 279, 281, 282, 283, 289, 291, 294, 296, 301, 312, 313, 328, 334, 335, 339, 341, 344, 345, 346, 347, 348, 349, 351, 358, 360, 362, 364, 365, 368, 370, 373, 374, 379, 380, 381, 385, 388, 390, 393
Dade County Adult Drug Court 371
Dade County Association of Chiefs of Police 339
Dade County Bar Association 36, 44, 128, 380, 385
  Committee on Children 128
  Juvenile and Domestic Relations Committee 165
Dade County Board of Public Instruction 54, 206, 285
Dade County Board of Visitors. *See* Board of Visitors
Dade County Children's Service Bureau 41
Dade County Circuit Court 28, 310, 367, 387, 390
  Domestic Relations Division 152, 387
  Domestic Violence Division 342, 374, 376
  Special Mental Health Program 374
Dade County Commission 29, 30, 38, 49, 50, 71, 81, 84, 93, 96, 97, 98, 99, 100, 101, 103, 104, 117, 118,

Index

120, 121, 123, 126, 137, 138, 154, 156, 172, 195, 246, 248, 272, 298, 302, 378, 380
  Juvenile Facilities Committee 79
Dade County Corrections Department 240
Dade County Courthouse 37, 74
Dade County Department of Public Welfare 92
  Division of Child Welfare 92
Dade County Farm for Boys 37
Dade County Grand Jury 82, 85, 90, 91, 92, 93, 94, 95, 99, 103, 118, 120, 121, 124, 133, 142, 239, 241, 242, 244, 245, 251
Dade County Juvenile Council 79
Dade County Juvenile Court 14, 16, 26, 31, 61, 72, 84, 87, 92, 159, 192, 211, 219, 318, 334, 346, 393
  Delinquency Section 310
  Dependency Court Intervention Program 319
  Dependency Section 311, 387
  Mental Health Clinic 148
  Probation Services Division 102
  Senior Judge Division 336
Dade County Juvenile Welfare Board 271
Dade County Juvnile Court
  Dependency Section 15
Dade County Mental Health Association 175, 208, 227
Dade County Personnel Department 101
Dade County Public Health Trust 180
Dade County Public Schools 288, 377
Dade County School Board 52, 69, 71, 143, 170, 179, 180, 205, 260, 268, 271, 288, 291, 294
Dade County School Counseling Unit 205
Dade County Social Workers 54
Dade County Times 55
Dade County Welfare Department 82, 96, 99, 101, 103, 123, 124, 142
Dade County Welfare Planning Council 99
Dade County Youth Crime Task Force 349

Dade Juvenile Hall 80, 90, 91, 101, 103, 104, 105, 110, 114, 117, 121, 122, 125, 126, 143, 147, 150, 154, 157, 172, 175, 176, 201, 242, 244, 245, 248, 249, 251, 260, 270, 300, 385
  Intake Center 201
Dade Marine Institute 198, 226, 297, 340, 371
Dade Public Defender's Office 148
Dade State Attorney's Office 93, 298
  Division of Child Support Enforcement 251, 316
Dade Women's Welfare Coalition 292
Dallas Park 43
Daniel (photography student) 308
Davis, Darrey 103, 124
DCF. *See* Department of Children and Families
DCF Children's Summit 345
DCMHA. *See* Dade County Mental Health Association
DDC. *See* dependency drug court
Deep South 167
delinquency cases. *See* under juvenile justice system
delinquency drug court 371
Democratic Party Convention 255
Democratic Party Executive Committee 30, 37, 71
Democrats 14, 61, 69, 72, 156, 211, 220, 316, 355, 358
Dennis 128, 129
Dennis the Menace 321
Dennis, George 128
Denver County Sheriff's Office 25
Denver Juvenile Court 24, 25, 275
Denver, Colorado 13, 20, 23, 24, 25, 30, 31, 116, 127, 147, 160, 170, 299, 379
Department of Children and Families 317, 328, 330, 331, 332, 333, 335, 343, 345, 346, 348, 349, 350, 351, 353, 355, 356, 357, 359, 363, 364, 374, 375. *See also* Department of Health and Rehabilitative Services

401

Department of Health and Rehabilitative Services 114, 132, 135, 136, 137, 139, 154, 155, 156, 158, 171, 173, 176, 178, 184, 188, 189, 192, 193, 195, 201, 207, 208, 209, 210, 211, 212, 213, 220, 222, 242, 243, 246, 248, 249, 250, 258, 260, 264, 267, 269, 270, 276, 283, 289, 300, 312, 313, 316, 331, 348, 383, 384
dependency cases. *See under* juvenile justice system
Dependency Court Intervention Program. *See under* Dade County Juvenile Court
dependency drug court 366, 368, 369, 371
Des Moines, Iowa 20
Destiny (juvenile delinquent) 325
Di Tomasso, Michael 357
Division 48 387
Dixie Herlong Chastain Building 155
DMI. *See* Dade Marine Institute
Dodgers. *See* Brooklyn Dodgers
domestic relations court 47, 48, 152
Donor's Forum 167
Driscoll, Amy 301
DUI (driving under the influence) 368
Duncan, Ted 93
Durant, Joe 173
Durant, Napoleon. *See* Durant, Joe

E

early intervention 16, 187, 192, 212, 216, 224, 227, 338
Eaton, Joe 238, 240, 243
Ebbets Field 167
Eckerd, Jack 199
Edelstein, Charles (Chuck) 276, 379
Eisenhower, Dwight (Ike) 78
Eleventh Judicial Circuit. *See* Dade County Circuit Court
Elks Club 52
Ellen, Mary 22
Elroy (student inmate) 265
Em's 229

Emory University 74
Episcopal Diocese of South Florida 182
Epstein, Gail 301

F

Faber, Robin 372
Fabrico, Roberto 260
Family Care Therapeutic Group Homes. *See under* CHARLEE
family court 15, 142, 161, 162, 163, 166, 169, 170, 171, 341, 387, 388, 390. *See also* Division 48
Family Division. *See* Division 48
Farina, Joseph 162, 310, 374, 388
Farris, Wayne 136
Faske, Adele 250
FDA (Food and Drug Administration) 144
FEI. *See* Florida Environmental Institute
Ferguson, John 162, 164, 165
Ferguson, Wilkie 17
Ferré, Maurice 298, 338
Fischl, Margaret 270
Fisheating Creek 189, 218
Fisher, Ida 28
Five Hundred Model Citizens 291
Flagler Street 63, 70, 75, 79, 80, 90, 162
Flagler Street courthouse. *See* Dade County Courthouse
Flagler, Henry 27, 40
Fletcher, Duncan 61
Florida 14, 16, 27, 28, 31, 32, 33, 35, 36, 37, 39, 42, 45, 48, 50, 51, 52, 56, 60, 61, 76, 81, 86, 87, 88, 89, 90, 93, 94, 104, 111, 119, 127, 129, 130, 132, 150, 151, 161, 177, 184, 187, 189, 191, 194, 197, 199, 202, 208, 212, 217, 218, 219, 221, 226, 228, 240, 252, 256, 258, 259, 261, 271, 278, 321, 323, 333, 340, 344, 346, 347, 356, 359, 376, 378, 394
State of Florida (government) 30, 81, 82, 93, 97, 99, 106, 117, 120, 121, 125, 126, 132, 135, 137, 138, 148, 154, 155, 156, 157, 171, 172, 175,

Index

176, 177, 178, 180, 181, 182, 184, 185, 187, 188, 193, 195, 200, 203, 209, 214, 220, 248, 267, 277, 283, 288, 298, 301, 311, 317, 320, 322, 330, 334, 336, 340, 347, 348, 350, 351, 355, 356, 358, 363, 375, 381
Florida A&M University 264
Florida Atlantic University 198
Florida Bar 31, 56, 86, 115, 161, 170, 171, 213, 267, 389
  Advisory Committee 213
  Commission on the Legal Needs of Children 389
  Florida Bar News 226
  Judge Hugh Glickstein Child Advocate of the Year Award 390
  Juvenile and Domestic Relations Committee 165
  Medical-Legal Committee 116
Florida Bar Association. *See* Florida Bar
Florida Child Abuse Death Review Team 332
Florida Commission on Community Service 300
Florida Conference of Circuit Court Judges 183
Florida Congressional Delegation 61
Florida Constitution 109, 113, 121, 131, 132, 133, 134, 135, 137, 155
  Article V 15, 108, 131, 134, 135, 136, 153, 155, 156, 171, 225
Florida Council on Crime and Delinquency 89
Florida Department of Children and Families. *See* Department of Children and Families
Florida Department of Corrections 189, 341
Florida Department of Health 271
Florida Department of Health and Rehabilitative Services. *See* Department of Health and Rehabilitative Services
Florida Department of Juvenile Justice 301, 323, 324, 341, 378

Florida Department of Law Enforcement 330
Florida Department of Transportation 368
Florida Environmental Institute 188, 189, 191, 197, 218, 219, 221
  Last Chance Ranch 189, 191, 197, 218, 221, 230, 264
Florida Fish and Game Department 44
Florida House of Representatives Judiciary Committee 132
Florida International University 157, 365
Florida Juvenile Court Judges Association 89
Florida Juvenile Justice Association 348, 394
Florida Keys 168
Florida land boom 27, 42, 44, 45, 64, 65
Florida Legislature 131, 156, 172, 183, 184, 185, 209, 213, 217, 222, 296, 342, 343, 368, 383
Florida's Strategic Plan for Infant Mental Health (Gladstone) 227
Florida State College for Women (old name). *See* Florida State University
Florida State Constitution 225
Florida State Police 57
Florida State University 58, 305
  Law School 164
Florida Supreme Court 56, 81, 132, 162, 175, 224, 226, 241, 318, 357, 387, 388, 390, 395
  Gender Bias Study Commission 324
  Judicial Qualifications Commission 137
Fontaine, Mark 348
Food Fair 164
Fort Lauderdale 189, 198
Fort Meyers, Florida 258
Fort Pierce, Florida 264
Foster Care Review Project 214, 225, 327, 345
Foster, Cornelius 263, 264, 267
Fox, Roberta 185, 248

G

GAL. *See* Guardian ad Litem
GAP (Girls' Advocacy Project) 323, 325, 327, 349
  Advisory Board 325
Gault 14, 15, 33, 56, 80, 82, 83, 108, 109, 121, 127, 129, 132, 133, 134, 136, 138, 139, 140, 141, 146, 147, 148, 149, 154, 155, 156, 160, 162, 168, 171, 203, 213, 214, 224, 225
Gault, Gerald 130. See also *Gault*
Gautier, T. N. 29
Gautier, William 85, 94
Gelber Gardens 287
Gelber, Barbara 262
Gelber, Daniel 262
Gelber, Edith 218, 262, 272
Gelber, Judy 262
Gelber, Seymour
  AIDS program 269
  assistant state attorney 238
  gang control 268
  Hard-Core Delinquents Reaching out through the Miami Experiment 265
  juvenile court judge 171, 192, 198, 239, 241, 261, 265, 272, 275
  Palace 273
  Profile of Dade County Juvenile Crime 252
  The Juvenile Justice System: Vision of the Future 224
  Where Have Our Heroes Gone? 261
General Assembly of Iowa 20
George (young burglar) 195
Georgia Fruit Growers' Exchange 74
Georgia General Assembly 64, 66, 72, 110
Georgia legislature. *See* Georgia General Assembly
Gerstein, Norman 248, 383
Gerstein, Richard (Dick) 93, 133, 135, 136, 164, 186, 238, 240, 243, 255, 261, 292
Gibson, Theodore 261

Gideon 127, 129, 130
Gievers, Karen 279, 334, 364
Gill, Joe 49
Girl Scout Council 62
Girl Scouts of America 52, 62
Girls Are People. *See* GAP
Gladstone, Adam 167
Gladstone, Essie 167
Gladstone, Irving 167
Gladstone, Lee 167
Gladstone, Marilynn 167
Gladstone, William (Bill)
  "Interruption" 229
  A Cry For Help 212
  election 163
  Florida's Strategic Plan for Infant Mental Health 227
  Gladstone Treatment Center 183
  interview 161
  juvenile court judge 15, 53, 136, 139, 143, 160, 163, 166, 169, 174, 182, 183, 184, 186, 191, 193, 198, 210, 211, 239, 240, 242, 243, 259, 267, 284, 314, 315, 318, 339, 341, 359, 380, 387, 388, 394
  private lawyer 168
  retirement 217, 220, 221, 225, 230, 310
  Tallahassee designer 188, 202, 205, 206, 221, 259
  William E. Gladstone Campus 224
  William Gladstone Award 226
Gladstone, Calvin 167
Gladview Center 262
Glen Mills Academy 286
Gold, Mike 203
Goldstein, Stanley 367
Goode, Ray 124
Goodman, Joni 184, 186, 215, 225
Goodrich, Mario 17
Gordon, Elaine 185
Gordon, Jack 156, 185, 259
Goss, Porter 220
Governor's Constituency for Children 207
Graham, Billy 230

Index

Graham, Bob 164, 183, 187, 188, 189, 191, 202, 207, 211, 218, 219, 220, 224, 280, 310, 383
Graham, Ed 261
Graham, Geralyn 329, 330, 332, 333, 343, 358
Graham, Pamela 329, 332, 333
Gray, Young 27
Great Depression 51, 60, 65, 74, 77, 78, 90, 92, 116, 189, 293
Greater Miami Chamber of Commerce 54, 254, 272
Greater Miami Crime Commission 186, 248
Greater Miami Jewish Federation Community Services Award 385
Green, Lex 61
Greenberg Traurig 327
Gross, Ludwig (Sonny) 205, 206
Grotegut, Joe 94
Guardian ad Litem 181, 184, 185, 186, 313, 327, 345, 364

H

Haast, Bill 144
Hall, Irvin 32
Hall, M. Lewis 40
Hampton, Bill 172
Hard-Core Delinquents Reaching out through the Miami Experiment (Gelber and Bailey) 265
hard-core juvenile crime. *See* juvenile crime:violent
Hardee, Cary 30, 31, 36
Harding, Major 226
Harper, Steve 362
Harris, Estelle 32
Harris, Marshall 164, 172
Harry (student inmate) 265
Harvard Law Review 23
Harvard University
  Kennedy School of Government 215
  Law School 23, 64, 73, 74, 215
Hazlett, Ira 79

Helen Williams 41
Henry Street 145, 158
Henry Street Settlement 22
heroin 144
Hialeah Junior High School 266
Hialeah, Florida 85
Hibiscus Island 44
Hilton, George 49
Hitler, Adolf 73, 78
Holland & Knight 82, 273, 274, 327
Holman, Hillis 97
Hoover, Herbert 57
Hopkins, Harry 293
Horvi MS9 144
Hotel Granada 54
House Juvenile Justice Committee 325, 340
House of Refuge 19, 22
HRS. *See* Department Health and Rehabilitative Services
HSC. *See* Human Services Coalition
Hubanks, Alan 192
Hubbard, Wally 220
HUD (U.S. Housing and Urban Development) 296
Hughes, Doug 268
Huizenga, Wayne 217
Hull House 20, 22
Human Services Coalition 279
Hurricane Andrew 168
Hurricane Katrina 358
Hyatt Hotel 68

I

IACCJ. *See* International Association of Children's Court Judges
IMHPP. *See* Infant and Young Children's Mental Health Project
Immigration and Naturalization Service 194, 195
in loco parentis 20
Independent Living Program 350
  Independent Living Advisory Panel 317
Industrial Claims Commission 141

Industrial Farm 49
Industrial Revolution 20
Infant and Young Children's Mental Health Project 322
Infant Mental Health Interventions in Juvenile Court (Lederman) 335
INS. *See* Immigration and Naturalization Service
Institute of Medicine 353
International Association of Children's Court Judges 88
International Conference of Juvenile and Family Court Magistrates 88
International Journal of Law and Psychiatry 325
"Interruption" (Gladstone) 229
Interstate Compact for the Return of Runaway Children 87, 88, 333
Intervention Program for Family Violence 322
IRS (U.S. Internal Revenue Services) 241

J

J (juvenile delinquent) 266
JAC. *See* Juvenile Assessment Center
Jack and Ruth Admire Foundation 295
Jackson Memorial Hospital 96, 177, 217, 270
  AIDS Clinic 270
  Child Guidance Clinic 123
  Psychiatric Institute 96
Jackson, Nakeil 287
Jacksonville, Florida 184
Jacobson, Gus 247
Jarvis, Verne 194
Jaski, Gerald 248
Jimenez, Julio 375
JMH. *See* Jackson Memorial Hospital
Joey (juvenile delinquent) 200
Johnson, Laurie 32
Johnson, William 370
Journal of the American Psychological Association 335, 336

Joyce, Israel 290
Judge Ad. *See* Atkinson, Henry
Judge Hugh Glickstein Child Advocate of the Year Award. *See under* Florida Bar
Judge's Journal 309
judicial activism. *See* activist judge
Julia Tuttle Causeway 69
Junior League of Miami 40, 41, 49, 51, 78, 79, 181, 185, 248, 296
Juvenile and Family Court Journal 224
Juvenile Assessment Center 298, 338
juvenile crime 33, 118, 119, 188, 203, 252, 258, 300, 384, 395
  female 257
  Latin 254
  violent 14, 91, 93, 119, 151, 181, 251, 314
Juvenile Justice 322
juvenile justice system 13, 16, 103, 178, 188, 191, 202, 203, 211, 217, 223, 224, 225, 227, 257, 258, 259, 263, 278, 288, 303, 307, 308, 310, 317, 323, 327, 338, 339, 348, 362, 371, 381, 391, 394, 396
  delinquency cases 16, 32, 53, 54, 61, 104, 143, 187, 199, 203, 208, 211, 213, 214, 216, 224, 253, 254, 257, 269, 284, 292, 294, 297, 298, 306, 310, 314, 323, 326, 337, 338, 341, 343, 380
  dependency cases 15, 16, 32, 53, 54, 61, 84, 104, 119, 121, 149, 152, 181, 184, 185, 186, 187, 201, 203, 209, 211, 212, 213, 215, 216, 224, 230, 307, 310, 312, 314, 315, 318, 319, 323, 327, 330, 335, 337, 341, 354, 363, 365, 380
Juvenile Justice System, The: Vision of the Future (Gelber) 224
Juvenile Justice Update (Rubin) 24
JWB. *See* Dade County Juvenile Welfare Board

K

Kansas City 330
Kansas City Chiefs 226
Karlan, Sandy 143, 341, 387
Kearney, Kathleen 330, 332, 334, 335, 344
Kellner, Leon 273
Kendall, Florida 49
Kendall Boys Center. *See* Kendall Children's Home
Kendall Children's Home 58, 75, 99, 101, 103, 110, 114, 120, 121, 124, 126, 129, 150, 155, 239
Kendall County Home for Children. *See* Kendall Children's Home
Kendall Hall. *See* Kendall Children's Home
Kendall Home. *See* Kendall Children's Home
Kendall Residential Placement Institution. *See* Kendall Children's Home
Kendall Youth Hall. *See* Kendall Children's Home
Kendall Youth Home. *See* Kendall Children's Home
Kennedy, John 133
Kent v. United States 82
Key West Juvenile Court 41
Key West, Florida 31, 41
Kids' Judge. *See* Lindsey, Ben
King, Larry 141
Kiwanis Club 51, 52, 54, 58
Klein, Herbert 367, 370
Knight Ridder 279
Knight, Dewey 97, 150
Kogan, Gerald 175
Kohl, Herb 220
Ku Klux Klan 25, 77, 125
Kyne, James (Jimmy) 165

L

Labor's Citizenship Committee 70
Lake Okeechobee 189, 301
LaMont, George 285
Langer, Lester 162, 212, 298, 310, 323, 338, 339, 341, 342, 343, 357, 388, 389, 390, 395
Langston Hughes Academy 288, 289, 290, 291
Larch-Mart 295
Larchmont Gardens 281, 293, 294, 304
Larrea, Mary 325
Last Chance Ranch. *See under* Florida Environmental Institute
Latin Builder's Association 272
Lawrence, David (Dave) 124, 180, 207, 225, 273, 279, 289, 330, 334, 343, 358, 394
Lawyers for Children in America 327
League of Women Voters 43, 212, 248, 272
Leatherman, Buck 59
Lederman, Cindy
  "Commandments" 322
  Characteristics of Adolescent Females in Juvenile Detention 325
  county court judge 319
  early life and education 352
  Infant Mental Health Interventions in Juvenile Court 335
  interview 352
  juvenile court judge 15, 53, 143, 162, 187, 192, 215, 223, 225, 227, 278, 306, 307, 310, 311, 317, 325, 335, 341, 343, 346, 347, 348, 349, 351, 354, 356, 357, 359
  Rilya Wilson case 329, 343, 347, 358
Leifman, Steve 373
Levi, Edward 241
Levine, Daniella 279
Levine, Jack 334
Levine, Steve 270
Levy, Bruce 299
Lewis, Fred 389
Lewis, Hamilton 71
Leyva, Jenny 288
Liberty City 125, 157, 190, 198, 262, 264, 282, 300, 304

Liberty Square 281, 295
Liberty Square Mart 295
Licko, Carol 334
Liege, Belgium 88
Lindsey, Ben 20, 23, 24, 25, 26, 116, 127, 147, 299
Literacy through Photography 309
Little League 294
Little Rivers Neighborhood Association 274
LiveScan 338
Loeb, Sophie 51
Louisiana State University 335
Lower East Side 22, 145
Loyola University 58
Lum's 255
Lummus, Martha 41
Lummus Park 77

M

Mack, Julian 20, 23
MADD (Mothers Against Drunk Driving) 366
Maloney, W. C. 27
Margolius, Rick 245, 246
Marianna State School for Boys 30, 50, 150, 175, 192, 200
Marianna, Florida 49
Mariel Boatlift 157, 193, 195, 259
Married Ladies' Afternoon Club. *See* Miami Woman's Club
Martindale-Hubbell Law Directory 160
Martinez, Bob 282
Marxist 73
Mary Ellen case 22
McAliley, Janet 268, 271, 272, 279
McCarthyism 78
McCloskey, Donald 77
McMartin family 181
McNayr, Irving 117, 118, 119, 120, 121, 123, 124, 125, 126, 138, 142, 146
Medicaid 315, 333
Meek, Carrie 303
Mellon, James 49

Menninger Clinic 143, 182
Mental Health Needs of Young Persons 208
Mercersburg Academy 160
Merriwether, Heath 295
methadone 144
Metro. *See* Metropolitan Home Rule
Metropolitan Home Rule 97, 99, 100, 103, 117
  Youth and Family Development Agency 295
Metro Justice Building 293
Miami 26, 27, 30, 31, 33, 35, 36, 38, 39, 42, 43, 44, 45, 46, 47, 50, 51, 52, 55, 58, 60, 61, 62, 63, 65, 68, 69, 74, 77, 78, 86, 90, 110, 111, 127, 133, 146, 148, 149, 151, 184, 193, 195, 198, 224, 256, 259, 264, 268, 292, 295, 298, 302, 306, 314, 342, 367, 368
Miami Beach 27, 43, 44, 66, 69, 163, 218, 247, 255, 268, 280, 373
Miami Beach Democratic Club 70
Miami Beach Elementary School 71
Miami Beach Municipal Court 65
Miami Boys Club 50, 226, 255, 257, 262
Miami Central High School 205
Miami City Charter 27
Miami Herald 29, 31, 41, 43, 57, 58, 69, 70, 71, 73, 74, 79, 82, 91, 100, 101, 102, 105, 114, 122, 125, 126, 129, 133, 134, 140, 143, 148, 165, 166, 172, 180, 192, 194, 201, 209, 222, 224, 225, 251, 252, 253, 257, 259, 262, 265, 270, 273, 278, 279, 281, 282, 283, 287, 289, 295, 297, 301, 305, 308, 313, 317, 322, 326, 330, 334, 339, 340, 343, 346, 348, 350, 351, 355, 356, 358, 359, 361, 365, 371, 372, 374, 375, 384, 395
  Spirit of ExcellenceAwards 303
  Spirit of ExcellenceAward 217
Miami Herald Publishing Company 254
Miami Historical Society 43
Miami Lions Club 40

Miami Mental Health Association 177
   Blue Ribbon Panel 177
Miami New Times 287, 335
Miami News 42, 43, 91, 134, 222, 241,
   242, 244, 245, 257
Miami Northwestern High School 205
Miami Organization of Junior League
   Girls. *See* Junior League of Miami
Miami Review 56
Miami River 43, 77, 78
Miami Safe Start Initiative 322
Miami Serpentarium 144
Miami Variety Children's Hospital 113
Miami Woman's Club 28, 29, 40, 44,
   78, 79
Miami-Dade College 300, 371
Miami-Dade Community College 175
Miami-Dade County. *See* Dade County
Miami-Dade Police Department 377
microlending 168
Miller, H. Dale 29
Milton, Israel 150
Mitzvah Camp. *See* Summer Fun for Kids
Modello Housing Project 281, 296
Monroe County, Florida 27, 80, 347
Moore, Andrea 357
Moore, Mark 215
Morphonios, Ellen 186
Most Wanted 333
MS. *See* multiple sclerosis
multiple sclerosis 144
Multiple Sclerosis Society 144
Myers, Ken 164, 172

N

Nathan, Ray 129, 130, 155
National Center for State Courts 380
National Children's Welfare Bureau 279
National College of Juvenile Justice 203
National Conference on Reciprocal
   Support 251
National Congress of Mothers 20
National Council of Jewish Women 181
National Council of Juvenile and Family
   Court Judges 208, 354
Juvenile Court Centennial Initiative 228
National Council of Juvenile Court Judges
   81, 86, 87, 88, 105, 187, 227
*Journal of the National Council of Juvenile
   Court Judges* 88, 105, 369
National Juvenile Court Foundation 88
National Probation Association 51
National Research Council 353
National Youth Administration 61
Nazi 73
NCJCJ. *See* National Council of Juvenile
   Court Judges
NCJFCJ. *See* National Council of
   Juvenile and Family Court Judges
NCJW. *See* National Council of
   Jewish Women
New Orleans 58
New York City 13, 19, 21, 26, 47, 48, 50,
   57, 60, 74, 113, 115, 119, 141, 145,
   149, 167, 268, 370
New York Society for the Prevention of
   Cruelty to Children 22
New York Times 47, 258, 260
New York Yankees 167
Nicholson, Robert 99, 101, 123
Nimkoff, Peter 128
1926 hurricane 40, 45, 46, 51, 57, 65
Non-Group 204
Norma (photography student) 308
North Key Largo 44

O

O'Laughlin, Jeanne 334
O'Reilly, Christine 320
Okeechobee Boys Training School 95,
   150, 176, 199, 206, 288
Okeechobee Corrections Center for
   Delinquents. *See* Okeechobee
   Boys Training School
Okeechobee, Florida 95, 176, 206
Old People's Home 49
Olympia Building 65
Oprah 181

original intent 14
Orlando, Frank 197, 198
Orr, Alexander, III 40
Orr, Jack 261
Orr, John 114
Osborne, Marie 301, 362
Osofsky, Joy 335
Our Kids 280, 345, 346, 347, 348, 350, 356, 358
Ozohu (plantation owner) 32

P

Pahokee Youth Development Center 301, 302
Palace. *See under* Gelber, Seymour
Pan Hellenic Club 43
Pancoast, Kay 40, 51
parens patriae 83, 203
Pariente, Barbara 162, 389, 395
Patrick (juvenile delinquent) 250
Paul, Dan 251
Payne, Walter 30
Peace Corps 292
Pedro (student inmate) 266
Penny, H. W. 30, 31, 36, 225
Perlman, Clifford 255, 256
Petersen, Thomas. *See* Petersen, Tom
Petersen, Tom
  "Rethinking Juvenile Justice" 297
  assistant state attorney 192
  chief assistant state attorney 292
  juvenile court judge 15, 141, 150, 279, 280, 282, 296, 298, 303, 318, 338, 359, 373, 377, 394
  juvenile court lawyer 149
  public defender 148
  resignation 303, 304, 305
  Schools and Neighborhood Consortium 292
  sociology professor 304
  VISTA member 292, 303
  What If Oswald Had Missed? (forthcoming) 306
Peterson, Pete 77

Phi Delta Delta 48
Piaget, Jean 191, 192, 208, 318
Picturing Ourselves Project 308
Pike County, Georgia 73
Pingree, David 209
Pinkney, Enid 44
Planas, J. C. 395
Polaroid Corporation 309
Pomerance, Rocky 255
Portland, Maine 35, 38, 47, 56, 62, 73
Pretrial Intervention Program 292
PREVENT 322
Pride Program 143
Probation and Parole Association (old name). *See* Florida Council on Crime and Delinquency
Profile of Dade County Juvenile Crime (Gelber) 252
PROven 144

R

Raiford State Prison 264
Ramsey, Laurie 212, 213
Ravlin, F. J. 49
Reader's Digest 118
Reaffirmation of United Family Court Plan. 388
Redfearn, Daniel 105
Regier, Jerry 328, 335
Reno, Doris 134
Reno, Henry 134
Reno, Janet 132, 134, 135, 136, 202, 212, 218, 219, 224, 268, 271, 272, 292, 298, 346
Report on Juvenile Offender and Victims; report override 395
Republicans 14, 57, 69, 199, 211, 220, 255, 280, 291, 316, 344, 349, 355, 395
Resource Support Program 260
Rethinking Juvenile Justice (Petersen) 297
Rhonda (prostitute) 212, 213
Rice, Richard 94
Rich, Nan 181, 182, 184, 185, 355
Richard Gerstein Criminal Court 374

Rilya Wilson case. *See under* Lederman, Cindy
Ripley's Believe It or Not! 82
Rippingille, Bonnie 376
Rivkind (judge) 336
Roberts, B. K. 241
Robertson, Pat 168
Roe v. Wade 369
Rogers, William 256
Ronald, Reagan 157
Ronnie Zamora case 251
Roosevelt, Franklin 51, 57, 61, 70, 152
Roosevelt, Theodore 26
Rosof, Robert 197, 198
Rotary Club 263
Rothman, Max 156, 157, 192, 246, 249
Rubin, Ellis 251
Rubin, Ted 25, 275, 277
 "Juvenile Justice Update" 24
 Behind the Black Robes 275
Ruden McCloskey 77
Runaway Compact. *See* Interstate Compact for the Return of Runaway Children
Rundle, Katherine 329

S

Sam Powers 146
Samika (photography student) 308
Samuels, Lawrence, the Fighter 264
Savannah, Georgia 38
Scared Straight 252
Schools and Neighborhood Consortium. *See under* Peterson, Tom
Schulz, Dave 73
Schuster, Jennifer 286, 288, 289, 291, 304, 377
Scoville, William 100
Sears, W. J. 61
Seigendorf, Arden 130
Seminole Indians 27, 28
Seminole Wars 27
Sheehan, D. E. 29
Shellow, Ron 164

Shenandoah Junior High 71
Sheppard, Ben
 childhood 145
 death 144
 doctor 111, 113, 116, 143, 144, 146
 election 114, 152
 juvenile court judge 15, 105, 109, 111, 114, 116, 118, 124, 128, 145, 146, 147, 154, 155, 158, 394
 private lawyer 146
 resignation 109, 130, 139, 142, 143, 146
Sheppard, Thelma 148
Shevin, Robert 151
Silbert, Jeffrey 210
Sills, Andy, "the Drinker" 264
Silver, Sam 167
Simon, Tobias 127, 129, 130, 141
Sims, Joyner 269
Sinclair, Upton 26
Sister City Program 208
Sisters of the Heart 376
60 Minutes 144
Smith, James 95
Smith, Marlyn 135, 138, 149, 158, 201, 209, 248
Smith, William 28
Snedigar, Fred 29
Society for Prevention of Cruelty to Animals 22
Socol, Sharon 308, 309, 310
Son of Sam. *See* David Berkowitz
South Dade 32, 164
South Florida 45, 111, 259, 328, 335
South Florida Calligraphy Guild 168
South Florida Evaluation and Treatment Center 374
South Florida Rural Services 156
South Florida State Hospital 177
Southridge High School 205
Spanish-American War 31
Spirit of Excellence Award. *See under Miami Herald*
Spock, Benjamin (Dr. Spock) 145
State of Florida (government). *See under* Florida

State of Florida Probation and Parole
    Association 86
Steinberg, Marty 273, 274
Stembler, George 29
Stepherson, Johnny 205, 206
Stetson Law School 36
Stetson University 60
Stierheim, Merrett 248
Stone, Donald (Don) 97, 98, 109, 110, 111,
    112, 129, 130, 131, 132, 135, 136,
    137, 139, 140, 141, 142, 148, 149,
    150, 151, 154, 155, 158, 171, 239
storaging 15, 291
Strange, Michael. *See* Oelricks, Blanche
street gangs 268
Sullivan, Dan 186
Summer Fun for Kids 385
Sun Bank 262
Sundberg, Allen 189
Sunland Training Center 383
Swan, Ed 145, 146

T

Tallahassee, Florida 29, 58, 69, 94, 133,
    155, 156, 187, 188, 202, 203, 205,
    206, 207, 209, 220, 223, 238, 257,
    270, 279, 280, 283, 316, 328, 332,
    335, 340, 344, 346, 351, 360, 364
Tampa Juvenile Court 52
Tampa, Florida 31, 52, 298
TAP. *See* Truancy Alternatives Program
Taro, Robert (Bob) 114, 138, 158, 194, 242
TCA. *See* Troy Community Academy
Teen Cuisine 287, 288
Temple Beth Shalom 373
Temple Judea 385
Third and Long Foundation 226
Third District Court of Appeals 17, 129,
    318, 333, 336, 357, 359
Thomas, Derrick 226
Thompson, Lawrence 114
Thursday morning conclave 260
Time 174

Titusville, Florida 38, 65
Toulmin, Harry 100, 101, 103
Trammell, Park 61
Transition Task Force on
    Juvenile Justice 216
TROY (Teaching and Rehabilitating Our
    Youth) 285, 286, 288, 289, 290,
    291, 296, 298, 304, 377
Troy Community Academy 286
Truancy Alternatives Program 299
Tuthill, Richard 20, 23, 24
Tutty, Ed 148, 259
TV Seven 136

U

U.S. Armed Forces 40
U.S. Attorney General's Office
    Office of Juvenile Justice 215
U.S. Attorney's Office
    Weed and Seed 343
U.S. Children's Bureau 26, 55
U.S. Civil Rights Commission 202
U.S. Department of Defense 169
U.S. Department of Education 289
U.S. Department of Justice 132, 279, 395
U.S. House of Representatives 55
U.S. Immigration Services 194
U.S. Navy Air Reserve 142
U.S. Securities and Exchange
    Commission 369
U.S. Senate 87, 191
    Subcommittee on the Judiciary 191
U.S. Supreme Court 14, 15, 33, 56, 78,
    80, 82, 84, 108, 109, 113, 124, 127,
    128, 129, 131, 135, 136, 139, 141,
    142, 151, 153, 154, 155, 196, 203,
    225, 314
Uniform Reciprocal Enforcement of
    Support Act 88, 251
United Way 212, 214, 294, 296, 346, 375
    Public Leadership Award 375
University of Alabama Press 265
University of Buffalo Law Review 323

Index

University of Miami 65, 116, 248, 304, 305
   Center for Treatment Research on
      Adolescent Drug Users 371
   Criminal Justice Program 136
   Law School 115, 116, 152, 365, 379
   Linda Ray Center 322, 369
   School of Medicine 325, 341
University of Southern California 379
Urban League 272
URESA. *See* Uniform Reciprocal
   Enforcement of Support Act

V

Veterans of Foreign Wars 252
Vietnam War 255, 264, 291
Vigilucci, Andres 282, 283
Visiedo, Octavio 285, 288
Visiting School Teacher Program 42
VISTA (Volunteers in Service to America
   148, 292, 303, 306
Voices for Children 186

W

W&S (Weed and Seed). *See under* U.S.
   Attorney's Office
Wald, Lillian 22, 28
Walsh, Beckham & Ellis 65, 73
Walsh, William 65, 66, 68
Walter Beckham Youth Hall. *See* Dade
   Juvenile Hall
Walters, Dave 146
Washington and Lee University 160, 168
Washington, D.C. 55, 58, 132, 169, 218,
   221, 280, 295, 360, 369
Watson, Cecil 38
Weather Bureau 46
Weaver, Sidney (Sid) 109, 151, 158
Weed and Seed. *See under* U.S. Attorney's
   Office
Weinberger, Casper 169
Welfare Board 48
Wells, Tom 144
Wetherington, Gerald 171, 203, 211,
   222, 250, 379, 380

WGBS 111, 118, 119, 123
Wharton, Frank 45
What If Oswald Had Missed? (Petersen) 306
Wheatley, Russell 299
Where Have Our Heroes Gone?
   (Gelber) 261
White House 26, 57, 58, 345
   Conference on Children and Youth 88
White House conference on orphaned
   and dependent children 26
Whited, Charles 148
Whiteside, Ellen 79
Whitlach, Walter
   A Brief History of National Council of
      Juvenile Judges 88
Wilcox, Mark 61
Willard, Ben 30
William E. Gladstone Campus.
   See under Gladstone, William (Bill)
William Gladstone Award. *See under*
   Gladstone, William (Bill)
Williams, Aubrey 61
Williams, Sylvia 242
Wilson, Fredericka 291
Wilson, George 31
Wilson, Gloria 329, 330
Wilson, Harold 29, 30
Withers, Ike 97
Women Lawyers 43
Women's Fund 167, 377
Women's Park Gallery Rotunda 378
Wood, Jane 134
Working Group 381
World War II 15, 40, 60, 70, 73, 78, 84, 86,
   90, 92, 116, 133, 238, 240, 245, 252
WPA (Works Progress Administration)
   61, 293
WWII. *See* World War II

Y

Yale University Law School 160, 168
Yankees. *See* New York Yankees
Yelvington, Arthur 29
YES. *See* Youth Environmental Program

YMHA (Young Men's Hebrew Association) 247
Youth Environmental Program 218, 220, 221
Youth Hall. *See* Dade Juvenile Hall
Youth Today 305

Z

Zabel, Sarah 317
Zamora, Ronnie 251
Zangara, Giuseppe 152
Zargula, Marco, the Charmer 264
Zebulon, Georgia 73
Zero to Three 187, 227, 230, 342, 343